Freda Kirchwey:
A Woman of *The Nation*

Freda Kirchwey, 1944

FREDA KIRCHWEY

A Woman of *The Nation*

Sara Alpern

HARVARD UNIVERSITY PRESS
Cambridge, Massachusetts, and London, England 1987

This book is printed on acid-free paper,
and its binding materials have been chosen
for strength and durability.

Library of Congress Cataloging-in-Publication Data

Alpern, Sara, 1942–
    Freda Kirchwey, a woman of the Nation.

    Bibliography: p.
    Includes index.
    1. Kirchwey, Freda. 2. Journalists—United States—
Biography. 3. Women journalists—United States—
Biography. 4. Nation (New York, N.Y. : 1865)
I. Title.
PN4874.K57A79   1987   070.4'1 [B]   86-25826
    ISBN 0-674-31828-5 (alk. paper)

To Joshua,
who will always be
"the son of the year"

Preface

In 1918, when Freda Kirchwey joined the staff of the *Nation,* there were limited opportunities for female journalists. But in those changing times, the *Nation* was no ordinary journal, and Freda Kirchwey proved to be an extraordinary woman. Throughout a career that spanned a half-century marked by the Great Depression, the rise of European fascism, World War II, and the dawn of the nuclear age, she helped fashion some of the century's most important domestic and foreign policy reforms.

In her college years, when woman suffrage, prison reform, and union organizing and strikes captured Freda Kirchwey's vivid imagination, she marched along with committed activists. She also wrote about the issues—in a charged, personal, on-the-spot style that caught readers' attention.

Her entry-level job on the *Nation,* one of this country's oldest and most prestigious political magazines (founded in 1865), developed into a lifelong career. From clipping articles for its International Relations Section, she quickly rose to editor, and then managing editor. In 1937 she purchased the journal, becoming owner, editor, and publisher of the *Nation.* Until 1955 she was responsible for its policies and personnel, its causes and editorial positions.

The varied issues on which the *Nation* and Freda Kirchwey took a stand included sexual freedom and birth control, democracy versus fascism and Nazism, the Spanish Civil War, pacifism and collective security, refugees and Zionism, McCarthyism and censorship, and, finally, the peaceful employment of atomic power.

Aided by her husband, Evans Clark, Director of the Twentieth Century Fund, and by a host of experts of varying viewpoints, Kirchwey used the forums of the *Nation* and the Nation Associates to examine issues that affected domestic and world affairs. The positions she took were not always popular, but in support of what she considered right, she risked the loss of contributors, circulation, money—even friends.

An early feminist, from a privileged and progressive background, Freda Kirchwey was determined to enjoy both career and marriage. Throughout the years, however, doubts surfaced as to whether she was combining them successfully. The early death of two of her three sons and strained relations with her husband led her to question once-accepted values and basic assumptions about her own femininity. Her experience provides insight into the problems faced by professional women in the first half of the twentieth century; it helps correct long-held beliefs about how they coped with the conflicting demands of family and career.

This book grew out of a study of Freda Kirchwey that I undertook years ago. I sought answers to questions that touched me as a woman, a historian, and a mother. How had this journalist succeeded in a male-dominated profession? How did she have time to be a good mother as well as a productive editor and publisher? How did she and her husband work out a two-career marriage? But instead of answers, I encountered more questions. I also discovered that after 1932 Freda Kirchwey, though she continued to care about better integrating women into society, focused her attention primarily on other issues of national and international significance. This biography is the story of a woman attempting to balance the public and private sides of her life while becoming a national force in politics and public policy.

Freda Kirchwey will be remembered as a courageous woman and a committed reformer, fierce partisan, faithful friend, and determined foe of tyranny. Her life was dedicated to making the world a better place for others.

January 1987   S.A.

Contents

Illustrations

Michael Clark, aged ten. (Photograph courtesy of Michael Clark.)

Jeffrey Clark, aged six. (Photograph courtesy of Michael Clark.)

Evans Clark at the helm of "Loon." (Photograph courtesy of Michael Clark.)

A *Nation* outing in Connecticut. (Permission granted by Schlesinger Library, Radcliffe College.)

American Field Service ambulance driver Michael Clark, 1942. (Photograph courtesy of Michael Clark.)

J. Alvarez del Vayo and Freda Kirchwey broadcasting from station WINS. (Permission granted by Schlesinger Library, Radcliffe College.)

The presentation to Freda Kirchwey of a $25,000 check on the twenty-fifth anniversary of her association with *The Nation*. (Permission granted by photographer Arthur Leipzig.)

A Nation Associates dinner in New York, 1945. (Permission granted by Schlesinger Library, Radcliffe College; photograph by May and Strauss.)

At the office of *The Nation,* about 1946. (Permission granted by Schlesinger Library, Radcliffe College.)

American Jewish Congress Awards dinner, 1948. (Permission granted by Wide World Photos, Inc.)

I ‖ *The Proper Rebel*

O n 1 May 1893 before 250,000 spectators, President Grover Cleveland officially opened the World's Fair Columbian Exposition. It included a Woman's Building, designed by women and filled with women's art and exhibits, which boasted "an unprecedented opportunity to present to the world a justification" of woman's "claim to be placed on complete equality with men."[1] A child born that fall in Lake Placid, New York, would one day stake her claim. On 26 September, Mary Frederika Kirchwey, called Freda, was born to George and Dora Wendell Kirchwey, parents of a five-year-old daughter and an eight-year-old son.

Freda, along with her sister Dorothy and brothers Karl and Georgie (born four years after Freda), was part of an extended family. For several years her paternal grandparents lived with their son; and George's two sisters, Clara and Mary (both of whom taught at the Horace Mann schools), as well as Freda's maternal grandmother (a minister's widow), sometimes lived with the Kirchweys. Dorothy remembered family dinners of eleven or twelve.[2] Amid the clanging of silver and the clinking of plates there was talk, lots of it. Conversation often centered on George Washington Kirchwey, Professor of Law at Columbia University, who, as a good progressive, described how law should be taught—not as dead dogma but as the vibrant stuff of life.

*

George Washington Kirchwey's background was not unlike that of others who would become reformers. His parents, Michael and Maria Anna von Lutz, had fled Germany separately following the overthrow of the revolution of 1848. After meeting in Saint Louis, Missouri, they settled in Detroit, Michigan, then moved to Albany, New York. Naming their son after America's first President, they made sure that he received a good education, culminating in Albany Boys' Academy. George next graduated from Yale College and studied law privately in Albany. After passing the New York State bar examination, he opened a law office in Albany in 1881; he married Dora Child Wendell two years later. In addition to a busy law practice, he edited New York State historical manuscripts between 1878 and 1888. In 1889 he was appointed dean of the Albany Law School. In 1891, he joined the Columbia Law School faculty, becoming its dean in 1901. Kirchwey founded the American Society for International Law and served as its director from 1906 to 1921.[3]

Seemingly a born reformer, George Kirchwey introduced changes into his law school classroom. His students did not memorize abstract principles, for he said none existed. He taught his specialty—contracts and corporation law—by means of the new casebook method of study, pioneered by Christopher C. Langdell at Harvard. But he rejected Langdell's emphasis on law as an abstract body of truth. Kirchwey instilled in his students a belief that the only laws that counted were living laws, laws forever changing to accommodate a changing environment. He, along with Oliver Wendell Holmes, Jr., Louis Brandeis, and others, were in large part responsible for the "legal realism" that became a part of the larger reform movement. Justice no longer had to be blind, for laws must be interpreted with human needs and conditions in mind.[4]

In Kirchwey's opinion, if courts did not interpret the law with the public will in mind, they did not deserve veneration. Loss of status for twentieth-century lawyers did not bother him; he felt that lawyers should earn the esteem of others through their public spirit. He taught, wrote, and spoke on all kinds of legal reforms in the optimistic spirit of progressivism.[5]

Kirchwey's major interest was in the new science of criminology. His positive outlook led him to stress the conditions that led to crime, rather than the consequences of breaking the law; to eliminate the root causes, one must understand human nature enough to rehabilitate the offender and return him to society as a productive member. He, like others of his day, rejected the notion of innate evil in reforming his fellow man and put his theories to the test when serving briefly as warden of Sing Sing Prison in 1916.[6]

Freda adored and respected her father more than anyone in her life, and he returned her love. "Dear Heart," he once wrote, "What I yearned for was one of those talks with you which do me more good than they do any one else—about your work and your aims in life and such highfalutin stuff which can be postponed with serious harm to either of us." Freda learned his values early. While she was still an impressionable teenager, he quit the deanship to devote more time to teaching. Time away from administration also meant more time to advocate peace. A leader in the New York Peace Society, founded in 1906, Kirchwey worked with Professor Samuel T. Dutton of Columbia University, the Reverend Charles T. Jefferson, Hamilton Holt, editor of the *Independent,* and prominent businessmen Andrew Carnegie and Daniel Guggenheim, among others, to promote peace. He was frequently asked to represent the pacifist cause in the New York area.[7]

Freda listened to her father's many public speeches, often at her mother's urging: "I know Papa would much appreciate having you there though he won't suggest it. You've never heard one of his Peace sermons, and it won't do you any harm!" Freda boasted of one of his talks, "He was *good.*" The whole family delighted in their "Papa Georgie," the eloquent speaker and dedicated reformer, looking distinguished with his cropped beard, his bright blue eyes sparkling out of the rimless glasses.[8]

The Kirchweys believed in reform and supported progressive causes. Dinner table slogans might include: Reform the Criminal! Give Woman the Vote! Support Unions for Workers! or Work toward Peace! Clara Kirchwey taught geography at Horace Mann High School and Mary Kirchwey taught sixth-graders in Horace Mann School; although they were not quite as active reformers as their brother, they were concerned, informed women who brought the world into their classrooms. All the Kirchweys read a lot. Dora shared their delight in the written word. She had taught English at Albany High School. One of her pupils, John Palmer Gavit, associate editor of *Survey Graphic,* remembered her as a model teacher.[9] When she was at home and strong enough to come down to dinner the conversation often turned to a book several of them had read.

Freda received her secondary education at the dinner table and at the Horace Mann schools, demonstration schools for Columbia University Teachers' College. An active youngster, she was interested in everything except her studies. "School is purgatory," she wrote in her junior year. In her diary she confessed to "awful" grades and wondered whether she had "flunked" everything from Grammar to Math to Cicero. One would think that living in a family of educators, with brother Karl excelling at Yale Law School and sister Dorothy doing Phi Beta Kappa work at Barnard, might have caused Freda deep distress about "awful" grades. Yet she was nonchalant. When a teacher asked her to share some of her "superb indifference" with an overly conscientious classmate, Freda asserted that he misunderstood her "hard working nature."[10] She worked at those activities she considered important. To those who equate intelligence with high marks, Freda might appear lacking. She was not bookish, nor did she care about idea systems. She was blessed with a sharp mind, and her "hard working nature" stretched it to observe people, discern values, and share insights.

Freda participated actively in a number of extracurricular activities. She swam, played basketball, and combined politics and writing through membership in the civics, literary, and dramatic clubs. She acted in the senior play, *The Rajah,* though in mortal fear of embarrassment. (She and her fellow actors were much too inexperienced to carry off the serious dialogue without being laughed at, she thought.) She drew and wrote for the high school paper. As news editor for the paper, student council member, and president of the sophomore class and vice-president of her junior class, Freda's activism flourished. She studied only when in fear of flunking—as she did after she failed the required Latin entrance examination for admission to Barnard. "I see long vistas of Latin prose compositions stretching down the years ahead of me," she moaned to sister Dorothy.[11] High school and college were dress rehearsals for a career in reform journalism, as Freda Kirchwey tried on strategies, roles, ideas, ideals, and developed skill in speaking, writing, and editing. Although her early writings were limited to immediate surroundings at home, in school, or on vacation, she constantly observed and wrote down her impressions.

Freda was interested in people from her school years on. She questioned what they looked like, what they thought, what they valued, how they treated each other. She sketched countless faces on art paper—just as, years later, she would doodle faces on office memos. She wrote numerous anecdotal social commentaries to capture character traits of the people around her and morals she derived from observing them. At the age of fifteen she drew on childhood memories for a story for the *Horace Mann Bulletin*. She recalled looking out the window of her 113th Street house at goats grazing and her neighbors, drinking and fighting. (The Kirchweys stopped patronizing the neighbors' dairy because of such behavior.) Freda did not disapprove of alcohol, but she disliked drunken scenes. Her moral judgment was not against insobriety, but unacceptable behavior. Another story told of an abstinent, Mrs. Hiram Lamb, pointing disgustedly at the "horrible example" of Spofford Fitch, the drunkard of a quiet Maine vacation village. But because Fitch spared the life of a kitten, Freda saw him as more humane than Mrs. Lamb, who scorned him saying, "He ain't even got the strength of mind to drown'd a kitten!"[12]

Freda was developing her values during high school as she wrote stories and read voraciously. The year she wrote "Spofford Fitch," she took as "fathers" Wells, Galsworthy, and Shaw, a "sort of unholy trinity." In "A Private Letter to H. G. Wells" Freda recalled adopting Wells: "I have an excellent father who offered me a cigarette and your novels at almost exactly the same time—when I was about sixteen years old. I imagine he knew I was likely to adopt you as a sort of secondary parent and was willing enough to share the job." She remembered riding on a train from New York toward the Adirondacks, reading Wells's *Ann Veronica:* "Beside me was seated a stout gray dignitary who knew my family. 'Does your father allow you to read that sort of book?' he asked me. 'I read them first,' I said, 'and then I decide whether to allow him to.' You can see that the Wellsian influence was already at work." She shaped herself in his image: "pert, undignified, irreverent, headlong, hopeful, ready to alter everything including myself into almost anything different."[13]

Freda's real family must have indulged and encouraged the spiritedness. Of the four children, Freda was the mischiefmaker. Once she wrote about a dream in which Puss in Boots begged her to become the Queen of Gooseland:

> 'I had to get some one of *most* foolish brand
> To rule o'er a laughable place like Gooseland!
> I went to your house once when you were in bed,
> And when I inquired your dear father said

That if I wished foolishness you'd surely do,
For you had enough of it, *quite,* to fit two.[14]

She also had tender memories of a family anecdote that she recounted many times in later years. Dorothy Canfield Fisher was
lunching with the Kirchweys when a fracas broke out among the
children in another part of the house. "Oh, stop that, Freda!" yelled
their father. When Fischer asked him how he knew who was the
instigator, he replied with a twinkle in his eye, "It's always Freda
when there's anything doing." Freda, lively and indulged, flourished
in this warm family home.[15] She may have become even more
spoiled when, following the death of her seven-year-old brother,
Georgie, 17 May 1905, eleven-year-old Freda again became the baby
of the family.[16]

Freda loved conversations, parties, dancing, and writing. About
an editorial she wrote on cheating, she admitted "Terribly pious but
I think it ought to be said." She joined the Delta Nu sorority and
enjoyed its trivial rituals. "Spent some time trying to squelch pledg-
lings, but I'm disgracefully nice to them." She was voted Horace
Mann High School's "Best All Round Senior." "Best all-round," she
recorded the honor in her diary, and added the word "(Joke)" next
to the entry. Then she crossed out that belittling judgment and let
the honor stand; she had begun to accept her leadership. As the
class yearbook characterized her, "her finger was always on the public pulse."[17]

And, she continued to write. During her formative years, Freda's
writing helped her determine her own social code amid the contra-
dictory messages of the books she read and the attitudes of the
people she admired. She explored the worlds of convention, adventure, and paganism, often pitting one against the other. Paganism
fascinated her as early as high school. In a poem glorifying paganism, she renounced civilization, where people "spent long years
studying from books and sometimes prayed without faith to a god
of their making." She much preferred her "friendly gods." In her
senior year she founded a Heathen Club, made up of girls who
could not qualify for membership in the Girls' League. Substituting
a heathen deity for a club officer, Freda deigned herself "the Golden
Calf."[18]

No doubt this would have upset Freda's Methodist grandfather,
the Reverend Rufus Wendell, who had hoped that his "Blessed

Daughter" would give her children a strong religious upbringing. "It is my wish and prayer that your own precious children may be taught the same comforting truth and be taught to order their lives in accordance with its requirements," he wrote in 1898, a year after Dora bore her last child. Freda was precious, but she did not order her life through religion. Her mother probably urged her to go to church, as she once urged Dorothy: "I think you would find it worthwhile not to quite eliminate that part of existence from your life!"[19]

Although Freda was free to explore a world without organized religion, there are indications that she set limits to her excursions. In particular, she found parental expectations for restraint hard to ignore. "Do be careful of my girl, not only of that dreadful beach but of other things of more or less danger. Promise yourself not to do one thing which you are conscious is risky or of which we would disapprove. Be your own sweet dear self all the time and all girls will be better thought of because of the few who represent the best." In an unpublished short story, Freda's autobiographical character Mary explores a D. H. Lawrence world of untamed nature, only to return, wondering desperately about her mother's love for her. Like Paul Morel, Lawrence's hero in *Sons and Lovers* (1911), Mary, almost fourteen, rebels against a superficial milieu and spends an "Afternoon of a Nymph."

Clothed only in a skirt and blouse, free of confining underwear, Mary runs from her home while her mother prepares lemonade for the Lattimers (who caricaturize the staid upper-middle-class). As she flees past the blackberry brambles and the pasture to the moss-covered rocks and the pond, she finds meaning in paganism through a union with nature. At the pond she kicks off her shoes and slips out of her clothes. "She was what she had wanted to be—a child of nature, naked, alone, close to the naked rocks." Looking at her breasts reflected in the pond, "She felt herself, the surprising fact of herself, and thought she could never again take herself for granted in the old sightless way." Mary presses her body against the earth and feels at one with nature. Having repudiated the world of affectations and constraints, she dresses and returns home, wondering, "How could she go back and climb into her old clothes and her old life?" She had to return, but vowed to keep the secrets of that day. "She made up a sort of prayer as she walked along to take the place of the senseless Christian prayers." At the very end of Mary's walk, horses stampede, swerving around her at the last minute. Terrified and excited, Mary thinks about the horses who have almost trampled her; they are innocent creatures of nature, incapable of evil. Even with them she feels at peace.

At home, Mary washes the grass and dirt stains from her body. As she combs her tangled hair, she realizes that "her lovely, mysterious body was being taken for granted again." She wonders about her mother's reaction: "Did her mother understand? Was it possible that her mother knew the wild places in Mary's heart, knew and loved her there? Or didn't her mother care at all, or even notice when she left home and when she came back? Not even enough to criticize?" Mary looks at her scruffy appearance and realizes that her mother must have noticed. If she had understood, then Mary could share some of the day with her: "not much, not the prayers, not her naked body on the earth, but the horses, perhaps, and how she hated ordinary, dumb people like the Lattimers. But probably her mother didn't care at all." Mary agonizes about her discoveries and wants to know if there are others like herself. She wonders especially about her mother. But, "Mary knew that she could never ask." In addition to a young woman's discovery of her sexuality, this story could well have been a sketch of an adolescent's quest to know and to be accepted by her mother. Mary, and probably Freda, wondered how other human beings could be admitted "to her living world." "A feeling almost of nausea swept her as she thought of their mean, busy lives, their cackling humor."[20]

The adolescent who felt uncomfortable and constrained in the story delighted in wildness. Once, leading a suffrage parade on horseback, dressed in a flowing white gown, she felt the horse's "pulsing gallop" and her own aliveness, "all thru my body a sense of tautness and strength." "I really think it ought to help a lot, don't you?" asked a friend about the rally. "Help? O-Yes," Freda, still feeling physically aroused, responded absentmindedly, pitying the friend who couldn't understand. "How could she know!"[21]

Freda's stories reveal the curiosity of a young woman in quest of a personal value system, a political persuasion, and her own sexuality. Yet in the story of the nymph, Mary did return home to wash up for the company; she kept the questions locked inside. Her stories made it possible for Freda to put into words her feelings of conflict between values of social rigidity and pagan freedom and moral restraint and sexual drive. A great observer of the tumultuous times, Freda sat enraptured, listening to the rasping voice of anarchist Emma Goldman. She admired passion and felt the magnetism of charismatic speakers. Years later, reviewing Goldman's autobiography, she would say: "Her collective emotions moved her as only private feelings move most of us."[22]

During college, the short pieces that explored male-female relations were playful, not unlike Freda's own freshman experiences at Barnard when she chatted about the many boyfriends in her life, with impudent disregard for any rejections: "Blaine loves me no more. I have changed, he says—for the worse" or George got "too chummy." At nineteen she toyed with possible scenarios for proper ways for girls to relate to boys. One story had a sleeping beauty motif: boy kisses sleeping girl and confesses it to girl, who confesses that she wasn't really asleep; boy tells girl she is no lady and should be terribly ashamed of herself. In another tale, girl takes care of boy recovering from motorcycle accident and lets him hold her hand because he is hurt. Boy replaces picture of his nasty girlfriend with picture of girl nurse, heroine. When he recovers, boy takes her hand, but she withdraws it, saying he must not take liberties. Boy replaces girl heroine's picture with picture of his nasty girlfriend.[23]

It is interesting to compare Kirchwey's innocent stories to those Rebecca West had written the year before, when the same age. Their writings were more than an ocean apart; they were worlds apart. Perhaps West's poverty-stricken background provided experience in survival that Kirchwey's family could never provide. When Cicily Fairfield decided to write for the *Freewoman,* a feminist weekly her parents had forbidden her to read, she adopted the pseudonym Rebecca West. A mature and sophisticated writer at nineteen, she deflated the then world-renowned forty-five-year-old H. G. Wells in a scathing review of his book *Marriage.* The review compelled Wells to meet the extraordinary woman who had the audacity to call him "the old maid among novelists," dismissing his obsession with sex in his novels as "the reaction towards the flesh of a mind too long absorbed in airships and colloids."[24] West's writings about sex showed no such reticence. She painted vivid pictures of white slavery, prostitution, wife abuse, and illegitimate children. She herself became an unwed mother at age twenty-one when she bore Anthony West, her son by lover, but never husband, H. G. Wells.[25]

Freda Kirchwey's college stories reflect a sheltered life. During those years she felt the tug of two very different kinds of rebellion:

the Wellsian and Lawrencian to abandon societal restraints, and the more playful Twain pull to be independent. Rather than adopt the sexual freedom of the more extreme influence, she took from it a fascination with paganism. For the most part she was much more comfortable with milder forms of rebellion. She loved the idea of nonconformity and saw as role models the adolescent Tom Sawyer and Huckleberry Finn. She invoked "the intrepidity of the great Tom Sawyer, the careless freedom of Robin Hood" when she and a friend stole out of her house, for a midnight bicycle ride "toward the sternest heights of adventure."[26]

*

At Barnard Freda continued writing, editing, leading, and having fun; and she became a little more enthusiastic about learning. A history major, she took courses with James Harvey Robinson, pioneer in what was once considered new social history. She studied politics with Charles Beard, economics with Henry Mussey, and anthropology with Franz Boas. Although John Dewey taught at Barnard, Freda did not take any of his philosophy courses, so her later pragmatic mode cannot be said to have originated at school, if indeed she was a Deweyian.[27]

She approached formal education with resignation and set her standards for achievement. After some failed chemistry quizzes during a summer session resulted in a "D" in freshman chemistry, Freda wrote her sister in disgust: "it makes me sick to have flunked—because I know I should have gotten through and when I fail to live up to even *my* low standards of scholarship it shows both a mental *and* moral deficiency—Let's change the subject."[28] Her greatest learning took place outside the classroom. She once wrote, "Things are real that are real to us; nothing else exists . . . The world should be open to its natural friends who can smell it and taste it and accept it without a struggle."[29]

Influenced by a family of reformers, Freda thought everyone should fight for better working conditions. In 1913, when shirtwaist factory workers struck, Freda left her classes, joined the picket lines, and came up against the strikers' stark poverty and lack of education. Guilt-stricken, she wondered if it was fair that she received an education while others did not. She asked one of the strikers, who reassured her, with "condescending kindness," that since Freda had good intentions, "the right idea about things," maybe when she graduated she could put the knowledge to good use making life easier for others. Freda agreed, but she was offended when the striker continued: "Gee, y'know, I'm not so sure we ain't better off'n you anyhow . . . Wot are you learning that you really need all your life that we ain't learning too . . . Except we live it an' you only read it." Aware of the distance between their experiences, Freda nevertheless resented the implication that she was "a dawdler, reading in books of the battles that she fought, studying the problems in which she was a live factor."

Freda learned most about such problems from books and newspapers; joining a picket line was a rare firsthand experience. Like many other reformers, she never starved, toiled in a sweatshop, sweltered in an overcrowded tenement. Her philosophical position was that all people, regardless of economic or social status, were equal. She knew the working class not at all, but was not a snob. Regarding the shirtwaist worker's attitude, she reflected, "the moment when I realized that she thought herself better than I, I knew myself to be at least as good as she, and the knowledge cheered me." Her mother's reaction was equally reassuring. When news stories announced that Freda Kirchwey, daughter of the former Columbia Law School dean, had led a contingent of pickets to support the striking shirtwaist working women, Dora proudly clipped the articles to send to Karl.[30] Though Freda was on the periphery of reforms, her family's prominence and her outspokenness gave her high visibility.

The Barnard years (1911–1915) might be subtitled "Enjoying Reform." Freda told a reporter that the strike was "the most interesting experience of my life."[31] This does not mean that she was not committed to the strikers' goals or that she supported their reforms as a lark. But she lacked the dedication of one whose life was devoted to a cause. In many ways Freda was born a reformer; her participation evolved naturally and unconsciously. Shielded from any personal suffering from inequalities, reforms represented challenge and adventure. College was a time to embark on crusades.

Such an attitude prevailed at Barnard. Freda and her classmates wanted to discover work that they liked "well enough to earn a living by." And, "through it all we want to have a good time." Freda did just that. Extracurricular activities provided the "elements of excitement and responsibility and companionship" that satisfied her "demand for fun." Curiosity sparked her interest and led to membership in the Intercollegiate Socialist Society. But more than once she cut a meeting to go out on a date.[32]

Suffrage Club work involved her more; it too was enjoyable. One summer found Freda piloting "the little Sulphite" car throughout Litchfield County, Connecticut, to urge support for woman suffrage. Some fifty years later her campaign leader wrote: "What fun we had! I remember you girls called me 'the conscientious slave driver.'" Back at Barnard that fall, Freda braved the puzzled, disapproving glares of many bystanders as she stood on a New York City street corner shouting the virtues of the suffrage publication *The Woman Voter.* "Why, she had been having the time of her life!" And, she announced: "I am infinitely better at selling papers than I am at chemistry."[33]

She campaigned for school office with that same zest. In spring 1913 she ran for junior class president and won. "Long Life to the President," cheered her "truant mother" from Pine Tree Inn, a New Jersey sanitarium. Dora was pleased not because of the influence her daughter would have but because of the "estimate in which you are now held by your associates." The quality of getting along with people was highly valued by Dora Kirchwey, and Freda personified that trait.[34]

The school year closed with another victory. During the year Freda had crusaded to abolish fraternities. A good progressive, she attacked the evils perpetrated by sororities (then called fraternities) in order to convince administrators to abolish them. Despite her own membership in a high school sorority, the maturing Freda now regarded such organizations, even though they provided opportunities for recreation, as despicable. Sororities represented discrimination, exclusion, and secrecy—all anathema to democracy, which was a college's "very birthright."[35] She especially objected to their exclusion of Jews. Sororities must go. "Barnard College Puts the Ban on Secret Societies" read the headline of a 1913 Sunday *New York Times,* and once more a picture of the lovely Miss Freda Kirchwey appeared in a newspaper article. The *Times* credited her with initiating and pursuing this successful battle. Her first crusade of words resulted in victory; she would choose to fight for various causes with words for the rest of her life.[36]

During the year she had made trips to see her ailing mother. She missed the love and care of "Mama Dodie" and had felt the emptiness of her absence. Dora had been in ill health for some time. Often she traveled to health spas or sanitariums to try the latest cure. Freda never became accustomed to the separations and visited her mother frequently. Once after Freda returned to Manhattan, Dora wrote:

I certainly have two very happy days to remember. It is a real comfort, after such long separations to come so quickly and closely into touch with you—the *real* you—again and feel that I know in part at least your point of view, your ideals and your purposes for your own individual life. I shall be grateful on more than one account, Dear, when I am once more a part of the home life and in daily contact with you and your precious Father. That way happiness and contentment lie.—

Goodnight, Sweetheart Fritzie. Bless you.   Mother.[37]

Later, Freda's stories and letters to her ill mother would include experiences as junior class president, while she electioneered for the office of president of the undergraduate association for the coming year. That runoff election between Freda Kirchwey and Sarah Butler, daughter of Columbia University president Nicholas Murray Butler, left Freda the victor by one vote. "Whom did you vote for?" a student asked Sarah. "Why Freda, of course. You can't vote for yourself." And whom did Freda vote for? "Well, I voted for myself, of course. If I didn't think I was the best person for the office, I wouldn't be running."[38]

By 1914 Freda was no longer reticent about her popularity. That same year she began a serious relationship with twenty-five-year-old Evans Clark, who had entered Columbia Law School in fall 1913. The rather tall, distinguished-looking man, with thick dark hair and blue eyes, had graduated with honors from Amherst College and briefly attended Harvard Graduate School before earning a Master of Arts degree from Columbia in 1913. After a year at Columbia Law School he accepted an instructorship in history and government at Princeton University. Teaching constitutional government, elements of jurisprudence and politics, he was especially interested in legal matters concerning labor relations.[39]

Freda had many boyfriends, but after her first date with Evans she commented to sister Dorothy, "He's awfully nice—don't you think?" She hoped he would not expect her to pay for supper and the opera that night though, as Dora said, "You never can tell what these feminist gentlemen mean." Freda, nicknamed Fritz or Fritzie, dated Evans, nicknamed Eve, the spring of her junior year and throughout her senior year. In her last year at college she was selected "Best Looking," "Done Most for Barnard," "Most Popular," "Most Famous in Future," and "Most Militant."[40]

Freda had always been casual about boyfriends. Imagine Evans' surprise when he met John Graves, another of Freda's beaux, at Princeton. Graves told his new acquaintance about the wonderful woman he planned to marry, and Evans discovered it was none other than the woman *he* hoped to win! Graves, who had been dating Freda since high school days, apparently had misinterpreted her attention; she had to explain her more serious attachment to Evans. Evans was relieved: "I'm very glad dear about John and I hope he feels the same way—I should hardly expect it, though seeing as how he's a man and his devotion's still unattached . . . It has all made me feel queer more than once—but I think you're wonderful about it."[41]

Freda respected her family's admonitions about proper behavior during courtship. When Evans proposed, she received some unsolicited advice from her father to respect Dora's strong desire that Freda not go to Princeton until she had made the "Great Decision." "Feelings are facts and strong feelings (whether justified or not) are important facts—mother's as well as yours." Writing to "reconcile" her "bravely and cheerfully," Papa Georgie reminded her, "After all it isn't as though she was opposing the course of true love—the way horrid mothers do."[42] Free love was inappropriate for a Kirchwey. Sex without marriage was unacceptable. Perhaps because Freda received her parents' unqualified support for political activities that many in society found radical, she did not or could not rebel against their sexual mores. She learned to control her passions and was once described as being "warm on the outside, but steely on the inside."[43]

Freda made her decision, and a delighted Evans received her answer in New York. On 13 March 1915 they became engaged. Her mother was pleased by this conventional step. Evans described his visit to his future mother-in-law as "a perfect day—wonderful." And Dora wrote to Dorothy, who was teaching economics at Smith for that year, "the expression on his face and clasp of his hand emphasized his words." One of Freda's classmates had announced her engagement the same day, with much fanfare. Dora compared this other young woman, who came to class "adorned with orchids and her new engagement ring," to "modest little Fritzie who shrinks from anything that suggests 'public announcement!'"[44]

The brief notice of Freda's engagement in the *New York Times* brought letters of congratulation and regret from many former beaux. A prospective father-in-law, her neighbor W. E. Lewis, was disappointed that the "sweetest of the sweethearts" had chosen to marry someone other than his son Tracy. A former boyfriend decided that Evans "must be a perfect wonder to have gotten the prize he did." Freda's special letter to John Graves received a gracious reply: "As for you and I—let us call it a mistake but never anything more or less than a sweet and pure and honest mistake. And we will keep our friendship unspoiled with any of those things that made our closer relations impossible. God bless you and Evans."[45]

"The die is cast . . . Don't you think it's a good idea?" Freda asked her sister for her blessing. Dorothy must have written Evans of her fear of losing Fritzie, for Evans reassured her, "may we not all gain something in place of what you lost?" Admitting that love may blind the lover, he nevertheless found in Freda "a very rare spirit, and a most beautiful woman." "It quite takes my breath away, Dot, time and time again—and I feel terribly unworthy at times . . . I come to her anyway with a genuine reverence, uncolored, I hope by any ideals."[46] The couple set their wedding date for November. The months between March and November were busy months of a full senior semester for Freda, with a job that started four days after graduation.

*

With all the offices Freda Kirchwey held at Barnard, her friends might have expected her to seek a career in politics. Few of her classmates knew that, after a year of study with Franz Boas, she dreamed of becoming an anthropologist. Fewer still would have believed the dread with which their valedictorian approached the delivery of her speech. She never lost this apprehension and, twenty years after graduation, still considered giving a speech "a cruel ordeal." She loved to talk on a one-to-one basis, and even to several people in a group, but with fifty people in front of her or, worse still, a thousand, she felt nauseous.[47]

Poised and seemingly at ease, Freda trembled inside. She wrote her father about it after addressing an outdoor rally of mill workers. As class orator of the Yale Class of 1879 and a lifetime public speaker, he responded that he understood her "nervousness": "Probably you will never get entirely over it. I haven't. Do you enjoy that part of your work or does it get to be a bore?" Then he added, "perhaps you, like your father, are a 'born speaker.'" Freda claimed otherwise. Once, preparing for a visit to Wellesley College, she declined to speak to its Economics Club: "Perhaps I am not a natural born orator; perhaps I need to be psychoanalyzed; anyhow, I can't speak to any Economics club."[48]

When Freda Kirchwey felt obligated to address a large audience, she forced herself to concentrate on her purpose or subject. When she accepted the honor of delivering the valedictory speech for the Barnard class of 1915, she wanted to explain the beliefs about public responsibility that she had formulated over her college years. She felt compelled to press herself and her classmates into action. Her speech echoed an earlier assessment: "Work of all sorts is waiting to be done." Traditional college spirit was a luxury in the midst of world problems; college activities became insignificant when compared with problems outside of this sheltered environment. "We might far better read the morning paper than go to a song-practice or a basketball game," she once exhorted her classmates. The *New York Times* headlines on commencement day erupted with reactions to Germany's sinking of the *Lusitania*. America had yet to enter Europe's war.[49]

Freda challenged herself and her classmates to solve problems closer to home. They must use "outside world" trade-union principles to effect change. The growing pains of a new world demanded creative solutions, and they must "test beliefs and feelings in the hot fire of experiment and experience." She confessed to her woeful inadequacy that year in failing to sustain enough group pressure to effect a major change in Barnard itself. Five of her classmates had tried to break the sex barrier at Columbia Law School, but were denied admission. As president of the undergraduate association, which voted a resolution of support for these women, she and others dropped the cause. Freda chose the captive audience at commencement to raise the issue again. She left Barnard, knowing that it shared some of the discrimination problems so prevalent in the "dark world" outside.[50]

Freda never questioned that she would work outside the home after graduating from Barnard. In college she had reviewed Mary Roberts Coolidge's *Why Women Are So,* an economic interpretation of history that showed how her mother's generation had benefited from the first burst of economic and social conditions that expanded opportunities for women. Freda's own generation profited especially, for, as she noted, their mothers had raised them "with a firm faith in our 'freewill' and potential economic independence."[51]

Extensive writing and editing experience in high school and college somewhat prepared Freda Kirchwey for a career in journalism. She enjoyed writing and felt it was worthwhile. She felt a strong desire to work for the good liberal causes that she had investigated early in her college years, and political journalism was a logical extension of her talents. She could continue to clarify issues that were important and do so in a way that was comfortable: the written media.

Impressed by her eagerness to write professionally, W. E. Lewis, publisher of the *Morning Telegraph*, hired her to cover general news and to write stories from the "woman's angle."[52] His New York sporting daily (famous for its racing news), was an unlikely paper for a young political crusader, but Freda saw an opportunity. She decided to publicize her father's penal reform ideas. George Kirchwey had become warden at Sing Sing Prison in 1916. His predecessor, Thomas Osborne, was a controversial warden because of his attempts to understand and rehabilitate prisoners. (He had earlier served a term in prison in order to study conditions firsthand.) As warden at Sing Sing, he provided inmates well-balanced meals, adequate exercise time, vocational training, and entertainment; he initiated a degree of self-government among the prisoners through the Mutual Welfare League. Critics charged that prisoners there had a better life than did law-abiding citizens. The criticism evidently escalated into fabricated charges accusing the warden of perjury, mismanagement, neglect of duty, and immorality. Osborne took a leave of absence from his post as warden to conduct a year-long successful legal battle against these attacks. His friend George W. Kirchwey, appointed in his place, assured the prisoners that he would continue Osborne's reforms.[53]

Among the press covering the appointment of the new warden was a reporter with the *Morning Telegraph*, his own twenty-two-year-old daughter. "The warden and I are rather old friends," she confessed to readers. Despite that fact, Freda waited four hours to conduct an interview with her father.[54] Pad in hand, she took notes as rapidly as he talked. He described the sweeping changes at Sing

Sing. What had been a life of inactivity, inedible meals, and boredom was transformed into a model humane prison, complete with a self-governing board and a convict court to maintain discipline.[55]

Part of Freda's interest in penal reform came from her father's fascination with his "boys." He once described the fundamental difference between the prisoners and Columbia Law School students: "My boys at Sing Sing had a little more kick to them, a little more pep, a little more of the spirit of adventure. With inadequate outlets, unfortunately, they satisfied their spirit by stealing and trying to 'beat the law.'" Freda respected her father's humane treatment of offenders and considered his work vital.[56] She considered penal reform, like feminism, one of the major elements of the "drama of the future." George W. Kirchwey was in the forefront of one and doubtlessly supported the other. In 1916 his wife and daughters became the first female honorary members of the prison's Mutual Welfare League; he initiated and supported the equality of women that membership implied. As warden he encouraged Freda to publish several articles in the prison journal.[57] She signed them Miss Freda Kirchwey, as she signed all of her writings, despite the fact that she had been married since November 1915.

For several months before her wedding, Freda had been writing for the *Morning Telegraph*. The separation was difficult for the couple, and more than once Evans admitted to loneliness: "O, how I yearned for you and your life giving touch, my precious one . . . This is going to be a poor session till we can get married." He was comforted by the knowledge that he could telephone and hear her voice, yet felt a "twinge of grudge" against Freda's friends, family, and fellow workers. "What a nasty, sneaky, disgusting feeling it is! I wish it wouldn't come. But perhaps it's a sign of how tremendously I love you." Again, he said: "If you'd only been with me there'd have been nothing else in the world but the glowing present. As it was there was a lot of past and future that held me back from real satisfaction."[58] Some of these confessions came after Freda expressed doubt about the relationship. She had felt some distancing on Evans' part, though he insisted that she was misreading his feelings: "It makes me shudder to think I could seem so opaque and cryptic when I feel so utterly transparent to you . . . Do let's get married as soon as the way's at all clear. It's fierce upsetting to both of us—this nearness and farness mixed up so bewilderingly." Freda's "Song" to Evans spoke of their new love:

We two love each other—and love is so sweet,
We two love each other, and love is so strong
So valiant and lusty, so sturdy and long.
My shy heart is whispering, secret and low
We two love each other and no one must know,
For love is so fragile, so wistful, so dear
That only we two can be trusted to hear.

The summer before their wedding Evans suggested: "Next summer, let's go, you and I—without a chaperone—and drink great draughts of it [Maine]—and of each other!"[59]

That the couple brought together love and a dedication to bettering the world did not go unnoticed. A friend of Evans described Freda as "some one with whom your added ability can incorporate who is interested in the big problems you have already confronted more or less alone." And Freda celebrated their commitment in "Comradeship," which ended:

How can the small inglorious minutes build a day
Radiant with the eager hope of a passionate year
On the far heights of courage—grave and gay?
Is it because we live them through together, dear?

Evans rejoiced in what they shared and admired Freda's openness to the "hotness of life," saying, "I always feel that you're closer to life than I am—at least you seem more to welcome it than I."[60]

One of the qualities that attracted Evans to Freda was her rebellious spirit. He once said, "I'm revolting more than ever before thanks to you!" Evans Clark's revolt from his patrician family had begun right after college. Attracted to the ministry because he considered the pulpit a good place to influence social change, and turning away from his Episcopalian upbringing, he decided upon the Congregational ministry and entered Andover Theological Seminary in Cambridge, Massachusetts. A comparative religion course in his first semester convinced him to leave, however, for he could not accept the teaching that any one religion was superior. In fact, from that point on, he began to develop an active hostility toward organized religion, symbolized by the upcoming civil marriage ceremony.[61]

Some of Evans' conventional relatives were concerned about the propriety of his fiancée's work. He had "quite a fight" over "the wisdom of young girls reporting for *Morning Telegraphs*." Defending Freda as a talented writer, Evans asked them to read her "Three Prayers for Ceres," published in the *Independent*. Overall he considered the exchange positive: "it'll open their eyes and heart a little to the feminist adventure—I felt all the while as if they were stripping and lashing me. But my s[ense] of h[umor] didn't all go and I've enjoyed the revelations it caused a lot since."[62] That "feminist adventure" was a shared one. Just a week before their wedding Evans promised Freda that he would reread the ending of Wells's *The World Set Free* a couple of times each year to remind him of her feminism. There the character Karenin says: "To think of yourselves as women is to think of yourselves in relation to men. You can't escape that consequence. You have to learn to think of yourselves— for our sakes and your own sakes—in relation to the sun and stars. You have to cease to be our adventure, Rachel, and come with us on our adventure."[63]

MISS FREDA KIRCHWEY MARRIED BY CONTRACT, blared the New York Sunday *Telegram,* announcing that the wedding had been performed in "secret ceremony" some six months before. The ceremony was secret only in that the couple had avoided publicity. Freda had asked her lawyer brother Karl to delay filing the marriage document in the county clerk's office until the end of the required six-month deadline. The newspaper ran the story, complete with picture, the day after the filing.[64] The ceremony had been very simple. Freda invited only immediate family and a few close friends to witness the marriage. George Kirchwey read some of Edward Carpenter's poetry, their views underscoring his daughter's unorthodox views on marriage. Justice Samuel Greenbaum, father of Freda's close friend Grace, witnessed the document. The marriage was not the norm, even in a family of reformers. The private wedding, the civil ceremony, and Freda's decision to keep her maiden name after marriage contrasted dramatically with her sister Dorothy's traditional Unitarian ceremony, attended by more than fifty guests, just two weeks later. The *New York Times* diplomatically mentioned Freda's wedding in its coverage of her sister's: "This is the second wedding in the bride's family in two weeks. Miss Freda Kirchwey was married on November 9 to Professor Evans Clark of Princeton. They attended the wedding."[65]

Freda and Evans returned from a honeymoon in Bermuda in time to watch Dorothy become Mrs. LaRue Brown, wife of a Harvard-trained Boston lawyer. Then the Kirchwey-Clarks took up residence in Princeton where Evans continued teaching government and Freda working at the *Morning Telegraph*. Using her maiden name was a statement of feminism, as it was for many of her contemporaries. Both Freda and Evans believed that women could combine careers with marriage.

She commuted daily from Princeton to New York City. A married woman with a career made her an anomaly in Princeton. One day Freda, unrecognized by two local women, overheard this conversation about her:

> "I've heard," said Lady No. 1, "that she doesn't live with him at all and they're not really married."
>
> "Well," said Lady No. 2 tentatively, "I've heard they're not really married, too, but she *does* spend week ends with him!"
>
> "It's a very queer situation," Lady No. 1 summed up darkly.[66]

New York was one of the few places that offered feminists alternatives to traditional marriages and sex-defined lifestyles, and some women moved there from parochial settings. Magazine writer Rheta Childe Dorr, a Nebraskan, and writer Susan Glaspell, an Iowan, were two of many feminists who consciously chose New York as a community where they could find free expression.[67]

Kirchwey matured in such an environment. Unlike some of her contemporaries, she never formulated a general theory of feminism. Her suggestions, like those of other progressives, were usually confined to political solutions to women's problems. She wanted to free women from political and legal discrimination. She saw women's rights as a natural outgrowth of democracy. She was convinced of the need to inform the public of the remaining inequities in the United States—and thereby bring about a solution: the change of laws. Faith in the workability of democracy seemed her most basic philosophical tenet; and that faith underlay her feminist ideals.

Kirchwey's resistance to dogma helps explain why she never developed a theory of women's rights. Like other feminists, she intertwined feminism and suffrage until the two seemed synonymous. But they were not. Some of the several million women who joined the cause of woman suffrage in the last decades of the battle were not feminists. Feminists or not, suffrage was the unifying cause for the General Federation of Women's Clubs, the Women's Trade Union League, and the National American Woman Suffrage Association.[68] Feminists like Kirchwey concentrated on generating an ever-increasing pool of suffrage supporters of all classes and world views.

*

During her year with the paper, the cub reporter interviewed playwrights about the theater, artists about Greenwich Village restaurants, convicts about Sing Sing, and judges about divorce court, as well as covering dance, style, hoboes, Wall Street, and dog shows. But most of all she used her forum, the *Morning Telegraph,* as a political instrument to support the enfranchisement of women. She presented the facts about woman suffrage as she saw them. If Freda suffered from any of society's inequities, it was from the disfranchisement of women, and she was aware of this. The more subtle sex role discrimination that she had already internalized remained unrecognized by her and, thus, never confronted.

The majority of her writing touched on women, and she extended her "woman's angle" assignment to include stories discussing the attempts of women to gain the vote. She reported on suffrage campaign strategies, actions, and results, even interjecting her own personal experiences as a campaigner for woman suffrage.

With her first piece for the *Morning Telegraph* Freda Kirchwey had established herself as a mediator. This was a stand she would often take as a political journalist addressing a liberal audience. She urged reconciliation between bickering factions of the woman suffrage movement, which had already split when the National American Woman Suffrage Association denounced the more radical Congressional Union because of its single-minded focus on the federal amendment. Keep silent about tactical differences, the journalist asked the two rival women's groups. Even at this early date, 1915, she used dissension to highlight the need for focus on the shared goal and unity against the common foe. Along with her rejection of dogma, she disapproved of divisions on theoretical or tactical grounds that could aid those opposed to the common cause.[69]

The maturing writer employed humor and irony effectively. Her strategy for reporting on suffrage and for converting the public to her views was to use autobiographical stories. Each had a suffrage theme of tactical or philosophical nature presented humorously. In "A Suffrage Swim" she analyzed the suffragist tactic of upholding the law: "it puts you in the effective pose of martyr, if you loyally uphold laws that you have no hand in making."[70] The story reported a campaign which took place in extreme heat; for relief, the suffragists took a long illegal swim in a public reservoir and were caught. The campaigners had not only broken the law, they had also disregarded their political strategy of upholding laws to gain martyrdom. Kirchwey, an active participant, laughed at herself and her colleagues by publicizing the story. She believed people should never take their causes so seriously that they lost their sense of humor. Her strategy was to catch antisuffrage people off guard, forcing them to see suffragists as ordinary people rather than revolutionaries.

Irony made it possible to criticize the suffragists by showing their frailties. In her articles Kirchwey sometimes disengaged herself from the cause and sharpened her objectivity. She was especially critical of suffragists' use of feminine wiles to attain goals. "A Suffrage Courtship" described the way some men thought about woman suffrage. A fictitious Mr. Harris was anxious to befriend Miss Cox, a suffragist, and could not understand why anyone so charming needed to vote. "You could make anybody vote the way you wanted him to—your father, or — or — your husband, or anybody," he argued, adding that her mere presence would influence the legislature. Miss Cox dismissed this despicable idea: "Feminine influence!—Why bribery and corruption are cleaner and better. It degrades women and degrades men; no end could ever be so desirable to justify such petty, sneaking means." Then she used precisely such "feminine influence" to entice Mr. Harris to join the suffrage parade. In an attempt to please her by pretending to support her cause, Mr. Harris was duped into donning a parade costume of white tights and gold Christmas trimmings. Miss Cox assured the irate participant that they both looked foolish in costume. But she led the parade in her costume of crown and robes, while he led two horses and a chariot in his degrading costume. Making the male character look and feel the fool gave Freda Kirchwey, through her alter ego, Miss Cox, public revenge for second-class citizenship.[71] The incident also exposed the shortcomings of a society in which a shallow individual like Mr. Harris had the right to vote simply because he was a man, while a woman had to beg for the ballot. Theoretically, suffrage would eliminate the need for women to exercise influence through men; it would give them power to exert influence directly.

Campaigning for suffrage taught Freda to accept expedient means to achieve ends. She had experience with political compromise through her reforming father, but during the suffrage campaign she observed and practiced opportunistic measures and also accepted and incorporated expediency into her general philosophy toward reform. "A Suffrage campaign is no place for a moralist," she concluded.[72]

Expediency linked Freda Kirchwey's suffrage struggle to the larger context of a means-and-ends approach to most progressive reforms: "Suffragists, like all good agitators, are passionately concerned with the end. Toward the means they have a certain indifference, or at least a tolerance, that might well shock a person who has never tried to get anything that is being forcibly withheld from him." Suffragists wrote their own grandiose press releases for local papers and planted questions in the audience to make certain that they would have the chance to deny a common fear that revolutionary consequences would follow a successful woman suffrage amendment. They solicited practical questions that the audience was usually too timid to ask. From her vantage point as a participant, Freda Kirchwey evaluated their actions favorably.[73]

Through the concurrent participation in campaign rallies and promotion of suffrage by means of the printed word, she became more self-confident. Apparently describing herself, she used another character in her story to voice the psychological change: "A girl starts out on a campaign timid about everything—afraid of crowds, afraid of the dark, afraid of her own voice. Before a week has passed she is bold as a lion . . . From it all she has gained a great respect for herself." Suffragists accepted their capabilities; they could speak and manipulate crowds of men and women. Freda valued what one of them called the "power of grasping public questions and helping shape the fabric of opinion."[74] This reinforced her own development as a journalist. Of the various people she had interviewed, she noted: "they even made me feel once in a while, that utter superiority inherent in representatives of the press so early taught to young reporters." Growing self-confidence helped her to explain the antisuffragists, and she quoted a cohort: "I believe antis are antis largely because unconsciously they have a deep sense of incapacity."[75]

A month before the New York State woman suffrage referendum, she covered the hundredth birthday celebration of Elizabeth Cady Stanton. Rather than focus on the outcome of the vote to amend the state constitution, Freda emphasized the number of people present at the dinner—one thousand—and stressed that many were prominent figures. Thus, she highlighted a victory or minimized a loss.[76]

Suffrage for women in New York did not pass that November. Undaunted, Freda Kirchwey attacked an unnamed political boss for categorizing it as "dead for the time being." She described, on the contrary, "a very lively ghost making plans for a new and concentrated fight of unprecedented vigor" at the New York State Suffrage Convention. She saw signs of consolidation among the contending factions represented there, and she praised the convention's willingness to see itself as a "party, thus indicating the growing 'political mindedness' of the members."[77]

Kirchwey covered the woman suffrage campaigns and strategies as an interested participant, using her *Morning Telegraph* pieces to evaluate programs, praise progress, and encourage moves toward eventual victory. But she was aware that her activities were controversial and attracted attention. She realized that privacy could be protected only if one avoided the public arena. She started one story claiming "the life of the private citizen is after all the only one worth living . . . the only one where he may in any degree hew out his own standards."[78] Yet she chose public life.

She stretched her writing assignments to keep the suffrage issue before readers, which meant manipulating assignments that had no connection with the subject. She took advantage of a dog show to muse: "It was called the Fifth Avenue parade, and it appeared a select company of true Fifth Avenue paraders, though not of the votes-for-women variety."[79] One piece surpassed all others for Kirchwey's injection of suffrage into an unrelated topic. She wrote about a Waldorf-Astoria bellhop who had made a fortune through investments. Commenting on his youth, the reporter concluded: "Just about old enough, I should say, to have voted for the suffrage amendment to-day."[80]

Kirchwey sometimes implied that an unnecessary fuss was being made about suffrage, for when it became law, it would not mean much change. On the other hand, many of her pieces implied that the vote alone would solve women's problems. Probing the broader meaning of democracy in which women lacked the vote, and in which the vote meant symbolic and real power, she argued that disfranchisement led to denigrating conditions and to an inferior self-image for many women. Yet, it is difficult to believe that voting rights could reverse some of the problems she herself documented.

She examined the attitudinal problems evident in prospective partners' expectations. Men and women had starkly different attitudes toward marriage, she wrote. In a story about a matchmaker, she discovered self-effacing female clients, willing to offer substantial money in exchange for mere companionship, while male clients unabashedly sought attractive women of means.[81] She argued that women who were dependent upon men tolerated this unbalanced search. Such differing desires and demands pointed to blatant disparities in social values for women and for men. Would suffrage erase these disparities? Would it give women self-esteem? She left these deeper questions unanswered, in fact unexamined.

But she did ask some tough questions of society. Why did some courts accept the word of the testifying man, but discredit the word of the woman? "The fact of the woman being a prostitute serves to injure her credibility. I don't see why this should be so. A man's morals have nothing to do with his credibility."[82] She hinted at some larger problems for which she would have been hard-pressed to expect political solutions. At times she expanded her vision beyond politics and offered readers a glimpse into economic factors that altered the texture of the world. Sent to gather information about unusual women in the work force, Kirchwey prodded Mary S. Snow of the Intercollegiate Bureau of Occupations for details about any women who worked in occupations atypical for their sex. Was there a female steeplejack or a female safeblower? Yet the journalist knew that it was not the spectacular woman who was changing the world for women, but the ordinary factory worker. Women had begun to enter the work force in great numbers. Kirchwey acknowledged that some seven million working women would force the real change; they formed "the real women's movement—which for the most part doesn't even know it is moving." Optimistically she hoped that the mere presence of the ideology of feminism would motivate these and other women to achieve. She concluded, "in these feministic days there is no limit to what these women will do," just as she perceived no real limits in her own chosen career.[83]

Interviews with four prominent New York feminists may have strengthened her career commitment. Sent to cover a controversial suggestion that women carry guns as part of a self-defense program, Kirchwey spoke to the initiator of the plan, Mrs. George Haven Putnam, former Barnard dean and a history professor there. The other three were Crystal Eastman (Benedict), chairman of the

Woman's Peace Party; Henrietta Rodman, education reformer; and Madeline Zabriskie Doty, lawyer and member of the New York State Prison Reform Commission.

Putnam's general program included training women to be physically stronger and economically self-sufficient and to overcome charges of "emotional instability." Eastman agreed with the plan, although she considered economic freedom the most essential freedom, since it "opens the way for the first time to freedom in love and activity and even thought." Rodman admitted that women needed spiritual courage, but she also thought physical daring might encourage them to have faith in their own ideas, so she supported Putnam's plan. Because the Putnam plan encouraged female initiative, Doty also concurred, for she believed progress depended on overcoming fear by cultivating skills. Although both men and women should increase individual incentive, it was especially true of women, "because traditionally they have been suppressed and discouraged from initiative and daring, particularly the physical sort." Inspired by these interviewees, Kirchwey considered "knocking down a policeman, but decided that that form of dangerous sport was not listed in the programme. I felt sure, though, that Mrs. Putnam must be right. It was still unanimous." She also thought well enough of herself to count her opinion among those of the prominent women polled about the plan.[84]

*

Kirchwey quit her job on the *Morning Telegraph* after a year, attributing the decision to one of "the accidents of fate that had punctuated my professional life, the arrival of a baby."[85] When Brewster Clark was born, 19 September 1916, Freda proudly recorded each minute detail in Evans' own baby book. She traced the youngster's tiny hand and foot at eleven weeks old alongside his father's hand and foot at twelve weeks. She recorded weight and height gains and Brewster's second tooth on 15 May 1917. At thirty-four weeks the health record stopped abruptly; Brewster died at just over eight months of age.[86] Freda did not write professionally for another eight months.

It had been a hard year for the couple. Evans lost his job at Princeton, and the couple moved from New Jersey to New York City after the 1917 spring term ended. Then came Brewster's illness and death. Evans was rejected twice for the draft because of a heart murmur. Both he and Freda were in poor physical condition and sought help from their family doctor, Billy Caldwell, who recommended exercise, fresh air, and sleep.[87] When Freda's sister bore her first child, Eleanor, on 1 August 1917, Freda welcomed her niece: "My! how pleased Eve and I are—and excited. We feel as if she ought to be just a little ours, too. We need her badly, Dottie."[88]

That fall Freda decided a new hairdo might help her mood. She encouraged her sister to do the same: "I've cut off my hair as I threatened. I look a little like a virtuoso and a little like a crusader but otherwise very beautiful. You'd better do it too. I'm sure your family will like you better. Mine does!" Living at 39½ Washington Square, she and Evans found jobs in New York early in 1918. He began working as research director and legislative secretary for the Socialist members of the New York City Board of Aldermen; Freda became an editorial assistant on *Every Week,* a literary and family publication, where she worked until 22 June 1918, the date of its demise. Her writing included assorted book reviews, news stories, and interviews she conducted. Some public interest pieces ranged from the theater to the circus to the proper care of children. Continuing her concern for women's issues, she reported that Marie Obernauer, industrial chairman of the National League for Women's Service, said that to support one man in combat, four men worked at home; of the four "men," one was a woman. Kirchwey also reviewed books and wrote general news items on specific countries, including Austria, Turkey, Germany, Spain, and Russia.[89]

"The importance of Leon Trotsky to Russia and to the world grows more instead of less," predicted Freda Kirchwey in 1918. She wanted to paint a picture of the revolutionary leader who had worked in New York City for a few months in 1916. Who was he? What did he look like? Her search led her on the "trail of Trotsky" to his desk at the newspaper *Novy Mir* and to a series of interviews with his colleagues Gregory Weinstein, B. Charney Vladeck, Henry Feuer, and Ludwig Lore. Vladeck explained that in Russia names were used to conceal identity. Trotsky had changed his name from Bronstein to Trotsky, adopting the name of his first jailer! Another friend described visits to Trotsky's home: "Always many glasses of tea, nothing else, and talk about Russia and Revolution. Trotsky was waiting day by day for the revolution. He knew it would come." Freda included a translation of "Moving Jaws," a Trotsky short story about Americans chewing gum in the subway. "It is like a dark religious ceremony, a soundless prayer to the God—Wealth." The article, "When Trotsky Lived in New York," with this original story, unknown details of the life and quirks of Leon Trotsky, and photographs, never appeared in print.[90] Bruce Barton, editor of *Every Week,* later to become known for his book *The Man Nobody Knows,* decided not to print the stories because he thought Trotsky would soon be forgotten. So Kirchwey's first scoop remained buried.[91]

The year 1918 was filled with short-lived employment. After *Every Week* went out of business, Kirchwey clipped "fillers" for the *New York Tribune* for two months, until she lost her job. Although she had never met Ernest Gruening, the *Tribune's* managing editor and later Senator from Alaska, she was fired along with all hired during his tenure. Gruening and his staff lost their jobs after he published a picture juxtaposing a Southern lynching with a parade of black troops returning from combat in France. Though Freda officially was terminated on 24 August 1918, she had already decided to leave.[92]

A college friend had told Freda of an opening at the *Nation.* Freda discussed the job possibility with her husband during their vacation and applied to the journal's editor and publisher, Oswald Garrison Villard, and managing editor Henry R. Mussey. She wrote Mussey, her former economics professor: "If you think I'm the man for the job, will you put in a word for me? I saw wood now better than I used to." Villard's response, questioning Kirchwey about "just what European experience" she had had and what languages she spoke, caused the applicant to hurry back to New York to answer in person. Satisfied with her competence, Villard hired her on August 27, and she began work the next day, in the new international relations section.[93] Freda Kirchwey arrived at the *Nation,* a crusading opinionmaking journal that had a fierce commitment to international and domestic causes.

Years later she reflected on two factors that may have helped her obtain the job. Villard had a "long-time friendship and admiration" for her father with whom he had joined in supporting several liberal causes. The editor also approved of Freda Kirchwey's own commitment to several movements that he considered important. At the interview the reporter stressed her involvement in the cause of woman suffrage and the peace movement. She recounted her experience as a member of the Woman's Peace Party. The night President Wilson declared war, she had been one of the female delegation demonstrating for peace at the capitol.[94]

A long and tumultuous relationship between Freda Kirchwey and Oswald Garrison Villard began in 1918. Born in 1872, during Reconstruction, and living through the beginning of the Cold War, Villard in many ways was representative of the antebellum reform tradition. His mother, Helen Francis Garrison (Fanny), grew up in the household of the abolitionist William Lloyd Garrison. Villard's father, Ferdinand Heinrich Gustave Hilgard (changed to Henry) had fled Germany in the aftermath of the revolution of 1848, as had Freda's grandparents. Villard believed that reform was an individual protesting the tyranny of the state. He was a deeply committed reformer, vigorously opposed to racism and injustice. The young staff he began to assemble in 1918 remade the *Nation* in the first few decades of the twentieth century. They never understood his devotion to E. L. Godkin (who had founded the *Nation* in 1865), and to older Mugwumps. If they had a complaint, it was that he opposed their attempts to modernize the format and the editorial policies of the journal of opinion.[95]

This was the beginning of what was to be Freda Kirchwey's lifelong career on the *Nation*. Through her upbringing in a politically active and aware household, and from her marriage, she had developed the sheltered and supported independence that she brought to her new position. Background, schooling, early writing, and her father's connections facilitated Kirchwey's early advancement as a journalist. But her own drive cannot be underestimated.

2 || *From Apprentice to Journalist*

At twenty-five Freda looked no older than she had six years earlier, when she walked into her first class with Professor Mussey; now he was one of her many superiors at the *Nation*. She had moved her desk to catch the best light in the dingy, crowded "barn," workroom of the International Relations Section (IRS), which was attached to the *Nation*'s main building by a fire door, "permanently latched open." Surrounded by copies of the Vancouver *Daily Province*, the Amsterdam *Handelsblad*, the London *Times* and Manchester *Guardian*, the Paris *Temps*, the Frankfurter *Zeitung*, the *Journal de Genève*, and the Shanghai *Celestial Empire Mercury*, Freda clipped any item of possible interest for the *Nation*'s sixteen-page international fortnightly supplement. Desks separated only by filing cabinets full of international and domestic clippings in English and foreign languages made conditions less than ideal, but no one seemed to mind. Motivated by energy, enthusiasm, and a feeling that something important was being done there, they assessed the world beyond America.[1]

Freda felt good about being part of what Villard called "the *Nation* family" and the people who became her teachers in her journalistic apprenticeship. Just behind her sat Emily Balch, absentmindedly nibbling raisins as she read clippings and wrote editorial paragraphs. She had lost her job teaching economics at Wellesley because of an outspoken pacifism during World War I; when Villard heard the news he offered her a job. Freda respected Balch for maintaining her convictions, for being "the least self-conscious woman" she had ever known, and for her enormous knowledge of foreign affairs, especialy about the Balkans.[2]

Nation work motivated Freda as formal college study never had because for the first time she became truly aware of the world outside of the United States. In many ways the *Nation* was a school of international affairs. Freda absorbed all that she could from voracious reading in social and political affairs and from endless talks with people she respected. William MacDonald, who was her immediate boss, as well as managing editor Mussey, and editorial writer Balch, were part of this dialogue; they, in turn, talked to a stream of foreign dignitaries.

Chaim Weizmann had traveled from Palestine to the United States to generate support for Zionism. After he dined with *Nation* editors, "subeditor" Freda Kirchwey met with him privately and deluged him with questions about the Balfour Declaration and the problems Jews faced under the British mandate. She later commented, "Nothing in my life had permitted me to understand, except superficially and intellectually, the meaning of Zionism." Weizmann impressed her most by his "sophistication in depth," the result of experiences surviving anti-Semitism in his homeland, Russia, and in leading the Jewish people to Palestine; he demonstrated dedication to "the best and broadest democratic aspirations."[3]

Firsthand experience was Kirchwey's best teacher, but when unable to observe things for herself, she sensed which people she could rely upon. She read widely—treaties, rules, newspaper reports, and books—then sought out trusted people of diverse opinions to find out their perceptions before she made up her mind about issues. She amassed information, assimilated it, filtered it through her own value system, used intuition, and developed a reasoned conscience. Freda worked hard, with "a consuming interest in the awful world." When she took the job, she was told to clip articles which might be used in the IRS notes. If her work proved good, she might try her hand at writing some of the notes—or even some editorial paragraphs in the front of the journal. Within months she was doing just that.[4]

The first week in November 1918, when Freda among others anxiously awaited news of peace, she received some news of her own:

"Dr. Nancy" [Jenison] affirmed that she was pregnant. Freda decided not to mention this at work until she became "much more indispensable." In fact she asked her sister to keep the news from the rest of the family. "I have decided that 9 months is too long to take getting a baby and that I'll shorten it to 5 or 6 by forgetting about it and not mentioning it abroad for a while." Seven months later, in June 1919, when William MacDonald became European correspondent, a very pregnant Freda Kirchwey replaced him as editor of the IRS.[5]

In Villard's quest to create a forum for his political views, in 1918 he had separated the weekly from its former newspaper companion, selling the *New York Evening Post*. Although much would be new about Villard's *Nation* after 1918, there was some continuity to the journal whose long tradition stretched back to the end of the Civil War. It maintained the idealism of its original editor, E. L. Godkin, or as I. F. Stone wrote, the *Nation* kept Godkin's "moralistic approach to politics and politicians." For the most part, the journal also adhered to its original commitment to the rights of blacks. Above all, it kept its independent spirit. "*The Nation* will not be the organ of any party, sect, or body," announced the prospectus for the "Weekly Journal of Politics, Literature, Science, and Art," first published 2 July 1865.[6]

The *Nation,* within the confines of classic liberalism, owed no allegiance to any political party or special interest group. Editorials had faith in the basic goodness of human beings. Good would prevail, conquering ignorance through reason. Kirchwey, along with her colleagues, wrote editorials urging individual freedom, personal equality, and social progress. They hoped to convince people that it was in their best interest to consider other people's needs as well as their own, that blending of interests could create a better country and a better world. Ideally a "universal dialogue" would provide the forum for solving problems.[7]

The liberalism of the *Nation* during the editorship of Villard, Kirchwey, McWilliams, and their successors would differ markedly from the laissez-faire liberalism of Godkin. From 1918 on, the *Nation* began to build a reputation as "a crusading liberal journal." It left behind its first editor's attitude toward reform and the qualities of "a staid literary magazine." The International Relations Section, which reflected the new look in the *Nation*'s expansive role in political affairs, achieved status by being the first to publish the idea of a

League of Nations, in a special supplement to the IRS in February 1919. General Jan Christian Smuts of South Africa, who wrote it, gave the document to Villard for dissemination rather than to the Associated Press. The *Nation* was one of the first American publications to print the new Soviet constitution. On more than one occasion its IRS scooped its rivals by bringing important fast-breaking events to its readers.[8]

Along with her work on the IRS, Kirchwey wrote unsigned editorials for the journal itself. Unlike the anti-Bolshevik propaganda prevalent in American papers, she brought a pro-Soviet perspective to her articles. She was acutely aware of a general negative view of the Bolsheviks in American papers. For example, a supposed Soviet massacre received much coverage by the American press. When a New York paper revealed that it was a fabrication, most American newspapers ignored the truth. Kirchwey chided them for unwillingness to curb their "lavishly-documented case against the Bolsheviki."[9]

Freda Kirchwey deplored Allied intervention into Russia to suppress the Bolshevik revolution and criticized American support of the anti-Bolsheviks. "We must not continue to abet the Allies' attempts to put down the Revolution," she argued in 1920. The failure of the United States to support the revolutionary government, its refusal to trade with that communist nation, led her to ask: "How long is the United States to connive in the throttling of the Russian people? How long are the leading men of the country going to approve by their silence our part in the shady diplomacy of the Allied Governments?"[10]

Evans Clark wrote *Nation* editorials from the same ideological viewpoint. He argued that U.S. economic and military expenditures to fight revolution in Russia were not advantageous to most Americans and that, although arguments against Soviet Russia fed on a fear of Bolshevism, monied interests in Allied countries determined their counterrevolutionary policies. A Soviet victory would result in profits returning to the Russian workers; foreign investors would lose money. A victory for the old regime, "dedicated to the unlimited private exploitation of public wealth," would give foreign investors "the whole loaf."[11]

Clark, who had already been labeled one of sixty-two of the "Who's Who in Pacifism and Radicalism" by Archibald E. Stevenson of the Military Intelligence Service early in 1919, no doubt acquired an even more invidious taint later that year when he began work as the assistant director of the commercial department of the Russian Socialist Federal Soviet Republic Bureau in New York. With a civil war raging in Russia, the Bolsheviks set up the closest office to a consulate as the new Soviet regime could have in the United States. Russian Ludwig C. A. K. Martens was its representative unofficially. By promoting trade in the United States the Bureau wanted to prove that the Soviet government was in charge; it also hoped that economic relations would pave the way to diplomatic recognition. In February 1920 Clark reported the Bureau's successful bid for the purchase of 135,000 pairs of army shoes and overshoes from the United States War Department.[12]

He resigned from the Bureau two months later to pursue another venture, this time helping American labor unions. Accepting his resignation with regret, Martens acknowledged the vital support "Comrade Clark" had contributed: "You joined my staff at a time when such a step on your part was a sacrifice and demanded some courage. I thank you heartily for this proof of your sympathy toward Russia and for the valuable work you have done for our Bureau and for our people." Such efforts were increasingly unpopular in an America beset by a Red Scare. Martens reported increased difficulty in continuing the work of his Bureau when the War Department found out that the shoes the Bureau had bought would be exported to Russia. In less than a year the Bureau would be closed and Martens expelled.[13]

Decrying Martens' deportation, Kirchwey continued to urge the United States to recognize the Bolshevik government, which she thought represented the will of the Russian people. "Recognize Russia!" Kirchwey demanded in 1921—as she would year after year until Franklin Delano Roosevelt's administration finally recognized the Soviet Union in 1933. She regarded the government's official policy of "no trade, no recognition, no invasion and no partition" of the Soviet Union as a policy of "militant inactivity." To her argument for recognition of the Soviet government was added the pragmatic view that Americans were losing financial profits by refusing to trade with the Soviets.[14]

Freda Kirchwey's strong support of the Soviet Union made her and the journal vulnerable during the Red-baiting that followed World War I. Henry Mussey pointed out that the *Nation*'s push for "tolerance and fair play" toward the Soviet Union were translated by some readers into "treason and 'bolshevism.'" Cancellations came in from "grieved and scandalized oldest subscribers." Ernest Gruening, managing editor since 1920, played a frightening prank on Freda, calling to warn her about an impending search of the Kirchwey-Clark home by a Department of Justice agent. In a frenzy she scoured her files for any Soviet documents she may have saved for the IRS. Relieved when Gruening confessed his practical joke, Freda recounted, "I hope it was a sign of the times & and not my gullibility that I believed him."[15]

In the 1920s Kirchwey took her job seriously, proclaiming that she considered gender irrelevant to the work. She was aware that there was discrimination against women in the publishing field, but she maintained that she had never personally experienced it, describing her career as "free from that sort of prejudice." In fact she boasted: "At the time I was made an editor it was apparent that I was engaged in the very pursuit that is supposed to hamper women in professional life. But nobody made any protest against the extremely pregnant Miss Kirchwey strolling about the office, interviewing foreign authors."[16] Villard "let me stay at work right up until my baby was born," Freda wrote. Shortly before she gave birth, a flustered Villard introduced her as, "This is Miss Freda Kirchwey, but she is really Mrs. Evans Clark."[17]

"It's a BOY," Evans wrote a friend. "Fritz was in grand form, bless her heart—read Galsworthy up to the time she went into the operating room." She was in labor from 5 to 7:45 P.M., 27 June 1919, when Michael Kirchwey Clark weighed in at seven pounds, four ounces. According to his baby book, his paternal grandfather had died at sixty-three of arteriosclerosis, but his paternal grandmother had "very good" health. His maternal grandfather was in "good" health, that of his Kirchwey grandmother was "delicate." Michael's mother's health was recorded as "tolerably good," and his father's was the same, though "nervous." Despite her "tolerably good" health, Freda had missed no work during the pregnancy.[18]

"I am a pretty intelligent girl compared to the one you hired," Kirchwey wrote to Villard soon after her son Michael's birth. But she confessed to a feeling that she had let her boss down: "Your constant generosity makes my conscience hurt me for the way I've gone back on you this summer, but as you say there isn't anything like a baby." Her impatience with the early days of motherhood surfaced when Freda suspected that her *Nation* colleague Albert J. Nock "looks upon me as a lost sheep and babies as inventions of the Evil One. In defiance of Mr. Nock . . . the infant is flourishing and I am feeling much better than I had any right to expect just two weeks after his arrival."[19]

She continued to be aware of her dual responsibilities as editor and mother. When she returned to work the next month, she told Villard: "I can assure you that the peaceful rest you encouraged me to take will make me a better editor as well as a better mother." Yet the push, the drive to fulfill both responsibilities well, remained an enormous pressure. Years later Freda described the trip from the *Nation* office on Vesey Street to her apartment at 62 Montague Street in Brooklyn Heights, where she and Evans had lived since she started to work for the *Nation*. She walked across the Brooklyn Bridge each noon to nurse Michael. "I did it for nine months. It wasn't easy and I don't say this admiringly—I think I'd have gotten a lot more satisfaction out of having a baby if I'd taken some time off. It was very hard."[20]

During her child-bearing years, however, Freda Kirchwey did not consider it advisable or proper to take more than the absolute minimum time off to have a child. Even then, she was always reading, observing, and digesting facts for her job. Recuperating at Ardnamurchan, the Clark vacation home in Nova Scotia, after Michael's birth, Freda commented on a *Nation* editorial about the Plumb plan (for government ownership of the railroads). The journal supported the plan, though it cautioned workers against threatening to strike if the government refused. Kirchwey supported workers' use of the strike as an effective pressure toward change. (In the years ahead, Evans Clark, serving as head of the Labor Bureau, Inc., an independent professional group of economic advisers and public relations counselors for labor unions, prepared publicity for striking railroad workers. He also wrote feature articles on strikes for the *New York Times*.)[21]

Freda Kirchwey shared her husband's commitment to bettering workers' lives by exposing the bleak conditions in which they lived and worked. Always ready to investigate social problems firsthand, in 1922 she accompanied Rabbi Stephen Wise's commission to the New River coal field in West Virginia where miners were on strike. "Destitution is an empty word," she thought before her trip. After interviewing operators and miners and their wives, "tasting, gingerly enough, the food they live on," she could make the word destitution "something concrete."[22] She saw torn tents housing ill-clad families who slept on the bare ground; meals were doled out by the United Mine Workers' Union. The desperate situation required action.

She admired the miners' wives, "slaves of slaves," who supported the strike. After interviewing one, Kirchwey pondered, "If she had been born into a different class, she would have turned out a militant suffragist." Compared to this "revolutionist," her former work for suffrage seemed a luxury. She doubted that the woman had read revolutionary theory or was familiar with Lenin or Trotsky; she "has little time for juggling dogmas." "She sees the world going wrong, and without stopping to reason about it, she sets out to make it right."[23] Freda envied such a woman, for she herself could be only an observer.

*

In private, as in her public life, Kirchwey was just beginning to use her emotions. When Evans and she married, they were both sexually naive, though Freda considered herself more mature, "more awakened, more expectant, less afraid." She was also "inwardly unyielding," which she attributed to her background of "independence and pugnacity." She expected Evans to be a catalyst, but though he was older, he too lacked sexual experience. Furthermore, he was reserved and had a "conscious objection to 'intense' or 'overwhelming' feelings." Freda tried to respect his reserve, even taking responsibility for his reticence by suggesting that he was reacting to "a resistance in me that we never fully realized. I wanted more 'help' in finding my way to a complete experience. I wanted an emotion that would sweep me over the barriers and the self-consciousness that kept me from the ultimate satisfaction."[24]

In her late twenties, Freda was open to learning of all kinds. She even tried nudity, which at the time was popular among many of her peers. She and Evans considered their nudity a private matter. On a summer vacation in Wyoming in 1921, they undressed to swim, but when they spied a fisherman nearby, they dressed and sought "a more sheltered nook."[25] After supper Freda talked anthropology with another camper. All sorts of questions kept her awake. "Were barbaric hordes of West Europe on a lower evolutionary plane than

Greeks of same period?" She jotted in her diary that night, "Yearned for Boas. Lay long awake recapitulating and repeating." A couple of days later, after hiking, Freda read some H. G. Wells aloud to an aching Evans, who lay down by the campfire.[26]

On another chilly August night Freda and Evans huddled around a campfire. With them Bert and Charlie, two blond trail hands, talked seditiously about disobeying gun registration laws. Freda was struck by the irony. Nobody would consider these cowboys disloyal, though in New York, those on the left who advocated socialist views might be considered traitors. New York state senator Clayton R. Lusk, chairman of a committee created to investigate the impact of Bolshevism, had recently suggested several ways to curb radical activities, including the expulsion of newly elected Socialists from the New York legislature. To Freda it was ludicrous to fear law-abiding Americans because of their political views, while tolerating those like Bert and Charlie, who defied the law. On her return she wrote an editorial recounting the campfire conversation and challenged Lusk to "look into . . . 'the extent' and aim of Americanism [as opposed to Bolshevism], how it can be rooted out."[27]

Kirchwey's editorials were drawn from experience and used irony. Her method did not vary: publicize the problem; put a message before the reader to motivate action. She had received support for and example of these tactics from her father and her mother. Dora once asked her daughters to publicize information on the poor treatment of illegitimate children in the United States, suggesting a "propaganda sort of article" to focus attention on laxity in dealing with this social problem.[28]

The Kirchwey family members reinforced each other's commitments to the social causes their values fostered. As chairman of the Child Welfare Committee of the National League of Women Voters, Dorothy prepared the League's case for accepting the Sheppard-Towner Bill, which provided hygienic instruction for maternity and infant care. Her mother wrote encouragingly: "It is a great asset to think on your feet. I'm glad you are being trained for so worthy a cause as the S.T. bill." Freda's editorials supporting the bill also pleased her mother. In one she read: "Babies . . . have little direct influence in politics . . . Since women have had the vote, however, the indirect influence of the babies is beginning to make itself felt. The fight for the bill is really the first test of the political strength of women because this particular measure, through the indifference of men and the persistent interest of women, has become peculiarly a women's bill."[29]

Infant mortality was no abstract issue for Freda and Dorothy. Freda had memories of Brewster's death. Dorothy had recently suffered the death of her daughter, Eleanor, in 1920, after the child's second birthday; she would not have another child. Together with others of various political persuasions in women's groups, journalism, and government, the sisters exerted pressure leading to congressional passage and presidential signing of the bill in 1921.[30]

At the time of its passage, Freda Kirchwey launched a campaign for a much more radical cause: the dissemination of birth control information. The right to planned pregnancies for all women was inviolable, and Freda wrote about it dramatically and often and with a knowledge that came out of her own experiences. Earlier she had written about the limitations childbearing placed on women, when, in a 1918 *Every Week* piece, she charged that once a Japanese woman married, she lost her personhood and became a "servant" of the husband; when she bore children the woman became "doubly enslaved." Years later, when Freda defended the need for maintaining protective legislation for women, she argued that one of the reasons women needed such legislation was to compensate for "certain physical handicaps—most particularly the handicap of childbearing."[31]

Although she viewed carrying a child a physical handicap, she also believed that having a child was a sign of a normal, well-adjusted woman. Many of Kirchwey's writings focused on the importance of having children, yet being able to limit their number and plan the time of their conception. "Generally speaking I don't like to speak generally about women!" she remarked, but some issues were so integral to women's lives that she did press them as women's issues.[32] She urged women who had worked for the passage of the Sheppard-Towner Bill to turn their energies to the harder task of "securing the repeal of all laws prohibiting education in the limitation of families."[33]

When the Cummins-Vaile Bill (1921) to legalize the dissemination of scientific facts on birth control came to a vote in Congress, Kirchwey urged an affirmative vote for a measure "designed to put science at the service of the people to order their own lives." She praised the Voluntary Parenthood League for its support, but asked, "Where are the other women's organizations?" Her staunch support of access to birth-control information separated her from the consensus of the League of Women Voters, as well as from the more radical National Woman's Party, to whom the mere discussion of birth control seemed inappropriate.[34]

In 1922, when the League of Women Voters sponsored a Pan-American Conference for Latin American women who wanted to form a similar organization in their countries, the sponsors deliberately avoided the topic of birth control. Speaking for herself and others of more radical sentiment, Kirchwey criticized the League: "If it fails to talk about birth control, that does not bother anybody except those of us who happen to believe that birth control information is more important to women than anything else in the world." She believed that knowledge of birth control had changed the morals and economic status of those women who had been able to acquire it and that such knowledge had modified "almost beyond recognition the middle-class home."[35]

*

She practiced what she advocated. Freda and Evans were one of an increasing number of dual career couples in the 1920s with well-spaced children and smaller families. Historian William Chafe has estimated that in that decade 450,000 women joined the professions and 100,000 women entered the business world. He cautioned, however, that increased numbers of professional women did not necessarily mean "startling advances" for them in new fields, since many entered professions traditionally associated with females.[36] Yet long accepted moral norms changed as this large articulate group of women interacted with male colleagues, husbands, or lovers, and then ran up against their own self-images as women. Some of the sanctions of the "old morality" ceased to have meaning in their new environment, most especially the belief that women should stay at home as the guardians of morality.

Most of this generation of college-educated women who left home chose careers in teaching, social work, and nursing. The few who persevered through graduate schooling in pharmacy, dentistry, medicine, or law found some support for their nontraditional careers. Freda Kirchwey, with only a college education, had secured a job in a male-dominated field: political journalism. She did have some female predecessors, however. She could have looked back to colonial times to Elizabeth Timothy, who took over the editing of the Charleston *South Carolina Gazette* in 1739 after the death of her husband. No inheritance was responsible for Anne Royall's choice of journalism. At the age of fifty-five she began to write her impressions in travel books; in 1831, aged sixty-two she began to publish exposés from the nation's capital in her paper, *Paul Pry*, and in 1836 in another paper, *The Huntress*. Royall's political stress was quite different from that of Sarah Josephah Hale, who a year later began to edit *Godey's Lady's Book*, which specialized in women's social interest topics. Kirchwey's place in journalistic history was rooted in the more political milieu of investigative reporting, personified perhaps by Elizabeth Cochrane Seaman, who wrote under the name of Nellie Bly. Bly feigned insanity to cover the treatment of the mentally ill on Blackwell's Island and won notoriety from her exposé of conditions there. Kirchwey knew Seaman as a family friend and her adventures in investigative reporting must have encouraged Freda's own variety of journalistic muckraking. Some slightly older accomplished female companions, such as socialist Crystal Eastman and labor activist Mary Simkovitch, had also paved the way.[37]

New York feminists who called their discussion group Heterodoxy reinforced Freda's commitment to her career. Elizabeth Gurley Flynn's tribute to the founder, Marie Jenny Howe, reflected the opinion of several members of Heterodoxy, including Kirchwey: "I treasure the friendships and stimulating associations it has given me. It has been a glimpse of the women of the future, big spirited, intellectually alert, devoid of the old 'femininity' which has been replaced by a wonderful freemasonry of women."[38] Evans also bolstered Freda's career. His moral support meant that she did not have to choose between him and journalism. Kirchwey and other women in their twenties and thirties in the 1920s were the "New-Style Feminists," as their contemporary Dorothy Bromley labeled them, who chose to have both a career and a marriage.[39]

Kirchwey was not only a "new-style feminist," she was interested in and wrote about other such women. She noted the wide-ranging implications of feminism: "It may mean a combination of short hair and knickerbockers or of babies and jobs. It may mean equal pay for equal work and equal pay for equal misbehavior." Despite the passage of the Nineteenth Amendment, "galling inequalities" still existed for American women. Accordingly, when the National Woman's Party advocated an equal rights amendment, she supported the concept, believing that to guarantee women equal protection under the law would eventually help change "age-long prejudices" against them. But in 1923 Kirchwey joined the many progressive women opposed to the equal rights amendment (ERA) as proposed, sharing their fear that its passage would mean the loss of protective labor legislation for women.[40]

To force political parties to consider other issues of concern to women, such as maternity protection and compensation and legalization of birth control information, she recommended a "vigorous nonpartisan organization of women." The fact that women were born with the unique capacity to bear children made these women's rights "nothing but human rights." She was aware of the difficulty women faced when they attempted to participate fully in society. She urged women to fight within the political parties: "For every party job, for every political office, for every legal change in the direction of equality, women will have to fight as women." She criticized the League of Women Voters' stance: "no policy for or against women in office."[41]

But Freda Kirchwey had no sympathy for the idea of a separate women's political party. Nor did she respect the strategy of the National Woman's Party, which urged women to vote for all female candidates who supported the equal rights amendment and "a general feminist program." She viewed women's struggle within the context of traditional progressivism and considered woman suffrage a progressive reform. The struggle for the vote, a "primary" right, united women with different priorities in a way that the struggle for full sexual equality never could, for: "women are going to vote according to the dictates of class interest and personal interest as well as sex interest." After experiencing firsthand the poverty of striking miners' wives, Kirchwey could not agree with the National Woman's Party that a women's bloc made sense. Life was more complicated than a world divided into men's and women's demands: "there are other revolutions going on in the world besides the women's revolution," and the National Woman's Party was wrong in urging "women voters to forget they are also human beings."[42]

Kirchwey's position paralleled the League's "No Sex Line Up" position, as well as that of many female political candidates who were unwilling to run as "women's" candidates. To them, focusing on gender questioned their commonality with men; they wanted voters to consider them as Republicans or Democrats, not as women. Emily Newell Blair, vice chairman of the Democratic Committee, explained that a woman's desire to be seen as a competent human being kept many from running as feminists. The dilemma of female political candidates was that they were voted against because of their sex and were not recognized as viable candidates because they lacked a power base. Party leaders gave only token support to female party members and did not confront the inequalities remaining for women. Ironically, those such as Alice Paul, Anne Martin, and Crystal Eastman, who advocated a women's bloc, were unable to convince the majority of women of this dilemma.[43]

Nor did they convince Freda Kirchwey, who wrote an editorial advising women to fight for their rights within the party structure. In 1924 she did push her progressive tradition to its outer limits when she urged feminists to ally with the Progressive Party to conduct that fight—"some such alliance of active partisan progressivism and feminism appeals to us." But Crystal Eastman, also using the *Nation*'s pages, challenged this assessment, arguing, "it seems to me most emphatically not true that the battle for 'equal rights,' must be fought within party lines. It can never be won there." Until major party leaders saw women as a bloc to be influenced and feared, gender would remain an issue in politics.[44]

Progressive leaders such as Carrie Chapman Catt, president of the League of Women Voters, and Grace Abbott, director of the Children's Bureau, were reluctant to call attention to their femaleness. They opted for attempted assimilation with men rather than sustained struggle as a women's bloc. They, along with Kirchwey, underestimated the tenacity of resistance against women's integration into the political and social structure. With disagreements between the two major political organizations of the women's movement and with many feminists wanting to assimilate with men and be finished with the fight that often pitted women against men, no focused strategy for combatting this opposition emerged.[45]

Without the sustained momentum that might have been provided by many former suffragist activists like Kirchwey, the battle for full equality splintered. The postsuffrage generation of female college students showed less interest in carrying on the struggles of their older sisters. When Freda went to Vassar to interview members of the senior class of 1923, she found the majority of them viewed a career as "a mere stop-gap before they are 'called' to the great and exclusive career of matrimony." After talking to a group of editors and managers of women's college newspapers, she was concerned by the degree of apathy they reported among fellow students. Exasperated by her encounters with such apathy and return to traditional values, she branded the group "The Languid Generation."[46]

Reports of overcrowded colleges sent Freda Kirchwey on "the great college tour" to explore and document that condition. But while interviewing administrators and professors of Eastern women's colleges she discovered that these administrators were limiting admissions to upper- and middle-class women, screening out working-class career-oriented women. One professor explained that admissions were limited to "nice girls," "conventional, well-brought-up middle-class girls—girls who will leave college and go back to their homes and never, never do anything worth doing as long as they live—nice girls." He wished admission depended upon "minds delighted by knowledge," that "no student would be judged by her personality or parentage or race or even by her willingness to 'contribute' to the life of the institution." Kirchwey decided that colleges selected those with malleable personalities and "Christian ethics." She compared their admitted bias with the fate of her working-class friend, Sonia Trotzky, who had worked days and studied nights to gain admission, only to be rejected as not "good college material." She decided that Sonia's "terrific need to know everything" would prevent her from ever fitting in as a "nice girl." Kirchwey did not always find what she expected, but she trusted her impressions and reported what she found. A tour to document lack of college space resulted in a *Nation* diatribe against college admission policies that fostered elitism and anti-Semitism.[47]

Along with Freda's own "terrific need to know everything," she gained experience and sharpened her writing skills. She continued to edit the IRS, and wrote *Nation* editorial paragraphs and pieces. Villard was aware that financial losses would mean changes on his journal. He considered whether, if he had to let some of his editors go, he should promote Kirchwey to managing editor. Norman Thomas, then associate editor, recommended her: "I think Freda would make a highly competent managing editor with Dorothy's help at the mechanics." A few months later Villard confided to one of his directors the drastic cuts he had decided to make in order to counter mounting deficits: "It is now settled that four of our editors are going—Carl Van Doren, Arthur Warner (whose name will, however, remain on the editorial page), Norman Thomas, and Dr. Gruening." He hoped to bring them back when finances improved. The fall before her actual promotion, those cuts left Freda, "three fairly busy people here at the office—myself, E. H. Gruening, and Mr. Schuum, proof-reader and make-up man." She wrote her sister, "I now sign myself (tho' my future is still undecided) as follows: Freda Kirchwey, Acting Managing Editor."[48]

At the time of the promotion, November 1922, Freda was three months pregnant with her third and last child, Jeffrey, and determined not to let the pregnancy interfere with her job. To be a good managing editor, she had to be a "planner, editor, contact man, traffic manager, and several things combined." She also felt that a managing editor should look for "new ideas and areas of interest." Just three days before Jeffrey's birth, Freda wrote Dorothy about her pregnant state. It was "blankedly uncomfortable," but she continued to enjoy her writer's life-style. "It's positively exciting to be able to bat around town and confer with people instead of sitting on one chair all day!"[49]

Once again she resolved to combine motherhood and career. In a letter she wrote Villard thirty-three hours after Jeffrey was born, Freda commented: "Even under these circumstances, it seems unnatural not to be at work—this being the first day I've cut this writer. If that sounds boastful—and I feel a little pride in it—at least I am boasting health rather than virtue." Reflecting the priority she placed on her job, she was pleased that pregnancy had not interfered with work. While others at the *Nation* that winter had suffered a variety of ailments, she and the baby had not: "I have felt as if Jeffrey and I were trying for a nonstop record!" The letter continued to spell out business details for which she had not left specific instructions prior to her hospitalization. She thanked Villard, "one of my chief helps in this winter's ventures." Then, referring to her motherhood, "I'm not going to let it hurt the Nation if I can possibly avoid it—and I'm sure I can."[50]

Hired help at home on Montague Street facilitated Freda's return to a full-time career: a nursemaid, who also cooked, and a daily cleaning woman. Freda followed doctor's orders to get her body back in shape: "Somewhere in the course of the 24 hours I'm supposed (in fact the future of my insides are said to depend on it) to do ½ hour of deep breathing—and that's the lowest cavern of hell.

I'd rather stand on my head for an hour than deep-breathe," she told her sister.[51]

*

Back at work, a burst of creative activity took place, and within six months Kirchwey prided herself on turning out a "fine" special issue of the *Nation,* commemorating the Soviet government's sixth anniversary. Freda, like many liberals and radicals of the 1920s, was enamored of the possibility of the new world the Russian experiment promised. After Stalin's rise to power and the beginning of collectivization, many became disillusioned, whereas Freda modified, but never completely rejected, the positive view of the Soviet Union she held in November of 1923: "In a world that is sick with the diseases that breed from capitalist-imperialism, the virility of Russia may hold out the best hope for civilization." By that time the Soviet Union was enjoying a period of relative internal peace following two years of economic recovery under Lenin's New Economic Policy (NEP). Lenin had compromised his Marxist ideology to reach an alliance between the proletariat and the peasants, and the NEP, which encouraged limited private enterprise and supported small businessmen, gave the illusion of a unity with capitalism without abandoning the goals of social and economic experimentation.[52]

In 1923 Freda Kirchwey used her authority as managing editor to compile a special issue about the Soviet Union. For the Soviet anniversary she chose articles that were "human and readable and not merely instructive."[53] She selected Jessica Smith's piece on the confiscation of a *dacha* once owned by a sugar magnate and its conversion into a proletarian cultural center; Dorothy Brewster's impressions of an omnipresent Lenin in Moscow; Max Eastman's description of the slower pace of Soviet life; Isaiah J. Hoorgin's analysis of the country's economy; and L. Talmy's description of the evolution of a brand-new Russian press, recruited from workers and peasants. The issue also featured the first of a series of articles on "The New Russian Women" by French writer Magdeleine Marx.[54]

Kirchwey introduced several cartoons in this issue, overcoming at last Villard's disapproval of them. Cartoons from Moscow's *Projektor* illustrated the Hoorgin article. She was genuinely pleased with the issue, as she wrote to Villard, then covering news from Europe: "Just at the moment we are recovering after a wild scramble to get out the Russian number. And now after flapping its pages over I have decided that it is a fine one." Life at home was hectic but happy: "What with the nicest baby ever born to nurse once in a while and a new (old) house to move into . . . I have yearned once in a while for a South Sea Island and a mango tree."[55]

Then Freda turned to a new idea: Why not publish a collection of articles reflecting the fascination of the 1920s with morality, especially sex? Beatrice Hinkle, Jungian psychoanalyst of the period, charged that so much conversation revolved around sexual morality, "one would be inclined to think it the outstanding problem of our time." Kirchwey agreed that sex was an important topic and believed that the increased number of women with careers made more interactions between female and male coworkers something new. She was aware of a general uncertainty about social mores. While some churches issued jeremiads, and much of the press sensationalized free love, she wanted to identify and understand the moral issues of the day. In 1923 Freda was experiencing an accelerating, stimulating career; she was married to a slightly balding thirty-five-year-old husband, had sons aged four and under one, and questioned how to blend the various parts of her life and what to claim as her own from the changing moral standards. At the age of thirty she had resoundingly rejected her earlier irreverence toward issues of morality. This was in contrast to her view in 1915 when, in a piece for the *Morning Telegraph,* she had viewed divorce court as a circus full of grimy stories, "all nationalities and at least two or three colors." Then she had scoffed at divorce as an issue; now it was part of a larger transformation in society.[56]

As Freda matured, she became more serious. She insisted that articles in the proposed morality series must take an informative, reflective look at current thought about changing values. Defending this approach to Villard, she said the *New Republic* had been criticized for publishing an article on sexual morality by Clement Wood because of the author's "trivial and smart and cocksure manner." Wood should not write on these subjects: "he positively leers while he does it." For the *Nation*'s series she sought persons of "authority or at least of some restraint"—who could write. "I think it will be well to avoid even the best of reformers if they cannot write. I am thinking in particular of such people as Dr. Stopes and Mrs. Sanger. It will be hard to avoid them because they all will want to write."[57]

Advance promotion of the series "New Morals for Old" read: "In a series of articles to appear in our next issue, *The Nation* will print the opinions of a few intelligent observers on the shifting moral standards of our day and on the difficult problems of modern sex relations." Bertrand Russell, Elsie Clews Parsons, Floyd Dell, Charlotte Perkins Gilman, Joseph Wood Krutch, Isabel Leavenworth, H. L. Mencken, Edwin Muir, Arthur Garfield Hays, Louis Fischer, M. Vaerting, Ludwig Lewisohn, Florence Guy Seabury, and Beatrice Hinkle were contributors. Freda's announcement to her sister was less serious, as she reminded "My dear Mrs. Brown" of her unrenewed subscription and warned what she would miss: "You will be interested in several of the special features we are planning for the coming year, particularly one on sex and moral standards, which, God knows, none needs more than you."[58]

"New Morals for Old" explored marriage (including common-law marriage), divorce, sex role expectations, children, birth control, monogamy, extramarital friendships, promiscuity, extramarital romances, prostitution, female economic independence, moral effects of crowded urban living, experimental psychology, eroticism, independence in mating, and sexual ethics. The authors questioned all assumptions about the sexes. As journalist Seabury said, by then so much had been written to create "the stereotype of Woman" that it was hard to know what women were really like.[59] Over the next several years Kirchwey would follow a pattern similar to this first series, which resulted in her being dubbed the *Nation*'s "'informal' morals editor." She liked her idea: a forum of experts to present facts, then to analyze, interpret, and suggest directions. The dialogue—whether within her own mind, at a meeting, or in the pages of her journal—was Freda's way to examine all sides of issues and attempt to find answers.

"New Morals for Old" included seminal topics, many on subjects that interested Kirchwey. For example, several articles detailed the effects of a double sexual standard for men and women; in their own life Freda and Evans defied this, holding to a single standard: each was free to have affairs. The much more typical double standard divided women into moral and immoral. Leavenworth asked if the virtue of some women was protected by the prostitution of others; and answered affirmatively. To close the chasm between women and men, she urged the ordinary woman to shed her unrealistic and artificial cloak of purity; she, like the ordinary man, must accept and enjoy sex, thereby erasing the artificial dichotomy between instinct and morality and allowing them to merge.[60]

The crowded urban life of the 1920s made it easier for couples freely to engage in sexual relations. There was more anonymity and more indifference to an individual's personal morality, argued anthropologist Parsons. Growing access to illegal birth-control information made the connection between sexual relations and childbearing optional. Sex, freed from the danger of pregnancy, could and did make new demands on relationships. In a marriage, reciprocity of passion and friendship could replace assumptions of duty and fidelity. According to lawyer Hays, spouses demanded "sexual and social compatibility"; divorce signaled that there had been a breach in that mutual commitment. He documented the extension of the grounds for divorce and concluded that such changes were drastic indeed.[61]

Rising divorce rates and the push for liberalized divorce laws reflected the demands of wives. Having become increasingly independent economically, women no longer needed to cling to marriage as the sole means of survival. Less dependent upon it for economic support, they could demand more of the institution, especially in its sexual and social dimensions. Parsons argued that the change in status of women—from being the property of men to owning property—created social independence for women, particularly independence in mating.[62] Also, as women gained access to various professions and worked with men, sex taboos dwindled, and women and men began to cooperate more and to develop companionships.

"Friendship between men and women is rather a new thing in the history of the world," remarked Dell. True friendship depended upon choice and equality, and women had only recently tasted the fruits of political equality and a degree of educational, economic, and social equality. Men and women could now become friends, and they did. In fact, the 1920s were fostering a dramatic increase in heterosexual friendships with a noticeable decrease of same sex friendships. There was also an increase of friendship within marriage: "More than ever before, husbands and wives are friends," said Dell. He also noted that if friendship was not found inside marriage, it could be found outside, in extramarital relations. Not that these were previously unknown; what was new was the number and the potential conventions that would evolve "to give social protection and dignity to extra-marital friendships."[63]

Extramarital relationships, extramarital romance, sexual equality, sexual compatibility—such were the topics addressed in the series. This was the 1920s: morality was changing, and women were in the forefront of the change. In most assessments written for the series, the new variable was woman. Indeed, psychoanalyst Beatrice Hinkle ascribed to women the role of "active agents in the field of sexual morality." In "Women and the New Morality" she pointed out that unequal economic conditions had previously allowed for a double standard. Men had controlled women's sexual conduct; women served as a symbol of virtue for men. Because women's thoughts and feelings about morality had been tangled in a web of anxiety about physical survival for themselves and their children, economic dependency had deprived them of the spiritual freedom to define morality for themselves.

Economic independence freed women from this dependent state; they could overturn the outdated double standard and determine, "in the true scientific spirit of the age" what morality was. In a word, women were participating in a revolt. Using highly developed capacities of feeling, intuition, and "superior psychological processes," they could create a "new morality." Hinkle did not delineate the elements of this new morality, but she did explain its dilemma. While women could look toward the generative potential of a creative, female, new morality, they also became susceptible to suffering "a general chaos of conflicting feelings." A woman who demanded to determine her own ego identity set herself apart from her biologically instinctive capacity as "race bearer." The critical question was: "How can she gain a relation to both racial and individual obligations, instead of possessing one to the exclusion of the other?" Hinkle wanted women to retain both functions; she regarded woman's biological role as "her greatest strength and value."[64]

Freda and Evans depended on Hinkle. At the time, Evans was undergoing psychoanalysis with her. He also interviewed her professionally and wrote a lead editorial for the *New York Times* on her theories about personality types.[65] Freda valued Hinkle's assessments of women and the new morality for the *Nation* series. When she edited these articles for publication of her 1924 book, *Our Changing Morality*, she relied heavily on Hinkle's analysis for her own conclusions. Kirchwey alluded to Hinkle's idea of the paradox for women vis-à-vis morality in the 1920s, that is, their active role in generating a new morality and their confusion about this amorphous process.

Giving the articles a common theme, Kirchwey said that they connected "the changing standards of sex behavior and the increasing freedom of women." But, she moved beyond Hinkle, and in fact beyond any of the articles, to conclude: "Certainly, of the factors involved in modern sex relations, women and economic conditions are the two that have suffered the most revolutionary change; and men's morals must largely shape themselves to the patterns laid down by these two masters of life." This is a powerful role for Freda to assign to women and, thus, to herself.

Freda Kirchwey concluded that a woman who was out in the world in competition with men confronted inconsistencies in sexual behavior for which her upbringing provided no answers. In generalizing about the series, she described her own dilemma: "slowly, clumsily, she is trying to construct a way out to a new sort of certainty in life; she is seeking something to take the place of the burden of solemn ideals and reverential attitudes that rolled off her shoulders when she emerged."[66]

Dora Child Wendell, Freda Kirchwey's mother, in 1881, at the age of twenty-five.

Georgie, Dora, and Freda in 1903.

Dorothy Kirchwey, aged twenty-two.

Freda Kirchwey, aged sixteen and a half.

Freda Kirchwey, aged twenty-two, about 1915.

Evans Clark, aged twenty-seven, about 1915.

The Kirchwey-Clarks at the Log Cabin; Mrs. Clark at the far end of the table, Freda Kirchwey facing the camera.

George Washington Kirchwey holding Brewster Clark, about 1916.

Freda Kirchwey and three-year-old Michael Clark.

Dorothy and La Rue Brown with Jeffrey and Michael Clark, about 1923.

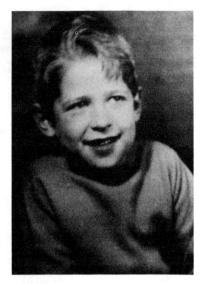

Michael Clark, aged ten.   Jeffrey Clark, aged six.

Evans Clark at the helm of "Loon," about 1930.

A *Nation* outing in Connecticut, about 1918. Left to right, front: Dorothy Van Doren, Mary Ross, Irita Van Doren, Freda Kirchwey; back: Joseph Wood Krutch, Mark Van Doren, Lewis Gannett, Oswald Garrison Villard.

American Field Service ambulance driver Michael Clark in the Middle East, 1942.

J. Alvarez del Vayo (second from left) and Freda Kirchwey broadcasting from station WINS, New York, during World War II.

The presentation to Freda Kirchwey of a $25,000 check on the twenty-fifth anniversary of her association with *The Nation;* 27 February 1944, Hotel Commodore, New York. Left to right: William Rosenblatt, Archibald Mac-Leish, Judge Thurman W. Arnold, Freda Kirchwey, Raymond Swing.

A Nation Associates dinner at the Waldorf-Astoria, New York, 25 June 1945.
Left to right: Freda Kirchwey, Dr. Thomas Mann, Secretary of the Interior
Harold Ickes, Supreme Court Justice Felix Frankfurter.

At the office of *The Nation,* about 1946. Left to right: Keith Hutchinson,
J. King Gordon, Joseph Wood Krutch, Freda Kirchwey, Maxwell Stewart,
I. F. Stone.

American Jewish Congress Awards dinner for distinguished service to Israel, 9 June 1948. Left to right: Eleanor Roosevelt, Freda Kirchwey.

3 || *A Search for Certainty*

"Moral standards are crumbling here and hardening there, and only those minds are to be pitied that find no interest in the flux and surge of impulses and ideas. Women, especially, are not to be pitied, for theirs is the central role in this modern drama. The future of personal relationships seems to be in their hands." Yet women also suffered the physical consequences of pregnancy. Evans and Freda conceived another child just six months after she made her observation, and within six more months she was aware that the fetus within her was dead: "It is patently and obviously defunct—as is proved by the fact that there's been a distinct shrinkage rather than the opposite in a month." It was a painful miscarriage, and Freda, who already practiced birth control, promised her sister to be "a wiser and much much cautiouser girl." By October 1924 Dora wrote Dorothy: "Freda looked tired but she insisted she is feeling well. Some task has that girl!"[1]

Dora hoped to lift Freda's spirits that Christmas with a warm red robe she had made for her, and she encouraged Dorothy to buy her sister something "more or less 'useless and pretty,'" for "she *never* spends money on herself except for necessities." Evans knew Freda loved "gay silk stockings" and "silk undergarments," even if they were frivolous. The successful professional woman loved feeling feminine. Freda and Evans were showered with gifts and hopes for the coming year. As the clock struck midnight on December 31 they climbed onto then jumped off of their chairs, their custom for welcoming a new year.[2]

For Freda the year began with final preparations for a *Nation* forum. She planned to gather experts and pose a question that plagued her personally: Is Monogamy Feasible? This forum was in part the result of the great interest in the *Nation*'s earlier morality series. Freda, who had been back at work full time since October, had secured Elsie Clews Parsons, anthropologist and writer, Dr. Alexander Goldenweiser, psychologist and anthropologist, and Floyd Dell, author, as speakers at the Fifth Avenue Restaurant symposium in January. Days before the dinner she counted the reservations, decided on the menu, arranged place cards for the head table, and fretted over her own role of chairman. She still hated making speeches to large groups, and it was especially hard at the time, for she still felt weak. The talks were "serious and, at the same time sharply provocative"; the discussion that followed was "so contentious that my powers as chairman were heavily taxed." Years later she recalled one of the exchanges:

> Said a dignified woman to Dr. Goldenweiser: "You have advocated legalizing birth control. Now I would like to ask you, Doctor, whether you meant to suggest that information about birth-control methods should be made available to young, unmarried women." Said Dr. Goldenweiser, partly rising, "Oh, yes." "Pardon me," said the questioner, "I'm not sure I heard the answer." "The answer," I told her after a glance at the speaker, "was yes." There was a pause, and then the audience broke into somewhat embarrassed laughter.[3]

Evans felt Freda "piloted" the dinner "with great dexterity and charm." Her mother said that even though Freda was nervous before the forum dinner, she had gotten over it or concealed it by the time she spoke. She was "exquisite in her simplicity and freshness of appearance. She looked 18." Her speech was "well thought out, clearly delivered and received with much enthusiasm," and she fielded the questions well.[4]

*

Toward the end of the year Kirchwey had given serious consideration to her career. She and Villard had had a row about one of her creative ideas that past summer, when she wrote, "We are printing this week a dazzling, lively, futuristic movie scenario by Robert

L. Wolf." Villard, furious, demanded an explanation. Freda defended her judgment: "I took it because I believed it to be striking and important and because I think *The Nation* ought to be proud to lead in this sort of modernism as well as other sorts." Villard disagreed and insisted that in the future any manuscripts that departed from the journal's traditional fare be submitted to him prior to publication. Freda wanted no part in what she considered censorship: "you are reducing my work to something I have no interest in. The only real function of a managing editor is to decide, in consultation with the staff, what material is worth using in the paper . . . the managing editor must have the general responsibility for accepting articles and planning the paper—or the job ceases to have any meaning."[5] Villard gave in and Freda remained.

A little later Freda received an offer of an attractive position with the Child Study Association of America, which fostered parent and family life education. The editorship of its quarterly, *Child Study,* would have paid a higher salary and given her a three-month vacation. "I could write a novel or climb a mountain or associate with my children or go to Russia!" After consulting her husband and father, Freda had decided instead to stay on the *Nation,* which covered "all fields on all continents." George wrote his wife: "You will be glad to know that the dubious plan of a new magazine editorship for Fritz has been dropped and that she isn't sorry." As Freda said, "too big a chunk of my life has gone into *The Nation* to permit me to leave it carelessly or without long thinking."[6] She had strengthened her commitment to the particular kind of journalism and the familial closeness of the working relationships she had developed there.

Indeed as managing editor Freda Kirchwey had quite a stake in her *Nation* family, including her authority to bring her immediate family into its pages. Both her husband and father had contributed articles. Not long before the Child Study job offer, she had solicited and seen into print a book review by her mother. In her review of *Colonial Women of America* Dora wrote: "The feminist of today will find her prototype among these early forebears of ours." She concluded by agreeing with author Elizabeth Anthony Dexter that women's freedom in the 1920s might be the result of "the respect by society and the self-respect which the working women of the earlier day quietly and unconsciously won for themselves." No doubt Freda credited part of her own place in life with the self-respect her mother "quietly and unconsciously won" for herself, despite debilitating poor health.[7] Recurring digestion problems, weakness, weight loss, fatigue, stomach pain, and an open wound on her knee afflicted her during her forties, fifties, and sixties.

For years Freda watched her mother suffer. Writing an invalid friend she remarked: "I think I partly know what all this must mean. I've seen my mother put off by sickness from things she yearned to be in year after year and the world is so hard to ignore these days. It takes a person with your or her indomitable spirit to face inaction." To her daughter, Dora was a model of strength, courage, and bravery. Yet Freda was aware of the frustration that occurred when her mother's "wretched old stomach" had to be considered in every plan. Dora's weight had dropped from 99 pounds in 1924 to 79 pounds in 1925, indicating a steady deteriorating condition, accompanied by "very severe headaches," "a curious paralysis of the right wrist," "a serious condition of anemia."[8]

Depression set in, and Dora did not want to see anyone but family members. Dorothy kept in close contact through letters and frequent visits from Boston; Karl Kirchwey, a New York lawyer who commuted from Port Washington, was not around as much as the sisters. Freda, who lived closest to her parents' 115th Street home, visited their mother most often, especially during the final months. Dora wrote Dorothy about "a good long call from Freda," who had "real color in her cheeks and had no end of interesting things to tell me of her own and her family's doings. That child's life is too full for her own good but it is highly entertaining to hear her tell about it."[9]

"Fritz keeps us in touch with their activities which are far too numerous for a lady with a job. The most entertaining thing this week was a Nation surprise party given at Freda's on Tuesday night for 'Papa' Schumm whose 70th birthday it was." Villard read imaginary telegrams while *Nation* book reviewer H. Van Loon played the violin. "Freda presented the huge gaily decorated birthday cake." Dora also noted about Freda's son: "Mickie has entered upon the religious phase of his existence . . . insists on saying his prayers in regular fashion on his knees! Freda is immensely amused—more I am afraid than is exactly befitting!" Freda also told her mother about having lunch at the Heterodoxy Club, hearing Alice Durer Miller, Mary Heaton Vorse, and others tell how they managed to find free time to write. "It must have been quite spicy as F. was quite keen about the ability shown by the women who talked."[10]

Dora was too ill to attend Freda's second *Nation* symposium, "Wages for Wives," in January 1926. The announcement for it read: "Is a wife a slave? Are her services as housekeeper, cook, nurse, furnace tender, interior decorator, gardener and general utility man worth more than merely board and lodging?" Doris Stevens, feminist activist author, discussed one side, and New York attorney Arthur Garfield Hays, the other. Freda thought the brief speeches from the floor were crisper than those of the chief speakers: "Clarence Darrow, cynical as always, but quite ultra-conservative about the subject in hand and our good Mr. Ratcliffe [S. K.] keen and snappy."[11]

Dora Kirchwey's health steadily deteriorated. In April she developed aphasia, and soon she became completely speechless. Freda, her aunts, and her father kept a close vigil. George said, "we have never lost our courage or the 'reasonable hope' that our brave fighter would win out."[12] Dora died on 30 June 1926. The "safe and gentle" music for her funeral included the Schumann "Traumereir," the last chorus of Bach's St. Matthew's Passion, "Sleep Take Thy Rest," and Chopin's Funeral March. Seven-year-old Michael regained consciousness in Presbyterian Hospital after a tonsillectomy to be greeted by the promised ice cream and the news that his "Mama Dodie" was dead.[13]

Many tributes were paid. "Dr. Nancy" Jenison wrote: "One thinks of her as the very spirit of courage—not making much of it but just quietly doing the things that would spread happiness and allow herself the truest kinds of happiness in life." Samuel Eliot remembered her as having a "buoyant spirit, a hospitable heart, a quick insight, a keen interest in things, in ideas, in nature, in events, in persons . . . Here was an affirmative nature, one that said 'Yes' more often than 'No.'"[14]

Dora Wendell Kirchwey's death left an enormous void in the lives of the family, just as these last months of her life had brought them closer together. George Washington Kirchwey said, "I had never had a stronger sense of the tie that binds us together and of the priceless companionship that has come to us out of the experience of the last few months." Her mother's death was a wrenching experience for Freda. Years later she responded to the death of friend

Otto Nathan's mother: "I understand from my own experience the mixed feelings of sorrow, exhaustion and relief—for her—that you are laboring under."[15] Freda felt her mother's death "shattering": "I am not yet adjusted to a world in which pain and death have come to occupy so large a place. It is easy to say that Mother was so ill and so hopelessly stricken that one could not wish for her recovery. The fact is that one feels only an added horror at the series of blows that finally broke down her brave fight. I am glad to have the children and an absorbing job to turn to these days."[16]

Freda made no mention of a supportive husband; after eleven years, she felt alienated from Evans. Overall, their sexual life left them frustrated; as Freda once told Evans, it held "a lot of joy and some disappointment." They began to experiment with others, which might not have happened if they "had wholly satisfied each other." Freda felt that it was "reasonable to suspect that the lack of completeness in our relationship helped to prod us in those other directions."[17] Such liaisons created a distance between Freda and Evans. When Evans began psychoanalysis with Beatrice Hinkle in 1924, Freda felt even more isolated from him. As he gained insights from analysis, she believed that he became more mature. Writing Evans some years later, she characterized the change: "You found yourself—and I lost you. Not entirely, but I lost an aspect of you that had meant more to me than I could have known." She complained that Dr. Hinkle knew Evans better than she did and speculated that had she too gone through analysis, she might have been able to adjust to her "new and grown-up husband!" But Freda was "afraid" to undergo analysis, and the couple drifted apart and into affairs.[18]

The death of Dora Kirchwey accentuated Freda's exhaustion caused by the emotional strain of her and Evans' extramarital affairs. She was beginning to realize that traditional values influenced her more than she realized they could. She "felt an utter alien" from Evans and their surroundings and yearned for an end to painful complications. She later explained: "I wanted to have you alone and feel the reality and peace of my family; I was sick of the desperate complications of my relations . . . You and I went off on terribly separate tangents and I was never so unhappy. From then on the vicious circle has revolved—with us in it like squirrels." Freda shut herself off from her husband, building walls that encouraged him to continue to find "warmth elsewhere," and admitted that her only protection from the pain was "detachment."[19] Behind her walls, however, she yearned for Evans: "It was as if my emotions had made some icy vow never to emerge until you wanted them alone. But how could you, when your warmth was met with ice?"[20]

*

Freda threw herself into her work at the *Nation* which had become a second home. She wrote Villard about an idea for a new theme, "some sort of series on women" that could tie in with a *Nation* dinner program she had planned for that February 1927. But she underrated her contribution saying, "I still seem to be only about half the person I ought to be."[21]

To cheer herself up that summer, she had her hair bobbed in the new, very short style. From a rented cottage in Manhasset, Long Island, she wrote Dorothy: "My son Michael fell on his face in the grass and swore never to look at me again . . . that I being his mother had no right to show my ears. It is rather startling and opinions differ—the female sex in general approving, the male not." But Freda could not deny that her health suffered: "I am slightly feeble. Last week the office took pity on me for my wobbly state and sent me off for four days rest." Later that month Freda told Villard that she had made progress on the series on "women and other similarly frivolous subjects." But she desperately needed a vacation: "I am tireder than usual even for this time of year and feel as though I were unlikely to have any intelligent ideas until I get off for a while."[22]

At Ardnamurchan in Nova Scotia, Freda rested and swam but wrote, "I still yearn for sun and nakedness and freedom from care." Despondently she pondered, on the eve of what would have been Dora's seventieth birthday: "Tomorrow will be a hard day for all of us—especially Papa Georgie. I wish we could all be with him on dear Mother's birthday. It's queer how hard these anniversaries are to get over. I still have desperate moments on little Brewster's birthday." Her father was equally concerned about Freda: "We must not let that beautiful spirit lapse into a state of ill-health. I am sure that the fine cooperative spirit which is the mark of all our tribe and which carried us back and all through the terrible experience of the last few months will enable us to pull our Fritzie out of this slough of dispond. I am, however, hoping that this vacation will have done much to bring her back to a normal condition."[23]

Writing was Freda Kirchwey's way of getting back to normal:

"some people write to make a living, but most people, including the professionals, write to get out of their systems thoughts and feelings that, left inside, produce uncomfortable ferment." Her words that tied together the first *Nation* series on morality also expressed her unanswered questions about changing morality. The second series (published in late 1926 through the summer of 1927) continued seeking answers. It asked seventeen professional women to address "the origins of their modern point of view toward men, marriage, children and jobs."[24]

The series, entitled "These Modern Women," contained sketches of a number of writers. It would have been logical for Freda to contribute as an anonymous professional woman. Her unusual position, managing editor of a major political journal, put her in the good company of feminist activist Inez Haynes Irwin, poet and popular writer Alice Mary Kimball, political commentator Mary Alden Hopkins—other journalists she selected for the series. Writing about "men, marriage, children and jobs" might have clarified some of her unresolved feelings. But Kirchwey did not choose to be one of "These Modern Women." Distress about extramarital affairs and concern for her eldest child's emotional well-being left her too involved in the ferment to write about it professionally. She preferred to limit herself to the safe role of editor. Or perhaps Freda unconsciously wanted her anonymous modern women to provide answers to her own confusing struggle to combine a career with a modern marriage and family.

Kirchwey wrote about the Soviet Union with a continuing interest, criticizing the United States for welcoming Kerensky, who predicted the collapse of the Bolshevik government.[25] She also commented on women as part of the news. For example, she editorialized about the book *Woman's Place* in the news section of the *Nation:* "the women's revolution," she wrote, "may mark the first half of this century more deeply than any other social change. The emotional conflicts that confront the modern woman, the profound choices that are forced upon her, the subtle interactions in home life, in the relations of the sexes, in factory and office are here discussed lightly yet with informed wisdom." She looked to a future, "when women shall have found their sea legs and the impressive activities of the advancing women of today will seem like the earnest and awkward yet somehow promising movements of a landlubber on his first day out."[26] Freda felt that she and other "advancing women" of the 1920s were having an impact on future society.

Because the advancement of women was dramatic, Kirchwey wondered about its impact on men. So she arranged a battle of the sexes. In February 1927 she was billed, "as near an impartial chairman as a frail woman can be," for the *Nation*'s "Men—What of 'Em?" symposium. It featured psychologist Lorine Pruette, journalist Ruth Hale, and author John Macy. *New Republic* editor Bruce Bliven, who was to have participated, left town, thereby "escaping the combat." Freda's father and aunts attended the dinner and "sat in the front row with the Gannetts and other members of Freda's official family." As usual she received glowing praise from both families.[27]

The dinner highlighted the series "These Modern Women," which had begun with the publication of Inez Haynes Irwin's "The Making of a Militant" in December 1926. Trying to figure out her modern woman's rebellion, Kirchwey asked of the first contributor: "Do spirited ancestors explain their rebellion? Or does it result from thwarted ambition or distaste for domestic drudgery?"[28] Many modern women like Irwin had modern marriages supporting their determination to fulfill themselves in careers. One contemporary expert, gynecologist Robert Dickinson, explained that "satisfactory sexual relations are necessary to fully adjusted and successful union." This new freedom to enjoy sex led in different directions. Paula Fass, historian of the 1920s, notes that the demand for mutual fulfillment in marriage during that decade meant that "sexual exclusiveness became the capstone of expressive love." But avant-garde couples like the Kirchwey-Clarks considered sexual exclusivity as a restraint on personal development. Ironically, freedom had its own limits. "Thou shalt not forbid extramarital affairs" could have been one of their rules for modern marriage; they saw fidelity as an artificial constraint.

Interestingly enough, of the women whose autobiographical sketches were included in the series, only atheist settlement house worker Elizabeth Stuyvesant even touched the sensitive subject of extramarital affairs, and then only in passing: "As I look back over eleven happy years I feel sure that our relationship would not have been harmonious or complete if either of us had stressed the conventional idea of exclusive mutual possession." The series might be as interesting to analyze for what it omitted as for what it included.

As a group, the essays presented no strategy for achieving equality for women. Even activist Crystal Eastman, who certainly had specific plans to achieve human equality, did not use her essay as a forum to advocate them.

The series made only brief mention of children, probably because only five of the women were mothers. A few stated briefly that they did not want children. Stuyvesant wrote: "With 'child-less old age' not so very far away, we still maintain that there is more genuine companionship to be had with chosen friends of similar age and experience than with immature fledglings of another generation." Another, children's book writer Wanda Gág, felt she must choose between her career and a family. Choosing an artist's career, she created "aesthetically" rather than "physically."[29]

Marriage was treated in a similar matter-of-fact fashion. "It is better to work hard than to be married hard," said poet Genevieve Taggard. "Marriage is too much of a compromise; it lops off a woman's life as an individual," Southern suffragist lawyer Sue Shelton White asserted. Phyllis Blanchard, a child psychologist who had married at the age of thirty, was delighted to have "both love and freedom, which once seemed to me such incompatible bedfellows." "I am married now, and I find that good too," remarked political cartoonist Lou Rogers. Neither of these women elaborated on what was so good in the marriage or how love and freedom could be combined. Refusing three proposals of marriage, writer Kate L. Gregg quipped of one of the men who had proposed: "One planned a house for me and insisted on a nice big kitchen. That was the end of him."[30]

Marriage was either dismissed cavalierly or praised briefly—strange, in a series purporting to give attitudes toward "men, marriage, children and jobs." What was given attention? The longest descriptions are of early relationships, remembrances of being a girl and all that being "born female" implied, and the authors' mostly varied career experiences. Perhaps these women talked less about marriage and children because they were uncertain about how to achieve a balance of career, marriage, and family. White, who so glibly dismissed marriage as a choice because of what it had "lopped off," admitted that the renunciation of marriage was lopping off something too: "We choose between the frying-pan and the fire—both very uncomfortable."[31]

The authors shared a sense that their difficulty was caused by being born a woman. One remarked: "women had all the children, men had all the fun." Another said of a delayed writing career: "I see quite plainly that it is the fact of being a woman which has delayed me fifteen years in reaching this point. It is nobody's fault." As much as these women remembered the early conditions responsible for their difficulties, they continued to see their failures in a personal sense. There is no recognition of societal expectations and pulls in different directions, which meant their sex, not their individual personalities, determined some of their problems.[32]

Another reason for the stress placed on early relationships rather than on marriage and family could have been that those who felt they had achieved the tenuous balance did not want to analyze it and thereby possibly jeopardize the balance. Or perhaps this particular group of women reflected some of the 1920s' fascination with Freud and saw more importance in those critical early human relationships.[33] Certainly, as editor of the series, Freda Kirchwey shared the reliance on psychological analyses. She even had had the life stories of her contributors analyzed by three different schools of psychology. To determine the meaning of "the underlying causes of the modern woman's rebellion," she selected behaviorist psychologist John B. Watson; neurologist Joseph Collins; and psychoanalyst Beatrice Hinkle.[34] Psychology was the authority of the day, and these three were representative experts.

Watson and Collins subverted their task. For analyses, they substituted derogatory, condescending personal diatribes against feminists and career women. Watson's analyses displayed prejudices against career women.[35] Placing the contributors in the general category of "militant suffragists" (an interesting characterization since suffrage had become a reality some seven years prior to this analysis), he described them as "Most of the terrible women one must meet, women with the blatant views and voices, women who have to be noticed." Watson did not like assertive women; he found their "militancy" and "restlessness" bothersome, and he wondered what they wanted. "These women were too modern to seek happiness; they sought what? Freedom." He made an interesting and not very logical link between the women's search for freedom and their militancy. That particular combination, he suggested, cost them a normal sex life: "When a woman is a militant suffragist the chances are, shall we say, a hundred to one that her sex life is not well adjusted?"

On the basis of the women he had seen as a practicing psychologist, Watson concluded that no militants, even the married ones, had a normal sex life. Looking for sexually adjusted women, he said: "I find no women shouting about their rights to some fanciful career that men—the brutes—have robbed them of."[36] Yet buried among Watson's mostly negative judgments, occasional perceptive comments are found. He mentioned, for example, that because of both husbands' and wives' pitiful lack of knowledge about sex, sexual adjustment occurred in only 20 percent of all marriages. He also voiced surprise that most of the women in the series did not acknowledge the extent to which their environment had contributed to the difficulties they experienced as women.

Watson's analysis reinforced assumptions about the inadequate sexuality of independent women and about confining sex roles. He assigned to women sole responsibility for preserving marriages; a career woman's divorce was her own fault. Of women whose marriages ended in divorce, he said: "And when they fail in that, as 80 percent do, restlessness sets in." Marriage and career were difficult for women to balance, and children represented "almost an insuperable barrier to a career."[37]

Joseph Collins (who chose from among the contributors the most and least agreeable companions) wrote: "The writers are all revolutionists; that is, they are all feminists." The nerve of these women—they "want to do something in the world and to do it themselves"! He was alarmed that they were so barren, that they ignored "their duty toward the race," which was of course to bear children—"from five to ten." He scolded the contributors for not having any or enough children, burdening them with an authority figure's guess: "I have a hunch that the sex-coefficient of many of these writers is low."[38]

That must have upset Freda Kirchwey. After consulting the experts, she was left without answers, only more questions. She knew it was not easy to do what she had undertaken with such enthusiasm and almost carefree abandon; to be a whole person in office, home, and bed was much harder than she had realized. How could she and the modern feminists in the series respond to accusations that career women were sexually inadequate? Even Beatrice Hinkle's analysis did not allay that fear. Unlike Collins and Watson, Hinkle took a respectful look at the women's life stories before making generalizations. She found that their feminism grew out of either supportive or oppressive families. Supportive families nurtured the women's quest for equality: "the feminism of these women was not born out of a sense of injustice and bitterness but developed as a natural growth from their own personality in contact with the special family environment." Their feminism resulted from exposure to the un-equal treatment of women in the larger society. On the other hand, families of "grinding poverty, conservative ideas, heavily burdened, unhappy mothers and a serious responsible childhood," produced a "fight reaction."[39]

In contrast to Freudian analysis, which diagnosed feminists as having a "castration complex" and saw their revolt as "an abnormal manifestation of an inner protest that they were not men," the fem-inist Jungian Hinkle considered such attitudes "a normal protest against collective restrictions." She found it important that the women's feminism came "directly from the necessities of their per-sonal life" rather than from principle. She left women with hope for the future. Modern women were in a transitional period, in which they struggled against "convention and inertia" and in which they were developing as individuals, "in contradistinction to the collec-tive destiny that had exclusively dominated their lives." Their very attitude was part of a movement toward the "birth of a new woman." Hinkle predicted: "From her a new race will be born for whom feminism or masculine antagonism will be but an echo of a dark age long past."[40]

Although she closed on this optimistic note, Hinkle touched a sensitive nerve when she concluded that although the anonymous women seemed to have reached "some kind of fulfillment, it is ob-vious in spite of their concealments that they have not achieved an inner freedom, or a real solution of their personal problems. They were weak on the side of their woman's nature."[41] It was as if to be independent human beings and to develop talents in a career the women had to renounce being "normal" women. Kirchwey solved the problem by creating a false dichotomy: she kept the career, while rejecting the label of career woman.

Freda and her peers disagreed with many nineteenth-century feminists who insisted that career and marriage were mutually exclusive. These twentieth-century feminists insisted that career and marriage could be combined. Even more important, they shared society's stereotypical views about many nineteenth-century career women as unmarriageable, masculine, and anti-male. Instead of viewing the professional women of the previous century as role models, many of the new generation of women determined to be as unlike their predecessors as possible, and they increasingly identified with men.[42]

Fear of labels like "man-hater" or "masculine" undermined their autonomy. The overall effect of the series on Freda probably increased her insecurity about her own femininity. Even though she had been chosen "Best Looking" Barnard senior of 1915, being a woman with an advancing career made her wonder if she were normal. Secretly she questioned her femininity, as if she alone experienced fears of not being normal—fears that were reinforced by the judgments of authorities such as her *Nation* series experts. She tended to view unfeminine women as abnormal. Once during her youth she heard a speech by political activist Emma Goldman. The speech had impressed her; Goldman's physical appearance did not. It obviously bothered her that Goldman looked "like a composite of my female teachers at the Horace Mann High School."[43]

Freda equated identity with paid work. Once describing possible companions for a Soviet tour, she remarked: "The man is a stock broker; his wife, nothing"; people were what they got paid for doing.[44] She tried to imagine herself as an ordinary housewife. Watching her first bridge game, she told Evans: "I felt a little superior to the bunch; but a little out of it too; I decided it might be pleasant to be a bridge playing lady and have a chance to ooh and ah over prizes and wrangle over plays. But no, I can't do it. I'll have to be satisfied with my superiority! It would take too much time and boredom to achieve regularity."[45] Kirchwey once referred to herself as "an earnest careerist," but this denoted a certain kind of career that she and Evans could accept. She once described a dean with whom she had shared a podium as a "'career' woman, but with all rather nice—humorous and genuine"—as if career women weren't nice, humorous, and genuine.[46]

Such a curious denial of who she was shows the pervasiveness of stereotyped views about career women. Certainly both Freda and her husband shared them. Evans liked women who were feminine in society's accepted definition of the term. Women should not be aggressive nor the dominant sex. During one of Freda Kirchwey's trips to England, she met Lady Reading, whom she described as "rather handsome, very dominating, vigorous, and overpowering, (the kind E. would hate!)."[47] Freda fought against "anti-feminine" traits in herself, even while she advanced into positions of increasing importance on the *Nation*.

Acutely aware that the demands and successes of her professional life went against traditional expectations for women, Kirchwey at some deep level feared the loss of femininity. Once in 1930, when Evans was again in psychoanalysis with Beatrice Hinkle, the analyst defined Freda as a "feminine creature." Freda, relieved by the judgment, indicated the depth of her feeling: "It's lucky I'm such a feminine creature—in spite of long doubts on that point! Knowing that, I may risk being a little more masculine."[48]

The tension between the masculine and feminine is revealingly discussed in Kirchwey's undated sketch of an anonymous female writer, perhaps herself. It shows her fascination with the tension between her feminine side of sensitivity and passivity and the masculine side (although she never calls it that) of mind and creative spirit. The writer, who looked much younger than her years, is caring, sensitive, helpful to others, generous, "very open-minded," attractive, and modest. Despite her modesty, she accepts her self-worth. She has great intelligence, a quick mind, organizational talents, and "courage to face difficult situations." She makes judgments impulsively at times, but in general they are "*good.*" Yet the writer occasionally reaches "a dead point," a state of depression that makes her indecisive and weak. Freda blames this passivity on the conflict "between the very virile spirit of this writer and her feminine sensitivity." But awareness of this persistent conflict, her "exceptional" temperament, and "her great sense of life" helps her shed these moods more quickly than most women would. This "wonderful, attractive," person, would make an ideal "friend and comrade," but not an ideal wife and mother. The writer is "so feminine and so sensitive but at the same time she is not fit to play a passive role—even when she plays it. On the ground of this study we would not want to advise any marriage with this writer." To Freda, "strict married life or strict family life" required the passive component of femininity, and her writer was "disinclined" to accept that consequence.[49]

Unlike the anonymous writer, Freda combined marriage and career, but she was painfully aware of the cost:

> But love I love you sadly in the midst of noisy mirth
> And the endless frantic business of the day

Where we lead our separate lives to prove our separate worth
And the fever of it drains our love away.[50]

A typical day found Freda at home after hours of investigative reporting and a long editorial conference. She had initiated a new "staff" member (her term for household help), in addition to reading the *New York Times* and the *Herald Tribune*. As she was rethinking an editorial, she greeted Evans' return home with a wave of the hand. He too had had a day of interviewing, writing, and conferring with colleagues at the *Times;* and he had even managed to get to a three-alarm fire, using his official fire department badge.[51]

*

Freda and Evans thought they could raise children without giving up any of their very busy lives, because they believed the experts who insisted that childrearing was the province of child development professionals. Like many modern parents of the time, they shared a fascination with parenting that resulted in the growth of organizations and child study groups such as the National Congress of Parents and Teachers and the Child Study Association of America. In 1925 Evans covered the first national conference on parenting sponsored by the Child Study Association. "Rearing of Children Becoming a Science" announced the *New York Times* headline of his long article. He detailed the appearance of new nursery schools from coast to coast, where children from under a year through six years of age received "expert care and attention conducive to their healthy development."[52]

Evans knew some of those schools firsthand, and he and Freda deliberately and carefully chose their children's professional educators. But years later Michael lamented having had so little contact with his parents when he was growing up. As an infant he was cared for by Tekla, a Norwegian nursemaid; by his eighteenth month he was already in the City and Country School in Manhattan. Following Tekla, a black woman, Virginia, cared for him at home. He had to be bathed, fed, and put to bed before 7 P.M., when she left for the day, which was especially hard during daylight savings time, as it was still light when Freda came up to kiss him goodnight.[53]

Michael did not care for the City and Country School. But he felt his mother liked it because Miss Caroline Pratt, its principal, thought children should be in the hands of professional educators rather than untrained parents. "My mother was only too glad to hear that."[54] Michael blamed his mother, rather than both parents, for delegating his early nurture and education to others.[55] He suspected that his father had little interest in raising children. Expert Hinkle gave an authority figure's blessing to professional childrearing: "Those parents who have no inclination for this profession will then, without shame or resentment, avail themselves of the nursery school for the more adequate care of their children than they are competent to give." Freda and Evans followed the advice of experts such as Hinkle and the same John B. Watson who critiqued "These Modern Women." Watson warned that excessive mother love was "a dangerous instrument." To avoid emotional reliance on the mother, he urged that children be left with nurses and other professionals. Freda was not consciously neglecting her children; she was following the advice of the experts.[56]

Freda illustrates an interesting conjunction of the "New Woman" and professional childrearing, but the result was not happy—at least for Michael, who described his mother as "emotionally cool, not very demonstrative, friendly, but rather non-emotive." He thought she lacked the "maternal fiber" and was "trying consciously to be a modern woman." Despite her attempt to combine her career with family responsibilities, the "career took precedence over the family."[57] Although feelings of that kind may not have crystallized in written form until much later, they must have been known to Freda. In 1952 Michael Clark wrote an extremely critical letter to both parents, in which he analyzed their parenthood; but he said that the letter was intended primarily for his mother.

In this letter Michael recounted the negative influence of all but his first nurse, Tekla, on his early development. After a description of other nursemaids and governesses who had looked after him, he continued: "With my own mother, who was trying to prove that the modern woman can have a career and a family too—the issue was alive thirty years ago but is, I hope, dead now in spite of the quaint neo-feminism of people like Dr. Edith Sommerskill—I was subjected to a regime of alternate acceptance and rejection. (I'm speaking of effect, mind you, not intention.)" In another part of this long letter, he concluded that he had once even fabricated an accomplishment, hoping it would make Freda love him "not part of the time, but always." While experts warned of excessive mother love and advised that child-development professionals raise children, Michael yearned to be closer to his parents.

But Freda and Evans trusted the experts. Against rigid disciplinarian regimentation, educational drills, and mechanized learning, they sought experimental education, which encouraged initiative, independence, and spontaneity. Both curriculum and method of teaching reflected the new values: "The child himself is the centre of this new universe." Evans had cited experts at the parenthood conference who urged parents to devote "less sentimentally emotional but more maturely responsible" attention to the child, and to recognize the child "as an individual from the day of his birth . . . who should be given every opportunity for growth according to his own particular bent, not a 'chip off the old block.'" The Kirchwey-Clarks felt the way to do this was to send their children to experimental progressive schools.[58]

Throughout her sons' formative years Freda publicly endorsed progressive education. Jeffrey apparently thrived in this atmosphere. In one *Nation* article his mother recounted how six-year-old Jeffrey brought home a book, "hand made from illustration to binding. The only thing the volume lacked was words." She said of her son: "The bookmaker said rather nonchalantly as he handed it to me, 'the bare places are for the stories.'" She used this incident to express her enthusiasm for progressive education, which gave people means to express their talents other than through the traditional written media. It was ironic that she overlooked the "bare places"—the skills that had brought success to her: a dedication to writing and a traditional education. She praised both modern psychology and modern education, which made it possible for a new generation to be able "to struggle through life without writing a book, poem, letter to the *Times,* or even a true confession."[59] Such meaningful education freed creative talents instead of stifling them in a rigorous, fixed academic curriculum. Experimental education was just the kind Freda would have enjoyed.

According to the progressive education theories, there was a need to consider the whole child. An uncompleted short story by Freda, probably written in the 1920s, illustrated the futility of the old form of education as a fixed end in itself. A travesty on Shakespeare, the story described Mrs. Hamblet and her son, William. Kirchwey described Mrs. Hamblet's marriage in a way that gave an interesting insight into the journalist's own concept of women and marriage:

Some women marry because they lack ambition, but Mrs. Hamblet married, rather against her will, because only through matrimony—Mrs. Hamblet was a virtuous woman—could she achieve the ambition that consumed her very soul. Mrs. Hamblet's ambition was to have a child who should graduate from Harvard University at an earlier age than any other child had ever done it.

Mrs. Hamblet began her rigorous education:

When William was six months old, Mrs. Hamblet used to recite Latin declensions as she nursed him, but she discovered that this was rather too stimulating and injured his digestion so she gave them up, and substituted little songs about German prepositions.

As the story progressed, it documented the enormous concentration of learning that enabled William to enter Harvard at the age of eight:

with so many advanced credits that during his freshman year he could take all the courses marked in the catalog "Post-graduate; open to specially qualified students." He finished college at eleven; having mastered 43 languages and dialects; twelve sciences, including *differential* calculus; and several other subjects that are never mentioned in polite society because no one in polite society could possibly pronounce their names.

At commencement, when a reporter asked Mrs. Hamblet what William would do with "all this highbrow stuff," it was obvious that "such a question had never occurred to her. William was finished, done, a work of art, an intricate machine if you will."[60]

The story satirized mere mastery of unconnected academic subjects, while the City and Country School offered children practical knowledge and fostered creativity. Kirchwey commended its attempts to instill a democratic spirit by urging children to "believe in their own right and the right of everyone else to grow into free and creative and individual persons." Unlike the public schools which, Kirchwey claimed, bred regimentation, prejudice, and punishment, the private school stressed respect and tolerance for differences.[61] But Michael later had reservations about the value of his education. He grew frustrated with schooling that did not teach him basic discipline and organizational skills, leaving him less than well prepared for the world. He felt that through the progressive education process of "'learning by experience' or of 'learning by doing,'" he had wasted time on "'projects—ponies, gardening, woodcraft, printing, weaving, music (percussion only), and 'fine arts.'" Michael considered progressive education "the school of short cuts, work soon abandoned and, worse still, of slipshod habits of mind. It is a stunting thing."[62]

While providing the latest methods to free Michael to be an individual, Freda and Evans ignored his personal need for a more traditional education and upbringing. The new practice of calling parents by their first names made him uncomfortable; he did not want to call them Freda and Evans and be their friend. Freda too had some difficulty in accepting the new concept of being a friend to your child. She saw no way that parents and children could be equals and said, "superiority wrecks friendliness." Ironically, she suggested that one of the best means of overcoming this condition was "by getting away from each other." This was just the opposite of what Michael craved, and at one point Freda saw his behavior as "very clinging."[63] She was frustrated that the experimental education and life style she gave her son seemed to upset, not free him.

In 1927, when he was eight years old, Freda took Michael in for psychological counseling; clearly his new-style education was not working. Freda wrote Dorothy that the doctor concluded what she and Evans had figured out: "that M's various difficulties arise from a sense of being disapproved by his pa and ma. That we've always demanded more rationality and adultness than his years would warrant." She had spent a great deal of time discussing her "childrens fate with various experts." The accumulated advice was: "The cure seems to be as much appreciation and affection from us as possible; as little tenseness and irritation, as much joviality and fun with us; as much time as we can give. She sees no need however for us to be with him this summer." Freda wrote that careful placement of Michael for the summer could mean a "new regime of smooth amiability after such a break," and she and Evans prepared to go abroad, leaving the children behind.[64]

What would be the best place for them? There was the Clark family summer place in Nova Scotia, but Freda did not want the children under the supervision of Evans' strict, rigid mother, Fannie: "I feel uncomfortable enough at best about putting the ocean between us and them. Ardnamurchan would be so grand if only it weren't full of theosophists and nature curers and table manners." She finally decided to leave them in the care of Margaret Kellogg

Smith, who, with her husband, ran a summer camp for children on a farm in Chestertown, Maryland.[65]

Worries about the children were overshadowed by the adventure of a voyage to England aboard the S.S. *Minnewaska* and anticipation of traveling through Europe with George Kirchwey that summer of 1927. Unfortunately, the damp cold of London left Freda with an intestinal virus, which laid her low for several days. Rest cured her illness and warmer clothing prevented future ones. It would be a summer of firsts. Freda almost wept during her first flight from London to Paris. Others were so casual about flying that, "I wasn't prepared for the violent emotions I actually experienced."[66]

*

Freda began to learn about Europe from personal observation as she and Evans traveled in England, Sweden, France, Austria, and Germany (where they met up with George Kirchwey). Evans, on assignment for the *New York Times,* worked so hard that Freda worried about the stress he was under. She was on vacation, but, surrounded by people and places she had written about all those years, she did her duty as a political journalist; the notes she scratched on the backs of newspapers, on napkins and scraps of paper, would become articles for the *Nation.* Over the years she would build on these early impressions.

In England, "apart from cold water, cold rooms, mutton, and cabbage" and "unbendable toilet paper," Freda noted social practices. She was surprised to find "astonishing respect from lower classes—except in House of Commons." There she observed quite the opposite during sessions in Parliament. Ellen Wilkinson, a representative of the Labour Party, told Churchill that "he might have the face of a pink cherub but he had the mind of Mephistopheles." Wilkinson, "small and lean" and "eloquent," delivered a speech attacking the antipicketing clause of the trade union bill. She reminded her peers that workers did not like strikes. Strikes took a toll on them and their families, but workers must be able to protest unjust working conditions. The Home Secretary, Sir William Joynson-Hicks, said that the "honorable" lady's mind was "warped," that "her mind is the mind of the trade-union leaders, and they will not see any right or fairness in the minds of the men who do not go on strike."[67]

Ever the observer, Kirchwey characterized the tension between labor and capital: "Labor, stubborn and resentful, flinging itself against a smooth wall of bland, assured conservatism, helpless to win from its opponents understanding of something which, after all, cannot be understood but must be felt; the Government, polite, almost playful, appearing to listen and weigh and reason, and then at the end falling back on the unimpeachable argument of its huge majority."[68]

Freda and Evans received an academic analysis of the trade union bill from their friend Harold Laski, who taught at the London School of Economics. Kirchwey had known Laski for years as a faithful member of the *Nation* outer circle. In 1927 she and Evans were able to visit with him and his wife, Frida. Freda and Evans wanted to hear their views about the controversial trade union bill that the conservative British government was pushing through Parliament. The general strike a year earlier had virtually paralyzed Britain, and only a tiny minority of even the Labour Party was opposed to eliminating the possibility of a similar strike. Yet many of liberal and radical persuasion thought the government's proposals for the trade union bill went far beyond the intention of eliminating a general strike. The bill seemed to outlaw picketing and almost all strikes and assured a loss of influence of labor unions. For an analysis of the bill and its consequences, Clark interviewed union leaders, industrialists, government representatives, and academics.[69]

Kirchwey reported some of the parliamentary debate on the bill, but she did not write as many other editorials as Villard would have liked. As she explained: "This trip will have to be put down to my general education, I think. I realise every day how terribly I need this first-hand contact with Europe and how much I need to absorb before I can write intelligently. I shudder when I think of the glib paragraphs I've written on world affairs! So if you don't mind, I'll go on sponging up what I can and not try to squeeze anything out just now."[70]

In Berlin, on the anniversary of World War I, she observed masses of demonstrators marching through the streets to protest future wars. Their banners proclaimed: "The Capitalists Are Preparing War Against Soviet Russia" or "Join the Red Front." The marchers were of all ages, but Freda thought many faces showed that "childhood had passed in the hungry war years." An American reporter beside her said of the demonstrators, "They're always pulling off these shows." Kirchwey said she had read that some 125,000 people were marching that day. He agreed, but "it doesn't mean anything." When she asked why, he answered, "O, because they're always demonstrating."[71]

But when Kirchwey arrived in Vienna, she learned that demonstrations there had meant something. Just a month before, workers, primarily Socialist-led, took to the streets to protest their "reactionary" Catholic government. Goading by some of the marchers and police brutality turned the protest into a riot, leaving property damage and more than one hundred dead. A pall of fear weighed heavily on Vienna. When Kirchwey interviewed Herr Breitner, Socialist head of the city's finance department, she wanted to know how the Viennese would react to the next day's scheduled execution in the United States of Sacco and Vanzetti. He said that all classes, even the "bourgeois," were bitterly critical, but no one would risk a mass demonstration. "The trouble in July came too close . . . a little more and it would have been revolution."

Her next stop, Heiligenblut, a small Austrian village, presented her with a different kind of gathering, a procession celebrating Marientag, the festival of the Virgin. "Heilige Marias" came from women of all sorts. Freda was struck by the "earnest faces," "terrible faces." "The faces of men and women who have spent all their years in a steady fight to draw life out of bare stony fields set up on edge against the sun. In no adult face was there a look of eagerness or humor or reflection. They were poor, bare souls." If need be, she was sure they would have marched to Vienna to protect it from socialists and atheists and concluded that these "grim and earnest workers" were on the side of the "old guard." They were the majority and would prevail against their striking counterparts in Berlin and Vienna.[72]

Toward the end of their trip she, Evans, and George read about the sense of doom pervading the United States, where Sacco and Vanzetti, arrested some seven years earlier, were about to be executed. Both George Kirchwey and Villard had written about them in the *Nation*. The case had become a *cause célèbre* on the continent as well as in America, Freda wrote after the fact:

> We've hardly talked about it—but every time we got within range of a newspaper we've rushed to it hoping, without any real hope that some miracle of mercy would have descended on the Governor or someone else. It was hard to sleep through some of

those nights. And everywhere we went—from Paris and Berlin to Heiligenblut in the Austrian Tyrol—people talked to us about it with horror and a complete inability to understand. This was true of people without any political feeling in the matter—casual companions in a railway compartment or in a hotel office.—And now they're dead. In spite of riots and bitter resentment, I feel, in people and in myself a distinct relief that, if it had to be, it is done. Anything is better than that strain of waiting.[73]

Earlier that summer, while traveling in England, Kirchwey had met Crystal Eastman, still angry that the conclusion of her "confession" for the "These Modern Women" series had been changed to end on a note of vigor and optimism; the passage ended with a tribute to Crystal's "almost perfect parents." She charged that her personality had been altered to suit the *Nation*'s whims. Max Eastman had written his sister, saying Villard had made the change. When Freda heard this, she "let Crystal think what she thought," but Villard, angry about being blamed, scolded Freda by letter. She retorted, "as I recall it, we all thought the article feeble in the end and hopeless—you included—and, with Polly's help, I tried to reconstruct a credible Crystal out of what seemed to be a worm." Freda said she would reread Villard's "mean" letter before deciding whether to return home at all.[74]

Freda and Evans returned to Paris for the last week of their trip. After dancing at the posh Deauville Casino, where she watched "rich and ugly people from all over the world doing the tango," Freda had long talks with her friends, political commentators Ludwig Lore and Robert Dell. She was impressed with Robert Dell's reports, but she wanted to check things out for herself. Just before she left Paris, she visited the working-class section. Walking around, she looked at the crowded houses and watched people talk and argue and children play. She sat in on local Communist and Socialist meetings. Though frustrated not to be able to understand the conversations, it was important to observe what she could. As she told Villard, "I should spend months everywhere getting really close to the life and happenings in these countries."[75] Yet she realized how much she missed because she could not understand French or German and suggested that Villard initiate "a continuation school" for those in his "plant," like Kirchwey, who needed foreign-language skills.[76]

＊

Freda and Evans returned and again became engrossed in their work. Evans wrote about general economic conditions in Europe; Freda put down her impressions of the various mass demonstrations she had witnessed. George Washington Kirchwey had remained in Europe to participate in a psychoanalytic conference, where he was introduced as "the outstanding criminologist in America and the man who had led the movement for securing justice for Sacco and Vanzetti." The family chuckled over his description of the confer- ence: "This is the true and orthodox psychoanalytic group, founded and led by Freud, and people like Jung and Adler and Dr. Hinkle and Evans Clark are rank outsiders. That gives me one on Evans!"[77]

The next time Freda and Evans entertained her father was as they packed for another move, this time from the pretty little red-brick Federal style house at 27 Vandam Street to a more spacious brown- stone farther uptown, at 146 West 12th Street. Freda wanted to have the family dinner at her house that Christmas but could not manage it. A couple of weeks before Christmas she wrote Dorothy, "We have a lovely Swedish maid who can neither talk English, clean or cook."[78] But by January, Freda had settled in and once again was addressing a large audience as part of her job, this time to pay tribute to Villard on his birthday and his new *Nation*'s tenth anniversary.

Unitarian minister John Haynes Holmes introduced Freda say- ing, "for years and years I have waited for the happy privacy of such an occasion as this to tell our next speaker how lovely I think she is. Every day she is growing older in the service of the *Nation*—and every day she is growing younger in beauty, grace and charm." New York's Hotel Pennsylvania was the setting for the celebration. Crys- tal Eastman, long over her tiff with the *Nation*, organized the event. She was, according to Holmes, "the chief conspirator in the foul and seditious plot of gathering together in this den of luxury of *The Nation* bolsheviks." Tributes to Villard came in from H. G. Wells, Harold Laski, Bertrand Russell, H. L. Mencken, and many others.[79]

Freda was on the podium with historian James Weldon Johnson, social reformer Florence Kelley, and *World* columnist Heywood Broun. She began her speech with an anecdote. She had overheard Villard reading over the "appalling list of distinguished speakers for this evening, looking for a head he could easily and with the least trouble cut off . . . 'Drop Freda, she won't be offended.' One look at me was enough to change his mind." She praised Villard's devotion to "the cause of man": "He attacks prejudice and privilege because he really believes he can overcome them . . . He likes to fight because he expects to win."[80]

Evans was captivated by Freda's charm and grace at the podium. Before putting his diary away, he recorded: "F. gave grand speech to 1000 people." Now, on the eve of a major career decision, he asked for Freda's ear. Rumor had it that he would receive an offer to head the Twentieth Century Fund, established by Boston merchant Edward A. Filene. The Fund, a nonprofit foundation, conducted wide-ranging economic research and often proposed government policies stemming from those studies.[81]

For Evans the job would mean a departure from his usual kind of work with politically radical causes.[82] He was still working for the Committee on Research of the Garland Fund, officially called the American Fund for Public Service. In 1922 Charles Garland, a socialist who inherited a considerable fortune, set up an institution to dispense money to radical, liberal, and labor causes. Among other projects, the fund subsidized the radical magazine *New Masses,* aided the defense of Sacco and Vanzetti, supported the National Association for the Advancement of Colored People's campaign for an antilynching bill, and put up bail money for arrested labor union organizers. While serving on the Garland Fund's committee, Evans Clark, as director of the Labor Research Bureau, had proposed and had received money from the fund to sustain his Labor Research Bureau work.[83]

Joining the liberal philanthropic Twentieth Century Fund would mean shifting to a more limited focus and a liberal rather than radical orientation. Before making such an important decision, Evans talked it over with Freda and her father. George described their evening as a "grand discussion."[84] Although there was no great enthusiasm, when Filene officially offered the directorship at a salary of $20,000–25,000, Evans accepted.[85]

Changes were in the offing not only for Evans. That same month Freda and Evans called George in for another family discussion. This time they would discuss a possible new job for Freda. When Mark Van Doren resigned as literary editor, Villard sought advice about a successor. Freda suggested drama and music critic Hiram Moderwell, but Ernest Gruening feared that Moderwell lacked the necessary "prestige or the special talents and training." Literary radical Max Eastman became the leading candidate, but Villard had "grave doubts" lest Eastman harm the *Nation,* "by strengthening the charge that we are bolshevick." He also worried that Eastman's former bohemian lifestyle, "his connection with the communist movement and his biographies of Lenin and Trotsky," might hurt the journal. Gruening agreed, and Villard offered the job to Freda. She was excited about the opportunity, for one of her major suggestions for *Nation* improvements had been: "MORE, MORE TIMELY, AND BETTER BOOK REVIEWS!" What better way to do this than to be in charge of the book review section? Freda Kirchwey accepted the job as the *Nation*'s literary editor, to begin in the fall of 1928.[86]

Joseph Wood Krutch, who had suggested another woman for the position, thought that rejection of his candidate meant that Villard did not want a female for the job. Villard corrected that perception: "we have put in Freda Kirchwey and I believe we shall have the best literary editor in New York—all of which is in answer to the report given to you that I did not want another woman. As a matter of fact, I did want another woman, but the same woman who charms us all!" Krutch supported the choice and asked Villard to give Freda his "oath of fealty—the King has abdicated—long live the Queen!"[87]

Before leaving her post as managing editor, Freda took the opportunity to air her position on two seemingly divergent issues. Heywood Broun had used his *Nation* page, "It Seems to Heywood Broun," to express editorial disagreements with his main employer, the *World,* for which he wrote a daily column; its editor fired him for "disloyalty." Kirchwey decided to air the incident in a printed forum of opinion. She sent copies of the documents—the offending article and the *Nation*'s coverage of the dismissal—to various editors asking for opinions about whether an issue of freedom of speech had been violated. William Allen White, liberal editor of the Kansas *Emporia Gazette* saw it as "just another newspaper row . . . No cause is involved, no principle at stake."[88] But in this instance, as in so many others, Kirchwey used the pages of her journal to put issues before her readers and to clarify the parameters of free speech, to her a sacred right.

Freda also cherished the right to dissent and decided to feature it by ridiculing blind patriotism. The month of the Broun forum, the

Daughters of the American Revolution were having a grand party to extol the virtues of democracy. Freda and others, who could have joined the DAR but distrusted its ultrapatriotic stance, decided to create a countergroup: the Descendants of the American Revolution. They had their own party and mocked the DAR. Freda asked her sister to send evidence that she was on the DAR "list"; "I want to prove to Lewis [Gannett] that I'm really on one." The Blacklist Party took place in New York in 1928; Freda covered the spoof in the *Nation*.[89]

Her skills in eulogy were called upon several months later, when she wrote about her friend and fellow women's rights advocate: "Crystal is dead. And all over the world there are women and men who will feel touched with loss, who will look on a world that seems more sober, more subdued." Hearing her speak had made Freda feel "just a little taller." Crystal Eastman carried the "breath of courage and a contagious belief in the coming triumph of freedom and decent human relations"; she was "a symbol of what the free woman might be." Eastman's last public appearance was the *Nation*'s anniversary dinner, which she organized and carried off despite ill health. This sad farewell to someone important in Freda's life was yet another death to be coped with.[90]

*

The late 1920s found Freda Kirchwey in an increasingly somber mood. She continued to try to make sense out of her personal morality by reading books that might help. Reviewing Margaret Mead's *Coming of Age in Samoa,* she found that Samoans loved without jealousy because of a lack of "emotional intensity." Freda concluded, "If love can be freed from conflict and life made simple only at the price of personal relations, who of us is ready to pay it? Most of us probably will read Miss Mead's impressive study and then continue as before to cling to our difficulties and our delights, with occasional impulses of escape to the expensive simplicity of the South Seas."[91]

It was a brash simplicity that Henry Mussey (back on the *Nation*'s payroll as managing editor late in 1928) thought he found in Kirchwey's book review of a biography of Susan B. Anthony. She wrote that Anthony "thought, worked, traveled, talked for the freedom of women." That she pursued this "single track" made her a fanatic to Kirchwey, though "a good fanatic." Mussey was furious: "It makes me shudder . . . the article struck me as ignorant, uncomprehending, lacking in historical background and perspective, immature—in a word, like Greenwich Village patronizing Susan B. Anthony." Kirchwey did not accept Mussey's criticism nor Villard's, which was similar; her reaction was unusual. Villard wrote: "I found her for the first time extremely sensitive to criticism. Other people did not share my opinion of it, she said . . . I have found that if I were to press further we might have tears. Again it is the only time in ten years when she has not taken criticism in the sweetest spirit."[92]

Yet she was unsparing in her criticism of H. G. Wells, who was too credulous for her taste in *Mr. Bletsworthy on Rampole Island* (1928). Sickened by the tales of countless deaths in World War I's brutal trench warfare, devastated by the deaths of family and friends, Freda shared a certain cynicism with many of her generation: "We have lost most of the brash impetuosity and expectant eagerness that characterized our pre-war years. We are not even as pert as we were. War and revolution and peace have combined to make us wary of programs and dubious of collective purposes, especially those developing from the enterprise of 'stronger and better men' than we."[93]

Freda decided to put her energies into a cause which she felt could never be oversimplified: the dissemination of information on birth control. Illegal abortions and drugs caused many deaths; women's excessive pregnancies caused others. Freda urged women to get "out of bondage" and termed the appeals for help collected in Margaret Sanger's *Motherhood in Bondage*, "a shout of protest." In the late 1920s both Freda and her father pushed for legalizing birth-control information. George Kirchwey spoke in support at the 56th Annual National Conference of Social Work held in San Francisco in July 1929.[94]

That summer Freda and Evans accepted an invitation from banker Maurice Wertheim to travel aboard his chartered steam yacht, the *Ianara*. Along with Charles Riegelman, a former Columbia law professor, Theresa Helburn, a manager of the Theatre Guild, and playwright S. N. Behrman, they boarded the *Ianara* in England and sailed to Norway, leaving Michael and Jeffrey with a friend. Cruising off the Norwegian fjords proved relaxing, although Freda did wish she were "in closer touch" with her children.[95]

Later she recalled the beautiful ocean and long talks on deck, but she remembered another incident more clearly. Once, when the captain had shut off the ship's engine in a Norwegian fjord, Freda took the opportunity to swim. As she floated, soaking up the sun she loved, the *Ianara* started up again, and Freda was thrust away from the ship. The harder she swam to get back, the faster the water carried her in the opposite direction. As the ship changed direction slightly, Freda's screams were heard above the engine's throb, and the crew pulled aboard its terrified passenger. Freda retold this story often, adding that if the captain had put the ship in reverse, the current could have sucked her into the yacht's propellers. She had sensed the chill of imminent death.[96]

Glad to be alive and feeling especially guilty about leaving Jeffrey, who had had a positive tubercular test in April, Freda was anxious to pick up the children in England and return to the United States. She thought of Jeffrey, so bright and cheerful; Mama Dodie once called him "the most radiantly happy small boy I ever remember to have seen." His gift of a book with blank pages for stories had inspired her last editorial before vacation. She could hear him saying: "When I grow up, I'm going to be a person that makes books. I'm going to paste them together and put the covers on and draw the pictures and fix them for people to write the stories in." She thought it fortunate that Jeffrey would not feel compelled to add his words to the flood of words passing an editor's desk. Yet Freda would not be editing "millions of words," nor would she be writing them for a long time.[97]

The previous April the doctors had suggested that Jeffrey spend the winter in the country. This fit in well with plans to send him to the Spring Hill boarding school in Litchfield, Connecticut, along with Michael. Jeffrey was ill at school that fall, but "lively (more so than's desired) and very happy and terribly amiable. He almost worries them by his cheerfulness about staying in bed, etc." Yet Freda confided to Dorothy that if her son's health did not improve, she must consider moving to "a warmer sunnier climate. Which would mean exile for him and me, and I hope it won't be necessary."[98]

Jeffrey did not improve. Evans was out of town that December, so Freda went alone to Litchfield to pick him up and bring him to a New York doctor, Dr. James A. Miller. Her father worried about her having the weight of the decision and then the arrangements for Jeff's care: "A bit hard for the poor girl with Evans away in Chicago. But she is equal to anything."[99] The world Freda knew and felt in the intense way that motivated her to improve it, to contribute to it, could no longer claim her sole attention. She took a leave of absence from the *Nation* for something more important: to help six-year-old Jeffrey regain good health.

On 10 January 1930, as they left for the railroad station, snow mixed with icy rain reminded Freda of why she had to take Jeff away from New York.[100] "It was such an ache to leave. I love you so terribly deeply. Goodbye, good luck, my blessed," she wrote Evans, as she would write him every day during the long ordeal. As the train rolled along, Jeff sat beside Freda, asking question after question while he busily cut and glued pictures into his "build it with scissors" book. Freda decided that she would survive the trip and the months ahead by "not trying to read or do anything consecutive or struggling against the tide in any way." A cable from Evans made her feel "happy and terribly despondent, both at once," for although his words made him feel close by, she knew that he was "hopelessly inaccessible—receding into the distance with every rattle of the wheels."[101]

Florida struck her as "a dismal state." Looking out the train window, Freda watched "endless wastes of pine and sand, flat, desolate, drab . . . It all looked about as tropical as Southern Jersey—except for the endless swamps." "Such hideous dismal flat country. Jeff kept exclaiming 'How gorgeous this country is!'"[102] She longed for the coast and water and beauty, but she was glad for the sun. "It is warm enough to make me feel that their (sic) will be sun and a chance for nakedness—for Jeff, anyhow."

They reached their destination. "Sarasota . . . a wretched town on the edge of a beachless bay." Yet Freda was determined to nurse Jeff back to health there.[103] Her life shrank to an unlikely room (rented by the week) at the Gulf View Inn on Sarasota Beach, where "the food is good and very plain (the people are ditto.)"[104] For the first time ever, Freda Kirchwey was a full-time mother with no nurse-maid, cook, or governess to help her. She would be all things to Jeffrey and mothering him would become her life.

4 || *The Missing Years,*
1930 –1932

Without the responsibility of the *Nation,* Freda was able to devote full attention to Jeffrey. She began the task of caring for her son with trepidation: "*Lord,* I wish I had real honest courage. The very thought of staying with Jeff and an old lady in a dingy 4-room house at the far end of a lonely beach gave me a lonely feeling that couldn't be mistaken for bravery or determination. I really felt lost and fearful."[1] But a day after she wrote this to Evans, Freda took charge of the situation: "From now on Jeff is going to be on a simple schedule of sunbaths and no forced feeding. I feel as if I were only now taking his case in hand."[2]

During their stay in Florida, Freda carefully recorded Jeffrey's temperature daily and supervised his diet and rest, waging a constant battle to help him gain weight and get the right amount of sun. In characterizing his frighteningly thin body for Evans, she scratched out the word "scared," substituting "hurts me," and admitted, "my fears have been so many—and very determined!"[3] Jeff, who had lost three pounds between the time he left school and left for Florida, now confessed that he had hidden his food except for soups, cereals, and milk. Although his mother made him eat more, his indigestion was continuous, and Jeff said he had "air" in his stomach and felt "awful inside." Freda noted "no gain in weight; temperature; indigestion and consequent lack of appetite," as well as "slightly swollen glands just under the corners of his jaw bone." She begged Evans to pass the pages of Jeff's diet, sleep, and activities along to Dr. J. A. Miller. Jeff's weight remained stable, but his glands became increasingly enlarged. Miller had told her not to be discouraged; treatment was "a long game," but the doctor simply alarmed and depressed her. Freda knew she had to be optimistic, to stop worrying; yet her fears conjured up bleak prospects for Jeffrey's recovery, hard though she tried to dismiss them as "having little basis outside my own brain."[4]

> Dear love, I wonder, too, when the end will be. May it be a year? And will Jeff need to be in the sun and away from children all that while? And, if so, how shall we work it? I suspect I'll bring him back and then have to go right up to the country with him. (Will I ever have a home with you, love?) The weeks do stretch on, and time goes both slowly and fast. This, if anything ever was, is a strange interlude. I hate to think of you in our house without me and of me on a sunny beach without you . . . Your letters, dear, are the very breath of the day for me. And when you come—![5]

Along with worries about Jeffrey, Freda wondered what would become of her marriage. The shared distress over Jeffrey's illness had broken through Evans' and her isolation from each other. On the verge of divorce, they called a "strange and lovely truce." How she had hated to leave her husband after the rekindling of intimacy in the days before her departure to Florida! Now, Freda reevaluated and wrote Evans about their relationship. She cherished the days before she left with Jeff, "even if there are no others like them"; she had found their union "real" and "wonderfully releasing." She believed Evans had returned to her not just to save the marriage or placate her feelings, but because he wanted to come back and that he too preferred monogamy, at least for the time being.[6]

Analyzing their marriage, Freda qualified her statements, cautious to assume no continuity or commitment from Evans and trying to make no demands or accusations. Once she referred to affairs as "foreign entanglements," then tried to lighten the judgment, saying, "tho I know you weren't entangled and that is merely a poor figure of speech!" Although she sought a "closeness we have both ached for," she admitted that it could not survive repression. She wanted to enjoy other men and women, "without plunging into the distracting whirlpools (excuse these exaggerated terms; I don't mean anything too sensational) of sexual intimacy, especially the long-drawn-out sort."

It was difficult to accept new rules for modern marriage that discounted repression and monogamy, while longing for traditional mores: "Even an interval in which we loved only each other would mean more to me than ten years of half-way satisfaction together, with a few outside attachments to fill the gap. But it can only happen if it happens. It can't be forced. And I'm not going to hope for too much.—I only know that I love you very much, so that it seems fantastic that we should rear difficulties and hazards and make love so hard."[7] She could not easily resolve the conflict between life as she understood it and the kind of relationships she wanted: "Sometimes I feel . . . 'Passionate friendships' seem possible to fit in with a more important and lasting love; and they seem inevitable. At other times I ache beyond bearing for a relationship which excludes—or at least leaves room for—no such outside sexual intimacies—kills even the desire for them."[8]

Freda was aware of Freudian concepts like repression; she could not return to what her new-morality generation considered an inappropriate restriction on freedom. So she tried to combine old and new values: "And *always* I believe that if one is deeply satisfied *most* of one's interest in and excitement about other people fizzes or expresses itself naturally in sociable rather than sexual intercourse."

But the shadow of Evans' former and possibly ongoing affairs made her solution unstable. She asked him to share with her his discussions with Dr. Hinkle concerning extramarital relations, hoping that their insights might help clarify her own position. Though Freda tried to be detached, dealing with the reality of sharing her husband with another woman was painful. She even envied Hinkle and admitted "a curious fear and reluctance" to know the details of their talks: "I suppose because I hate to think or hear about your other loves—whatever their kind or degree—and also because I shrink from analyzing too much the problems of our own relationship—just as you always have. But I came thru the reading unscathed!—and still feeling close to you." She looked to Evans to work out their mutual problems: "let me cling to you—even while we look steadily at our miseries and mistakes."[9]

Freda desperately wanted Evans to share some of the awesome burden of caring for Jeff: "I can wait indefinitely if I know you are actually coming." The weeks in Florida were emotionally draining.

In February she met a surgeon, Dr. Pullen, a "swell person with the rare gift of creating confidence . . . I almost wept the first time I talked to him—and then realized how much worry I'd been suppressing."[10] In March she was "tired and shaky and scared. Had a chill and a long spell of wakefulness and panic." That same day she begged her husband to reassure her that Jeffrey would recover: "he'll get well, won't he. Sometimes a wave of absolute terror bowls me over. But most of the time I feel that time and patience will do the job."[11]

Freda saw any delegation of responsibility for Jeffrey as abandonment, even when he played with children.[12] Looking forward to being alone with Evans when he came to visit, she hoped, "Jeff will surely be well enough by that time to stand desertion." For the time being she wanted to remain in charge, have total responsibility for her son. "I get sort of satisfaction out of the job, anyhow, you know, darling."[13]

Over and over Freda insisted that she wanted to devote herself to her son, that she did not miss her work. While claiming that she did not resent this, and denying that she objected to the strain and the boredom, her words reveal a desperation for the long ordeal to end: "Don't think beloved, that I begrudge these weeks to Jeff. I really have no craving to do other work; or if I have it's an abstract one. Jeff is in and on my mind almost all the time and I couldn't detach myself or free my thoughts and feelings enough to write even if I had a chance."[14] She even began a piece, "Life on Sarasota Beach," thinking she could salvage an amusing sketch about life there, but what came out detailed a day divided into mostly thirty-minute intervals of care for Jeff.[15] She compared her life in Florida with that of her husband in New York: "You sound so busy and normal in the midst of things that it makes me feel more than ever in exile in a strange—and unreal—land."[16] At best Freda was bored with a "day broken into tiny pieces."[17]

Much of Freda's correspondence during Jeffrey's three-month rest reveals how low her spirits were. To Villard, she commented, "I have some time to read, if I don't do anything else."[18] Florida life was so foreign, empty of the world of news, cosmopolitan people, work—and the delegation of the children to responsible child-rearers. She considered renting a car, but it seemed "a foolish extravagance. Why do I feel so lost without it?"[19] Villard tried to bolster her morale: "It's terribly hard to think of you as being so far away and I find myself combatting every now and then the desire to go to the telephone to get your opinion on this, that, or other important subject." Freda replied: "I had begun to feel very remote and deserted, and the news and comments from you gave me a feeling that the real world kept going on even while I lived in exile." She had to work in "5 minute snatches" and could read that way, but not write.[20] She had to get up to care for Jeffrey at least five times while writing the letter. "You see there's no peace even for an idle woman in Florida!"[21] The days ran together into waves of undivided tasks and painful emotions: "I have settled down to a feeling of permanence and reality about this place. In one way, it is more reassuring and less painful. In another, it is a bit terrifying. It makes the rest of the world . . . seem more remote and unattainable . . . I can't tell the days apart as I look back at them."[22]

Freda and Jeffrey suffered together in Florida. She endured the emotional strain, Jeffrey the physical. Jeff was lively despite his declining health. He promised to be quiet one day while Freda wrote Evans, but he kept interrupting, "'Can't I even send Evans my love?' 'Sure,' said I. 'Or tell him I'm having a fine time?' 'Sure enough,' said I." Freda promised to write all those things to Evans for him in a minute; Jeff timed her on his alarm clock. She had to stop her letter to Evans to write Jeff's: "I am having a good time . . . I am sending you my love. These things are kisses. So never you mind if they look like something else because they're kisses xxxxxx. Goodbye." Another time Jeff wrote Evans in one breath: "I am having a fine time. My glands are going to be pricked. I am finding lots of shells . . . We are having gorgeous weather and mother is letting me go out on the sand some—I wish you could come down, dear Evans. Love from Jeffrey."[23] Just before the planned visit from Evans, Jeff and his mother shared an exchange of "confidence." Jeffrey said, "Evans won't like me trotting in in the night. He'll want to sleep and not be disturbed."[24] Freda was glad to have her husband arrive in Florida. The doctor had decided to operate on one of Jeffrey's glands. At last Evans could absorb some of the responsibility she had carried alone. But within days, after he left, Freda was even lonelier.[25]

Evans returned to New York and talked to George about Jeff and Freda; news spread of Freda's "vigil in the sands of Sarasota."[26] "The loneliness and anxiety" were "a heavy strain on her." Her father felt guilty: "I should have gone before this but for my work, which makes it out of the question." He asked Dorothy if she could go to Florida, but it was rapidly becoming too late. As George Kirchwey sadly reported, "Jeff is only 'a shadow of his former self—wasted to a skeleton.'"[27]

Freda had increasing difficulty coping with Jeffrey's rapidly deteriorating condition. "I am stumped and scared in spite of reassurances . . . It is almost as hard a time as I have ever lived thru and a thousand times worse because you are so far—so terribly far away . . . Now I'm going to bed—alone. With warm milk and bromide as my helps. Goodnight my dear thoughtful loving and discerning Eve. I'll try to think you are back in that room with me. Dear Lover."[28]

Jeff's consistently high temperature and weakened condition made daily telegraphs to Evans necessary. "The little thing has seemed rather plaintive and feeble all day—but gosh, why not! An enema, 4 or 5 poulticings, 2 one-hour sessions of hot cloths, innumerable feedings he didn't want—Why shouldn't he protest and grow tired?"[29] From the middle of the month Freda recorded only sporadic readings of his temperature for various times during the days. When his condition worsened further, Evans came to Florida to assist in bringing Jeff to New York for hospitalization. The day before their departure Freda wrote thanking Villard for his concerned notes. The timing of her letter might seem "foolish," but she explained that she had been unable to acknowledge his notes earlier, for she could not recount Jeffrey's heartbreaking battle against illness. Even in this desperate hour Freda remained aware of the *Nation,* and she enclosed a clipping for its anonymous human interest feature, "The Drifter." Telling Villard that she would call him after she had reached home and found her bearings, she added, "The enclosed I thought too good to go unnoticed. It's work [for] a Drifter."[30]

The trip to New York weakened Jeffrey. The tubercular infection had spread through his body. He no longer had a "good fighting chance" to live, only a "fair chance." Less than a week after his arrival at New York's Presbyterian Hospital, Freda Kirchwey ended her diary: "Jeff died—4:30."[31] She never wrote in it again.

The autopsy on Jeffrey revealed extensive tuberculosis and spinal meningitis. The report called the case interesting: "practically every tissue is involved. Tubercles are found in such unusual sites as the myocardium (or heart muscle), pancreas, skeletal muscle and thyroid. The meningitis is characterized by the presence of amazing numbers of bacilii."[32] Dr. Miller's insistence to Freda that medical knowledge could not have saved her son fell on deaf ears. Consultation with her own family doctor left her both comforted and appalled. She asked: "Is there no way of discovering a lurking infection like that?—no way of guarding against its becoming active? It makes me perfectly sick." Dorothy assured her: "What you did about Jeff might not have made any difference from the time he was six months old on—that the intestinal tb came long before any of the other things and that more or less rest and so on probably wouldn't have affected that in the slightest."[33]

After the funeral Villard handed Freda and Evans the keys to Rockledge Farm, his country retreat in Connecticut. Their recovery would take much longer than the few days they spent there. Freda told her sister: "Oh, how tired and empty and limp we felt. And how queer the world looked. It's going to be a slow job accepting a life without Jeff in it."[34]

Freda grieved in quiet ways. On a sympathy note sent to her she wrote, "lonely, lonelyness, loneliyness," over the words of sympathy. It was probably then that she expressed the depth of her anguish and anger in a poem:

> The night God died was a dark night—heavy with stars but black.
> The man that killed him sneaked along the road
> And hid where the brook slips under the railroad track
> He washed the blood and star dust from his hands and then
> When morning came picked up his dusty load
> And started off along the road again
> The day was nice. He whistled. Then he tried a song
> People he passed smiled at him as he strode
> Obviously no one knew a thing was wrong—[35]

Sympathy notes abounded. "Fate seems to have been cruelly unfair to you in regard to your children, but of course fate is notoriously unfair in all respects," said *Nation* colleague Arthur Warner. Norman Thomas, who had suffered the death of his son Tommy, shared "a peculiarly vivid and poignant sense" of her grief, but hoped she would take "a certain cold comfort that death after meningitis is better than the maimed life mentally and physically which sometimes survives." Edwin Markham, who had won an international prize for a sonnet that year, typed a copy of the poem and dedicated it to his "friend, Dr. George W. Kirchwey," in memory of Jeffrey. Freda's father, the last to give up hope in Jeffrey's losing battle to survive, was stricken by the death. Yet, "Out of the whole strain his strength seemed to rise absolutely intact and dependable. Gosh what a man!"[36] Freda wrote.

Michael tried to avoid the subject of his brother's death at first, but then he asked many questions and wanted to know if Jeffrey had been in pain. Freda felt Michael "seemed quite mature and understanding about it all," but he had recurring nightmares and a panic fear of death for years to come.[37] The weight of the responsibility for proper care of her children haunted Freda. Two of the three children had now died. Years later, after Freda and Evans had spent much time planning a trip to Moscow, she canceled the trip because of Michael's ill health. She explained to colleague Louis Fischer (who was to have been their guide in Moscow) that she could not leave her sick child: "The decision was less on account of *The Nation* than on account of Mickey's health which has not been good this spring. I am unwilling to be so far away from him for so long, especially since he is to be in Mamaroneck under the doctor's eye. This is a terrible disappointment to us both—and I might add to Mickey, too. We tried to talk ourselves into thinking it would be all right to go, but it didn't work."[38]

*

Although George, Evans, and Michael suffered Jeff's loss, Freda's response worried the family the most. Her reaction was atypical, even considering the deaths of Brewster and Dora. Work could not pull her out of her suffering this time. When Villard offered her a less demanding job, she shared with him her ambivalence about going back to work. She did want to put her "mind" and "what energy" she had to work, but she didn't want him to create a job just to get her back in the office. "Let's wait till a real job turns up." She also admitted that now even work at a real job was out of the question: "I am a little afraid that for a while I'll have to go easy, at best. I'm tired down through layers of my being that haven't ever before been reached, I think."[39]

Freda retreated to the countryside of West Cornwall, Connecticut. She hired John Gordon, "an unusually nice boy," to be eleven-year-old Michael's summer companion and tutor. She also brought

Michael Gannett, a friend of her son, with them. The house was big enough for all four of them and Evans, when he could come up from New York to write.[40]

Meantime, Evans escaped into his job. He resumed working for the Fund and continued to write feature articles for the *New York Times*. In those beginning months of the Great Depression he analyzed the realities of "mass financing" of an America living on consumer credit. He documented that $2,600,000,000 a year was advanced to wage earners in small loans from a range of creditors, from pawn shops to personal finance companies.[41] When Evans visited West Cornwall in mid-June he brought pages of exhaustive research for another article on American philanthropic organizations. He analyzed his figures and documented the kinds of issues and the activities American foundation monies supported. He credited the Garland Fund as "sole contributor" to "the promotion of birth control, the maintenance of civil liberties, the support of labor unions and strike relief work." He also applauded the Twentieth Century Fund as "the only one primarily devoted to the improvement of the world's economic organization and technique for the common good."[42]

Freda was always ready to lend Evans a hand, editing copy or clarifying ideas even before he put them into print. Yet this June, Freda was mostly glad just to have Evans near her: "It's grand to have him around in spite of his labors." To Villard she laconically observed: "The Nation seems to me good these days, though I find myself not very politically—or publicly-minded."[43]

Freda was trying to decide what life meant after so much of it had been taken away from her. Twice a week she traveled from West Cornwall to Washington, Connecticut, to seek the help of psychoanalyst Beatrice Hinkle. She got "tired suddenly and unaccountably." She recorded, "my states of mind vary with a speed that is alarming to one of my usual calm nature, but I sleep much better and feel miserable much less of the time." Yet she felt too weak to work. Villard wrote Krutch: "We don't get very reassuring accounts of Freda . . . She needs very much to build herself up and guard against anemia. Poor girl, she finds it hard to settle down to anything."[44]

When Evans traveled to gather material for another article, Freda decided to accompany him. At the Hanover Inn at Dartmouth College she was the "wife" of a foundation director.[45] It was a strange position; she did no work of her own. She decided then to try resting in Nova Scotia at Ardnamurchan. Her father was dubious: "I don't see this as the most desirable place for Freda. There is far too much going on, too much unconscious but still compelling demand for participation in all sorts of activities to permit one to play the role of a semi-invalid such as Freda requires." In December the Kirchwey-Clarks moved to a spacious house in Mamaroneck, New York.[46]

The new year found something new in the way of work for Freda. She put together a panel of women to address a topic she had struggled with a long time: "The Independent Woman," a course to be offered at 11—12:30 on 6 January 1931, at the New School for Social Research: The catalog described the course:

> No single aspect of recent social development has given rise to such exaggerated hopes and fears as the entry of woman upon a wide variety of independent careers, in industry, business and the professions. Economic independence for women has now become so solidly established a fact that the debate pro and con must give way to a deliberate examination of the opportunities open to women, the various methods of reconciling the business or professional position in the family; psychological consequences of the new activities upon women; the effect upon established institutions.

Kirchwey wrote that the lecturers would provide a "fresh view of the several problems involved."[47] She convinced her friend Grace Greenbaum Epstein to talk about shopkeeping, and Sarah Butler, vice-chairman of the New York State Republican Committee, to speak about politics. Margaret Mead, Theresa Helburn, and Amelia Earhart were among the other "good" speakers.[48]

Aside from this work and several book reviews for the *Nation*, 1931 found Freda still unable to return to full-time work. While she had been nursing Jeffrey, Villard had brought in Henry Hazlitt to assume her job of literary editor. Despite her absence, Villard had kept her as one of his three associate editors, along with Dorothy Van Doren and Arthur Warner. Mauritz Hallgren, who had begun a writing career on the *Chicago Tribune,* and had most recently been a member of the Berlin staff of the United Press, joined the *Nation* as an associate editor in October 1930. Villard waited until January 1931 before designating Freda a contributing editor rather than associate editor, and she joined the list of those who wrote only occasional pieces. The next month she reviewed *The Education of a Princess*, the memoirs of Marie, Grand Duchess of Russia. She found it hard to believe that Marie, who had experienced so much death and destruction in her life, fainted at the sight of lower-class sailors and their ill-clad female companions in her former royal box. "I can only conclude," Freda wrote, "that box and sailors suddenly lost their material identity and loomed as symbols of all that was gone, and that Marie's nervous system responded with a general collapse such as her cool intelligence would never have tolerated."[49]

This revealing review was her first piece of writing in a year. For one who equated life with paid work, inactivity signified a serious malaise. In contrast, Evans handled the pain the way Freda once had, by vigorous involvement in work. When Dorothy was ill, Evans warned her about her "too hectic life." He confessed that he had been working too hard: "I'm cursing myself for not having been easier on myself this past year and I'm in a state of missionary zeal about warning other people!" Of his and Freda's lives for years past, he wrote: "I think that our too hectic life all these years has taken a lot out of both of us which a bit of leeway all along would have avoided." He also reminded Dorothy, "Jeffrey died a year ago this afternoon—its strange how much anniversaries can mean, isn't it?"[50]

Freda continued her search in psychoanalysis, which became a way to structure meaning out of torment. If she could understand, she could cope. She trusted analysis to free her to verbalize the strong feelings she had inside and used it and the time free from work to reflect on relationships. Freda urged her sister, who was experiencing difficult emotional times of her own, to gather up her courage and begin psychoanalysis. "No matter what the outcome I can't think it a bad thing to know one's inner workings!" She advised Dorothy to "rest and think and read a little!" and to "build up a little wall of detachment and become a bit more egocentric if you hope to keep well." Freda, who had been reading the letters their mother had written Dorothy, admitted to her sister: "I think all these admonitions are a rather oblique reflection of Mama Dodie's letters on which I've spent the afternoon. They are fascinating to me."[51]

Dorothy was grateful for Freda's advice, which surprised her sister and caused her to reflect on their relationship. Early in life Freda consistently sassed her sister. A childhood friend recalled hearing a scolding eleven-year-old Freda received from Dora. "Why are you so mean to Dorothy, Freda? She loves you so." "I know," replied Freda, "but she's too damned bossy."[52]

Freda had carried this flip, brusque facade in interactions with her sister into her mature years. She wanted to change the pattern for, as she explained to Dorothy: "I have never felt I could be much use to you because some ancient little-sister pattern always turns up and makes me behave in an off-hand and hard-boiled manner that belies my real desires and feelings . . . I'm thankful, my dear, if any of my experiences and emotional excursions and efforts to find more satisfying ways of life have given you the least bit of help." She reiterated her advocacy of analysis: Dorothy's thoughts "might be clearer [inside] after a little spell of analysis . . . So try it, no matter what!"[53]

In the fall of 1931 Evans wrote that Freda was better than she had been for two years. "She went to a big Yiddish Halloween party with Grace & Co. that lasted till 5 a.m." On 9 November Freda and Evans' sixteenth anniversary, she wrote Dorothy, "Give L[arry] my love. I'm glad he's playing Badminton but it doesn't take the place of analysis!" Analysis had permitted Freda to work again. It was natural for one who sketched faces on *Nation* memos to sculpt a woman's face of clay. "That's what p.a. [psychoanalysis] has done for me."[54] The anniversary was special to Freda and Evans. The tragedy of Jeffrey's death had brought them together in a way that no force could ever pull apart. They yearned for another baby, but Freda could not get pregnant. "I saw Billy Caldwell to ask why I seem not to be having babies. He insists I am elegantly equipped for it except for a slight acidity. But both E and I are going to have a few tests."[55]

Freda continued to review books. In Emma Goldman's autobiography she confronted the dilemma of feeling versus intellectualizing life:

> She is contemptuous of any intellectualizing that stands in the way of faith and action. Always she feels first and thinks later— and less. I realize that I am describing here a process common to the rest of the human breed, but a difference is created by the range and strength of Emma Goldman's capacity for emotion, which render insignificant by comparison the "wishful thinking" of most of us.
>
> How attractive and how terrifying is this unabashed acceptance

of feeling as the test of action! The primitive passions are justified, even harnessed to high and impersonal aims; the laborious processes of analysis are made to appear sterile; realism becomes something rather anemic and cynical. Life itself is lent color and warmth and meaning. We may reject such satisfactions as immature, but some part of our being remains envious, feels itself "petty and unblest"—and unfulfilled.[56]

Goldman, exasperated by much of the American reaction to her book, wrote: "it is true, there is no one in the States who has the understanding, the feeling, and the equipment, to do justice to my book. True, Mrs. Freda Kirchwey, in the Nation, has done excellently, far better than any man's review, but even she has not grasped the depth and the compelling motives of my life."[57]

*

Although Freda had spent a long time in the "laborious, process of analysis," she admired Goldman's emotionality. Eventually feelings would bring the journalist back into the public world, but a deep sense of purpose was required to force her to action. She wanted no part of battles that could not be won. She had recently lost two of them: her mother and her son. Work on the *Nation* must count. By the summer of 1932 Freda Kirchwey had recovered enough to consider a return to that work, and she began to negotiate with Villard. Originally he promised a salary of $100 a week, but he reduced the offer to $90, explaining: "it will make trouble in the office if you should come in at a higher rate than Joe [Krutch] or [Henry] Hazlitt. I think you will agree with me that there should be complete equality in starvation wages." She agreed to come back, "on the basis of a flat starvation rate all round pending adjustments to be made when and if possible." She was concerned about more than her own salary. She insisted upon reading the journal's records, for she wanted an understanding of the "financial structure of the paper," admitting, "I've always been far too ignorant of it." She was also interested in Villard's long-range plan to retire as the *Nation* editor and to divest control in a board of directors.[58]

Kirchwey's return to the *Nation* came only after careful thought and extensive consultations with many friends and colleagues—and of course with Evans and George. Taking the sharp right turn off Orchard Drive, Freda and Evans drove down the tree-studded road leading to the Wertheim home, far from any Cos Cob traffic. The evening came alive with *Nation* talk. Maurice Wertheim, a big backer of the *Nation*, liked Freda, and the feeling was mutual. She had come to him for advice, and he had invited Joseph Wood Krutch to join them. After all, in his proposed organization plan Oswald Garrison Villard had verbally agreed to relinquish "control" to a group of editors. Of them, Freda Kirchwey and Joe Krutch would have the major responsibility for running the paper. That evening's conversation and "elaborate study of the ownership and financial control of the paper" convinced Kirchwey to return to the *Nation*.[59]

Once back, she explained to a reporter that she had "spent three years 'having a breathing spell.' 'Perhaps'—she half apologized . . . 'perhaps it's the disease of my generation not to be sure of 'the way out.'"[60] In effect she admitted that her generation had not discovered the means to achieve the tenuous balance of career and family. She was surprised to hear from another reporter that other Barnard alumnae seemed to feel that the combination of home and career was not difficult. "Do most alumnae find it easy?" Freda asked. "Though both ran smoothly, I always had a feeling of strain, of never being caught up with myself. That is true of a lot of my friends, too. They all know that they can carry on homes and jobs, but it's pretty overwhelming. I don't mean that one should choose one or the other, but there should be a greater effort to find a balance between them." She had thought long and hard about the pressure she had lived with, taking as little time as possible off work when she had babies. By 1932 she concluded: "I think that's silly. It is a strain that is fair neither to the woman nor the baby."[61] Through analysis she had concluded that women should have more time to relax during pregnancy and after childbirth. Nevertheless, she told a reporter, "I don't want women who must stay at home through force or circumstances to feel like worms."[62]

Yet what Freda called the "perennial question" of "Women and Careers" had yielded no answers. No matter how many sides she looked at, no certain answers emerged, only more questions. Although she continued to appreciate the flow of ideas about the issues, in general, she stopped pursuing women's issues publicly. She emerged from her inner struggle committed to journalistic goals that could be achieved.

5 || *A Desk with a View*

At age thirty-nine, Freda Kirchwey returned to the *Nation*'s offices at 20 Vesey Street sobered by the years of personal struggle. Some four months later, in January 1933, Villard, who had supported her throughout her long ordeal, officially retired as editor, remaining as publisher and contributor. Freda became the "de facto executive editor" of the new editorial board, "a directorate of equals." Her equals included Joseph Wood Krutch, Henry Hazlitt, and Mauritz Hallgren (soon to be replaced by Ernest Gruening). During the next several years the composition of the board changed, but Kirchwey remained. In earlier years the younger editors had used "cajolery" and "mild sabotage" to get their ideas across to Villard. Freda considered such "juvenile stratagems" tiresome, and negotiated real, as opposed to nominal, editorial control for the board as a condition for her return; the "child-and-father relationship" that Villard's paternalistic style of managing had encouraged was abandoned.[1]

Villard's surrender of control over editorial decisions left in charge the woman who never raised her voice, listened carefully to her colleagues, and conveyed a sense of self-confidence on the job. Amid the journal's strong-willed, highly articulate writers, eager to get their passionate views in print, Freda Kirchwey, the diplomat and mediator, fared well. From her earliest days at Barnard she had cherished the idea of an open forum where ideas could be aired and shared, and she put it in practice at weekly editorial conferences where the board sorted out policy, designated crucial national and international issues, and negotiated writing assignments.

Often as she passed Caroline Whiting's desk, Kirchwey snagged her silk stockings on its splintered wood. The battered furniture, a sign of the journal's precarious financial picture, reflected the country's economic plight during the Depression. To stave off economic ruin, with the help of business manager Hugo Van Arx, she and Krutch adopted an austerity plan designed to stabilize the journal. Cutting the pay of even star writers like Robert Dell and Paul Y. Anderson from two cents a word to one cent, they "starved the paper into temporary solvency." Their own reduced salaries were worthwhile sacrifices to keep the *Nation*'s message in print at a time when fascism stalked Europe.[2]

Freda Kirchwey, buoyed by the optimism of her progressive-era upbringing, insisted that ideas were worth fighting for. She increasingly used the *Nation* as a "propaganda journal," devoted to "fighting with words."[3] Crusading was not new to the *Nation*. What was new was a developing stress on the fighting nature of the journal and its use as a weapon against fascism. For Kirchwey, fascism was not the invention of Hitler or Mussolini, Horthy or Mannerheim: "It is merely the form assumed by the counter-revolution in an age equipped with highly developed instruments of destruction and of deception. Fascism is merely tyranny stream-lined, mechanized, and thus capable of new triumphs of terror. It is tyranny geared to twentieth-century techniques, sustained by the peculiar brands of social and political unrest characteristic of twentieth century economic life." Of even greater concern was its appeal to primitivism, for it was "no genuine primitivism, but rather an attempt to escape from the frustrations and fear of modern industrial life by a steep dive into the sub-rational, the collective, the instinctual." She wrote, "What reason cannot deal with must always be disturbing to the reasoning mind."[4]

What could be more alarming to someone who believed that people could be convinced by rational arguments, than the threat of a base appeal to instinct. The myths that provided fascism's "slogans and incantations" created a "mass flight from reality." Fascist propaganda manipulated that "steep dive into the sub-rational" becoming as much the enemy as actual bullets. In these extraordinary times, Freda Kirchwey, who had always longed to be a participant in the world instead of an observer, took on the challenge of using words as counter-propaganda weapons.[5]

Over the years she had mastered the use of the *Nation* as advocate. Unlike a daily newspaper, whose job was to report as much of the news as possible, Kirchwey viewed her journal's task as one of influencing the public by articulating a particular point of view: "From the days of Godkin down *The Nation* has in the strictest sense been a propaganda journal. I mean simply a journal devoted to fighting with words for the particular set of beliefs which its editors and owners have held."[6]

The *Nation* now gave structure to Kirchwey's life; it became her vehicle to fight fascism and the ills it perpetrated. Meanwhile, a new-found comfort in her relationship with her husband enabled her to break through the years of isolation, and she moved increasingly into the world of his political interests. But Freda's immersion in the *Nation* surpassed their shared interest in the world. When she was not at the office writing editorials or conferring with colleagues, she was home devouring the latest news, writing more editorials, or telephoning reporters and colleagues. With a Tuesday deadline, weekends were rarely free from work. The couple often spent weekends on their boat, the *Southwind*. While Evans enjoyed the sail, with Michael (when he was home from school), Freda pored over the stack of newspapers, clippings, and books she had brought on board.[7]

A spoof about the Kirchwey-Clarks preparing to leave for a weekend on the water began: "10 a.m. any Saturday morning," with Evans asking, "Are you ready, Fritz?" and Freda replying: "All but getting dressed and calling up Muriel [Gray] and Peggy [Marshall] and Maxwell [Stewart] and Max Lerner." Freda continued dressing, "by sitting on the bed with a pile of proofs." A two-hour delay found the rest of the family at the dock waiting for Freda who had decided to write her editorial before she left. The editorial in this spoof gives an inkling of her life.

> Up to the time of going to press, two-gun Hitler had not said the final word. The prospect is bleak, for what can be expected of a gangster who has not the common decency or human consideration to state his position before our Tuesday deadline? The time for vacillation is past. Karl and Prue must declare their hand. If Hitler's army moves one inch into the Sudeten territory Father

and Tante Mary must take the 11:15 train for Mamaroneck. Poland can still be won over, late as it is, if we can get the laundry to Mrs. Kay tonight.

There is just one faint chance left. If all the European cabinets will only state their positions firmly and unequivocably by midnight, Monday, we can still make this week's press.[8]

Although Freda kept in close touch with her son Michael, who was attending Phillips Exeter Academy in New Hampshire, and saw her immediate family and a few close friends as often as she could, her mind was seldom far from the *Nation* and world fascism. Although Evans shared Freda's commitment to a better world, he worried about the consequences of her intense involvement with the journal: "O, beloved, let's *enjoy* these next years together—do shake yourself loose from the pressures you've been under. I'll not let my job get me either. Let's go to the theater and have good evenings at home and dance, and sail."[9] But during the 1930s they rarely spent relaxing evenings at home.

From 1932 to 1939 Kirchwey deplored news of Mussolini sealing control of Italy, Hitler consolidating his gains in Germany, and Franco forcing the Loyalists out of Spain. Fascism's brutal march through Europe in the 1930s pushed the last decade's preoccupation with sexual morality far into the background. The ultimate moral question remained: would good or evil prevail? Kirchwey believed the hope of the world depended on "a successful resistance to international fascism."[10]

But the economic imbalance of a world replete with grave discrepancies between industry and its workers and a staggering number of unemployed provided a breeding ground for chilling solutions, "universal slavery," and "state absolutism." Wall Street's slogans of free enterprise made no sense when industry refused to pay workers enough money to buy the goods they produced. "The question is not, how can we save free enterprise in a free market, with all the subsidiary freedoms that are supposed to flow from those two. The question is rather, how much freedom can survive the degree of collective control necessary to keep the industrial machine going: and where is that control to be lodged?" Democracy provided one answer, fascism another, and the latter was "most likely to result from either a failure to get there in time or a refusal to attempt any answer at all."[11]

The *Nation* put its readers on alert against domestic demagogues.

It blasted Louisiana Senator Huey P. Long who had built national recognition from his local campaign: "Hitler had to burn the Reichstag to get what he wanted. Huey merely filled the legislative halls with armed men." On another occasion, after Long got forty-four bills through the Louisiana legislature, the *Nation* said he had made himself "dictator of his State."[12] His announced "Share the Wealth" program, which would tax the rich to give every man $5,000 and a home, promised easy answers to hard economic and social questions.

Terrible poverty and continued unemployment resulted in receptive ears to another man the *Nation* considered a threat: Father Charles Coughlin, the Detroit radio priest who renounced his support for FDR and announced his National Union for Social Justice. Raymond Gram Swing, a *Nation* editor, listened to Coughlin's intended programs and warned that none of them mentioned "democratic government" or freedom of speech.[13] Coughlin insisted on protecting "the natural right to private property." Like Hitler and Mussolini before him, he attacked the big industrialists and bankers, but the *Nation* warned: "If his following grows, as similar movements did in Germany and Italy, it will ultimately make its peace with big industry and finance, and if it obtains control we shall be ruled by the same kind of fascist oligarchy." A little later the journal pointed out "the fascist technique in his attack on recent labor legislation."[14]

The real threat lay in the combination of the Coughlin and Long movements. "Their programs, for all their glamorous radical sound, are capitalist radicalism." They relied on the profit motive and railed against socialism. Hitler and Mussolini had both found cooperation with big business, and Swing warned that in America fascism might look different, but the basics were the same, and available for manipulation: "For fascism is the reorganization of society by undemocratic means to maintain the capitalist system. It is a movement, first of all, of passion and prejudice, growing out of the despair of disillusioned, impoverished people. Then comes the collusion between demagogue and big business."[15]

Unlike many of her middle-class counterparts, Kirchwey never considered democracy synonymous with capitalism, nor did she see the world divided into capitalist versus popular revolutionary camps. Exposure to workers' conditions at home and abroad, to Evans' work with various labor causes and her own work on the

Garland Fund, convinced her of an urgent need to alleviate the bleak conditions of the masses. She was not convinced that capitalism could meet the depth of these needs and argued that "revolutions never happen unless the masses are driven either by hunger or by oppression or both together past the limits of endurance." To its victims, mob rule brings no alternative but violence: "Then men will fight, because it no longer avails them to vote, or talk, or appeal to their elected representatives or the courts."[16]

Freda Kirchwey's impatience with capitalism's failure to meet the needs of the masses, her remembrance of Western democracies aiding the counterrevolutionaries against the Bolsheviks during the Russian revolution and civil war, and her judgment that eventually the Soviet Union would deliver its promise of a worker state reinforced a basic acceptance of that country as a legitimate power and a logical ally. Yet many of the middle class regarded the abolition of private enterprise inherent in both communism and socialism as antithetical to their way of life. Many could be persuaded to acquiesce to dictatorship because fascism's emphasis on private property made it seem a lesser evil to them than communism.

The Nazi takeover in Germany showed what could happen if fascists played on middle-class fear of the masses' susceptibility to communism. Kirchwey knew that in the United States the middle class was the pivotal group in achieving victory for democracy; she must help prevent them from being manipulated. She must motivate them to meet the needs of the poor as they had been motivated to do during the progressive era. "Freely functioning" capitalism's time had run out, and Kirchwey sought "some form of widespread social control or ownership and social planning." She looked to fundamental economic and social reforms to stave off the dread system that threatened a world made vulnerable by the Depression.[17]

*

In 1932 Norman Thomas, the Socialist Party presidential candidate, seemed most likely to offer a vigorous solution to such problems in the United States. Despite its third-party status, Freda considered his candidacy "more than a political flurry." To the editors of the *Nation*, the incumbent Herbert Hoover represented "the tragic failure of rugged individualism."[18] A month before the election the journal reviewed his record: he refused to do away with the tariff; he did not take decisive substantive action to alleviate underlying economic ills; he consistently minimized the effects of the

Depression; he "steadfastly" opposed a dole; and he asserted "that prosperity was just around the corner." All of these factors convinced the *Nation* that Hoover would be "overwhelmingly repudiated at the polls."[19] Indeed he would be, though not by Norman Thomas. Once Franklin Delano Roosevelt (FDR) won the election, Freda lent the new President a receptive ear. She hoped that the comprehensive program of unemployment relief he had created while governor of New York signaled the possibility that the needs of the masses could be met nationwide. Recognizing his goals as central to answering what she perceived as the country's needs, she wished him well in establishing "a democracy based on full economic, as well as political, equality."[20] Impressed by his "sense of vigor and action," his "friendly, personal tone," she concluded that he was "a person of courage and candor."[21]

FDR and the United States needed courage. When Roosevelt took office in 1933, the country's unemployed numbered some 13 million. Years later Kirchwey remembered the New Deal as the *Nation*'s "special assignment and charge. We functioned a little like a political Watch and Ward Society."[22] Although the journal took FDR to task for not going far enough to solve the grave problems of the Depression, its editors reluctantly accepted whatever was new about the New Deal as better than what they considered the do-nothing policies of Hoover.[23]

Once Roosevelt was elected, the *Nation* hoped he would lead the country out of the devastating plight it was in. In many respects the journal reflected the ideals of many of the intellectuals Roosevelt brought to his administration. As historian Arthur Ekrich wrote, the New Dealers were "at home in the world of ideas." Roosevelt had consulted liberal reformers during his governorship and throughout his campaign, and they followed him to Washington. Sherwood Anderson described that city after the emergence of what would be called the Brain Trust: "There is a curious exhilarating feeling. You cannot be there now without a feeling of the entire sincerity of these men." They were convinced that ideas could be put into practice, and the *Nation* shared their belief: "The life of the country is at low ebb. Mr. Roosevelt need not fear to try new leaders and new ideas, and to venture boldly into untrodden paths." The "gravest crisis in its peace-time history" made it imperative for Roosevelt to be bold.[24]

Roosevelt hung onto capitalism, yet he pushed for a more positive state and for more government controls.[25] As the New Deal began he steered a middle course between the 1920s' glorification of private enterprise and the growing move toward social welfare. After a few months Kirchwey judged Roosevelt's many programs as diversions rather than as representative of sound economic theory. She wanted answers to some fundamental questions. How could a planned economy "exist within the shaky framework of the profit system?" A rebuilt economic structure required a different tack from the one Roosevelt was taking.[26]

Judging the National Industrial Recovery Act (NIRA), which set up the National Recovery Administration (NRA) code agreements with major industries and guaranteed workers the right to unionize, a "promising first step" to economic reform, she thought its plan "to prevent the downfall of capitalism and create temporary prosperity" left other conditions unmet. She wanted the federal government to take over the banking, transportation, and communications industries, thereby removing private profit and giving labor a fair share of wealth. Answering her question "Can Controlled Capitalism Save Us?" negatively, she stressed the unmet need of stretching economic prosperity to cover the people as a whole. Yet she acknowledged that the United States had not elected President Roosevelt "to usher in a collective society," and she was willing to judge his administration by its success along the path to equality. At least FDR had abandoned the laissez-faire practice of keeping the government out of business. But in June 1933 the *Nation* thought "Mr. Roosevelt could have and should have moved farther to the left."[27]

Kirchwey continued to look at the NRA with skepticism. She and Evans Clark, in his work for the Twentieth Century Fund, wrote of the necessity for the government to "enforce some regard for public welfare as well as private profit." Of the chances for achieving this in FDR's administration, she wrote: "To translate its good intentions into accomplished fact will take courage and determination beyond anything that capitalist politics has taught us to expect."[28] Reviewing Roosevelt's actions at the end of 1933, Kirchwey acknowledged his commitment to "prosperity based on social control and a wider distribution of social benefits." The results were much less evident.[29] Yet both of them must have felt more confident of the NRA's worth by 1935, when Clark accepted an appointment as "impartial chairman" of the New York State NRA adjustment board.[30]

On another piece of legislation the *Nation* was critical. "Where Is Security, Mr. Roosevelt?" it asked of a social security package which made no provisions for domestics, farmers, or migrant workers, neglected the serious problem of millions of unemployed, and lacked adequate federal standards. "Defeat the Wagner-Lewis Bill!" Kirchwey argued that it was better not to pass the act than to create an act with so much missing and such cumbersome administrative problems. The *Nation* continued this advice in July when the bill came before Congress.[31]

The social security bill that Roosevelt signed in August 1935 was scathingly attacked for the *Nation* by Abraham Epstein, the same social security expert whose ideas formed the basis for the Twentieth Century Fund's research on social welfare programs. Epstein detailed the history of the act from original support for the plan to the final project. After several amendments, the act came out with serious deficiencies. Unlike other insurance systems with "government contributions derived from the higher-income groups," America's plan was to be "self-sustaining," requiring contributions of worker and employer. This would cost the worker twofold: he would have to pay into the plan and, because the employer would not want to pay his own share out of the profits, he would pass costs on to the consumer. The exclusion of the wealthy from any responsibility for the vicissitudes of life caused by mass production and the lack of inclusion of various kinds of workers in the provisions made this plan "socially unwise."[32]

The *Nation*'s insistence that the federal government tap the resources of the wealthy to correct the excesses of capitalism was evident in its endorsement of spending public money for low-income housing. The journal joined the executive director of the Twentieth Century Fund in urging support for the Wagner-Ellenbogen Public Housing Bill of 1936, which proposed that federal money be used to assist with construction costs and to subsidize rents of public housing for low-income groups. Evans Clark spoke in favor of the bill at a Bankers Club meeting in New York City. He presented public housing as "a business problem . . . a challenge to businessmen" and documented how the increase in construction would promote business. He pointed out a "men of good will" appeal—"the hearty, natural desire of slum dwellers for decent houses"—and called this aspect "the kick in the drink for business men." However, that motivation was not "kick" enough, and the bill failed to be enacted.[33]

Continuing their collective effort, Clark and Kirchwey had better luck supporting the National Labor Relations Act (NLRA), commonly called the Wagner Act. It would become a much stronger act for labor than the previous NIRA, which some businesses had subverted by setting up company unions. Employer-dominated company unions would disappear as bona-fide collective bargaining units under the supervision of the proposed permanent independent National Labor Relations Board (NLRB) created by the Wagner Act. The NLRB would guarantee and police collective bargaining and would restrain business from committing "unfair labor practices." The *Nation* ran one positive editorial after another praising the 1935 bill, and, when critics attacked it in public hearings, brought out Twentieth Century Fund ammunition. The Fund's Committee on Government and Labor made an independent study and recommended strengthening the Wagner Act by giving the NLRB additional power to enforce collective agreements that either party subsequently violated. The *Nation* recommended that the power be added to the bill.[34]

"Can Labor Enforce the Wagner Bill?" the journal asked after its passage. It answered in the affirmative, pleased with the guarantee of collective bargaining that made possible "an ultimate shift in economic power from employers to workers." While crediting Senator Wagner for the act, the *Nation* criticized the President for not openly supporting the bill.[35]

Characteristically, the *Nation* seemed hard on the President in 1935, as it consistently prodded him toward further social welfare legislation. Paul Ward, author of the *Nation* series F.D.R.—the Boss in the Back Room, charged that the progressive legislation embodied in the Wagner Act was forced on the President. The title of one of the articles—"Roosevelt's Hollow Triumph"—gave the flavor to the series which evaluated FDR. Ward, calling Roosevelt's victories "empty ones," blasted all but the Tennessee Valley Authority (TVA), "the best of New Deal measures."[36]

Ward's articles were particularly critical; but *Nation* editors in general were disappointed. Looking toward the election of 1936, the journal concluded: "Roosevelt, measured against what he might have been, cuts a far poorer figure than he will present next year in contrast with the choice of the Republican Party." FDR could have done so much more, but the Republicans would do even less. When the President courted business support late in 1935, the editors argued that his actions represented not only "bad politics" but "bad economics." They declared: "The New Deal Ends."[37]

As 1936 unfolded with a split Socialist Party, the left faction supporting Norman Thomas and the right faction adding its numbers to organized labor union support of FDR, the *Nation* decided: "we must have general principles, tested always by pragmatic action. A socialized future is the only adequate political solution for a mass-production world. To chart the specific American path to that future is our primary task."[38]

Despite all its criticism, the *Nation* did not encourage a leftist third-party challenge to Roosevelt in 1936. It would take until 1940 to educate the public about "the idea of production for use rather than for profit." The implication was that it would be better to wait until then to run an alternative to FDR. Several months before the election, while still criticizing the President for a discrepancy between his promises and his delivery, the *Nation* cautioned against a radical alternative for this election: "For the present, American radicalism must curb itself because it fears the uncharted future and because no new leadership has yet emerged." Privately, however, Freda Kirchwey voted her conscience and cast a vote for Thomas.[39] Following the election, the *Nation* ran a favorable assessment of President Roosevelt and his administration. Stuart Chase wrote: "Short of revolution, he has brought about reforms and breaches of the old order so colossal as to stagger the imagination."[40] Although the New Deal was insufficient, it was at least a partial answer.

Even earlier, as fascism continued to grow in Europe, as Father Coughlin and Huey Long increased their popularity in the United States, and as the Supreme Court declared unconstitutional both the NIRA and the Agricultural Adjustment Act (AAA), which gave farmers federal price supports, Kirchwey and many *Nation* editors looked to some continuation of New Deal legislation as essential solutions to poverty and social problems that could lead to fascism in America.[41] They agreed with Max Lerner who argued that the Court was "smashing the best legislative efforts of the community."[42]

The views of Freda Kirchwey, Heywood Broun, Joseph Wood Krutch, Maxwell Stewart, and Max Lerner were reflected in unsigned editorials that sharply criticized the Court's decisions blocking New Deal legislation: "Safety against fascism is not in statutes but in a just economic order." They feared the conservative strict constructionist interpretations of the laws that reinforced states' rights at the expense of broad federal powers inherent in much of the New Deal legislation. The *Nation* seemed to come to life about the issue of curbing the power of the Supreme Court. It supported the President when he talked of initiating a constitutional amendment to do this. After Roosevelt had "forfeited many golden opportunities we think that he now has the best issue of his career."[43]

By 1937 the reality of international fascism pushed Kirchwey to view the jeopardized domestic policies of FDR as minimal answers to basic needs. She feared that the Court's stamp of illegality on New Deal reforms would allow social and economic injustices to remain uncorrected and provide the breeding ground for "fascism." Therefore, when the President proposed a judicial reorganization plan which would have given him the power to appoint an additional Supreme Court justice for each judge over seventy years of age who refused to retire, up to a maximum of fifteen justices, the *Nation*—always careful to protect constitutional safeguards—practiced expediency and announced its support.[44] The editors would have preferred a constitutional amendment to wrest social and economic legislation from the Supreme Court's grasp, but because of the time an amendment would require, most of them were willing to settle for preservation of New Deal legislation by any means— even the controversial "Court-packing" scheme. Kirchwey and most of her *Nation* colleagues thought that the President's proposal would "dynamite the reactionary judges into retirement."[45]

The Supreme Court reorganization plan, which would increase presidential power (and decrease the power and prestige of the highest Court) worried some liberals, like former Roosevelt adviser Raymond Moley.[46] Many of them had criticized decisions that struck down the NRA and the AAA, the heart of the first New Deal, yet they considered FDR's attempt to tamper with one of the three branches of government an ominous venture indeed—one that threatened the preservation of democracy.

Kirchwey, probably with the support of Lerner, Stewart, Broun, and Krutch, argued with those who criticized the plan as unconstitutional, an attack on judicial independence, or "*psychologically* a step toward fascism and dictatorship": "There is not the slightest sign of such a dictatorship in Mr. Roosevelt's plan. On the contrary, we regard it as one of the necessary steps in blocking the road to fascism." The *Nation* editors blamed the Court: "The soil of economic chaos out of which fascism grows has been amply supplied by the court's refusal to allow national action for economic control." A month later the journal escalated the critique, calling for "Purging the Supreme Court." Along with a detailed critical yet supportive analysis of Roosevelt's plan, the editors presented a list of candidates for the hoped-for Supreme Court justice positions that FDR's plan would create and urged their fellow "progressives" to "overcome" the "myth of Supreme Court divinity."[47]

The *Nation*'s majority view on the Court issue chagrined former publisher and editor-in-chief, Oswald Garrison Villard, and current publisher, Maurice Wertheim. Others were equally distressed. Unitarian minister John Haynes Holmes wrote of his "profound sense of depression and almost despair." The Court fight activated presidential usurpation of power. Liberal editor William Allen White wrote to Kirchwey: "I line up in this court controversy with Mr. Wertheim and Mr. Villard . . . I do not think we should give the power of precedent to any president to deliberately—recast the personnel of the supreme court." Villard asked, "What Is *The Nation* Coming To?" Wertheim echoed him: "It is unthinkable that a progressive and liberal journal should actually advocate any plan by which new judges are placed on our supreme tribunal who will decide cases on instructions, or who will be believed to have decided them on this basis."[48]

For some time Wertheim had been uncomfortable about the direction the *Nation* was taking. He wanted less radicalism, according to Hugo Van Arx, who wrote: "He is getting a licking from his down-town click."[49] The rift over the Supreme Court issue finally made him decide to get rid of the publication. While the *Nation* became much more supportive of FDR's program, Wertheim had become increasingly critical of the New Deal. Although he allowed the journal complete editorial freedom, he could not help but be bothered by the growing divergence of views. The solution he attempted was to hire and fire, bringing in journalists he felt would express views similar to his own. From the start Kirchwey challenged the banker's idea of adding someone new at an executive rank to support his beliefs. She said she would not remain under such circumstances: "My ego and my ideals would trip me up at every turn. I'm interested in working out plans with my fellow editors and then carrying them out as effectively as we can. I'm not even slightly interested in carrying out somebody else's plans—be he the best planner this side of Moscow."[50]

Nevertheless, when Wertheim brought in Max Lerner, Kirchwey did not leave. Lerner supported the New Deal and did not serve "to neutralize the Nation's political position." The three-person editorial board of Lerner, Kirchwey, and Krutch seemed cumbersome, and by the summer of 1936 the staff consensus was that there should be one executive editor: Freda Kirchwey. Evidently Wertheim had considered selling the magazine to its editors as early as June 1936, but he apparently changed his mind, and tension within the *Nation* continued.[51]

That summer while Kirchwey was on a forced vacation at Perry Mansfield Camp in Steamboat Springs, Colorado, to recover from insomnia and acute migraine headaches, Evans Clark wrote "of the staff's eagerness to have you back to pull things together." He said, "the feeling in the office is apparently running so high that if you are not given a free hand there is real danger of wholesale resignations." Associate editor Krutch, considering "what should be done to save the Nation," wrote: "It's a terrible thing to wish on you but how about coming back to be managing editor? Seriously it's the only solution I can think of. But get healthy first. You'll need strength." And Van Arx: "You are the only hope, the only member on the editorial board who possesses those (sic.) catholic knowledge and tendencies that would make for an editorial executive."[52]

To the *Nation* staff the solution was executive editorial control by Freda Kirchwey. She communicated the desire for that centralized authority to Wertheim and nominated herself for the job. Wertheim did not support the reorganization plan; nor did his dismay about the journal lessen. Another of the writers he had selected, Heywood Broun, also supported the *Nation*'s views instead of Wertheim's. Wertheim became more disgruntled at the ever-increasing ideological tension between patron and journal. "His business partners, he reported, no longer said good-morning to him; taking little stock in his obligations to keep hands off editorial policies, they held him personally responsible for every 'wrong' view expressed in *The Nation*." As Kirchwey acknowledged, "Kicks and blows must be much harder to bear when you have nothing to do with the offenses for which they are administered."[53]

A few months after the February 1937 Supreme Court editorial, a particularly sharp thorn to Wertheim, he decided to sell the *Nation*.

At a meeting with Krutch and Kirchwey in June 1937, he announced that he would sell it to Kirchwey, "whom he considered a true liberal, or he would sell it to the first person who would take it off his hands—no matter who, or what his views." Kirchwey proposed that a syndicate buy the journal, but Wertheim insisted on either her sole ownership or sale on the open market to the highest bidder. So, Freda Kirchwey recounted, "I bought *The Nation,* using money from a small trust fund my husband had inherited from his mother." (She paid $15,000 outright and took an interest-free loan from Wertheim's Civic Aid Foundation for the other $15,000.) "I felt I had no choice and Evans backed me. Fortunately—or was it fortunate?—neither of us could clearly foresee what my commitment would mean."[54]

In his public statement of the sale Wertheim mentioned the Supreme Court issue as an example of views on which he and the journal differed. He felt he would best serve the journal by giving "centralized control" to "its senior editor, Freda Kirchwey," elaborating that her many years of work there gave her "a unique apprenticeship for the full responsibility of ownership and control."[55] In the next issue, the editors announced "*The Nation*'s Future," boasting: "we believe that militant liberalism has come of age and can pay its own way."[56]

*

From 1933 on Kirchwey and other *Nation* editors had advocated that the United States adopt a "new role" in Europe. They wrote to gain support for the country's move toward collective security. Gone forever were the days when the journal found it difficult to determine which countries were the world's "aggressors."[57] Daily advances for the fascism of Hitler, Franco, and Mussolini led the *Nation* to urge economic boycotts. After Italy invaded Ethiopia, Kirchwey, once again in collaboration with Evans Clark, documented that the major powers, except Italy, produced at least two of the major commodities: food, machinery, iron and steel, coal, oil, and chemicals. "Italy cannot fight the other nations of Europe unless they sell it the materials to fight with." Since the U.S. was Italy's largest source of imports, any system of economic sanctions needed American cooperation. Based on the Committee on Economic Sanctions' research, amassed under the auspices of the Twentieth Century Fund, Kirchwey and Clark urged an international economic boycott of Mussolini's Italy.[58]

After the Japanese attack on Manchuria in 1931 and the League of Nation's subsequent investigation, Kirchwey in 1933 implored the United States to "Back the League!"; in order for League sanctions to succeed, they needed the support of both America and the Soviet Union (which were not then "even on speaking terms"). Nonrecognition of the Soviet Union was ludicrous, and Kirchwey urged Roosevelt to recognize that nation promptly. Although she would have preferred quicker action, she praised him in November 1933: "The resumption of normal relations between Russia and the United States will, we believe, stand out as a major accomplishment of the New Deal."[59]

Dealing with fascism meant giving up "all dreams of international justice and the substitution of law for force," for the future of the world depended "solely on the national interests of the major powers." Fascism had changed the rules. The *Nation* watched Hitler force his will on Germany, from the time of his appointment as Chancellor to his "election." After the death of President von Hindenburg, Hitler flew his personal flag alongside the German Kaiserreich. Kirchwey decried the desecration of Germany with Hitler's swastika, which stood "for the abolition of personal liberty, for prejudice, for reaction, for race hatred and persecution, for terror and murder." She detailed Hitler's early atrocities: his attacks on Jews, Socialists, and liberal members of the Reichstag, and the murders of Communist leaders. "What other perhaps more horrible outrages are taking place behind the veil of censorship can only be guessed at."[60]

German truculence at the disarmament conference increased fear of what lay behind Hitler's censorship. By the summer of 1933, when Kirchwey first backed collective security, she believed that changing "the unjust treaties" that had allowed Hitler to seize power must await his overthrow. He could not be trusted: "Hitler's current protestations of peaceful intent can hardly be taken seriously in view of the blood and iron which permeate his whole philosophy." The awesomeness of world events made it imperative that we "no longer dodge international responsibilities." Americans should oppose Germany's aggression.[61]

The descriptions of Nazi repression provided by fleeing German refugees made the challenge more pressing. And even their experiences paled in comparison to Hitler's public statements of his intentions. In September 1933, reporting a huge Nazi demonstration at

Nuremberg commemorating World War I, Kirchwey reviled Hitler's defense of his "Jewish policy," which he claimed was necessary in order for Germany to rid itself of "the dominant Jewish influence—which is decadent." As chilling was his mad prediction that "all other nations will be forced to adopt tactics of a similar nature" and his orchestrated mass-hysteria demonstrations, which sent 150,000 uniformed men into fury in their parade and incited Jew-baiting in the thousands more crowding around them. "Atrocity stories would be superfluous," Kirchwey concluded. The *Nation* reported Hitler's profound assault on the world as news of the week, printed scathing editorials revealing Nazi support in the United States, and tried in other ways to confront Americans with the vile presence of Nazis.[62]

Although the *Nation* reported Nazi hostility toward Jews, much of the American press relied on German newspapers for information. A German Jew, whose letter to her son in Zurich was printed in the *Nation,* cited the outrageous American gullibility in believing German reports that claimed: "No Jew is molested and everybody may attend to his affairs in greatest peace whatever business he may be engaged in." The realities were quite different. Already proletarian women, wearing white armbands reading "Buy German Goods Only," picketed Jewish stores. Already it was illegal for German municipal or federal employees to buy from Jews. Four of their close friends had committed suicide rather than live in what she called *Hexenkessel* (witch kettle). Each day brown uniforms, swastika flags, and military music swept even the youngest, from three to six, into Jew-baiting, yelling "Tueff, tueff, tueff [the sound of a train], there comes another Jew!" Whether by choice or by force her son's best friend now wore a Nazi uniform; she could never visit his family again. Escape was the only answer, but "it is not so simple."[63]

Jew-baiting was not confined within German borders. Calling the anti-Semitism in neighboring Poland an "old disease," Kirchwey reported in 1936: "the present epidemic, in form and violence, suggests that the source of the infection is its next-door neighbor. Germany should be forced to post on its door a sign reading, 'Unclean!'" She exposed "gangster" Hitler's "war against the Jews." During the anniversary of the Armistice, Nazi youths in party cars "smashed and plundered Jewish shops, burned synagogues, beat and arrested thousands of helpless Jews." "Never were mass cowardice, mass brutality, and mass destructiveness so gruesomely displayed"; the attack was "degenerate brutality," "an orgy of terror."[64]

Just as Hitler's propaganda incited the masses, Kirchwey consciously used the kind of language that would attract the attention of *Nation* readers. She understood propaganda, calling it "persuasion applied to the collective mind," whose use could be "honest or crooked," "violent or restrained," "dogmatic" or "reasonable." Dictatorships and democracies alike found it "a necessary instrument for forming or informing the public mind." Propaganda Minister Goebbels boasted of his efficient persecution of the Jews, which could serve as "a blueprint of action for the anti-Semitism that lurks just under the surface in all countries." Rather than accept this grim outcome, Kirchwey insisted that Goebbels' stories of blatant persecution of Jews would horrify the ordinary person rather than stimulate him to follow suit.[65]

She recalled Robert Dell's early assessment: "the more Hitler gets, the more he will want." His terrible treatment of dissenters and unimaginable treatment of Jewish nationals made his policy "an outbreak of primitive barbarism unchecked by any of the restraints by which the conduct of civilized people is regulated, with which it is useless to reason, and which cannot even be judged by ordinary moral and intellectual standards." How could talks about peace pacts have any meaning? How could one value Hitler's signature on any such pacts? "The man is clearly a criminal lunatic."[66]

Hitler's mania also expressed itself in an obsession with increasing the Aryan stock. This meant women's forced return to *Kinder, Kuche, Kirche* (children, kitchen, church). Kirchwey publicized that policy by detailing its effect on German sociologist Mathilde Vaerting. Vaerting had taught at the University of Jena since 1923, but the Nazi government could not allow her to continue research documenting that men's domination of women was based on sociological rather than biological foundations. As a prominent female faculty member of a significant German university she belied the government's prescription that all women should contribute to the German state by staying home and bearing children. The Nazis could not abide her, and Mathilde Vaerting was fired. Kirchwey reported in 1933: "Her dismissal is the most striking overt act so far committed in the Nazi war against the freedom of women."[67]

With such grim news for women coming out of Germany, it is not surprising that Freda Kirchwey celebrated the legalization of the dissemination of birth-control information in the United States.

"Birth Control Wins" shouted the *Nation*'s cover, displacing other news of that week in January 1937.[68] Birth-control legalization represented a victory against a mentality that regarded women as breeders of soldiers for the front. Battles to preserve the rights of women had to be fought and could be won. The Nazis who relegated women to childbearing, pushed them back into "a dead past."[69] American woman's twentieth-century victories, "the late and rather fragile fruit of the democratic process," advanced them toward human equality. Women's rights were "nothing more than a single aspect of democracy," and to retain recent gains women must develop "a fanatic attachment to the institutions and vital concepts of democracy." Continuing advanced education was particularly important. Fascist denial of educating women as full human beings meant that "the college woman of today stands, of necessity, on the front line."[70] Her battle was a part of the larger battle between democracy and fascism.

Kirchwey increasingly found herself advocating a warlike posture. She had abandoned the pacifism of earlier days in favor of a more militant stance and once wrote a dialogue clarifying her thoughts and externalizing her dilemma.

SELF I: How do you like being attacked as a militant?

SELF II: Don't like it. Makes me feel uncomfortable. Not guilty, but uneasy.

SELF I: A fine line to draw. Sure it isn't guilt?

SELF II: Sure. But associations are sometimes stronger than convictions.

SELF I: Like what?

SELF II: When people throw 1914 at me or 1917, I remember things. Peace demonstrations on the steps of Congress. Bitter attacks on people who thought that war could make democracy secure or that Britain had more of it than Germany.

SELF I: I thought so. You feel guilty. You think that nowadays you may be advocating a course that will lead to war . . .

SELF II: No. That's not it. I am advocating the only course that seems to me to give us a chance to dodge a war—us as well as the world . . .

SELF I: What course are you talking about? I've heard a lot of people say you haven't advocated any definite policy at all. Just a general up-and-at-em line.

SELF II: That's a libel. I've advocated a change in the N.L. [Neutrality Laws] so we can ship goods to nations that are attacked . . . I'd favor sending over an army if it appeared likely that Europe would otherwise be overwhelmed by German armies.

SELF I: It appeared certain in 1917—but you were against our going in.

SELF II: Fascism wasn't invented in 1917.

SELF I: No but old-fashioned capitalist imperialism was. Are you sure there's much difference?

SELF II: I'm sure. I never was more sure of anything in my life, than of the basic unarguable difference. It is measured by the difference between Hitler and Chamberlain, by the difference between tyranny in Germany and the relative democracy of England. It's measured most of all by the difference in the ways of life and thought in Germany under Hitler and in England even under Chamberlain.

That basic difference gave Freda Kirchwey hope for the preservation of European democracy, despite her belief that fascism was "the natural outgrowth of capitalist-democracy at a certain point in its decadence." Although she could not guarantee that the democracies would not turn to fascism after the war, the only chance to rid Europe of "the certain blackness of fascism" lay in Hitler's defeat.[71]

Hitler exploited the open wounds of World War I's peace of vengeance, and it bore fruits of aggression in the 1930s. As Germany began to rearm, the *Nation* wrote: "Let Hitler, let Mussolini, let Stalin testify to the correctness of the words, 'The Madness of Versailles.'" Hitler had already outlined his war of expansion, and, although in the early summer of 1935 his speeches were often conciliatory, the *Nation* remembered *Mein Kampf* and gave a negative answer to the question "Can Hitler Be Trusted?"[72]

The hope of the world lay in unity against Hitler, but many nonfascist countries feared the communism of the Soviet Union as much or more, especially because of the communist intention of spreading its ideology throughout the world through the Comintern, the Communist International. By 1935 the Comintern had abandoned its propaganda for international communism and called for unity with all groups opposed to fascism. Kirchwey, relieved and encouraged by Moscow's "olive branch," said: "It may well be that the basic conflict of the next ten years will not be between capitalism and revolution but between fascism and democracy—a struggle in which the forces of revolution must support and win the support of all the friends of democracy, while the forces of capitalism will gradually, and often unwillingly, form an alliance with the cohorts of fascism." She knew that it would take some time for the "revolutionary lions and the liberal lambs" to come together, but she hoped that they would. "If they keep their attention fixed on the universal enemy, an honestly united front may emerge, based on the compelling logic of self-preservation."[73]

*

But a vicious ideological struggle between Stalin and Trotsky jeopardized a united front against fascism. After Stalin expelled him from the Communist Party, Trotsky lived in exile. Stalin's Great Purge to rid the Soviet Union of those he considered counterrevolutionary traitors began in 1934 and continued through 1938. The most spectacular were the Moscow Trials, at which party leaders Kamanev, Zinoviev, Radek, and even Bukharin, along with many others, publicly confessed to treason and were executed.

The *Nation* editors criticized Stalin, though minimally. For example, of the outrage of some 66 to 71 suspects who were rounded up and shot in 1934, Kirchwey wrote: "This summary act will echo in every country in the world." But sustained criticism would have sabotaged her strategy of minimizing Soviet wrongs to focus on the larger goal: unity among antifascist forces. Her view of the trials was similar to Louis Fischer's early assessment: "I believe that even the Zinoviev, etc. trial will not stop the growth of democracy. That growth is the product of economic improvement and social peace the existence of both these phenomena is not subject to the slightest doubt." Fischer blamed the trial on the Soviet Union's transitional phase: "The shift from dictatorship to democracy is not only unprecedented, it is also difficult and tortuous. It takes time."[74]

The Moscow Trials were uncomfortable but not demoralizing to Kirchwey. Reporting some new executions, she acknowledged that the total numbered over one hundred. She thought Stalin might be trying to gain support of "the bourgeoisie world" by "exterminating revolutionary extremists" and criticized that strategy: "The recent executions have, in fact, provided a field day for the enemies of Moscow at a time when Soviet policy in Europe needs all the friends it can find."[75] She did not focus on the question of guilt or innocence or concentrate on the horror of unjustified murders; such issues were secondary to what she considered a greater issue. The collective security system against fascism was at stake. She adopted a moral stance of good versus the evil of fascism and an expedient stance regarding the Soviet Union. Because she regarded the Soviet Union as a flawed but necessary ally, she put it on the side of good and downplayed Soviet totalitarianism, which she considered temporary. A moralist against fascism, she was a relativist toward the Soviet Union.

Expediency also influenced Kirchwey's participation in the ideological conflict between Trotsky and Stalin. An original member of the American Committee for the Defense of Leon Trotsky, she resigned as soon as the committee obtained "safe asylum" for him. Because she was not a follower of Trotsky, she could not continue as a member of the "partisan group," and she objected to the pro-Trotsky, anti-Soviet tone of the committee's publicity. "The partisan passions of those who attack the Soviet Government and of the Communist Party are, in my opinion, jointly creating a chasm so deep that the world-wide popular opposition to fascism is in immediate danger of foundering in it."[76] The day after she resigned, she went to Mexico for a much-needed vacation. Interestingly, Kirchwey, who trusted her firsthand observations, wanted no such confirmation about Trotsky. She assured her son that her trip would be strictly a vacation: "I surely have no plans to interview Trotsky or see labor leaders or do any investigating in Mexico."[77]

The fate of Spain far overshadowed the Trotsky–Stalin controversy for Kirchwey. Spain offered a chance to destroy fascism. The Nazis and the Italians aided Franco, while only the Soviet Union gave support to the Spanish Loyalists. "Franco's success," the *Nation* predicted, "would encourage the Nazis to go and do likewise in Czecho-Slovakia, Danzig, the Polish Corridor, or anywhere else. Defeated in Spain, Hitler would be sobered and checked. He would also be weakened by the expenditure on Franco of several hundred million dollars . . . If the fascists are beaten in Spain, they are weakened everywhere." The plea went out: "The supreme test of an antifascist is not what he says but what he does for Spain."[78]

Because Kirchwey considered the Spanish crisis the "most crucial of all issues," she selected a foreign affairs expert to give their shared argument more weight. Vera Micheles Dean, head of the Foreign Policy Association, acknowledged in "A Challenge to Pacifists" that the Spanish Civil War raised the possibility of a Europe divided between fascism and communism, neither system acceptable to Western democracies. To avoid an alliance with the Soviet Union, the democracies chose to remain neutral. Pacifists wanted to avoid war at all cost. To Dean, Kirchwey, and others, such views prepared the way for eventual defeat in Spain. Bowing to dictators became the price of peace. Dean urged "realistic pacifists" to arm against "aggressive dictatorships"; "Democracy must not be left unarmed." Kirchwey echoed the awesome significance of the Spanish Civil War: "political realism would demand that it be understood for what it is—a single maneuver in a general war."[79]

But Congress disagreed, voting to extend United States neutrality laws to include civil wars. A group called the "Friends of the Debs Column" advertised in periodicals to recruit Americans to support the Spanish Republic. Now, with the new neutrality law, the U.S. government announced the imposition of legal penalties on those who aided recruitment. The *Nation* decided to refrain from publishing further advertisements, but under the guise of announcing compliance with the law, Kirchwey, the practical strategist, highlighted the desirability and "generous" effort of the "Debs Column."[80]

With continued aid to Franco by the Italians and the Germans, and nonintervention on the part of Britain, France, and the United States, the cause of the Spanish Republic was lost. In February 1939, with the defeat of the Loyalists in Catalonia, Kirchwey urged Britain and France to admit the significance of "democracy's war" in Spain, although she doubted that they would do so.[81] In fact in late February 1939, when Britain and France foresaw the impending defeat, they facilitated Franco's victory by refusing to help the Loyalists obtain arms—a move the *Nation* branded "a futile as well as a shameful maneuver."[82]

When the Loyalists capitulated, in March 1939, Kirchwey directed her editorials against recognition of the Franco government. The Stimson doctrine, which refused to recognize territories gained by force, could be used as a reason not to acknowledge the defeat of Loyalist Spain.[83] She disagreed with the U.S. characterization of the war as a strictly civil war; it was an international war of manifold consequences, which symbolized the battle of fascism against democracy. Denouncing French recognition of Franco's Spain, she noted that German and Italian troop withdrawals should have been made a minimum precondition to recognition. Problems of reprisals, slave labor, and refugees tainted the supposed "'Peace' in Spain."[84]

Passionate ideological struggles among the left in the United States resulted from Spain's war. During the crisis, Louis Fischer, the *Nation*'s Soviet Union correspondent, bitterly criticized the journal for publishing anti-Loyalist views. But although Kirchwey followed a "general formula" of Loyalist support for "fighting fascism," she thought it important to publish other viewpoints and told Fischer in 1937, "To say otherwise is to say *The Nation* ought to be a party organ. The whole value of its function is to be analytical and critical and free to present varying views without any inhibitions resulting from partisan control or even rigid ideological limits." This meant clarity and consistency in the editorial section, a wide diversity of views in the correspondence section, and uncensored unsigned articles which "fairly" closely reflected the editorial opinions.[85]

A little later that year Fischer asked his editor to answer the charge that the *Nation* had become "a hive of Trotzkyites." She waited to "cool down" before responding that she was trying to follow an "honest and unbiased course," which included support of the Loyalist Spanish government against "illegal actions by Communists as well as the activities of Anarchists and other dissidents." Anti-Stalinist propagandist Anita Brenner was so enraged at the *Nation*'s position that she stopped speaking to Freda Kirchwey. To Dwight Macdonald's criticism that she would not print an article by Brenner, Kirchwey explained: "I want to admit to you without any shame, however, that we will not accept articles that play up out of all proportion and with seeming bias the outrages that have been committed behind the lines—by Communists or anyone else. Neither the whole truth nor the Loyalist cause is served by centering attention primarily on them. It would be equally unjustified to deny that they exist or to pretend they don't matter; and we have done neither."[86]

Stalin did receive some *Nation* criticism. Kirchwey told Fischer: "We cannot take the position that such issues as the Soviet purge and the policy of the Comintern should be discussed only by those who have no criticism of Soviet policy." However, she did not want to print "the opinion of committed partisans," except to let them "blow off steam in the letter pages." Within the context of a general Popular Front framework, balance was important, and she reiterated: "our job is to keep our editorial position clear; and for the rest, to permit freedom of expression to a variety of left points of view. Our whole critical function would be sacrificed by a rigid co-ordination of opinion throughout this paper."[87]

*

Meanwhile, ideological positions at the *Nation* hardened, reflecting painful choices for liberals. A significant issue thrashed out in its pages was the correct stance of American liberals toward Roosevelt. In 1937 Kirchwey adopted a mediator role when two of her key writers took issue on that subject, on the Court-reform plan, and the possibility of a third-term presidency; she tried to stop an editorial war between Villard and Broun, both of whom wrote weekly columns for the *Nation*. Broun, a staunch Roosevelt supporter, put Villard in the general category of liberals, "who know not what they do" and can therefore be used by "sinister groups." He concluded: "Liberalism will never be a useful force in America until the children of light have made up their minds that they must be at least half as smart as the children of darkness. Oswald Garrison Villard please note." Villard described himself as "the target of unlimited abuse" and "liquidated from the ranks of the desirables." Kirchwey decried exaggerating the differences between liberals because this gave aid to the "enemy": "If liberals and progressives are going to be at each other's throats all the time it will make it very easy for the enemy to walk off with the victory."[88]

Disagreement with the political views of other journals also reaffirmed her own stance as mediator. At one point she addressed specifically charges she and the *Nation* received from the right in the *New Leader* and the left in the *New Masses*: "Either the *New Masses* or the *New Leader* must be wrong about us; we can't possibly be Trotskyite assassins, enemies of the Soviet Union, and Communists all at once."[89] Answering Granville Hicks's accusation that the *Nation* printed anti-communist book reviews, Kirchwey insisted that the journal sought "writers who still remain outside the intellectual trade barriers that surround the various totalitarian camps."[90]

*

Kirchwey's belief that the Soviet Union was the leader of the anti-fascist forces and the Soviet dream promising a worker state affected her judgment. Even throughout the purges, which she watched "with an anxiety born of the new dependence on Soviet power," she continued to romanticize the country's international role. The

USSR was "the chief element of hope in a world from which order and sanity have almost vanished." On its twentieth anniversary she admitted that it had undergone many years of purges, but she believed it more important that the Soviet Union maintained "the objectives of socialist control and construction." She supported it because a victory for fascism would mean "the end of socialism and the Soviet government and the essence of western civilization as well."[91]

In 1936, after a remilitarized Germany had reoccupied the Rhineland, France and Great Britain made only feeble protests. Hitler's Berlin-Rome Axis and the Anti-Comintern Pact with Japan signaled determined aggression, yet the West's appeasement policy prevailed. Freda Kirchwey had internalized the public horrors of Hitler and argued that the results of his victory would bring consequences "that don't bear thinking of."[92] To her, Max Lerner, and others, the collective security of the remaining countries was the only means of stopping Hitler before it was too late. They believed fascism had to expand or die. In *It Is Later Than You Think,* Lerner called for a "militant collectivist democracy"; and Freda Kirchwey called for "militant liberalism" to stop fascism.[93]

Continued Soviet repression made it difficult even for Kirchwey to focus on collective security. Branding the Bukharin trials, "Russian Tragedy, Act III," she worried about the effect of the injustices: "The trial of Bukharin and his fellow-oppositionists has broken about the ears of the world like the detonation of a bomb. One can hear the cracking of liberal hopes; of the dream of anti-fascist unity; of a whole system of revolutionary philosophy . . . wherever democracy is threatened, the significance of the trial will be anxiously weighed." Although admitting that "terror and plotting and espionage have become a commonplace in the Socialist fatherland," she concentrated on the causes of repression. She understood residual grievances over foreign intervention against the Bolsheviks during the Russian revolution and civil war, but she warned what fears of conspiracy had become: "Repression came to be identified with justice; opposition with treason."[94] Yet privately she still argued, "in spite of the trials, I believe Russia is dependable; that it wants peace, and will join in any joint effort to check Hitler and Mussolini, and will also fight if necessary. Russia is still the strongest reason for hope."[95]

After all, the world was beset by an implacable Hitler: "he knows what he wants and he intends to get it." Kirchwey judged European diplomacy as inept largely because it failed "to recognize a gunman when he's dressed in the uniform of the head of a state."[96] Hitler and his fascist allies used weapons against the democracies "that those countries—with all their faults—would never use."[97] "Austria was murdered," she wrote of Hitler's takeover there under the pretense that "all Germans must be united under a single flag." "The Great Betrayal" at Munich ended hope for a united collective security system against the fascists for a while. Excluding Stalin from the Munich Conference and the "brutal and irresponsible betrayal of the Czechoslovak republic" there paved the way to war.[98] Kirchwey agonized over the state of Europe:

> If only the people of Europe had known as much about what was happening to it as we did! . . . the end was sorrowful—for Czechoslovakia which is already, in despair, falling into line with Germany; for France, which is now a second-rate power without a friend in Europe save only Britain, and even for Britain, which has proved to Hitler that for the present at least he can go as far as he likes. I suppose Spain will be sold out next. But the worst part of it all is the sure fact that a new era has begun in Europe and that not only France and Britain and Spain and Czecho. but the democratic system itself is on the skids.[99]

Freda and Evans watched Europe on the eve of war with the added worry of their son's travel there. Evans recorded: "Every night we listen to the broadcasts from London, Prague, Paris and Berlin till midnight and get up for the early news bulletins the next morning. Freda has been writing the leading editorials on the European situation so you can imagine the pressure on us here at home. It's a full time job to read and listen to the news much less write about it."[100]

Kirchwey, persistent in her attacks against ineffective appeasement policy, saw Hitler's takeover of Czechoslovakia in 1939 in a wider context: "Hitler marched not only into Czechoslovakia; he marched into the United States as well. And we are not ready for him." Americans must support all those who fight the Nazis. It was not a case of affection for Chamberlain or Daladier, but the singular fact that "we love Hitler less."[101] Time was short to achieve unity against fascism.[102] She scoffed at the shock of certain statesmen when Hitler seized Czechoslovakia: "A good deal of trouble might have been avoided if *Mein Kampf* were made required reading for statesmen. They would then at least be spared the succession of surprises that makes their progress toward general defeat unnecessarily painful." She feared a Nazi victory, not by a direct air attack, but by "the gradual crumbling of the economic and political and cultural relationships of men and nations until we all shall be forced, in order to survive, to fit into the framework of a Nazi world."[103]

That summer after Czechoslovakia's fall, when American liberals and radicals agonized over their position on the Soviet Union, Freda Kirchwey held to her belief in the unity of all antifascists. The Committee for Cultural Freedom, an outgrowth of the Dewey Commission on the Moscow Trials, was in part formed to fight for intellectual freedom against totalitarian doctrine.[104] The *Nation* published its manifesto. But Kirchwey criticized the Committee, charging that it gave a false reason for its existence. Discounting its claim of a commitment to broad based intellectual freedom, she argued that it was created specifically to attack Soviet totalitarianism and the Communist Party. Its denunciations created a divisive issue among the left, a "counsel of disruption."[105]

She considered a schism among the left to be very dangerous. She had few delusions about the Communist Party, which was "a nuisance or menace to all its opponents. Whatever its line may be, its tactics are invariably provocative and often destructive." Despite its faults, however, "the Communists perform necessary functions in the confused struggle of our time"; they were acceptable, albeit not completely desirable, allies. The Communist Party became, for her, one of a number of leftist groups dedicated to the antifascist struggle. Regardless of ideological and substantive practical differences or even repressive actions on the part of the Communists, Kirchwey sought an alliance with them and, thus, unity of the left against the increasing numbers of rightist groups: "The task of re-creating unity and hope and strengthening the organs of democracy is not to be accomplished by insisting upon differences and crystallizing them in manifestos and committees. While moral rearmament engrosses the right, a little factional disarmament might well be tried on the left. There is virtue in merely refusing to shoot."[106]

Kirchwey aligned the *Nation* with the Soviet Union against fascism.[107] Liberals who considered Stalin as great an enemy as Hitler found Kirchwey's position unconscionable. Sidney Hook acknowledged his debt to the *Nation* for its "formative influence" on him. He felt that the *Nation*, which had stood against injustice of all kinds, had "changed sides" during this controversy, and he argued against Kirchwey: "It is really hard to reconcile your pleas for all-round disarmament with your attack on the Committee. I believe in all-round disarmament also but not in *moral* disarmament." He explained the intensity of his immediate response to her original editorial:

> if my rejoinder to your editorial is heated, it is a measure of the relatively high esteem I had for the Nation before you so unjustly attacked the Committee for Cultural Freedom. I have not always agreed with the Nation's policy on specific issues, the Lord knows. Differences are compatible with a common set of ideals and especially a common method. But it is those ideals and that method which the Manifesto of the Committee for Cultural Freedom eloquently affirmed and which the Nation's editorial in effect denied.[108]

Kirchwey disagreed, insisting upon the danger of an increasingly split left. A scathing attack of the Committee for Cultural Freedom, signed by four hundred people who supported the USSR, was published in the *Nation* but with Kirchwey's sharp critique. She said that, though their letter was addressed "To All Active Supporters of Democracy and Peace," it did not have the endorsement of the majority opinion on the *Nation*, notwithstanding the signature of two members of the staff. She agreed that there was "a basic difference" between Stalin's Soviet Union and the fascist dictatorships; she too wanted unity among American progressives. She agreed that members of the Committee for Cultural Freedom created dissension on the left and generated anti-Soviet feelings. Yet she disapproved of the new group's "uncritical approval" of the USSR: "To my mind the effort to promote unity on the left will fail if it is predicated on a categorical declaration of faith in the virtues of the Soviet Union."[109] Again calling for unity, Kirchwey accused the pro-Stalinists of being a divisive group. Responding to their letter a week later and just after the signing of the Nazi-Soviet Pact, she wondered how many of the group would have supported the letter had they foreseen that alliance.[110]

What did Kirchwey think of the Nazi-Soviet Pact? Although she called it "a solid and menacing fact that cannot be figured out of existence," she reasoned that "the long-range ambitions of Stalin and Hitler are bound to clash." She saw the alliance as temporary and never considered it as reprehensible as others did. She was less alarmed than Villard and Louis Fischer. Villard felt the pact meant that "two conscienceless men" had joined together "for mutual advantage." Dramatically reversing his pro-Soviet stance, Fischer called the pact "totally indefensible"; he felt it made Stalin and Hitler "full-fledged partners."[111] The Kirchwey prediction of temporary alliance proved correct. Hitler invaded Russia in 1941; within six months, the Soviet Union was an ally of the West.

Despite Stalin's two-year alliance with Hitler, Kirchwey had not viewed the Soviet Union as an enemy. Although she denounced its December 1939 invasion of Finland with the strongest language, she did not conduct a sustained criticism of the Soviet Union for its totalitarian tactics. Spain had convinced her that division among socialists handed victory to the fascists. Nor was there room for isolation. International fascism must be stopped:

> We can't insulate ourselves against it: we must defeat it. The chance of doing so is small. The time for doing so is short. But in one sense the crisis itself gives us a fighting chance: only in extremity will the non-fascist nations act. They are in extremity now. Perhaps they will act. At least they should have behind them all the force that all the decent parties, groups, journals, and individuals can put there. I should hate to see *The Nation* left out of this particular international brigade.[112]

"Let's Mind Our Own Business," she argued in language likely to catch the eye of American isolationist Senators Nye, Johnson, and Reynolds. But her message would diametrically oppose theirs. Americans must stop fascism from growing.

> We surrendered our chance to mind our business in Spain; we were too intent on keeping out of trouble and minding Chamberlain's business. We allowed democracy to be slaughtered in Spain . . .
> Today the United States is the grand arsenal for triumphant fascism . . . It is our business to stop providing these three aggressors with arms and the goods necessary to the manufacture of arms and the conduct of war.[113]

The pacifist of 1917 had become the militant liberal of 1939. It was only a matter of time before her pleas for American economic intervention would escalate to appeals for military intervention in a battle to save civilization as she knew it.

6 || *Political War Years,*
    1939–1944

In the summer of 1939 the presence of Michael Clark, Freda Kirchwey's only surviving son, in an unstable Europe made her "uneasy and unhappy": "No one knows the true meaning of Litvinov's resignation. Nobody knows whether Chamberlain has been pressing Poland to compromise, nor what is going on in Italy between Ribbentrop and Ciano. Nobody, in short, knows whether Hitler will back down or win another Munich victory. Nobody knows anything. But for that very reason I wish you were in America, my blessed son! If war should suddenly seem imminent we'd cable you money . . . immediately and count on you to make a swift and efficient get-away." Kirchwey thought back to the notorious Munich agreement of September 1938, in which Chamberlain and Daladier had agreed to Hitler's annexation of the Sudetenland in exchange for his promise of peace after he brought German-speaking territories into his Third Reich. Hitler's flagrant breach of promise made the appeasement at Munich even more repugnant, and a symbol of defeat. After the Nazi-Soviet Pact in late August 1939, the immediate Polish Nazi takeover of Danzig, and Hitler's final list of demands to Poland, Kirchwey decided: "War would be preferable to another deal with Hitler, and war would be preferable to the continued struggle of nerves and diplomacy that has exhausted the peoples for the past months. I say that in full realization of what the words mean."[1]

When Germany invaded Poland on 1 September 1939, and Britain and France within days declared war, Michael was safely back from his travels in Europe, and his mother was able to trace the new "Nazi-Soviet line through Poland" on the huge map he sent for her forty-sixth birthday. "What days and what news. My forebodings are too unpleasant to talk about tonight," she wrote him. In "Munich Bears Fruit" she reminded *Nation* readers that appeasement had failed. Statesmen finally realized what most ordinary people had accepted and what most of the "independent press of the world" have known: no bargains could be made with Hitler. The war presented a stark choice: no matter how blatant the deficiencies of the democracies, they must be preserved against "an organized system of persecution."[2]

What of the United States? During the next two years Kirchwey would ask that question in various ways. While the President tried to keep the country out of the war as well as work toward an Allied victory for "the survival of democracy and the safety of the United States," she asked, "Can We Stay Neutral?" Appeasement could not be an answer for the United States any more than it had been for Britain or France. We must stop providing goods to their enemies.[3]

Democracy and fascism competed with answers for an increasingly complex modern industrial world. Societies that needed major regulation had to choose where to rest that power and whether to keep a degree of freedom from collective control. Pointing out the dangers of the efficient but undemocratic fascist system, Kirchwey urged Americans to examine their functioning democracy critically; those who equated democracy with freedom needed to recognize the dangers to it. Democracy was not only threatened by the fascism abroad; its failure to confront and to solve important social and economic problems at home opened the door to fascist appeals.[4]

Kirchwey brooded about Father Coughlin's vicious anti-Semitism and other "public, and both verbal and physical" attacks on Jews that were not reported by American newspapers, not even the *New York Times*. Kirchwey speculated in public speeches that they had consciously decided not to publicize what was surely a new and "important development in American public life" lest the facts increase "ill-feeling between sections of the community or religious groups."[5] This silence, "an inexcusable and entirely ill-advised effort to bend the news to produce a particular social result," raised her ire, for it prevented the citizens of a democracy from getting their facts "straight and uncensored."[6]

Kirchwey charged the House Committee on Un-American Activities with overt repression of the press and labeled its chairman, Martin Dies, "the one-man Gestapo from Texas." She argued that the Committee, which had been set up to investigate subversive activities, overstepped its bounds and infringed upon the civil rights of many innocent groups and individuals.[7] The Dies Committee became a vehicle for a "national forum, to inform as well as shape public opinion." It became a conservative, anti-New Deal mouthpiece and labeled many New Deal liberals subversive. Kirchwey opposed this reactionary force: "Dies isn't after sedition; he is after you and me and the President."[8]

Deeply committed to democratic practices, she warned Americans not to succumb to fear of communists and fascists to the point where the civil liberties of any group—even those at cross-purposes with democracy—could be threatened.[9] With Clark, she looked for new legal means to monitor partisan activities and "prevent the slander of racial or religious groups."[10] Kirchwey hinted, however, that more than strictly consistent democratic means might become necessary: "We do not want to shut out, or shut up, the expression of even the most distasteful doctrines. But somehow, within the limits of our democratic procedures, we must find a way to meet this invasion. For the spread of race hatred and contempt for democratic government is not only a provocation of violence but is itself a part of a program of violence."[11]

The maintenance of civil liberties during the war years continued to be important. Even the American Civil Liberties Union reverberated with arguments about the meaning of liberty when, after a long and heated trial, its board voted to expel Elizabeth Gurley Flynn because of her membership in the Communist Party. She had been a Party member since 1937, and had been reelected to the ACLU Board of Directors in 1939 with full knowledge of that membership. However, the shock of the Nazi-Soviet Pact later that year, which made the ACLU consider the Communists as much an enemy as the fascists, divided the organization. Some, like Corliss Lamont, insisted that even this did not permit the abridgement of an individual's rights, but the faction with enough votes to expel Flynn took a different position. The chairman, John Haynes Holmes, argued that board membership should be restricted to those who believed in liberty. He and the majority charged that Communists did not believe in liberty and used civil liberties to undermine democracy.[12] Freda Kirchwey wished that the divisive incident had not occurred. She questioned why the ACLU had reelected Flynn to its board after she had declared her Party membership. However, once re-elected, she should not have been expelled. Kirchwey considered the expulsion "untimely"; ultimately it hurt the cause of civil liberties because it fed the negative popular sentiment "against all extreme elements."[13]

*

Mostly, however, Kirchwey focused her campaign on fascism abroad. By the late 1930s she had supported collective security; now worsening conditions in Europe made her broaden that concept. Germany's conquest of Denmark and Norway, its invasion of Luxembourg, Belgium, the Netherlands, and France, and Britain's evacuation of Dunkirk led her to advocate universal military training.[14]

The adversarial positions taken by Kirchwey strained relations with Villard. The two had disagreed especially since she began to guide the *Nation* away from its pacifist stance and toward support of American acceptance of international responsibilities. Villard's weekly "Issues and Men" continued to differ ideologically from the rest of the journal. He argued that Roosevelt's 1940 "meeting-force-with-force-speech" was a victory for Hitler; Kirchwey and the other *Nation* editors considered it "a far-fetched assumption—namely that Hitler will feel pleased to death because America is building a big navy . . . However you and I may disapprove of a huge American navy we must, I am afraid, assume that Hitler will feel the same way. What he wants is to have his potential enemies remain completely unmilitaristic (like Norway) and as ineffectual as possible so that he can handle them easily and at his own convenience."[15]

Kirchwey feared the influence of pacifists like Villard and challenged his "dream world."[16] Fascism, a system of highly organized tyranny, had enveloped Europe and threatened the world. Neither appeasement nor ignoring the threat would do. If the United States did not fight and defeat fascism, it must recognize Hitler and his puppet governments and compete with a forced labor economy. An unchallenged Nazi Germany meant "the end of democracy."[17] She constantly underscored the false neutrality of a policy of inaction that actually aided those supplied by fascist powers. The demise of the Spanish Republic proved this, she believed, and she reiterated the mistake of the Western world in dealing with Loyalist Spain.

Once Kirchwey called for universal military training, Villard decided that he could no longer write even a protest column for the *Nation*. In a "Personal and Private" letter to her, he severed his ties with the journal, scathingly refusing to contribute to an "extraordinary, and, what seems to me, insane course." He accused her of shaking hands "with all the forces of reaction against which *The Nation* has battled so strongly." Villard concluded with the "profoundest regret" that she had "prostituted the *Nation*" and hoped that it would "die very soon or fall into other hands." In a less severe public statement Villard sadly ended his forty-six years with the *Nation* in conflict with Kirchwey and with the journal's increasing commitment to collective security.[18]

The *Nation* and its editor were becoming the target of many leftist and progressive groups that disagreed with its stand. Major criticism came from those who saw no moral differences between Hitler and Stalin and blamed Kirchwey for not concurring. One reader charged that her earlier acceptance of Stalin's appeals to collective security "at face value," resulted in her selling her readers "a Russian bill of goods"—an opinion undoubtedly reinforced by Kirchwey's interpretation of Stalin's pronouncement of "a coming Socialist revolution." Kirchwey said that although one could view the Soviet Union's former cooperation with democracies "all a sham," she preferred "to believe that it has been moving away from its revolutionary internationalism toward a strongly nationalist state capitalism and that today all talk of the first is designed to fortify and enhance the latter. The fate of Finland may serve to confirm or dispute this belief."[19]

Peter Viereck, then a student at Harvard, wrote such a biting caricature of the *Nation* for the *Atlantic Monthly* that Lewis Gannett, a former *Nation* editor, demanded the retraction of "libelous" allegations that the *Nation* essentially "endorsed" Soviet policy. Viereck responded: "If by 'endorsed' Mr. Gannett means 'approved the general tendency of,' as evidenced by past editorial policy, then I stick to my guns and say that is exactly what I intended to imply." Viereck said others were much more critical of the *Nation*. Editorials by Eugene Lyons in the *American Mercury* had called fellow travelers "carbon copies of the views cynically manufactured in Moscow for export . . . The domination of the fellow travelers amounted to intellectual terror in many fields . . . The test of a True Liberal *Nation* style, is how loud he yells hurrah for the slaughter of poor peasants and the shooting of Old Blosheviks in Russia." Viereck did not judge the *Nation* that harshly, but he did maintain that its writers, "well meaning, basically decent liberals," were "temporarily hoodwinked into their Russophilism."[20] Freda Kirchwey took these criticisms in stride.

Kirchwey's bitter denunciation of the brutal Soviet invasion of Finland in December 1939 mollified some of her critics for a while. She lashed out: "The horrors that fascism wreaked in Spain are being repeated, in the name of peace and socialism, in Finland." It was an inexcusable blatant act of aggression, and Kirchwey ignored "the shocking nonsense" of Soviet press justifications. Viereck welcomed her criticism of the invasion with "delighted surprise." It proved that the *Nation* "had at last cut loose from the fellow-traveler 'party line' and was again a magazine of decency and integrity."[21]

*

Early in 1940 Freda Kirchwey used the occasion of the *Nation's* seventy-fifth anniversary to review in a special issue the journal's history and to take stock of "American liberal democracy" as well as the country's heritage, problems, and "capacity for survival and growth." But as she planned the issue, she wrote her friend Archibald MacLeish: "It's hard these weeks to look far ahead or to think of anything besides the possible consequences of Stalin's next move."[22] Kirchwey worked with MacLeish, Lewis Gannett, Paul Kellogg, Elmo Roper, and Joseph Blumenthal on this issue, which included contributions from Carl Sandburg, Eleanor Roosevelt, Thomas Mann, I. F. Stone, Max Lerner, Joseph Wood Krutch, Carl Van Doren, Reinhold Niebuhr, and others. The request for a message from the President received a "100%" endorsement from the Democratic Committee, and Eleanor Roosevelt mentioned her participation in the issue in her nationally syndicated newspaper column, "My Day": "I have always had a great respect for anyone who was good enough to write for the 'Nation,' so perhaps I may be forgiven if I feel a little puffed up at being permitted to be a contributor to this important number."[23]

Among other international pieces, the issue assessed the Soviet Union after twenty-two years as a Communist nation. As usual, Kirchwey put different points of view into print. Managing editor

Robert Bendiner ironically defined "Peace"—"all Southeastern Europe cringes before the Russian olive branch"; and "Semi-fascism"—that phenomenon which the Soviet Union deigned as worse than fascism; "it is what they are fighting now in Finland." He implied the folly of sympathizing with the Soviet Union: "It is better to let politics afflict you with strange bedfellows than to let a choice of bedfellows afflict you with strange politics." Kirchwey, less critical of the Soviet Union, found the issues more complicated: "It seems to me that non-Stalinist lefts have to teach the public how to draw distinctions between the ideas that went into the revolution, the achievements that still live . . . and, in our own country the hopes of the left-liberal elements between these and the products of Stalinism in Russia and here . . . We face the need of making and popularizing discriminations that are damned hard to put over."[24]

"I like it," she said of Louis Fischer's longer discussion. His general philosophical description of Soviet ideology and actions detailed the disillusionment of those who had originally greeted the Soviet experiment as the chance to end imperialistic wars and to usher in "a new socialist democracy," which would be "purer than bourgeois democracy." The attack on Finland reduced Soviet-support among liberals in capitalist countries to the "lowest ebb since 1917." This fed Red-baiters everywhere, at a time when, Fischer and Kirchwey believed, "Everything depends on whether socialism and democracy are compatible."[25]

Kirchwey's "Old Liberties for a New World," was a passionate plea to preserve democracy, which she equated with freedom. It was clear that the United States must contribute "both to the defeat of fascism" and following the end of the war, to "the equally difficult task of constructing an organized peace."[26] Kirchwey had not yet reached the point of advocating a declaration of war, but the European conflict was constantly on her mind, especially since her son had not given up hope of joining the Allied effort. She begged him not to go: "E and I hope with all our might that you'll give up the idea of going to France. Leave it another year; then the war may be over. You aren't needed there and we want you to stay whole and alive." Evans Clark also wrote of their concern. "You can't faintly imagine what it would mean to lose you. I don't need to elaborate within the special circumstances which, added to our love for you, make the thought a ghastly one."[27]

Michael returned to Harvard the fall of 1940, but in the spring term, he dropped out of college to become an ambulance driver in the British-American Ambulance Corps. His unit boarded the unarmed *Zam Zam,* which, though under British admiralty orders, flew the Egyptian flag. The ship was bound for Egypt via Mombasa, where the ambulance drivers were to have disembarked before traveling overland to join units of the Free French forces fighting the Italians in Eritrea. On 17 April 1941, the *Zam Zam* was shelled by a German surface raider in the South Atlantic. But for a "lucky shot" which destroyed the *Zam Zam's* radio transmitter, an SOS would have been sent, revealing the German ship's position. In that event, for its own protection the raider would have destroyed all evidence of its presence and left the scene immediately. However, because no distress signal had been sent, the Germans had time to remove much needed food supplies from the stricken vessel—and to rescue its passengers and crew—before sending the *Zam Zam* to the bottom of the ocean with a charge of dynamite.[28]

Days of agony for Freda and Evans followed news of the sinking, before word came that the passengers were still alive. Letters of condolence poured in. Lewis Gannett's was perhaps representative: "It must be utterly shattering—unless there is more hope than our city desk knows . . . All I can say is that, for whatever it is worth, we are all with you . . . You and Michael were and are one; responsible rebel youth; that's you, that's been *The Nation,* and I have always loved you both for it. I love you still." When Freda finally heard that Michael was safe she told Caroline Whiting: "I cried and that's the first time in years and years and years that I've cried." After the good news came in Norman Thomas wrote Freda: "I want you and Evans to know how sincerely I, a non-interventionist, admire the kind of stand Michael took in support of his beliefs, and how overjoyed Violet and I are, for your sake and his, that he is safe." Freda "carefully" filed away a long, moving piece by the *Jewish Daily Forward:* "Freda Kirchwey—Gentle and Idealistic Woman. Her only son was a passenger on the sunken ship Zam-Zam," which traced her ordeal and the dilemma she faced as a mother and an antifascist.[29]

Kirchwey replied to more than a hundred letters of condolence with the news of Michael's survival. Meanwhile, he and the rest of the passengers, including several groups of missionaries on their way to Africa, spent thirty-three days in cramped conditions on board a German supply and prison ship. When the ship finally made port in occupied France, the enemy nationals were sent to prison camp; the Americans went home—all but the ambulance drivers, whose fate remained uncertain. Although they held U.S. passports, their Geneva cards had been issued by the British. Michael and the other ambulance drivers were detained another month while the Americans negotiated for their release.[30]

Ironically, the very day of the *Zam Zam* attack Freda had written Michael about their shared commitment to the war and about her determination to keep the *Nation* afloat for its part of that battle:

> I consider the *Nation* a small but not unimportant part of the war effort and I don't want to sell or drop it. I feel this all the more because our last circular brought such a vicious response from the isolationist pacifist elements of the left—not only Communists— that I am determined to fight all the harder for the anti-Nazi position. Those elements are, of course, a minority even on the left but so noisy and so troublesome at moments of decision that they need to be countered vigorously all the time—and more than ever in a period of bad news. They use discouraging news as propaganda against American help.[31]

Now that Michael was safe, she concentrated on *Nation* worries. She unburdened herself to Louis Fischer: "The hour has struck and I am spending my time trying to finance *The Nation's* survival. But don't talk about it generally." When Villard resigned in 1940, he took many readers with him; the *Nation* lost pacifist readers "by the thousands." "Pro-defense, anti-Hitler liberals" started to replace them, but there weren't enough. Skyrocketing costs of publishing during wartime added to the difficulties, and by 1941 the *Nation* had lost some $10,000. To bail out the journal, Kirchwey began a major appeal to readers and influential friends. She asked Philadelphian Jacob Billikopf of the Labor Standards Association for a list of people "who might be interested in seeing *The Nation* survive." Earlier that year, when criticism of the *Nation* had become so vitriolic that business manager Hugo Van Arx, worried about sales, had suggested that the editor soften the pro-defense position, she had refused, adhering to the *Nation's* "fighting quality."[32]

A German victory would threaten civilization itself. True, she admitted, she could foresee problems for any society victorious over Hitler, but a victory for Hitler "would be not merely bad but intolerable." Its selection of factors and its weight of plans of action would secure for the *Nation,* "the greatest area of genuine democracy and the most effective promotion of the fight against Hitler."

She dismissed criticism that the journal was FDR's mouthpiece, reminding Van Arx of the issues over which the *Nation* continued to disagree with and criticize the President. She cited the journal's "need of opposing manifestations of domestic Hitlerism." The time was wrong to assuage opponents: "We should look upon our journal as a weapon—not a pair of scales—and make it as sharp and deadly as we can."[33]

But now, several months later, Kirchwey still was unready to advocate war. When, in July 1941, the *New York Post* published a front-page editorial calling for a declaration of war, the *Nation*, like the *New Republic*, deemed this too drastic a step. A month later the *New Republic* came out "For a Declaration of War." Kirchwey leaned in the same direction, without formally committing herself: "The United States has only one thing to decide—where and how and when it can intervene with the greatest possible effect." And: "We must realize that the death of freedom in Europe spells disaster to this country as certainly as the loss of our shipping routes in the Western Pacific. We must learn while there is still time to act."[34] Kirchwey encouraged the President to prepare Americans for war. By the fall of 1941 she wrote that Americans must reconcile themselves to fighting: "Before its total, uncompromising demands are laid upon them, the people of America must learn that this war is their war; that they cannot dodge it or buy their way out of it; that they must fight it because fighting is the only alternative to surrender."[35]

Freda Kirchwey was convinced that the war must be fought in more than the military arena; it was a political war as well. She assembled a staff sharing that commitment and, on 13 September 1941, introduced Norman Angell, Jonathan Daniels, Louis Fischer, Reinhold Niebuhr, and Julio Alvarez del Vayo as contributing editors: "They are not merely eminent as writers and thinkers. They are also fighters," who joined the staff "as active participants in the many-sided struggle for the survival of freedom and the creation of a democratic world to which *The Nation* is unalterably committed."[36]

*

The mass exodus from homelands overrun by Franco, Hitler, and Mussolini created a growing stream of freedom-loving refugees. Where were they to go? Time and again Kirchwey reiterated "America is a refugee nation." Recounting her own family's story, she reminded readers and audiences that she would not have been in the

United States had the country not welcomed her paternal grandfather, a "young rebel," who fled Prussia in 1848. She considered her family's story typical: "Aliens. Refugees. Exiles. These are America."[37]

By the twentieth century, however, immigration laws did not encourage foreigners, especially from southeastern Europe. The gravity of the war situation now challenged those restrictions. "Let in the Refugees!" Kirchwey implored. "Now is the time to prove that the right of asylum is not dead in the United States." "Bring Them Out!" shouted another article about the anti-Nazi and antifascist refugees in France in 1940: "The future will pay tribute to their heroism; the present cannot ignore their plight without revealing its own spiritual bankruptcy."[38]

When Kirchwey appealed to "the conscience of all Americans, including, above all, the President of the United States," to save lives, she offered the American public a rare detailed description of the condition of refugees in occupied and unoccupied France. "Nightmare in France," she called the plight of the estimated hundreds of thousands of antifascist refugees and their nonpolitical counterparts, trapped there. She attributed the failure to obtain their release to "the grim efficiency of the fascist terror which systematically closes avenues of escape" and "the timidity and procrastination of the governments that should speed the task—our own government in particular."[39]

Freda Kirchwey and the *Nation* especially wanted a sanctuary for the Jews. She wanted America to open its borders; even more, she sought safe asylum for them in Palestine. From 1934 to 1939 so many Jews had fled to Palestine that they more than doubled the immigration of the preceding twelve years; by 1939 there were more than a half a million Jews there.[40]

The *Nation* urged Britain to open up the mandate to a new exodus and charged that its unwillingness was a "logical extension of Chamberlain's appeasement policies." The infamous White Paper of 1939 that set Jewish immigration at 75,000 over a five-year period ("if economic conditions permit!") was "no more than a sop to the world's conscience."[41] The barrier to Jewish immigration was even more unconscionable in light of Hitler's "crusade against the Jews" later that year: mass deportations. When Villard reported from The Hague in 1939 that Jews were being herded into camps to do forced labor, Kirchwey wrote of the "unimaginable horror." "The reservation has become a place of death and a center of infection." Like many liberals, Kirchwey considered the cause of Jewish immigration to Palestine "a matter of elementary justice." Speaking of Zionist leader Chaim Weizmann, she described her own compassion for the Jews: "He does not think of Jewish suffering as I do, with sympathy and anger and the repugnance of a person whose whole personal life has been, naturally and without effort, a repudiation of the concept that underlies that suffering."[42]

She came to link the struggle of the Jews with the struggle for democracy. As she wrote about fund-raising specifically for Jews, she felt identified with "a crucial American movement": "I am here, in short, to plead the cause of American ideals. The Jews of Europe are surely in need of help; but not in greater need than you and I and our fellow Americans. Thousands of European Jews will die, unnecessarily, if we do not reach them with our life-giving dollars. But American democracy may die, too, and that is equally important." The future of Jews was at stake; but their fate also represented "the values of civilization." If Americans failed to aid the Jews, the nation would cease to stand for the ideals it had always stood for. If that happened, Kirchwey said, "Let the Nazis have it [America]."[43]

She was horrified by Hitler and his persecution and extermination of the Jews; to her he was a symbol of evil against good. Fascists represented "a wholly lawless brutal counter-revolution—an organized terror—aimed at exterminating "all political opposition."[44] Time and time again Kirchwey reminded her readers that, although millions of innocent people were being killed in the war, Hitler's killing of the Jews was of a different magnitude: "the Jews have died *as Jews,* selected for obliteration to satisfy the race mania that underlies the whole dogma of Teutonic fascism . . . this systematic murder of a race is without example in history. It is too vast and too terrible for the normal mind to grasp, indeed this is its protection."[45] The realization that "only Jews" were being killed because "they belong to a single religious-racial group"[46] made Kirchwey, a non-Jew, wonder: "It must make other groups examine their souls with some mistrust and ask themselves: Is there in us some taint of barbarism, too, some lurking fascist infection, that we are less hated than the Jews?"[47]

The Jews were the symbol of all that the fascists were attempting to destroy: "Jews the world over have reason to be proud . . . they have become the flaming symbol to all the world of humanity and freedom." Persecution of them was directed against "the spirit of humanity, of free inquiry and tolerance, of reason as opposed to blind will . . . the living symbol of those qualities that make life worth living and civilization worth struggling to preserve . . . the values the Jewish people symbolize belong in the end to all men and women of good will everywhere." Freda Kirchwey wanted to fight along with them. "The war is a war not for power or prestige—not even for a race or a culture—but for a way of life, the way of generosity and peace and reason and good will. You people . . . are in the very front lines in that war, you occupy exposed positions, and you fight against great odds. I hope you will let me join you in these trenches."[48]

Hitler continued his mass murders, and Kirchwey continued her way of fighting. Although confirmation of reports of the murders had appeared by December 1942, people did not pay attention to the extent of the horror. Historian David S. Wyman blames America's abandonment of the Jews on "unemployment, nativistic restrictionism and anti-Semitism," but he also believes that a lack of media exposure of the Holocaust prevented public pressure on the government to rescue them. Although about half a million Jews had been exterminated by January 1942 and the major concentration camps began operating in the summer of 1942, even by 1943 and 1944 the mass murders received very little coverage in neutral and Allied newspapers or in official Allied dispatches. In contrast, the *Nation* and the *New Republic* published the horrid reality of Jewish extermination very early on as they tried to force American and world attention on the exterminators.[49]

Philip S. Bernstein's *Nation* series on the fate of European Jews was "one of the earliest and most comprehensive accounts to appear anywhere." Bernstein wrote of the "vastness and the ghastliness of the Jewish tragedy in Europe," about Jews "being slaughtered . . . wherever the Nazis can lay hands upon them." What was happening to the Jews was an omen for all mankind: "The oppression of the Jew has been the symptom of decay." The world must do something because "the future of the world is bound up with it."[50] Yet even the *Nation* could scarcely accept the degree of the horror. Even sometime after 1943, when Kirchwey and others attended an American Jewish Congress luncheon where Ben-Gurion gave "a shocking report of mass executions," few credited the magnitude of the exterminations. "Later it became evident that his information had been limited. The facts were much, much worse."[51]

Albert Einstein helped form the International Free World Association, an antifascist group composed of émigrés from all parts of Europe. Such renowned figures as Gunnar Myrdal, Julius Deutsch, Rustem Vambery, and Count Carlo Sforza joined it to work for the defeat of Hitler and the establishment of a democratic peace. When the association published the first issue of its monthly journal, *Free World,* the group and its publication were endorsed enthusiastically by Kirchwey. She not only supported their efforts by highlighting the subjects discussed in their journal but also lent her editor Robert Bendiner to serve as their managing editor, and her bookkeeper, Adeline Henkel, to help with the accounting. As a member of their International Board, she devoted time to the organization.[52]

*

Her association with this group undoubtedly strengthened Kirchwey's belief that the war had to be fought on more than a military level. "If it is true, as I fully believe, that this war can only be won by a combination of political and military effort, the Free World movement should receive the fullest encouragement from all the people of this country who favor the defeat of Hitler." One Free World Association member, Julio Alvarez del Vayo, Republican Spain's last foreign minister, became a *Nation* editor. By the time he joined the staff in 1941 (probably through the prompting of Louis Fischer, who suggested that he write about Spain under Franco), Del Vayo already had contributed many articles to the journal. Distracted by his halting English, Kirchwey once commented, "I hope Del Vayo spoke intelligibly; I'm worried about his career as a lecturer." Another time she said, "tho' his English was at its worst, he made a big impression." Soon, fired by the zeal of shared causes, she ignored his imperfect speech and began the task of reworking his articles into better English.[53]

"World War III?" impressed Kirchwey especially. In it Del Vayo put the world of 1942 into the historical context of other wartime periods. He discussed the compromises made against the interest of the popular majority in the 1814–1815 Congress of Vienna in Metternich's time with the compromises made at Versailles after World War I. In both cases the priority of achieving a balance of power made the participants anxious to maintain the status quo and to suppress the popular forces. Conditions during World War II seemed uncomfortably similar. Once again a desire for balance of power was accompanied by a strong fear of socialism, which many of the Allies saw as upsetting that balance. Some of them had come to see fascism as a positive counterbalance to socialism. Because the elements of reaction would continue in their power positions, Del Vayo warned that this mentality would lead to the probability of another war. To avoid World War III, he insisted that "anti-fascist and progressive leaders" must gain political power in their respective countries, for, "in the end, it comes back to the men and to the forces that move them."[54]

As she often did with issues she regarded as significant and controversial, Kirchwey made this article the subject of an open forum among prominent people of different disciplines from several countries. Veteran Italian diplomat Count Sforza agreed to participate saying, "Only my hating to answer no to YOU, decided me to write," though "General discussions of this kind are in the present moment more useful among Americans."[55] Others from whom Kirchwey solicited written responses to "World War III?" included theologian Reinhold Niebuhr, *New Republic* editor Michael Straight, and Russian socialist Theodore Dan.

An interesting dialogue ensued. Not all agreed with Del Vayo. Niebuhr, for instance, was more sanguine about the chance for a durable peace that did not depend "altogether upon the victory in the domestic struggle of the traditional radical and labor forces." Straight did not think a third world war would result from the power politics: the "foundations of world organization . . . already in existence . . . cannot be destroyed by a political settlement, however bad." Sforza, on the other hand, shared some of Del Vayo's skepticism, citing several democracies that had sold out under pressure from "realists." After World War II, he said, the new League [the United Nations] must admit to membership only those states, "which are governed according to the freely expressed will of their citizens." Dan reiterated and supported Del Vayo's thesis: "The destiny of the future peace depends upon the social forces that shape that peace."[56]

Kirchwey obviously agreed with Del Vayo. His article and the subsequent forum probably provided the last incentive to initiate a broader and continuous forum for ideas on how to wage war and plan for peace. Pooling talent from Free World Association members, in 1942 she launched a special section of the *Nation,* "Political War," in the hope that it would increase the journal's value as a "weapon in the fight for a democratic victory." The weekly four-page section would feature the political expressions of popular forces in various countries, with attention being paid to political émigrés, those who were "profoundly involved in the ideological and moral aspects of the struggle" against fascism.[57] It would serve as an open forum of ideas; its editor, Del Vayo, promised that "no single personality" would dominate and that it would include articles by "all people who really understand the character of the present war."[58]

Kirchwey thought World War II must be seen as more than a military confrontation; it was a political war as well. The fears of some American and Allied leaders about the increasing power of the masses and a popular challenge to the old order were, she felt, foolish, even dangerous. U.S. relations with Vichy France disgusted her: "Vichy is only the most obvious and striking example of our diplomatic insulation against the revolutionary challenge of Hitler's war. The traditionalists of the American State Department, by habit and persuasion, shun the reality of revolution. They hope to win the war without using—or losing—the forces of democratic resistance; they hope to defeat fascism with near-fascism, or at least with the vestigial remnants of pre-war conservatism."[59]

Economic and social imbalances in the world were, to Kirchwey, a breeding ground for ever-threatening fascist propaganda. The world must solve its economic and social discrepancies through a commitment to popular voices and aid for popular uprisings. Those who were willing to make war against the Axis powers, while ignoring the political policies of those nations, were preventing the only chance for a victory for democratic forces and lasting peace. To probe beyond the strictly military aspects of the war became the purpose of the Political War section: "We intend to underline the revolutionary character of the war and help develop a political strategy through which the democratic elements in all countries may overcome the forces of reaction and capitulation, and free the peoples of the world from the tragic conflict of fighting under colors not their own."[60]

In October 1942 Del Vayo called for an internationally coordinated political war strategy. He visualized an "Inter-Allied Council," similar to a war council, to coordinate political war plans.[61] It could, for instance, decide the wisdom of the Allies' maintaining diplomatic relations with Vichy France. Although the plan never was implemented, the Political War section continued throughout the war, providing suggestions and analyses. Among its many prominent contributors were Carlo Sforza, who wrote about Italy; exiled German writer and editor Leopold Swarzschild, who analyzed Nazi propaganda and other political war subjects under the pen name Argus; and S. K. Ratcliffe and Harold Laski, who examined Great Britain. Ralph Bates covered Yugoslavia and Russia; Jules Moch, former French minister, detailed plans for the DeGaulle government (among other things); Fritz Sternberg also commented on France; Dr. Juan Negrin, ousted Spanish premier, and of course Del Vayo, wrote extensively about Spain. Political War subjects ranged from an exposé of Nazi propaganda designed to split the Allies to a discussion of the fascism remaining in Italy after Mussolini's death.[62] A forum for exiled political leaders, it allowed them to fight with words. Freda Kirchwey, who saw Spain as the true test of democracy, considered Del Vayo a legitimate leader who could continue to lead the good fight. Having him as editor brought her close to the front lines of what she considered the war of good against evil.[63]

*

By the time Del Vayo took charge of Political War, the United States was at war. Kirchwey had completed more than a decade of active coverage of world events and had merged her public and private lives as never before into a life on the *Nation* where she and Del Vayo could work together to help defeat fascism. It was a good time for her to mobilize energy and commitment to such an important battle. Work would help fill the void left by the deaths of her father and Aunt Mary Frederika, both in March 1942. George Kirchwey had remained involved in penal reform organizations after his retirement as the head of the criminology department of the New York School of Social Work in 1932. He was also chairman of the National Board of Review of Motion Pictures and a board member of the American League to Abolish Capital Punishment. Four years before his death the League organized an eighty-third birthday party in his honor. President Roosevelt, who had been at Columbia University Law School when Kirchwey was dean, could not attend but had sent along his wishes to his "old friend," who appreciated encouragement from the "Chief," saying the birthday greetings "brought healing on its wings." But Kirchwey's condition was deteriorating; less than two years later he began to be forgetful and shaky. As Dorothy described him, "all of a sudden he is an old, old man," and it was "painful to watch" how disoriented he had become. During the war years George Kirchwey had shied away from association with his German heritage, but in the final years of senility, he began to speak German phrases from his youth. Freda, mourning her father, mused: "somehow since his death I have found myself drawing closer to the days before his mind and personality became dimmed."[64]

She and Evans attended funeral services for George Washington Kirchwey at Saint Paul's Chapel at Columbia University. Dr. Harry Emerson Fosdick of the Riverside Church conducted the service, which was attended by many friends, Columbia Law School faculty, and "a few ex-convicts." Now the daughter of this progressive force for justice sublimated her grief, pouring her energy into the battle against fascism.[65]

*

James Wechsler, who worked with Freda Kirchwey on the *Nation* for several years, recalled her as "a compassionate, spirited and conscientious woman who seemed to suffer personal pain at each unfolding of this century's horrors." The stakes were high. Nothing must interfere with the defeat of fascism. India's quest for independence from British rule won Kirchwey's attention, but not her unqualified support. "The deadlock between Britain and India imperils one important sector, both political and military, of the battle line of the United Nations. It is from this point of view—which places victory over the Axis above all other considerations—that the issue must be judged and a solution pressed." She was critical of British intransigence and sympathized with India's Congress Party, but "our sympathy does not blind us, as their bitterness blinds them, to the cold fact that an Axis victory would not only end India's chances for independence but destroy the freedom of the rest of the world."[66]

She persuaded Louis Fischer, who had just returned from India, to write a feature article on Mahatma Gandhi; breaking the low-rate precedent, she offered him $100 for it. He accepted and began a series of detailed controversial pieces about India, highlighting Gandhi's civil disobedience campaign and the Cripps Mission. (In March 1942 Sir Stafford Cripps had been sent to India to seek a

settlement with political leaders there.) Fischer disagreed with Kirchwey's criticism of Gandhi's civil disobedience. She replied: "My
honest belief is that Gandhi should not have launched the civil disobedience campaign even after the breakdown of the negotiations.
He should have gone on trying stubbornly and patiently to reach
some sort of an agreement, and he should have refused to do anything which could precipitate civil disorder in the midst of the war
. . . None of this excuses the British. I think intransigence on both
sides is inexcusable at a time like this."[67]

Nevertheless, Louis Fischer attempted to use Kirchwey's connection with Supreme Court Justice Felix Frankfurter as a way of influencing President Roosevelt to back the plan for India's independence. Frankfurter denied her request, saying that he did not try to
influence the President; furthermore, "the least one can do if one
cannot advance an Indian settlement, is to avoid stirring the mud-
died water."[68] Fischer's first article on the controversy "disturbed"
Frankfurter. In it Fischer detailed reasons for Sir Stafford Cripps's
failure to negotiate an agreement between England and the various
Indian political parties. Cripps, he claimed, had promised India an
immediate national government with full powers, but pressure from
headquarters forced withdrawal of the promise. But Kirchwey told
Fischer that Frankfurter had "the *best possible first-hand reasons* to
believe that the failure of the mission was not due to any such
maneuvers."[69]

British officials telegraphed a direct denial of Fischer's accusations. One official charged the author with "the most glaring errors
of fact and understanding." Kirchwey printed the replies and entered the controversy by publishing Fischer's rebuttal to her own
coverage of the touchy British–Indian negotiations. "You cannot
mean—can you?—that we are fighting for the British Empire,"
Fischer asked. She decided to print his letter and her reply instead
of her usual editorial: "The British Empire is a fact—slightly frayed
around the edges but still fairly substantial . . . And it isn't territory
alone that is at stake. You know that. The most important asset the
empire brings us is the bond of mutual responsibility." She admitted
that India had not been allowed to choose whether to enter the war.
Although she supported self-government for India, she focused on
the main goal: defeat of the Axis powers. "We have a war to fight
and our side has to be united in all our faults and virtues or we shall
face defeat together." Reinhold Niebuhr called her analysis of the

Allies vis-à-vis the British Empire, "absolutely first rate, and in my opinion the best political thinking that has been done on this subject."[70]

The controversy continued, with Kirchwey printing some British views and Fischer demanding a chance to refute them. After several months the *Nation* editors decided too much attention was being focused on India, "however central and important the debate may be." When managing editor Robert Bendiner directed Fischer to condense his article-long response to critics into a letter to the editor, Fischer threatened to resign. Kirchwey asked Bendiner what he thought of capitulating and publishing Fischer's comments as an article, and he replied: "I don't think that appeasing the Louis Fischers of this world is a paying proposition. You know him much better than I, of course, but I would bet that he was bluffing (where else would he go?) . . . That's just my feeling as an editor. As a person, I really sympathize with you and I imagine I would do the same thing in your place. But next time, my dear, please deal with that big potroast yourself."[71]

Kirchwey decided to run Fischer's article but, a bit ruffled, warned him: "Nor do I like ultimatums. The fact that yours succeeded doesn't make me like it any better . . . We'll use your answer next week. I'm extremely sorry this disagreement arose; I hope it will be the last one, ever." To Fischer the issue seemed "in part, only in part, political." As he told Kirchwey: "You had taken the pro-empire attitude . . . Can't you see that we are already losing the peace? India for me is a question of the peace." But her position was focused on winning the war.[72]

*

That goal was responsible for many hard decisions. One meant abandoning the principle of absolute free speech. Even before the United States entered the war Kirchwey thought it necessary "to stop the Nazi campaign of lies." Hitler had to export ideas to create a sympathetic attitude toward Nazism, and she saw his propaganda as an enemy. "Nazism cannot live unto itself alone. It prides itself on its dynamic nature. It claims the earth as its empire. It needs pro-Nazi feelings in other lands."[73] Because the United States advocated the free expression of ideas, it was fertile ground for Nazi propaganda. Kirchwey believed that the Bill of Rights should not be used "for the wiping out of the very rights it aimed to protect and our devotion to it should not lead us to commit national suicide." In

1939 she had felt that fascist propaganda could be curbed by coun-terpropaganda and legal restrictions on fascist activities.[74] She had been considering Evans Clark's suggestion for a specific plan of ac-tion to combat Nazi activities, "without doing violence to American ideals of free speech, free assembly, etc." Such possibilities included restricting the wearing of fascist uniforms, prohibiting the carrying of weapons, seeking a way to give authorities "the power to prose-cute Nazi agents who attack Jews as a race," and requiring "Nazi organizations" to disclose financial records.[75]

Following the Nazi-Soviet Pact, the House Committee on Un-American Activities pushed for new anti-alien and anti-radical leg-islation. Kirchwey worried about the "lavish, undiscriminating way" Congressman Dies collected testimony and accused the administra-tion of "sheltering thousands of Communists" in the federal govern-ment. The Committee itself was the danger because it generated fear: "Now is the time for all good men to come to the aid of de-mocracy. We have not gone to war, and no excuse exists for war-time hysteria. Neither Communists nor even [German-American] Bundists are enemy agents . . . They deserve to be watched but not to be persecuted . . . The real danger is that general detestation of Communists and Bundists will lead to acts of outright repression supported not only by reactionaries but by disgusted liberals . . . Democracy was not invented as a luxury to be indulged in only in times of calm and stability. It is a pliable, tough-fibered technique especially useful when times are hard. Only a weak and distrustful American could today advocate measures of repression and coer-cion, or encourage a mood of panic. Now is the time to demon-strate the resilience of our institutions. Now is the time to deal with dissent calmly and with full respect for its rights."[76]

The Nazi invasion of Norway challenged Kirchwey to examine her commitment to civil liberties. Because Norway had "permitted 'legal' Nazi activities and trusted in the loyalty and sober sense of its vast democratic majority," its fate revealed a dilemma. While admit-ting that the only way a democracy can exist is with "the uncoerced support of the majority," Kirchwey hinted of a move away from an absolute commitment to democracy's preservations of freedom of speech and assembly with the questions: "When do circumstances cease to be normal? At what moment does it become necessary to limit the freedom of everyone in order to suppress the danger lurk-ing in a disloyal handful?" Norway, she decided, "missed the moment." The United States had its own "fifth column," but "the moment for drastic repression has not arrived, and the task of liberals in America is difficult but clear. They must fight to preserve the democratic safeguards contained in the Bill of Rights, while applying to Nazis and their supporters the equally democratic methods of exposure, counter-propaganda, and justified legal attack . . . Otherwise the Nazi invasion of Norway is likely to end in a victory for Martin Dies in America."[77]

Then followed Hitler's conquest of the Netherlands, Belgium, and France, his massive attack on the Soviet Union, and the Japanese attack on Pearl Harbor. The United States declared war, and within months Freda Kirchwey demanded that the government "Curb the Fascist Press!": "The fascist press in the United States should be suppressed. It is a menace to freedom and an obstacle to winning the war." Reversing her previous arguments, she said: "To protect it in the name of democracy is an evidence of timidity, not of self-confidence. A self-confident nation takes whatever steps are necessary to secure its existence; it does not allow its institutions to be used by enemies as weapons for its own destruction." To Attorney General Biddle's argument that the repression of fascists could lead to repression of any number of other groups of legitimate dissent, she was willing to take the risk, warning that Biddle underestimated "the danger of an unchecked fascist press."[78]

This stand presented difficulties for the civil libertarian who believed in the sanctity of freedom of speech. The First Amendment could be curtailed only with "compelling state interest," when speech presented a clear and present danger to national security. Furthermore, to suppress a fascist press presented difficulties in the definition of "fascist." Kirchwey admitted the difficulty, but included "out-and-out pro-Axis papers, Jew-baiters, Britain-haters, and foes of democracy like Coughlin" in her definition. It was not enough to watch the fascist press and wait, for in the meantime, fascism could continue to grow by dramatizing American democracy's real and serious flaws. "Racial discrimination, poverty and insecurity" could be exploited to arouse Americans to exchange their imperfect democracy for the promises of fascism. Americans could not risk giving the enemy the forum to rally toward defeat. Remedies of democratic counterpropaganda and forced disclosures of fascist funds offered insufficient resistance. Nor was it wise to wait for fascists to commit an act that threatened national security.

Reversing her earlier arguments, Freda Kirchwey decided that the very existence of a "treason press" in the United States was "an integral part of the fascist offensive . . . They should be exterminated exactly as if they were many enemy-machine-gun nests in the Bataan jungle." The country should protect itself and not participate in Europe's "democratic suicide."[79]

Kirchwey's view of fascism and the peculiar nature of its propaganda finally moved her to what must have been a very uncomfortable stance, one that raised the ire and concern of more rigorous civil libertarians. A reader demanded: "Is it really you who pick up Fascist allegations that democracies disarm themselves by practising democracy?" "We anti-Fascists are too few to exercise dictatorship." Kirchwey disagreed: "propaganda must be looked upon as a weapon to be snatched from the enemy just as one would drop a bomb on an ammunition dump. In fact, we see no essential difference between a munitions plant and a fascist propaganda plan, though one may be more or less destructive than the other . . . we don't believe civil-liberties-as-usual fits the realities of the fight against fascism."[80]

A dismayed Norman Thomas protested "Curb the Fascist Press!" and accused Kirchwey of betraying liberal principles: "It is a rather terrible thing that liberals should now be the spokesmen for a jittery program which, if it means anything, can only be interpreted to mean no criticism of the Administration except from us." Democracies must do no more than stop "immediate overt acts" or apply "the well known theory of clear defense and immediate danger." To go beyond this defense jeopardizes opposition in general: "In ten years or less it won't be the people you want to suppress now who will be suppressed and stay suppressed by your theory; it will be yourselves along with many others, unless, indeed, you want to go farther than I think you do in support of a Roosevelt totalitarianism. Don't forget that neither Roosevelt nor anybody else is immortal. The principles once established are apt to outlive men."[81] Kirchwey, who did not see the issue as one of free speech, responded that propaganda "is a weapon not different from others used by the enemy," and "I don't think the opinions expressed by the advocates and defenders of fascism can be treated like mere dissent from the prevailing point of view."[82]

When the American Civil Liberties Union expressed its intent to defend the freedom of the fascist press during wartime, Freda

Kirchwey resigned her membership. Her friend John Haynes
Holmes accepted her resignation but admonished: "I would fight
to the death to maintain their [fascists] liberties, not for their own
sake, but for the sake of a democracy which disappears when such
liberties are withdrawn . . . Indeed, it is no longer a democracy, but
to the extent at least that civil liberties are denied, has already itself
become a fascist state." Holmes urged Kirchwey to return to the
ACLU after the war, when "You will be yourself again!"[83]

Kirchwey had spent her early years opposing all kinds of censorship. In 1929, when birth-control advocate Mary Ware Dennett was
jailed for distributing sex educational information, Kirchwey wrote
of the necessity to defend absolute freedom of speech: "Freedom to
teach birth control or the facts of sex, or to publish a novel whose
language seems vulgar to police magistrates, or to proclaim the
coming revolution, or to express one's faith in Darwin and one's
disbelief in God, these must be defended—as they are opposed—
together." Thus, some thirteen years before, she wrote a critique
that now could be used against her: "Repression is one thing, and
those who try to differentiate the forms it takes make a mistake both
in logic and human consequences."[84] But during the war she believed that abandoning her commitment to absolute civil liberties
was a lesser evil than giving over free expression to the manipulated
half-truths of fascism, which could lead to defeat from within.

*

Early in 1942 Victor Serge, French novelist and journalist, wrote
his friend Dwight Macdonald, editor of the *Partisan Review,* about
a "slander-campaign" against him and four other European émigrés
living in Mexico. The Mexican Communist Party had accused them
of being Nazi agents and introduced a resolution to the Mexican
Chamber of Deputies demanding their expulsion. Deportation
would mean almost certain death. Macdonald and Sidney Hook
composed a letter of protest to Mexican President Avila Camacho
detailing the series of vicious lies. They hoped to have it signed by
hundreds of influential Americans, so they organized an Initiating
Committee of "prominent Americans" to solicit the support of hundreds more. John Dos Passos' response to Macdonald indicated the
committee members' diverse political views: "I absolutely disagree
with most of the things you write nowadays but I certainly think
this sort of thing you do is highly useful."[85] The Committee included Hook, Dos Passos, Kirchwey, Roger Baldwin, John Dewey,

James T. Farrell, Quincy Howe, and Reinhold Niebuhr. Kirchwey not only endorsed the letter as one of the Initiating Committee but also agreed to have replies sent to the *Nation*. She made this plea to Eleanor Roosevelt: "The enclosed documents tell their own story. I hope you'll want to join us in signing the letter to President Camacho."[86] Six days later she wrote asking Macdonald to remove her name from the list.

Admitting it "unspeakably careless," Kirchwey confessed that she had not read the final draft of the letter to Camacho carefully. Whether this was the case, or whether she had become uncomfortable with the letter's political implications, she vehemently disagreed with its portrayal of all five émigrés as "important anti-fascist fighters": "I think the letter should have stuck exclusively to the main issue which is not the importance or political standing of the men involved but the nature of the attack upon them. I'm against illegal machinations and plots and false charges—not to mention assassination—per se, without regard to the character or politics of the victims."

The final letter went beyond the issue of sanctuary for the émigrés to a justification of anti-Stalinists against Stalinists. Privately Kirchwey confided to Secretary of the Interior Harold Ickes: "I don't see why Stalin doesn't call off these stupid agents and put an end to the vendettas they are endlessly pursuing."[87] Her withdrawal was so sudden that her name appeared on the sponsoring letter, which contained 160 signatures, and she was mentioned in the *New York Times*'s coverage of the letter. Kirchwey decided to air both sides in the *Nation*. After publishing Richard Rovere's blast, "Ogpu at Work," which branded the charges against the five as false, she printed a heated reply by Stalinists, who insisted that the men were connected with "the Nazi fifth column" in Mexico. She wanted to stay out of the debate: "The editors of *The Nation* do not want to enter into an argument with the distinguished Mexicans and European exiles." She did give a strong endorsement of Gustav Regler (a former high officer in the International Brigade) and less firm support for Serge, but she ventured no opinion of the other three: "We cannot answer for the character of all the persons who have been under attack in Mexico." While withholding judgment and challenging the Stalinists to submit proof of their charges, she gave credence to their accusations. Norman Thomas admonished: "I think so weak is your rejoinder that it undoes the good that you started to do with the matter at hand." He reminded her that she did not point out that the Mexican Communists threatened their enemies with Trotsky's fate—axe murder—and asked: "The exigencies of war require many strange things, but do they require that that which is monstrous, when practiced by Hitler, is pardonable when practiced by Stalin?"[88]

A charge of undue influence by Del Vayo brought a furious private reaction: "I'm not going to fight the Spanish war all over again . . . but I would like to remind you that *The Nation*'s attitude toward the role of the POUM [Partido Obrero de Unificación Marxista, a working-class party] and of the Trotskyists in Spain long antedated the presence of J. Alvarez del Vayo on our masthead." Explaining that Del Vayo had not been consulted about the original Rovere article or the editorial replies, Kirchwey continued, "your invidious suggestions concerning his influence are particularly uncalled for." The question was not one of defending the men in question or of their positions, but whether there was an "excuse for Communist threats and instigations to violence." A scathing critique by Dwight Macdonald continued the controversy. When Kirchwey edited his letter to the editor, she deleted several specific references to herself.[89]

However, in an attempt to clarify the *Nation*'s position and to answer Macdonald "and then drop the subject for good," she publicly answered his basic question: "Does one or does one not become a tool of fascism, in *The Nation*'s eyes, if one opposes the present conduct of the war as imperialistic?" She called his query a "political catch question." The real question was not opposition to the way the war was being fought but opposition to the war itself. She acknowledged that opposition to the war did make a person "a tool of the fascists," but "a tool is not an agent . . . The attitudes and activities of these men do not make them 'Nazi agents' or justify threats against them or attacks upon them by Communists."[90]

*

Any opposition to the war against fascism worried Freda Kirchwey. Earlier in 1941, when Germany attacked the Soviet Union and the Soviets joined the Allies, she focused on unity within the collective security system she had supported since 1933. That Stalin in 1941 used the anniversary of the October Revolution to announce Maxim Litvinov's appointment as ambassador to Washington signaled closer cooperation with the West. When Stalin dissolved the Third International in 1943, Kirchwey praised the action as "an act of political war," "an offensive blow against Hitler's one remaining political weapon—exploitation of the fear of Communist Revolution."[91]

In June 1943 she was concerned about some activities in the American government and responded to I. F. Stone's offer to arrange for an anonymous exposé of FBI infringements on civil liberties which could be published in the *Nation:* "There was a time when I would have objected to printing any anonymous article in *The Nation* which made serious charges against individuals or government agencies." Although she realized the seriousness of the charges and the necessity of confidentiality for the government source, she reminded Stone: "When [Attorney General] Francis Biddle calls me up the day after the first article appears, I want to be able to say that I know who the writer is, that I consider him a responsible and reliable person, and that I can vouch for the authenticity of the facts." But Stone was unable to convince the government official that his identity could be entrusted to her.[92] So Kirchwey traveled to Washington to investigate charges that the FBI's "character investigation" of government war agency workers violated their civil liberties. Talks with a Cabinet member, the head of a federal agency, and two other prominent government officials convinced her that "the inquisition was aimed at ridding the government service of as many New Dealers and other progressives as possible." Based on these facts, trust in Stone's integrity, and the importance of the charges, she risked the consequences and published the two-part "Washington Gestapo."[93]

The exposé also included Roosevelt: "President Roosevelt himself could not qualify for work in a war agency. Does he not entertain the Soviet Premier, Molotov, in the White House? Busy as he is with questions of global war, he perhaps does not mark the steady weeding out from his agencies of those who could be counted on to push rather than sabotage his war program." Kirchwey was less than pleased with this part of the attack: "in the middle of a war when one is forced to denounce the President it is probably better strategy to do it in an extremely serious, dignified way—however bitterly."[94]

The heated controversy lasted for weeks. Some readers wrote the Department of Justice directly. One letter charged: "The articles in the July 17 and 24 issues of *The Nation* on 'The Washington Gestapo' and Freda Kirchwey's 'End the Inquisition' in the July 31 issue are very disturbing to all liberal minded people. We urge you to use your power to stop this inquisition before all forward thinking people are forced out of federal service." J. Edgar Hoover, FBI director, responded: "I have not dignified the particular articles with a public denial because of the anonymous character of the first two and the tendency of the Nation to engage in a campaign of smear against the FBI over a period of years." The FBI had been amassing a file on Freda Kirchwey for some time. In 1944, however, the Bureau stopped investigating her as a key figure, admitting, "no specific information has been developed in this case indicative of subject's membership in the COMMUNIST PARTY or her engaging in some form of subversive activities this case is being closed," though it continued to update her file periodically.[95]

Shortly before the FBI series came out Freda Kirchwey was diagnosed as having pneumonia. In April she went to Tidalholm, a resort in Beaufort, South Carolina, to recuperate. She wrote Villard: "At this serene distance from the world and my job I feel as if pressure and anxiety were the two things to guard against in these desperate days (Just how to do it I haven't figured out!)" She recovered her strength in time to travel to Britain that summer to cover the war firsthand. Arriving in London from Scotland, she received what she called her "greatest personal triumph in Britain": a description of her by the Chief Officer for West Scotland to the Ministry of Information Press Officer in Manchester:

MISS KERCHWAY IS ESSENTIALLY AN ATTRACTIVE PERSON. A LITTLE FRENCH, TRES CHIC ET TRES PETITE. SHE IS WEARING A NEAT BLUE HAT WITH A WIDE BRIM IN FRONT, WHICH IS INCLINED TO CONCEAL QUITE A LARGE PART OF A VERY PRETTY FACE. SHE IS WEARING A BLUE CLOAK WHICH FALLS FROM HER SHOULDERS OVER A CHARMING SCARLET AND BLUE COAT AND SKIRT. SHE IS CARRYING A BLUE SUITCASE AND A SMALL CANVAS HOLD ALL. SHE HAS VERY NEAT LEGS AND FEET. SHE IS VERY MUCH MORE EXCITING THEN YOU SOUND, BUT I WILL TRY AND CHEER THE DESCRIPTION UP A BIT.[96]

Once in England, Kirchwey tried to be diplomatic with the British Ministry, which expected her to be most interested in the Women's Division. She was not and recorded "Discover as I go along that my preoccupation with politics and with foreign policy in particular hasn't the slightest relation to what the Ministry wants of me." She wanted to talk with as many people as possible and find out as much as she could about the war and predictions for postwar Europe. She interviewed war workers in Scotland and England.[97] And she conferred with Lady Astor and other British officials. Her friend in the Labour Party, Harold Laski, considered her visit a "refreshment." "It meant the more to me because I have felt that many of the Americans I care about, and some even of those I care about most, have not been fighting the war I have been fighting, but have been content to assume, first, that victory is an end in itself, and second, that we can trust leaders who have shown not an atom of zeal for a new world," he wrote. Kirchwey returned to the United States with only the clothes on her back, having left all other clothing, jewelry, and shoes to be given away to alleviate in a small way the need she had witnessed.[98]

*

Kirchwey returned in the fall of 1943 to a journal which was finally improving its financial state. The last few years had been a battle for survival. Following Villard's departure and an increase in production expenses, the *Nation*'s deficits had escalated. In 1942, to offset losses, Kirchwey had pursued the idea of merging the *Nation* with the *New Republic,* which also was undergoing financial duress. Evans Clark, negotiating for Kirchwey, told *New Republic* editor Bruce Bliven that Freda would be interested in a merger if she could share "editorial management" and had "equal control" of the business management. Bliven's response ignored the conditions: "We do not believe it is possible to give formal recognition to a continuing ownership in the joint property on Freda's part . . . We are prepared to bring Freda into the office as a full editor, at a proper salary and have her share fully with me in the daily work of getting out the papers." But, he insisted: "I ought to have the final veto power." Clark said there was "no basis for further negotiations."[99]

Early in 1943 Kirchwey decided on a reorganization plan that could rescue the *Nation*. Divesting herself of ownership, she would create a nonprofit organization responsible for the journal. That would assure readers that the constant appeals for funds were not bringing her personal profit. She proposed the sale of *The Nation*, Inc., which she owned, to the new creation: Nation Associates. By this transfer, announced in February 1943, Kirchwey remained editor and publisher of the journal and became president of Nation Associates. An appeal was sent to subscribers to become members of Nation Associates; contributions from $10 to $100 entitled them to varied degrees of involvement. They were informed that if the plan did not generate the needed $25,000, the *Nation* was in danger of ceasing publication. Readers responded with a flourish of support. Thomas Mann sent encouragement with his $50: "I am not a rich man, but with the enclosed small check I want to indicate that I should consider it a great misfortune if the NATION whose reader I have been ever since I have lived in this country, would disappear." John Gunther wrote: "You hit me at the worst time in the whole world. This is because of a lot of reasons, personal and otherwise, which I don't need to go into. But anyway here is my check for $100, which must mean that I truly love you very much."[100]

Numerous other loyal readers bailed out the *Nation*. By May 1943 Kirchwey repaid an outstanding debt to Maurice Wertheim and acknowledged the success of her appeal. The *Nation* had netted some $36,000 after expenses, and with current charges paid, $20,000 was left to work with that year.[101] The Nation Associates was officially established. It supported the publication of the *Nation* and was to serve as an instrument to promote "the principles of a progressive democracy." Its fundamental objective was "to help focus the energies of the progressive forces in our country through an accelerated program of political education aimed at enlarging the awareness of the American citizen of his responsibilities for building a world society aimed at extending the democratic way of life."[102]

The Nation Associates educated the public by amassing facts on timely topics and by sponsoring public forums. In October 1944 it hosted its first conference: America's Opportunity to Create and Maintain Lasting Peace. Speakers addressed the question from a variety of vantage points. Reinhold Niebuhr talked about American foreign policy and its relationship to peace; Ray Joseph, author of *Argentina Diary,* talked about South America's role in the postwar world; Henry Lee Moon, former Regional Racial Relations Advisor to the Federal Public Housing Authority, spoke on postwar expectations of blacks; Lawrence K. Rosinger, who covered Far Eastern affairs for the Foreign Policy Association, spoke about "American Far Eastern Policy."[103]

The concept of an open forum was central to the purpose of the Nation Associates and the *Nation.* In February 1944 a dinner forum arranged by a private group had put a capstone on Freda Kirchwey's career. Including many of the same people who had financed the Nation Associates, Raymond Swing's Kirchwey Dinner Committee organized a testimonial to honor her twenty-five years of service on the *Nation*. Yet another Sponsors Group was solicited to honor her service to the journal and recognize "her great services to the liberal cause in America."[104] The committee, organized in October 1943, worked for months to plan the occasion and raise at least $25,000 to enable Kirchwey "to intensify and expand the work of *The Nation*."[105]

The familiar (albeit a bit tired) smile of the affable editor high-lighted the full portrait cover of the Tribute dinner program. Her equally familiar signature titled the page simply "Freda Kirchwey." The booklet was as well done as the dinner. In addition to listing the speakers and a printed staff tribute to Kirchwey, "as editor and as human being," it contained a letter from President Franklin Del-ano Roosevelt and an impressive list of some 1,430 sponsors. A roll call of persons who sponsored the evening reads like a who's who of prominent figures: Albert Einstein, Thomas Mann, John Dos Passos, Justice Hugo L. Black, Lillian Hellman, Judge Dorothy Kenyon, Walter Lippmann, John Dewey, Carl Becker, Carrie Chap-man Catt, and Beatrice Hinkle, to name but a few; 1,217 in all came to the Commodore Hotel to pay tribute to Freda Kirchwey.[106]

As Freda prepared for the dinner, Del Vayo urged her to put herself "emotionally and mentally in the position of a political leader," making her speech "as less personal as possible." She should accept the tribute money "not to a magazine, not to a person, but to a political fighting position."[107] The speakers that evening ex-tolled her virtues and those of the *Nation*. Judge Thurman Arnold spoke about the journal's influence. Looking around at the impres-sive array of guests, he asked: "What magazine with circulation of over a million would receive the tribute from the diverse economic groups and the different political parties which has been given to *The Nation* this evening?" He concluded that the journal influenced the world by influencing people who influenced others—newspaper writers, college professors, and governmental leaders, for example. *New York Post* columnist Dorothy Thompson praised the *Nation* for seeing the war as "in essence a struggle of mankind for its own future."[108]

Reinhold Niebuhr, chairman of the Union for Democratic Action, praised Freda Kirchwey for being "at once a political idealist and a political realist." He was grateful that she took over the *Nation's* editorship, "before the world and America were forced to confront the catastrophes of our age." He credited her with helping to overcome a "sentimental note in liberalism. She understood the tragic alternatives which faced us in this present conflict and recognized, as many liberals did not, that when evil becomes embodied in tanks and airplanes, it has to be challenged by the same embodiment of physical force."[109]

Evidently Kirchwey achieved the balance Niebuhr sought that year when he urged the "children of light" to cure their "blindness" to the forces of darkness, arm themselves with the "wisdom of the children of darkness but remain free from their malice." "The preservation of a democratic civilization requires the wisdom of the serpent and the harmlessness of the dove."[110] That night he shared his hope that the *Nation* would continue to be "an organ of the conscience of the nation." Of Kirchwey, he said: "May she, through the instrument of this great journal, continue to search the conscience of the democratic cause, stiffen the courage of democratic purpose, and also, possibly, sweeten its temper."[111]

In her own speech Kirchwey focused on the ideological aspect of World War II. She traced her writing on the *Nation* back to the compromises that came out of the World War I peace conference. She and others had recorded the "bargains of the statesmen" that sold out popular forces. In effect, this sellout had dictated a "process of democratic defeat" begun in 1919. World War II proved no exception, for even democratic America had placed an embargo on Republican Spain, preferring "to accept the aggressions of the fascists, rather than chance the results of a people's victory."[112]

Looking ahead to victory and another peace, Kirchwey sought assurance that this kind of fear would not dictate yet another unsuccessful peace; but she found none. In the United States as in Britain, power "is still largely in the hands of men who hate fascism less than they fear social change." Repeating the arguments she had made since she started the Political War section some years before, Kirchwey vowed that the *Nation* would continue to urge American leaders to grasp this important aspect of a broader struggle to fight more than a military war. She called for them to help create a "New Deal for the world" by recognition of and cooperation with worldwide popular forces that sought to replace the "old system." "Some form or degree of collectivist control, under democratic sanctions" was needed, for "only a New Deal for the world, more far-reaching and consistent than our own faltering New Deal, can prevent the coming of World War III." She committed her journal to wage the fight for that world New Deal.[113] Accepting the $25,000 gift—$1,000 for each year of service on the *Nation*—Freda Kirchwey promised to put the funds to immediate use. "The time has passed when a fighting journal can afford to interest itself only in survival." Action was necessary.

A difficult job awaited her, for, as she confided to her son: "Never since 1920, I think, has there been as little progressive feeling in the country; the understanding of the war itself does not increase with our increasing participation. There's a tough period ahead and the worst part of it is that reaction will be reflected in a foreign policy even less generous and realistic than that of the past few years. But all this only indicates a need to work harder and speak more clearly . . . I've been reading a life of Tom Paine and it has put new heart in me!"[114]

The issues Freda Kirchwey addressed at her tribute dinner occupied her thoughts and actions in the years to come. She pledged the *Nation* to help get Allied support to create a truly representative international organization; get rid of Allied support for the monarchist faction in Italy; recognize DeGaulle's French Committee of National Liberation; break off relations with fascist Spain; support "Free People's movements in every occupied country"; sustain the "development of a Jewish national homeland in Palestine"; and back democratic regimes in Latin America. Such foreign policy positions were critical. Yet, as she pointed out, no American president could construct any "responsible foreign policy" without the aid of the Congress. In fact, in 1944, Kirchwey, probably recalling the Senate's role in killing the League of Nations, said: "The future of the world will be largely determined in the Congress of the United States."[115]

She realized the critical nature of other support: that of an increasingly powerful Soviet Union. When she said that the security of the USSR "demands neighbors who prefer peace to conquest," she used the same justification the Soviets would use when they moved into Eastern Europe. As always, she argued for unity among progressive forces: "We must find our allies; we must overlook our smaller differences; and we must move." She saw that movement as one against fascism and concluded her remarks with a call to defeat fascism and win the war. Expressing the horror of the Second World War, she argued that all ordinary people wanted were "the opposites of these products of fascism and war." Kirchwey, the commonsensical woman of "good will," set out "to help create a world fit, not for heroes, but for ordinary men and women."[116]

The *Nation* staff showed its vigorous and steadfast respect for their editor-in-chief in a tribute that honored her both personally and professionally:

FREDA KIRCHWEY

It is one thing to expound high principles in print week by week. It is another to put them into practice day by day. And we who work with Freda Kirchwey think it relevant to depose and say that her liberalism begins at home. As editor-in-chief she has had the wisdom and courage to establish a genuine working democracy of which the tone and temper are set by her own respect for other individuals and their opinions, her humor, and her sense of fair play. As employer her sympathy and understanding for every human problem have won for her the freely given loyalty and friendship of every worker in the shop. In *The Nation* world liberty, equality, and fraternity, the four freedoms, collective security, and the union shop prevail. We who work in it find it good. We recommend it to the larger world, and on this, the twenty-fifth anniversary of her connection with *The Nation* we salute Freda Kirchwey as editor and as human being. May her anniversaries increase.

THE STAFF OF THE NATION[117]

7 || Postwar Fighting,
1945–1950

Freda Kirchwey's tribute dinner reflected the support—or at least respect—she received from a number of people with strikingly different views from her own. Her position on the Soviet Union, however, increasingly alienated her from some of them, including many who wrote for the *Nation*. Through the 1940s the front of the journal, which accepted the legitimacy of the Soviet Union and urged greater rapport with it, coexisted with a back section, the literary section, which was becoming increasingly anti-Stalinist. In March 1943, for example, the editorial page proclaimed: "No one in his senses—unless he were an Axis agent—would knowingly stimulate the growth of a feeling against Russia. Close relations between the Soviet Union and its allies are essential—today, for winning the war, tomorrow, for establishing a peaceful Europe." Meanwhile, Diana Trilling's scathing review of a pro-Soviet novel characterized the back: "Except for members of the Communist Party or a few sentimentalists who think that the fine victories of the Russian army justify all the sins of Stalinism . . . it is hard to know who can take seriously Ruth McKenney's long and serious new novel, 'Jake Home.'"[1]

Kirchwey made room for this dialogue. But the editorial pages were becoming more pro-Soviet than liberals like Louis Fischer could tolerate. Yalta's meeting of the Big Three—Roosevelt, Stalin, and Churchill—in 1945 won Kirchwey's approval. Diana Trilling, Sidney Hook, and others, however, felt the Allied concessions regarding Poland as unforgiveable as Kirchwey had considered American refusal to aid Loyalist Spain. But Kirchwey reasoned that the political unity of the Allies at Yalta offset "even the Polish settlement," which she deemed "a pretty decent compromise." In fact, she saw Poland used as a rallying cry for those who hated the British, feared the Russians, and wanted to spread those feelings.[2]

She clung to the belief that the Soviet Union and the United States were on the same side. The surrender of Germany in May 1945 left the task of avoiding a war between those two powers. "Russia, with all its differences of policy and system, is 'on our side.' Not even its most ruthless and arbitrary acts have been able to kill the popular belief that the Soviet government has tackled and begun to solve the strangling problems of modern economic life." To Kirchwey *"permanent cooperation"* between the world powers offered the only hope for peace. British and American liberals and leftists had to "point out the immense dangers of their governments' foreign policies and to demand increasingly a change in men and in actions."[3]

When the war in Europe ended, Louis Fischer decided he could no longer continue to be listed as a contributing editor to a journal with such "misleading" coverage of current events. After a twenty-two-year association, he noisily resigned, accusing the *Nation* of having a "line" and charging that it had "become very much like a party organ. Its opinions appear to be determined by loyalties to organized groups and to governments rather than to principle. *The Nation* is playing politics; that distorts its policies."[4] The *Nation*'s reply, though regretting Fischer's departure, made his implied charges specific:

> We assume that he is charging *The Nation* with a bias in favor of Russia and of communism. We suppose he considers that to be our "line." We suppose he is charging us with ignoring, out of "expediency," the bad behavior of the Soviet Union; of failing out of policy to denounce the Soviet power for suppressing "small, weak states" . . . We can only answer quite flatly that he is wrong. We say what we believe. What we believe is very different from what Mr. Fischer believes.

The editors elaborated on why they feared the growing American suspicion and hatred of the Soviet Union: "We believe Russian policy is primarily a security policy, not an imperialist one; it can become dangerous to the world, therefore, only if Russia decides that the other major powers are plotting against it . . . It would be dishonest to pretend that we think Russia's foreign policy is as great a threat to the basic purpose of destroying fascism and its political and economic roots as is the foreign policy of Britain and the United States."[5]

Kirchwey and others at the *Nation* were more worried about the Allied obsession with defending the "crumbling status quo" than with the rising power of the Soviet Union, and Fischer charged them with a double standard. "I resigned because I did not want to give even the appearance of responsibility for *The Nation*'s partial and therefore wrong presentation of world affairs. I think your reply proves my point."[6] The debate continued as Kirchwey reported the vigorous response the issue generated among readers; agreement with the *Nation* position won three to one. She ended its volume in June 1945 with a full page of readers' comments. Reinhold Niebuhr's position was particularly telling in that it predicted a major issue which would later force even him off the *Nation*. Although he disagreed with Fischer's position, Niebuhr was troubled by the journal's response and privately wrote:

> You declare that despite Russian mistakes it has a more rigorous policy of anti-fascism than we have. That seems to me a too simple and naive way of describing the situation. It is not quite true for one thing because Russia is using fascist forces in Rumania and Hungary. But more important is the fact that this fascist and anti-fascist business is a too simple category for the problem . . . Our primary mistake may be not the use of fascist forces but the general lack of a creative economic policy.[7]

With the war over, Niebuhr moved away from his position in *The Children of Light and the Children of Darkness*. He, and others like him, abandoned the uneasy alliance with the Soviet Union and began to call Stalinism, totalitarianism. Kirchwey, on the other hand, continued to focus on the antifascist battle. The war was over, but her cause was not yet won: fascism still ruled Spain. The "sin" George Orwell ascribed to "nearly all left-wingers from 1933 onwards," that "they have wanted to be anti-Fascist without being anti-totalitarian," could be aimed accurately at Freda Kirchwey during the next decade of her editorship.[8]

*

She covered the formation of the United Nations in San Francisco, hoping that an international peacekeeping organization could prevent the abuses and carnage of war. As delegates laid the ground rules for the world organization in April through June 1945, she listened to the debate and interviewed some of the participants. An impressive array of dignitaries, including Soviet Foreign Minister Vlacheslav M. Molotov, U.S. Secretary of State Edward R. Stettinius, and Czech Prime Minister Jan Masaryk, hammered out the delicate compromises which set up what she hoped would be a "new security machine."[9]

Kirchwey, reporting firsthand, wrote about her sense of the political realities and the feelings that had to be overcome in order to achieve even a semblance of an effective organization. The United Nations, which provided the sole mechanism for world peace, merited support: "The security organization will at least provide the instrument which, assuming the United Nations remain united, can be used for peace as the present alliance has been used for war. Without it there is nothing. With it there is a hope and a machine."[10]

She disagreed with critics who warned that "unless we make the world over *first,* the security organization will be nothing more than an instrument to enforce injustice," but she did believe that a machine could be only as good as its parts. At the time of the UN's creation and often during the years that followed she argued that the United Nations should consist of countries whose governments accurately reflected the popular will.[11] She sought representation of ordinary people, "workers and intellectuals in particular."[12] Although Kirchwey spoke in all-encompassing terms, her acceptance of the Soviet Union's consolidation in Eastern Europe contradicted absolute representation. She, like many on the *Nation* and the *New Republic* at this time, remained optimistic that the USSR would become less defensive. Optimism determined her argument that the United Nations could become "a security organization founded in democracy," for "the free world *remains to be made.*"[13] The League of Nations had failed because its foundation was "a system of society that was obsolete," but "it collapsed because the nations that made it up were unable to create equality and stability, because democracy itself was crumbling."[14]

For the new United Nations to be effective, Kirchwey felt that the Soviet Union had to be an equal bargaining agent with the other former Allied powers. When news came of the certain defeat of Hitler, Kirchwey turned her attention to what she considered the most important task in San Francisco: "the job of welding the Soviet Union into the security set-up." She agreed with an unnamed veteran reporter there who felt a huge job remained, that of overcoming memories of twenty-five years of hostility and suspicion, which had culminated in the "freezing out of Russia at Munich." Whether people viewed the Soviet Union "as a hope or a menace," it was "the pivot around which this conference revolves."[15]

She was troubled by the Western press's characterizing Soviet policy as "unique." At the United Nations all countries pursued self-interest policies. Look at the other great powers: "Their methods may be more discreet, their manners nicer, but are they sacrificing any measures of national protection to the general plan?" She thought not. Less critical of Soviet action in Eastern Europe than some, Kirchwey felt the USSR had the right to protect itself from attack. That the Soviet Union intended to ring itself with friendly governments to her did not seem too different from Britain's hold on liberated Italian colonies in Africa under the trusteeship plan. She explained away the incident of the Soviet Union's arrest of several prominent Polish resistance leaders: "And how much worse was Russia's arrest of the 'sixteen' Poles than the arrest last summer of the Greek delegates from the E.A.M. (the Greek leftist popular resistance movement), who went in good faith to Cairo to confer with the British?"[16] "If each delegation would admit for the duration of the conference its own interested motives and forswear self-righteous accusations of the others, a start might be made toward the honest and realistic relations which must form the basis of even a limited system of collective action."[17]

Kirchwey conceded that the United Nations had many flaws. Its charter was "a great-power alliance rather than a world government," and she compared it to "frontier justice to a world just emerging from lawlessness."[18] "It will not create international government. It will not produce justice as between nations comprising the security organization." Nor would it assure a democratic society. Labor was not represented. Neither were the popular liberation movements, people still fighting repressive regimes in Bolivia, El Salvador, and Argentina. Their absence posed a significant political fact.[19] As she had done throughout the war, when she argued for a political victory as well as a military victory, she reiterated: "*The Nation* has tried with stubborn persistence to prove the indivisible nature of this war."[20]

Early in 1946 Kirchwey was invited to Argentina to cover elections in that dictatorship. She decided to accept if Clark could accompany her. At the last minute, when he got an assignment that would partially cover his expenses, the two were on their way by train to Miami and a flight to Buenos Aires. As usual, Kirchwey talked to many people, including the leader of the Buenos Aires Jewish community, Dr. Moisés Goldman, and "most of the American correspondents and radio people." She interviewed primarily centrist and leftist Argentinian politicians. Foreign Minister Cooke was the only influential pro-Peron person she talked with. After spending some time with presidential candidate José P. Tamborini, leader of the Union Civica Radical, she wrote: "I liked him but found him unimpressive. Sincere and intelligent but without much color." She liked his devotion to "genuine, old-fashioned, liberal democracy." But when Juan Peron defeated Tamborini, Kirchwey drew the following moral: "you can't lick 2½ years of military-fascist dictatorship, plus a demagogic but very shrewd campaign aimed at the 'masses,' by a few months of propaganda based on broad, abstract democratic ideals."[21]

Although Peron's fascist military government was represented in the United Nations, that of his counterpart, Franco, still was not represented. Kirchwey and the Nation Associates took some credit for keeping fascist Spain out of the UN by constantly calling attention to Franco's actions. For years Kirchwey had decried America's acceptance of Franco's professions of neutrality. The Generalissimo, helped into power by the Fuhrer's economic and military aid, repaid him by sending skilled and unskilled Spanish workers to Germany and a symbolic Blue Division to augment the German invasion of the Soviet Union. Kirchwey reminded Americans that Franco had betrayed his own people by aiding Hitler.[22]

To highlight this unofficial Nazi alliance, early in 1945 the Nation Associates staged a demonstration in New York City's Madison Square Garden. Its goal was to convince Americans to sever diplomatic relations with Spain and give "moral and financial assistance to the democratic Spanish elements." "If the War has not taught us that democracy and peace will never be secure as long as any section of the world continues under fascist domination, it has taught us nothing."[23] Thomas Mann, Reinhold Niebuhr, and Helen Gahagan Douglas agreed, as did the political groups that sponsored the demonstration: the Union for Democratic Action, the Congress of Industrial Organization, the American Business Congress, the American Labor Party, the Abraham Lincoln Brigade, and the Free World Association. A tireless Kirchwey recounted the defeat of Loyalist Spain, reminding the audience that the military defeat was also "the greatest *political* defeat the democracies have suffered in the past eight years." Once again she stressed that the political war was "an integral part of the military war."

She urged the President to keep his promise that "this war was not being fought to keep fascists or near-fascists in power." To demonstration participants, she said: "We have a right to ask our leaders to make good these promises. It is for this and no other important reason that we elected Franklin Delano Roosevelt." The purpose of the gathering was "to demand of our government that it end its relations with the fascist regime in Spain and, in so doing, permit the people of Spain to liberate themselves from a brutal dictatorship operating under the direction of the Gestapo in behalf of our enemies." The mistakes of 1936 should not be repeated. "Shall the United States betray democracy again? . . . The answer must be *NO*."[24]

Diplomatic as always, Roosevelt, appreciative of the conclusions of the demonstration, explained that the "maintenance of diplomatic relations with any government does not of itself imply that the American Government approves of the regime and system of government." Although the United States does not "interfere in the internal affairs of foreign countries," FDR acknowledged that we can have friendlier relations with those governments "based on democratic principles similar to ours."[25] Kirchwey could not have been pleased with his restatement of truisms and lack of commitment to any policy change toward Franco's Spain.

The Friends of the Spanish Republic, organized at the January demonstration, set out "to show the integral connection between Spain's fascist regime and the total fascist conspiracy." When World War II ended, Kirchwey continued her work for that committee, trying to persuade Americans to finish the war and fight fascist Spain. She admitted the difficulty of convincing some leaders that "the struggle against fascism is not only a military struggle but is even more a social and political struggle. Since they fail to accept this fact, they also fail to see that you cannot fight fascism with fascists."[26] Her recurrent plea would continue to be nonrecognition of Spanish fascism. In addition to speeches and organizational work, the Nation Associates prepared a number of reports about Spain for the United Nations as well as for the United States government. As early as 1945 the Associates claimed their first victory against Franco's Spain at the UN conference: "Largely as a result of efforts initiated by this organization, the San Francisco conference voted to bar Franco Spain from membership in the United Nations."[27]

*

On 12 April 1945, at the age of sixty-three, Franklin Delano Roosevelt died, leaving behind a stunned world and a grieving nation. Liberals were concerned as to what would become of the United States without his leadership. As historian Alonzo Hamby points out: FDR "had made the New Deal the very definition of American Liberalism . . . In a very real sense, he *was* liberalism; there was no separate, organized movement with an identity which transcended Roosevelt's personality and political appeal."[28]

Freda Kirchwey had viewed Roosevelt as the symbol of the "hope of security and freedom, of release from intolerable oppression." His death marked the "End of an Era," she noted. "When people lose a friend they grieve; when they lose a cherished symbol their world is shaken." Despite the assurances of incoming President Truman that he would continue FDR's programs, there would be "a basic change." Truman might try to salvage the New Deal, but he would never captivate his followers in the way that Roosevelt had, nor would they see him as a living symbol of democracy.[29]

Kirchwey viewed the new era with trepidation, realizing that the United Nations could work as a collective system only to the degree to which "each nation accepts such a system as necessary to its own survival."[30] The tenuousness of survival became more than an abstract worry with the news bulletin of 6 August 1945: "Sixteen hours ago an American airplane dropped one bomb on Hiroshima, an important Japanese military base . . . It is an atomic bomb. It is a harnessing of the basic power of the universe."[31] Historians still argue about whether the bomb was necessary for victory,[32] or if this "weapon rather ostentatiously on our hip,"[33] laid claim to America's supremacy over the Soviet Union.[34]

At the time Kirchwey wrote:

The bomb that hurried Russia into Far Eastern war a week ahead of schedule and drove Japan to surrender has accomplished the specific job for which it was created. From the point of view of military strategy, $2,000,000,000 (the cost of the bomb and the cost of nine days of war) was never better spent. The suffering, the wholesale slaughter it entailed, have been outweighed by its spectacular success; Allied leaders can rightly claim that the loss of life on both sides would have been many times greater if the atomic bomb had not been used and Japan had gone on fighting. There is no answer to this argument. The danger is that it will encourage those in power to assume that, once accepted as valid, the argument can be applied equally well in the future. If that assumption should be permitted, the chance of saving civilization—perhaps the world itself—from destruction is a remote one.[35]

Freda Kirchwey did not ask why the bomb was dropped. She accepted its reality and speculated on the consequences: "if anything is sure about the atomic bomb it is that no physical protection against it will ever be possible." The resulting weaponry escalation could lead only to stalemate or destruction, never to protection. The powers that possessed atomic knowledge—the United States, Canada, and Britain—could not hope to monopolize that knowledge for long. Countries lacking the atomic bomb could not be expected to accept assurances of non-use by those who had it. The United Nations, dominated by the great powers, could not assure control of atomic weapons. A "World Government" was needed to control atomic weapons and save the world from the threat of atomic destruction. The choice was "one world or none."[36]

Along with a world government, Kirchwey believed that understanding the problem was the key to a solution: "If we are to survive our new powers we must understand their full meaning."[37] So the Nation Associates sponsored one of the first major forums to discuss the realities of an atomic era. The editors announced the *Nation*'s forum on atomic power: "We must study, think, and act . . . The forum is intended to add to the knowledge and crystallize the opinions of American progressives and so to increase their ability to influence policy in Washington." A later announcement stressed the idea behind the conference: "the purpose of the forum is public education—followed by public demand for a wise policy in Washington."[38]

Three editorials raised the issues to be discussed at the conference. In "Russia and the Bomb," Kirchwey stressed that the atomic bomb was not just another more sophisticated weapon. The magnitude of its destructive capabilities made it impossible to keep as a monopoly; it was only a matter of time until other nations constructed atomic bombs. For Americans to want to keep the monopoly of the "secret of the bomb" was "Natural, but futile, and therefore stupid." "The Bomb Is a World Affair," reminded King Gordon (managing editor since March 1944, when Bendiner went into the army). Truman's (November 1945) statement announcing a plan to give atomic bomb control to the United Nations Organization was reached after consultation with only Great Britain and Canada. Gordon argued that the Soviet Union must be included in the creation of any form of effective international control. "Economics in the Atomic Age," the final editorial in preparation for the conference, acknowledged that the "overwhelming concern must be to prevent its use in global suicide." It speculated about the enormous advances possible if scientists could be freed from the military preoccupation about atomic power; they could then more fully determine its peacetime applications for relieving economic problems.[39]

Scientists, government officials, foreign dignitaries, and journalists addressed the six hundred people who attended the Nation Associates' December 1945 three-day forum: The Challenge of the Atomic Bomb. The tone was somber. Atomic bomb scientist Harold C. Urey stressed the need to "impress people with the seriousness of the situation": "We have made technological warfare so dreadful that we cannot survive if we practice it. We have that choice to make." Columnist Edgar Ansel Mowrer said: "The only way to prevent mankind from atomizing itself is to make sure that atomic weapons will never be used; finally, the only sure way to do this is to make sure there will be no more war." Participants agreed that there must be an end to war, but they stressed different methods to achieve it.[40]

Most conference participants advocated (for different reasons) cooperation between the United States and the Soviet Union. Several of them, including Kirchwey, were committed to peaceful coexistence. Lessening the tensions between the superpowers was the key to others. Representative Helen Gahagan Douglas asked, "Why in hell don't we stop screaming about who owes who and try to *help* Russia?" Why not replace fear of Russia with friendship, "The most powerful weapon for peace." "Share and Share Alike," urged New York *Herald Tribune* columnist Walter Millis when he spoke of our "secrets of the bomb." He asked his listeners to imagine how they would feel if the Soviet Union had made the atomic bomb discovery first and had refused to share the knowledge. The United States must change its policy and share technological knowledge. This would prove good faith and would solicit the Soviet Union's aid and expertise in finding some "international control of the atomic horror."[41]

Kirchwey reported to her son that the conference was "Terrific in every way—work, expense, but also success." It culminated at a dinner attended by two thousand, with the same number turned away for lack of space. The keynote speaker, Harold Laski, "imported from England," considered socialism the only system that could avoid war.[42] "There is no middle way. Free enterprise and the market economy mean war; socialism and planned economy mean peace. We must plan our civilization or we must perish." Thomas K. Finletter, a lawyer, had another solution: world government. Yet in a lengthy description of how it would work, he noted the problem of American acceptance: "World government adds up to—world government, the setting up of something more powerful than the Government of the United States. It is not surprising that there is this search for a middle ground." There was no middle ground, said Edgar Mowrer: "If you accept the fact that mankind must banish war, then inevitably—if you can think straight—you reach the conclusion that mankind must achieve world government. Nothing less can do the trick." Not so, according to Australian Foreign Minister Herbert Vere Evatt: "What is necessary is to concentrate on making the existing United Nations organization a success."[43]

Whether world socialism, world government, or a strong United Nations, some kind of international control seemed necessary to counter the possibility of atomic destruction. Drawing on scientific expertise, MIT professor Ivan A. Getting echoed what Freda Kirchwey had expressed so early on—the lack of defense capability against atomic warfare: "The conclusion to which we are driven, as men experienced in designing equipment and seeing it put into the field, is that there is no adequate defense possible against atomic explosives when the enemy has a free choice of all the possible technical ways of delivering such explosives." World cooperation was the answer to this awesome threat; mutual distrust led to escalation. An arms race not only threatened war but also lessened the peaceful applications of the new source of energy. Millis reminded the audience that "the situation is also calculated to cripple the non-military development of atomic energy and nuclear research in general."[44]

According to Dr. Harold C. Urey, who had helped split the atom, the potential for peacetime use of atomic energy was hampered by its potential for war: "The peace-time applications of atomic energy are of no importance whatever unless the danger of atomic bombs is banished from the earth." Economist Stuart Chase recommended spending two billion dollars to educate social scientists to deal with the problem of atomic power: "Perhaps after some time in the laboratory and plenty of courage and effort, they can show us how to live with the unbelievable power the physical scientists have loosed upon us." Boris Pregel, President of the Radium and Uranium Corporation and expert on radioactivity, was more optimistic. He looked forward to the peaceful use of atomic power as a means of equalizing the status of people in economically backward areas of the world and concluded: "the atomic energy era means—equality, peace, and happiness."[45]

At the last session of the conference, delegates made some specific suggestions to meet the reality of an atomic world. Freda Kirchwey articulated a number of resolutions that reflected "the sense of the forum." A resolution for a world government was not feasible because there was insufficient time for discussion and for agreement; instead the delegates supported "establishing atomic control" through a strengthened UN. The veto in its Security Council, which made such control relative and therefore ineffective, must be abolished. "Private monopolies, national or international, over the industrial exploitation of atomic energy" should be avoided, and a resolution proposed nationalizing the production of atomic energy. The U.S. Congress should work out the details for control: in particular, "a federal control commission must be composed of representatives of the people as a whole . . . including government and military." That commission, however, must remain "under full civilian control."[46]

Seventeen years later Kirchwey, not one to boast, credited the conference's demand for "civilian control of atomic power" with results: "It is not far-fetched to believe that Washington's decision to create a civilian A.E.C. was partly influenced by the eddies flowing out from that gathering." In 1946 two different plans for the control of atomic energy were introduced in the Senate. James O'Brien MacMahon (D, Connecticut) proposed civilian control; Senator Arthur H. Vandenberg (R, Michigan) wanted the military to be in control. The Atomic Energy Act of 1946 was a compromise between the two bills; but on the important issue of control, MacMahon's provision for exclusive civilian control prevailed.[47]

*

On 12 September 1946, at the French Embassy in Washington, D.C., Freda Kirchwey was made a member of the French Legion of Honor for her work during World War II. In congratulating his wife, Evans Clark made an interesting comment about her politics: "*Congratulations* on your Legion of Honor award—that's marvelous—and so well deserved. Did anyone so far left ever get one before?" Kirchwey shared the title of Chevalier of the Legion of Honor with Waverly Root, newspaper man; Raymond Swing, radio correspondent; Elliot H. Lee, executive vice president of American Relief for France; and Reginald Townsend, president of the French Institute in the United States. Also honored at the ceremonies at the French Embassy in Washington, D.C., were Henry Morgenthau, Jr., former Secretary of the Treasury, Archibald MacLeish, former Assistant Secretary of State, and Oscar Cox, former administrator of the Foreign Economic Administration.[48]

Kirchwey's unswerving support of the Free French after Hitler invaded France and had set up the Vichy government under Pétain was probably behind the award. She had been horrified by American recognition of Vichy, and in one instance had dramatically pitted her views against those of the American State Department. Early in 1942, when Free French Vice Admiral Emil Muselier liberated Saint Pierre and Miquelon, islands off the coast of Newfoundland, Secretary of State Hull rebuked him severely. "Shocked" by the State Department protest, Kirchwey called for Hull's resignation and wondered if President Roosevelt had had knowledge of the protest: "If the President knew, then the very principle of freedom has been betrayed by its most respected and powerful defender." She concluded that Roosevelt did not know and that the State Department had acted on its own. The *Nation* telegraphed words of sup-

port to Muselier: YOU AND THE FREE FRENCH FORCES AND THE
PEOPLE OF ST. PIERRE AND MIQUELON HAVE THE UNQUALI-
FIED SUPPORT OF ALL PATRIOTIC AMERICANS WHO FEEL
NOTHING BUT SHAME AT THEIR GOVERNMENT'S BETRAYAL OF
OUR COMMON CAUSE. And she printed Muselier's response: I
KNEW IT WAS NOT POSSIBLE THAT THE NOBLE AMERICAN NA-
TION WOULD NOT BE WHOLEHEARTEDLY WITH US IN THE
CAUSE OF LIBERTY AND IN THE SACRED RIGHT OF PEOPLES TO
SELF-DETERMINATION.[49] Readers' response ranged from calling
the *Nation*'s treatment of the incident, "a most gratifying bit of jour-
nalism," to "ungenerous and unwise at a time when we are trying so
hard to unite all of the many forces that must be united if we are to
win this war."[50]

Also in 1946 the eleven-month-long Nuremberg trial meted out
justice to Nazis who had committed crimes against humanity.
Kirchwey wished that the German people "through revolution"
could "have purged itself of the poison of fascist tyranny." To be
meaningful, "'denazification' must come from inside." But the Allied powers chose to set up an International Military Tribunal to try
the war criminals. Kirchwey considered the Nuremberg trials "outside the law," but she felt that some good had come from them: the
evidence proved that "the Nazi regime . . . was as unprecedentedly
evil as the world knew it to be." The testimony of concentration
camp survivors was "an unforgettable lesson in the meaning of terror." Even the "quite unjustified acquittals" did not take away the
good of setting a precedent for defining "crimes against humanity"
as violations of international law.[51]

*

According to Kirchwey, the world that survived Nazi war horrors
required U. S. rapprochement with the Soviet Union. The *Nation*'s
position upset not only American conservatives; the then anti-
Stalinist *Partisan Review* bitterly attacked its stand. When it began
publishing in 1934, with William Phillips and Philip Rahv at its
helm, the *Partisan Review* had supported the communist cultural
and political movement. Financial difficulties led to its collapse in
1936, and when it was reorganized in 1937, Phillips and Rahv, joined
by Fred Dupee and Dwight Macdonald, challenged the Popular
Front position. For many years the *Partisan Review* had taken an
opposing stand to the *Nation* where communism and the USSR

were concerned. In 1946, outraged by events in Eastern Europe, it accused the *Nation,* along with the *New Republic* and *PM,* of being a "'Liberal' Fifth Column."[52]

This attack was aimed at the "totalitarian liberal."[53] Recalling the liberals of 1946, when he joined the *Partisan Review* as editor, William Barrett wrote: "The love affair between American liberals and the Soviet Union had gone through varying fortunes from the 1930s to the end of World War II." Part of Barrett's education had been gained from *Partisan Review* editor Philip Rahv as he attacked liberals for encouraging an aggressive Soviet policy; he quotes Rahv: "Those goddam Liberals . . . they'll end by giving away the whole of Western Europe to Stalin. He won't even have to push for it, they'll make a present of it to him."[54] Rahv and Phillips considered the liberal-backed appeasement policy toward the Soviet Union dangerous. With no previous experience in political polemics, Barrett wrote an editorial, "The 'Liberal' Fifth Column." It was unsigned, which signified the concurrence of the journal editors as a whole.

The editorial referred to liberals as the "foci" of an "infection": "a powerfully vocal lobby willing to override all concerns of international democracy and decency in the interests of a foreign power." To characterize them as "Fifth Column" advocates of the Soviet Union, Barrett divided them into three categories: "international revolutionary," "patriot," and "Fifth Column." International revolutionaries would support some higher principle over their own government. The *Nation,* the *New Republic,* and *PM* did not support any coherent ideology like "international socialism," so they were not international revolutionaries. If they were patriots, they would support the U.S. government, "however imperfect or circumscribed." Because the three publications did not give such unqualified support, they were not patriots. A "Fifth Column" may "persistently override the interests of the government under which you live for the sake of some foreign government from no general principle except that . . . well, you are for that foreign government." Since the liberals did not fit into the first two categories, the *Partisan Review* argued that they belonged in the "Fifth Column." As Barrett later reminded 1980s readers, the phrase had a more ominous ring in 1946, when it evoked memories of Franco's boast that he would conquer Madrid with the help of a fifth column inside the citadel.[55] The pro-Soviet position of American liberals made them an American version of a fifth column. The three journals attacked the British Foreign Ministry and the United States State Department, but they were uncritical of the Soviets. When Ralph Ingersoll of *PM* wrote, "We must be neither for nor against Russia, but we must try to understand her," Barrett retorted sarcastically that such illogic could have been used about Hitler's Germany.[56] Although this "virtual Fifth Column" was not "officially designated and paid by" the Soviet Union, it contributed to the success of Stalinist plans.

Years later Barrett "reread the piece with some embarrassment, aghast at how strident it is," and historian Richard Pells recently explained that *"Partisan Review*'s hysteria might be excused as a reflection of the growing tension all writers felt over the Cold War." But to the editors of the *Partisan Review* and to others who became increasingly anticommunist, no compromise was possible with the totalitarianism of the Soviet Union. It had to be fought with the same kind of diligence used to fight fascism during World War II. Agreeing with Hannah Arendt's thesis in *The Origins of Totalitarianism,* they saw no qualitative difference between Soviet totalitarianism and German fascism.[57]

The crux of the difference between Freda Kirchwey and a growing number of anticommunist liberals stemmed from their crucially different assessments of Soviet communism and German fascism—of Stalin and the Soviet Union, on the one hand, and Hitler and Germany, on the other. While some liberals grew more convinced that Soviet totalitarianism was as grave a threat as fascism, Kirchwey grew more adamant that those who saw the two as the same phenomenon were wrong. No matter how authoritarian Stalin's regime became, Kirchwey did not see him as another Hitler. Despite the fact that Stalin eventually had abandoned the Loyalists, she continued to remember his support during the dark days of the Spanish Civil War—although the memory of the Nazi-Soviet Pact tempered her sympathy. In the postwar decade Kirchwey held to her view of a world divided into fascists and antifascists, and despite many imperfections, to her the Soviet Union was antifascist.

In the 1940s and 1950s, as Americans reevaluated their opinions about the Soviet Union and the Communist Party, many felt Kirchwey's support of the Soviet Union was wrong. Her critics came from various sides of the political spectrum, as fierce divisions among radicals and liberals surfaced. Sidney Hook, in a 1947 *Partisan Review* symposium about the future of socialism, wrote: "democracy can best be *defended* against the danger of totalitarianism by socialist measures. But I do not believe that these relationships can be made credible to those who confuse socialism with Stalinism."[58] Arthur Schlesinger, Jr., who moved to the right as he attempted to protect New Deal reforms, lashed out in a militant anti-communist *Life* article in which he bemoaned the Communist Party's effect of dividing the "non-Communist left." A new magazine, *Commentary,* emerged, with its editor, Elliot Cohen, promising "a reaffirmation of 'our possibilities in America.'"[59] Most liberals shared an increasingly critical view of the Soviet Union. Kirchwey remained where she had been during World War II.

Tied to criticism of her position was the serious charge that her pro-Soviet stand was the result of inordinate influence by *Nation* foreign editor, Julio Alvarez del Vayo.[60] Anticommunist writer and editor Benjamin Stolberg considered Del Vayo "a Comintern agent," who exercised an onerous influence on Freda Kirchwey, "a prisoner of the Communist point of view."[61]

These conclusions were unfounded, although Del Vayo and Kirchwey did make many sympathetic assessments of the Soviet Union for the *Nation.* What rankled anticommunist liberals even more was their criticism of American policies. That dismay still continues, and in 1982 historian William O'Neill wrote: "*The Nation* went on believing that however deplorable Soviet policy might be, America's was worse."[62] Not sharing their fear of Soviet strength, Kirchwey encouraged Americans to understand the Soviet Union. Her voice was one of many in a ceaseless debate among liberals on the role of Soviet-American relations and of the real or false threat of communism.

*

The debate took place during a postwar period of major reevaluation. Predictably Kirchwey and the Nation Associates held a conference in September 1946 to examine The Challenge of the Post-War World to the Liberal Movement. What was not known was the publicity the conference received after one of its key speakers, Henry Wallace, resigned from his cabinet post as Secretary of Commerce. Speaking out against growing right-wing tendencies in the Democratic Party, Wallace "converted the conference of The Nation Associates into a political convention of the independent progressive forces of the [West] Coast." But other viewpoints were expressed there. Harry Girvetz of the University of Santa Barbara deplored the move to the right and urged liberals to create a new organization, which would seek reforms but disavow communism, without making "the mistake of identifying communism with fascism." Kirchwey labeled his as the "right liberal" position.[63]

Communism must be reckoned with, said Girvetz, and organized labor did its share of coping with the threat of "communist penetration" in their organizations. At the eighth annual convention of the Congress of Industrial Organizations (CIO) its president, Philip Murray, put together a group of six (three holding procommunist and three, anticommunist positions), to work out a compromise for the organization's policy toward communism. To avoid a likely floor fight and a more devastating policy, the left-wingers agreed to a basically anticommunist compromise which promised to: "resent and reject efforts of the Communist Party or any other parties and their adherents in the affairs of the C.I.O."[64]

Increasingly the issue of communism divided liberals. In his memoirs, Norman Podhoretz, later to become editor of *Commentary,* discussed the development of anticommunism among his contemporaries: "Whether they became conservatives, socialists, or liberals, their ruling passion tended to be a hatred of Communism and a suspicion of Communists. Having been Communists themselves, or having seen and dealt with Communists at close range, they had all come away from the experience with the conviction that Communism was a great evil—as great an evil as Nazism and possibly even greater."[65]

Cold War tensions mounted, and the political climate in the United States became increasingly conservative. Such an overwhelming number of conservatives won congressional victories in 1946 that liberals reevaluated their stands and began to formulate appeals to the public to combat the conservative avalanche. Kirchwey considered the period an opportunity for the revitalization of liberals: "The Roosevelt era died bit by bit. Now that it has been officially interred, despite the nominal survival of Truman, progressives are free to abandon both pretense and illusions and get to work laying the foundation for a new beginning."[66] Within months of the congressional elections, in which many conservatives had won by charging their opponents with procommunist sympathies, two organizations were formed to lobby and educate the public: the Progressive Citizens of America (PCA) and Americans for Democratic Action (ADA).[67] At the very time they most needed to unite, liberals divided. The question that divided them was: What will we do with communists? *New Republic* journalist Helen Fuller agreed with Kirchwey: "The immediate result of the latest conferences held by liberal groups is to emphasize the differences between them—and this is at a time when unity among liberals is desperately needed."[68]

PCA and ADA each had its own prescription, which stemmed from profoundly different assessments about the Soviet Union and communism. PCA, founded 29 December 1946, combined those in the former National Citizens Political Action Committee (NCPAC) and the Independent Citizens Committee of the Arts, Sciences, and Professions (ICCASP). Many in PCA disapproved of Truman's foreign policy, regarding it as unnecessarily belligerent; they did not view the Soviet Union as intrinsically expansive, but believed it expanded in the interest of national defense. They were bitterly critical of Truman's treatment of Henry Wallace; many of them looked to Wallace as a leader of a future third party, with PCA as its nucleus. PCA's policy allowed anyone, including communists, to join. Leadership included the former chair of ICCASP, sculptor Jo Davidson; former head of UDA, Frank Kingdon; former national director of ICCASP, theatrical agent Hannah Dorner; former head of the Farm Security Administration in the New Deal, Calvin B. ("Beanie") Baldwin; author Bartley Crum; and, for a time, CIO president Philip Murray.[69]

ADA was created in January 1947, by members of the Union for Democratic Action (UDA), some of whom had broken away from the Socialist Party in 1941 to advocate American intervention in World War II. Almost bankrupt, UDA announced a conference and a fund-raising dinner to pay off its debts. Economist John Kenneth Galbraith, former Office of Price Administration chairman Leon Henderson, head of the United Auto Workers (UAW) Walter Reuther, *Nation* associate editor Robert Bendiner, Reinhold Niebuhr, and Eleanor Roosevelt were a few of the representatives of labor, politics, and journalism in attendance. At this January 1947 conference UDA dissolved, and ADA was formed.[70] Basically the group wanted to keep a liberal movement intact against the growing conservative trend in the United States, and it wanted to increase commitment to the welfare state. Like the UDA, it wanted no communist affiliation: "We reject any association with Communists or sympathizers with communism in the United States as completely as we reject any association with Fascists or their sympathizers."[71]

Arthur Schlesinger, Jr., drafted a very strong anti-Soviet statement of principles for consideration. James Loeb, Jr., onetime Socialist and former UDA executive secretary, as secretary of ADA's organizing committee, bemoaned the press's publicity of a "'split' in liberal ranks." Yet in his disclaimer, he reinforced the firm anticommunist position of the ADA which made any alliance with PCA impossible: "We believe millions of Americans want to identify themselves with a movement dedicated to liberty, tolerance and justice that recognizes liberalism as a positive and militant credo and that instinctively and wholeheartedly rebels against suppression and terrorism in any form or any disguise."[72]

Freda Kirchwey had been on the board of directors of UDA, but in this controversy she refused to take sides. Playing down their differences, she criticized the two separate liberal organizations. Why couldn't PCA and ADA lambaste the conservatives, "under one name—and one overhead?" As so often in the past, she urged progressives to unite against the common enemy. The separation into ADA and PCA seemed to her "as unnecessary as it is unfortunate."[73] Yet when the same tension between liberals surfaced in the *Nation,* she published the differing views. Robert Bendiner wrote praising ADA membership policies that excluded Communists. The exclusion was warranted:

> The police state, both Communist and fascist, is a slave state. A slave may have his preference of masters, but the question of choice is a strange preoccupation for men determined to keep their freedom.
>
> The A.D.A. unequivocally rejects this choice, and in so doing it brings to an end a shoddy era in the history of American progressivism.

He saw ADA as the hope for American liberals because it "rejected utterly the choice of totalitarian extremes."[74]

Freda Kirchwey published a very different view from that of her associate editor, insinuating that his outlook represented that of a tiny part of ADA's membership. The issue of communism that divided PCA and ADA was exacerbated, she felt, by a minority within each organization; communist-sympathizers in PCA were few in number, and only a fraction of ADA members equated communism with fascism. She wanted these minority groups "eliminated," for they "prefer factional infighting in support of their own interests to common action." She hoped that talks among the majority of PCA and ADA would reach some "union—or at the very least a method of liaison."[75] The *Nation* should not take a stand but should build a bridge between the two organizations and "work to strengthen the anti-factionalists in them."[76] But at a meeting at her home intended to achieve this, the outcome was bleak. Fierce differences about communism divided them so much that one who was there wrote: "There was some clarification of position, but almost no hope that these two groups can or will ever get together."[77]

*

The extreme difference in viewpoint between Kirchwey and Bendiner was a common occurrence on the *Nation,* which had to deal with these ideological differences in the journal itself. Responding to one of the many letters about this particular PCA-ADA split, Kirchwey wrote: "I think the *Nation* is the place to thrash out the whole situation confronting liberals today."[78] Quite often a sympathetic portrayal of the Soviet Union in the front of the journal (the editorial section) was counterbalanced by an anti-Soviet book review in the back (the literary section). By the 1940s Margaret Marshall, the literary editor and a former Soviet enthusiast, had become increasingly disillusioned with that country. Her disillusionment found expression in the book reviews she selected. As Diana Trilling said, defining the opponents of "the anti-anti-communist spirit": "*Partisan Review, Commentary,* the back pages of the *Nation* were the most impressive of the journals of leftwing intellectual anti-communism."[79] Kirchwey sometimes printed Marshall's anticommunist views in the front as well,[80] and she always gave her authority for the back of the journal. Marshall once said: "She never interfered with my conduct of the book section, though she was certainly unhappy about many reviews and articles that appeared in it—including many of my own."[81]

Marshall's absolute responsibility for the literary section continues to be the subject of controversy. William Phillips insists in his memoirs that Kirchwey controlled the back of the journal: "Margaret Marshall denied taking orders from above or telling Rahv and me that as Trotskyites we were not welcome at *The Nation,* but we know that memory is often at the service of one's guilt." Yet many others concur with Margaret Marshall's memory of absolute independence in the selection of reviewers. Trilling, fiction reviewer for the *Nation* from 1941 to 1949, recalls how extraordinary it was to have such a remarkably different front and back of the journal. Although extremely critical of Kirchwey's last years of editing, Trilling credits her with "a principled stand" during the years of Marshall's literary editorship. Bendiner also said she "endured the dual magazine" for a long time and that this was extraordinary.[82]

As the Cold War tension increased, so did tension between the front and the back of the *Nation*. Quite probably Kirchwey saw it as a healthy sign, reflecting an open forum of ideas. Only occasionally did she find it necessary to convey dismay. One of those times she wrote a vigorous rebuttal to a review by Arthur Schlesinger, Jr., of former Trotskyist James Burnham's book, *The Struggle for the World*.[83] Burnham's book argued that the Soviets and the Americans were pitted against each other in a struggle to establish a "universal empire" and that the imminent danger of Soviet world domination required the United States to adopt stringent anticommunist policies. Schlesinger's favorable review was qualified; considering Burnham's virulent anti-Sovietism, he commented, "one is glad he is not Secretary of State." Yet, Schlesinger contributed to the continuing tension among liberals over the issue of communism. He anticipated some liberals' criticism of Burnham for not contributing to "Anglo-American-Soviet-unity" and argued against their position and for the necessity of Burnham's attack on the USSR. Schlesinger considered communism and fascism so similar as to require the same treatment, and he criticized those liberals who did not agree with him. "Arguments considered beneath contempt when urged by conservatives against the foes of Nazi totalitarianism are now trotted out occasionally by liberals against the foes of Soviet totalitarianism. The arguments do not improve with age and use."[84]

Kirchwey deplored Schlesinger's analysis. She was surprised that an avowed liberal could write such a sympathetic review of a book "destined to become the bible of the 'Bomb Russia First' boys" and concerned lest the book and Schlesinger's review increase fear of the Soviet Union. "Liberals Beware!" she warned; such fear of the Soviet Union could foster an awesome ideology. "In other countries, when fear of Russia sent liberals scurrying toward the campfires of the militant right, the final result was something worse than communism."[85]

Schlesinger was a cofounder of ADA, but Kirchwey criticized him as a person, saying that she hoped his distrust of the Soviets and acceptance of Burnham was his own individual response and not representative of the majority of liberal thinking. Her strategy was to underplay the widespread acceptance of his kind of liberal thinking and convince undecided liberals to adopt her arguments instead. Nevertheless, she admitted that "an alarming percentage of liberals" tolerated loyalty oaths and investigations by the House Committee on Un-American Activities as "a healthy resistance to communism." President Truman's loyalty program and his new foreign policy, the Truman Doctrine, provided official support for this growing phenomenon. "The threat of communism in this country is insignificant; while the threat of reaction is explicit in the Washington red-hunt and implicit in Mr. Truman's new foreign policy."[86]

*

In March 1947, when Truman announced his massive aid to Greece and Turkey, calling it the "necessity of helping free peoples to maintain their free institutions," Kirchwey labeled his policy, "Manifest Destiny, 1947." Truman had extended the Monroe Doctrine's "hands off" to the whole world, and Kirchwey blasted the doctrine as "a plain declaration of political war against Russia." The *New Republic* also castigated the policy: "Repression, as long as it might represent itself as anti-Comintern, could count on the support of Harry Truman's method for sustaining 'free peoples' everywhere."[87] Kirchwey criticized the Truman Doctrine for setting off a chain reaction: every such American attempt to curtail the spread of communism predictably fed a Soviet reaction to consolidate its power. She described the Soviet Union's inroads in Hungary that year as such "counter-moves" and bemoaned the "mounting political warfare" that continued between the USSR and the West.[88]

Kirchwey found it frustrating that the American government refused to admit "the indigenous character" of revolutions like those in Greece and Turkey. The United States should not continue to aid governments whose people wanted them ousted: "stabilizing an economic system that needs to be routed out and strengthening a government that needs to be overthrown—or at least invited to resign—are not going to provide a lasting substitute for thoroughgoing social change."[89] Democracy could not be preserved where it did not exist; backing reactionary regimes was not the answer. The people of Greece and Turkey have "'had enough'—and more. They want a change. And they will not thank the government that spends billions to prevent it."[90] Poverty and instability made countries receptive to communism. If the United States wanted to prevent communism from spreading, it should create prosperity in poverty-stricken nations. To Kirchwey, socialism was the answer: "It is impossible to doubt that a planned and controlled—that is, a socialist—economy is necessary for the revival of Europe." America must support revolutionary changes: "By a paradox that seems to me a simple fact, peace and prosperity will be more secure in America if we accept the process of revolution in Europe and the East instead of subsidizing resistance to it."[91]

In contrast to the dismay over the Truman Doctrine, liberals, including Kirchwey, praised the Marshall Plan, announced in June of 1947. The economic plan directed "against hunger, poverty, desperation and chaos" was one "all liberals could applaud," said the *New Republic*'s lead editorial. When Secretary of State Marshall told reporters that his program would invite the Soviet Union "and the countries it dominated" to participate, the *Nation* called this "a wise move," despite Kirchwey's suspicion that it was less than sincere. Because the Plan switched "from anti-communism to recovery," the *Nation* praised its relief possibilities and supported its premise—an interdependent world: "If we do not aid Europe to become our partner in prosperity we shall surely find ourselves her partner in misery." Kirchwey supplemented these arguments, saying that the need for the U.S. to devote billions of dollars to help European recovery was "an expression of long-range intelligent self-interest, not of charity."[92]

A Soviet boycott of the Plan left untested its offer to include aid to that country. Kirchwey wrote that the United States now could avoid hypocrisy and openly fight communism in Europe, abandoning "all pretense of general relief and reconstruction." Still, she wanted the Plan to succeed, for aid meant Europe's survival: "American liberals and leftists—Communists apart—cannot possibly advocate a defeat of the Marshall Plan; it is not their stomachs that would go empty."[93]

In April 1948 the $6,098,000,000 budget for the European Recovery Plan (the Marshall Plan) included $425,000,000 for military appropriations. Kirchwey accepted the idea of helping Europe recover and thereby, "incidentally, and almost politely," help it "resist Communist aggression," but she bitterly criticized mixing "guns, goods, dollars" and "the military-political purposes they represent."[94] "What the President has proposed is to change the Marshall Plan into a Truman doctrine for Western Europe by promising to go to the rescue of nations threatened by Communism."[95] The Soviet Union shared the blame because its pressure on Finland (including demands that the Finnish president visit Stalin) created fear of a coup similar to the 1948 coup in Czechoslovakia.[96]

Although the USSR received some blame from Kirchwey for U.S. military aid to Europe, she denounced the United States for contributing to the coup in Czechoslovakia. She recalled 1919, when the West refused aid to Hungarian premier Count Michael Karolyi, who had to relinquish his government to Communist Bela Kun. Although the *Nation* remembered the Soviet Union's March 1948 coup in Czechoslovakia as "the aggressive designs of a foreign tyranny," Kirchwey pointed to faulty American policy which had made that coup easier.[97] Fearful of communism and socialism, the United States had refused to lend money to the Czech regime: "Is this to be the American role whenever the great issue is joined—to weaken or openly fight the democratic forces in each country and so help prepare the way for dictatorship? And then to view the outcome with alarm, and remonstrate, and blame the victim for not making a bold stand?"[98]

Kirchwey failed to mention another crucial fact bearing on the Czech situation: that the Soviet Union had dissuaded its Eastern European bloc countries from taking advantage of the Marshall Plan. In early July 1947 Czech leader Jan Masaryk had accepted an invitation to go to Paris to plan a joint request for American aid under the Marshall Plan. Czech Communist chief Klement Gottwald informed Masaryk that Stalin was surprised by this, since the real aim of the Marshall Plan was to "create a western bloc and isolate the Soviet Union." The Soviet Union "would regard [Czech] participation as a break in the front of the Slav States and as an act specifically aimed against the USSR."[99] In less than a year the communists destroyed Czech democracy and Masaryk was dead under questionable circumstances. Three months later President Eduard Beneš resigned rather than sign a constitution legalizing one-party rule in Czechoslovakia. "He could do nothing to modify communist repressions . . . Like Masaryk's death, Beneš' resignation must be regarded as the final product of a sentence of ill-intentioned or stupid acts permitted by all the great powers over a period of many years," Kirchwey concluded.[100]

*

As an active participant in the Cultural Congress for Peace at Wroclaw, Poland, in August 1948, Freda Kirchwey witnessed the bleak conditions of postwar Europe firsthand. Touring Poland, Czechoslovakia, and Italy after the conference, she wrote of America's failure to comprehend the depth of the war's effects, both the emotional pain and the physical devastation: "Intense feelings & pol. reactions related to war experiences wh. have dug deep into nerves and brain cells of human beings. From distance these effects invisible—or recorded only in ways that do not dig deep into *our* nerves & cells. Put flatly we don't understand how Europe feels even when we've read all the facts." Americans dismiss some of the facts as "unreasonable" or "propaganda," while the Soviet Union accepts "these powerful emotionally-rooted attitudes."[101]

The Congress itself included six hundred delegates from Europe, North and South America, and Asia. Kirchwey described the American delegation, which included a "Far Left," a "Center Left," and a "Further Right." She included herself in the "Center Left," along with sculptor Jo Davidson, former U.S. Assistant Attorney General O. John Rogge, radio producer and writer Norman Corwin, and economist Otto Nathan.[102] The Congress, mostly polemics, provided a forum, which she saw as hope for future forums leading to peace.[103] She viewed this Congress as the political world, "with the right wing amputated," and noted that it was dominated by the communists and their allies.[104] A savage attack on the United States by Soviet novelist Fadayev pushed noncommunist Western delegates to defend or praise American policy. Dismayed by the lack of true discussion, Kirchwey wished that the liberals had organized, but, she lamented: "they were unorganized, impeded by their own doubts, qualifications, and discriminations, as well as by a temperamental dislike of verbal free-for-alls."[105]

Back in the United States, Kirchwey was disturbed by a group of liberals who did organize. The PCA created the Progressive Party and wanted Henry Wallace to serve as their presidential candidate. Kirchwey considered the move ill-advised. She saw important differences between the Democratic and the Republican 1948 platforms on foreign policy, inflation, and labor; despite weaknesses, the Democrats deserved liberal support. "The result of the P.C.A.'s decision, if Henry Wallace agrees to run, can only be to confuse enough progressives to assure a Republican victory without establishing a mass base for a future third-party movement."[106]

The *Nation* had supported third-party candidates in the past; it came out for Robert LaFollette in 1924 and Norman Thomas in 1932. The 1948 election, however, had too much at stake to risk a third-party protest. Calling the PCA's politics "quixotic," the *Nation* caused a stir among its readers. J. W. Gitt, long-time friend and liberal editor of the *Gazette and Daily* (York, Pennsylvania), wrote: "I am still infuriated by the piece in THE NATION a week or two ago in which the Wallace candidacy was referred to as 'Quixotic,' and the smug, sophisticated manner in which it was written. My God, woman, all my life I have been engaged in what some people have called 'Quixotic' endeavors, and, if I may be pardoned for saying so, I fear that you have been too. At least I thought so."[107]

Most *Nation* editors discredited the candidacy of "Wallace, the Incomplete Angler," as Bendiner dubbed him. Kirchwey said that the *Nation,* in the company of "many millions of progressives," would decide "not to 'stand up and be counted' for Henry Wallace." Without the support of labor, his bid for the presidency was "foolish." Furthermore, communists had too much influence upon his candidacy, and she reminded readers that the communists' decisions were "controlled by interests unrelated to the needs and desires of Henry Wallace's 'common man.'"[108] Despite Del Vayo's firm support of the Wallace candidacy, Freda Kirchwey stuck to her original decision.[109] She urged Wallace to withdraw from the race and use his influence "to help remake Democratic policy," and, when that did not happen, her *Nation* editorial refused to endorse anyone: "This is a year where independents would be happier if they could vote against rather than for the candidates."[110]

The *New Republic* supported Harry S Truman. Its policies from this time diverged from those of the *Nation*. In a relatively short time the *New Republic* and its publisher, Michael Straight, had traveled a long political journey. It was Michael Straight who had recruited Henry Wallace to be editor of the *New Republic* in September, 1946, just one week after Truman forced Wallace to resign as Secretary of Commerce. Straight liked Wallace's innovative ideas and hoped his name would increase circulation. The union was brief. In March 1947 Wallace's adviser, Harold Young of Texas, invited Straight to a party at Jo Davidson's house with Wallace, Calvin B. (Beanie) Baldwin, Hannah Dorner, and himself. Young said:

"Mike, you've been keeping Henry to yourself for long enough. We've decided that it's time that he got out and met the people again." Wallace began to travel about the country in opposition to Truman. Straight was confronted by a tough decision: "I had bound *The New Republic* to Henry Wallace. He, in turn, had allowed himself to be bound to the P.C.A. To whom was the P.C.A. bound? I asked myself that question and I feared the answer." When Wallace formally decided to head the Progressive Party, he wrote his last editorial as editor of the *New Republic* (5 January 1948). Straight did not denounce the Progressive Party immediately, but it was only a matter of time before he wrote Wallace of the *New Republic*'s intention to endorse Truman.[111]

"Dewey Defeats Truman" read the *Chicago Tribune*'s premature headline. The outcome of that 1948 election was so uncertain that the *Nation* felt it too close to call and instead published an open letter "To the Victor." The editors urged whoever won to keep "two snarling worlds from literally blasting society to bits" and hoped he would "deal firmly . . . but not belligerently, fairly but not fatuously" with the Soviet Union. Americans did not want war with the Soviet Union, but neither did they want their country to become "an exposed island in a totalitarian sea."[112]

The editorial anticipated the tensions of 1949, which Eric Goldman has called the "Year of Shocks."[113] Although Italy and France rejected communism and northwestern European countries joined the United States and Canada to form the North Atlantic Treaty Organization (NATO) to guard against possible Soviet attacks, it was a jarring year for Americans. Despite extensive American aid, the Nationalist Chinese government fled to Taiwan in August, leaving China to the communists; a month later the Soviet Union exploded its first atomic bomb, ending the Anglo-American monopoly of atomic weapons. Americans also faced the shock of Whittaker Chambers' accusations of Alger Hiss's previous Communist connections. Charges originating at the August HUAC hearings reached a deadlocked jury in July 1949, at the conclusion of the first trial.[114] The hunt for espionage raged on.

The *New Republic* vigorously endorsed Truman's foreign policy. Pells captures the change: "As the *New Republic*'s sense of urgency mounted, so did the harshness of its rhetoric. The journal's characterizations of Soviet policy sounded increasingly indistinguishable from those of James Burnham, Philip Rahv, and George Kennan."[115] In contrast, the *Nation* criticized Truman from the very beginning. First it was his inaugural, full of anticommunism, which stated what would become NATO. Kirchwey labeled it "a new declaration of cold war."[116] The Atlantic Pact worried her. Although it was supposedly in agreement with the United Nations, she interpreted it as a vote of no confidence in that organization: "The pact is a statement that the Western nations, led by the United States, no longer believe that the U.N. can deal with threats to the peace emanating from the Eastern nations, led by Soviet Russia." She also lashed out at the Soviet Union for helping to write the pact, "by threat and denunciation, by ruthlessness and self-righteousness. You can generate a spirit of war even by shouting 'war monger' if you do it loud and often enough!"[117]

Despite her criticism of the Soviet Union, Kirchwey was the target of anticommunist liberals. In 1949 in *The Vital Center,* Arthur Schlesinger, Jr., categorized the *Nation* and the *New Republic* as journals of the progressive, "the fellow traveler or the fellow traveler of the fellow traveler." He qualified his remark in a brief footnote, which admitted that "the *Nation* is now in good part liberated from the Soviet mystique"; nevertheless, he commented on Del Vayo's pro-Sovietism and the "pious genuflections by Miss Kirchwey herself." Using a Civil War term that meant "northern men with southern principles," Schlesinger talked about "doughfaced progressivism"—"democratic men with totalitarian principles." Sentimentality and incurable optimism blinded this "doughfaced progressivism" to the evil of totalitarianism; it became, "if not an accomplice of totalitarianism, at least an accessory before the fact."[118]

The *Nation* reviewed *The Vital Center* quite favorably. The reviewer, Robert Bendiner, was out of step with others on the journal, considering himself, like Schlesinger, an anticommunist liberal. But even Bendiner criticized the author's overstated critique of progressives. Schlesinger made them out as more theoretical and ignorant than they were in fact. He condescendingly berated them for their paucity of knowledge of crucial political realities: "People who had barely heard of Spain in 1934 became world-champion Spanish experts by 1937, though if you asked them what a Carlist was they would have been hard pressed for an answer." These faults, however, were secondary to Schlesinger's "really profound exposition of the fatal lure of totalitarianism."[119] Bendiner agreed that the progressives were being drawn too much toward communism, and that hope lay with anticommunist liberals. To Schlesinger, "The non-communist left has brought what measure of hope there is in our political life today . . . The health of the democratic left requires the unconditional rejection of totalitarianism."[120]

Schlesinger's book, which chided liberals considered to be lax toward communism, gave a name to people who espoused his views; they were the "Vital Center." Bendiner saw that "vital center" as a new alignment of liberals and conservatives who had more in common with each other than the liberal "has with the Communist or than the conservative has with the fascist." He looked toward an alliance against totalitarianism: "The extent to which they present a solid wall to the totalitarians, both Communist and fascist, is the extent to which the 'vital center' will have political validity."[121]

*

In March 1949 the Cultural and Scientific Conference on World Peace met at the Waldorf-Astoria Hotel in New York City. Kirchwey characterized the makeup of the gathering, sponsored by the National Council of the Arts, Sciences, and Professions, as being similar to that of the 1948 Wallace party: "Communists, near-Communists, and assorted liberals who believe peace requires a policy of conciliation with Russia."[122] Not all foreign delegates were able to participate, because they were refused visas. Kirchwey said the U.S. State Department demonstrated "lack of confidence in the capacity of America to survive without damage the brief visit, and not so brief oratory, of a handful of assorted European leftists."[123]

The conference further divided the anticommunist and the anti-anticommunist American liberals. The announcement of a conference on peace resulted in Sidney Hook's offer to deliver a paper entitled "Science and Free Inquiry," to refute "the idea that there are such things as national truths, racial truths or class truths in science." This was a direct challenge to the ideology of the Stalin years in the Soviet Union which argued that truths had class components and must be interpreted by the Communist Party. Hook was surprised that his paper was accepted for the Waldorf conference, since he thought that the sponsors were fellow travelers. His surprise did not last long. When he was not notified of the time for his presentation, he called, only to discover that he was not listed on the program. Protests were to no avail, so Hook decided to collect the remnants of his anticommunist colleagues from the old Committee for Cultural Freedom and others who opposed the Waldorf conference. They met at Dwight MacDonald's house to discuss their positions, form their own organization, and plan a counterconference. MacDonald, Hook, Norman Thomas, Mary McCarthy, Arthur Schlesinger, Jr., Herman J. Muller, George Counts, Bertram D. Wolfe, and others adopted the name American Intellectuals for Freedom (AIF) and arranged an AIF Freedom House Conference. As the historian O'Neill has pointed out, the "remarkably diverse group" was united by a commitment to answer pro-Soviet propaganda.[124]

In many respects the AIF was a rebirth of the Committee for Cultural Freedom of the 1930s. This strongly anticommunist group of intellectuals pressured noncommunist liberals to withdraw from the Waldorf conference, which they later characterized as "an intellectual fraud." Kirchwey criticized the AIF for these actions and for distorting the conference as "a Communist frame-up." She acknowledged that the Waldorf conference was one-sided; it was sympathetic toward the Soviet Union. But it was not controlled by the Soviet Union. The conference lacked the "genuine discussion" of an open forum of more varied views. As far as Kirchwey was concerned, however, the AIF conference fared no better. Their preconference publicity and conference sessions laden with overt hostility toward the Soviets matched the Waldorf conference's equally determined sympathy for the Soviet Union.[125]

Hook did not take Kirchwey's criticisms lightly. "The record of Miss Kirchwey's 'totalitarian liberalism' has been spread on the political pages of *The Nation* during the last ten years for all to see. It has been a record of moral double-dealing." To prove his point, Hook included brief quotes from former *Nation* pieces. Kirchwey published the attack and refuted its charges: "As for my past, I shall try to correct a few of Dr. Hook's distortions and for the rest stand on the record. I did not deny, as Dr. Hook charges, 'that there was any such thing as red totalitarianism' nor did I insist 'that the Communist Party was an integral part of the liberal movement.'" Her final comment holds a curious foreshadowing: "It seems odd that Dr. Hook and his political allies should have wished to appear time after time in a journal which is no longer regarded as an organ of liberal opinion. Odd, too, that an illiberal editor with a ten-year record of 'intellectual and moral double-dealing' would go on printing these people. For the first time I have realized how very odd it is."[126]

Concerning the Waldorf conference itself, Kirchwey charged that Hook had attributed to her more sympathy for it than she actually had; "I disagree with a large part of what I heard there." She doubted his statement that, unlike the Waldorf conference, the American Intellectuals for Freedom were willing to have speakers of differing views participate at their Freedom House conference. That they would have allowed communist participation, she called "wholly disingenuous." Both organizations were clearly partisan. "Why can't Dr. Hook admit the simple, not very shocking or fraudulent fact that when partisan organizations, left, right, or center, hold meetings, they act like partisan organizations, favoring people of their own general point of view and rejecting most of those who detest and oppose them?"[127]

What the country and the world needed in this time of escalating Cold War was an open discussion, Kirchwey felt, so a Nation Associates forum was held later in April. It opened with the question: "Peace. How Can It Be Achieved?" Herbert V. Evatt, foreign minister of Australia; William O. Douglas, U.S. Supreme Court Justice; Moshe Sharett, foreign minister of Israel; Romulo Gallegos, Venezuelan president-in-exile, and Freda Kirchwey addressed that topic. Kirchwey criticized the growing ideological split signaled by the recent conferences: "Many sensible words were spoken but they were almost drowned out by the deafening clash of ideologies."[128]

*

The ideological differences in the Cold War between the United States and the Soviet Union no doubt motivated a change in policy concerning Spain both in the United States and at the United Nations. During the 1940s the Nation Associates fought to keep the issue of fascism in the limelight. "Franco Spain is the unfinished business of the war," stated one of many reports.[129] Page after page of painstakingly documented efforts proved the illegality of the Franco regime and demanded that it be kept isolated. In 1946 the UN banned Spain from specialized agencies and recommended that its member nations recall their diplomatic representatives from that country. However, later in the postwar period, when the USSR remained steadfastly opposed to Spain and fear of communism spread in the United States, friends of Franco repeatedly tried to reverse the UN decision. In the spring of 1949 it seemed likely that they would succeed. The United States, ready to support a move to overturn the 1946 UN decision, was in favor of Brazil's plan to admit Spain to specialized UN agencies and restore ambassadors there.[130]

Kirchwey headlined the disheartening news to liberals, who "believe that concern for a democratic Spain is not the exclusive prerogative of the Communists or the Soviet bloc." She urged them to protest the proposal to admit Spain to the United Nations, for "Peace cannot be built on a rotten alliance with the last remnant of Nazism still in power."[131] The fight continued with letters, telegrams, and memoranda. Kirchwey appealed to the General Assembly of the United Nations to remember the intent of its Declaration of Human Rights and other decisions which protected the kinds of liberties Franco denied. She reminded them that the 1946 resolution barring Franco's Spain, "expressed the moral indignation of the community of nations."[132]

Meanwhile, liberals such as Irving Howe and Diana and Lionel Trilling worried about other countries. They deplored the Soviet Union's consolidation of power into an Eastern European bloc and considered Kirchwey's position on Spain hypocritical. Although she criticized instances of Soviet aggression, she did not conduct a sustained critique of Soviet transgressions.[133] She used a double standard when assessing oppression; she did not apply the same criteria to the Soviet Union's movement through Eastern Europe as she did to Franco's continuing suppression of Republicans in Spain.

Liberals like Malcolm Cowley had minimized some of the Soviet Union's wrongdoings during World War II because of the necessity to fight against only one enemy at a time; during the postwar era, however, they turned against the USSR. Unlike them, Kirchwey had never seen the Soviet Union as the lesser of two evils. She felt that it was committed to the ultimate improvement of the quality of life of its people, and she saw its opposition to the Franco regime as proof of the Soviet Union's good intentions. George Orwell, on the other hand, had seen the Soviet stand on Spain as strategic rather than principled.[134]

By 1950 Kirchwey's dream of a free Spain suffered a bitter defeat. Benjamin Cohen of the American delegation to the United Nations informed her of the vote to admit Spain to specialized agencies in the UN and to send a U.S. ambassador to Madrid. Kirchwey voiced her anguish at the decision, which she considered "a defeat for the

morality and integrity of the United States and the United Nations."
She would never accept Franco as a legitimate leader and continued
the battle to restore Republican Spain.[135]

*

In the spring of 1946 Kirchwey stopped in France en route to
Palestine, a place she had always wanted to visit. Evans Clark was
angered to hear that her first night's sleep in Paris was interrupted
by a call from Nation Associates director, Lillie Shultz. "You can't
escape her even across the ocean can you? But I'm sure it was *very
important*."[136] The lives of the Kirchwey-Clarks had changed dras-
tically since 1930, when Evans had poured his grief over the loss of
Jeffrey into his work, and Freda retreated from hers. Now Evans
wrote that his life held "nothing of any special interest . . . which is
so different from your life, dear one."[137] He found their apartment
"dismally empty" without her, but "at least there aren't Kings [Gor-
don], and Lillies [Shultz] and Diegos [del Vayo] and Izzies [Stone]
endlessly on the phone or right here in our midst . . . How you can
take so much of it and them I can't see."[138] He missed his "distant
darling": "Sometimes I wish I weren't so damned attached to you
when you're off on these long jaunts and life seems so sort of trun-
cated . . . but I spose the rawness of the feeling will eventually wear
off."[139] On other occasions, however, Evans' work took him away.
Once Freda wrote to him in Brazil: "Life seems very unnatural with
you away—and so endlessly far away—especially in its more lei-
surely hours."[140] But Evans considered that, for the most part, it
was Freda's immersion in the *Nation* that took the greatest toll, at
least on him:

> I've put in many hours since you left pondering on our life to-
> gether these past few years . . . especially your hectic part in it and
> its effects on me. Some day I'm going to write a long letter about
> it . . . so much of it has been bad for both of us, although you've
> so far, stood it better . . . I love you so deeply and dearly my
> darling one, that it's hard to be objective, especially when you're
> near me.[141]

*

Freda set out for Palestine that spring as the *Nation*'s correspondent. Adding to the pleasure of the trip was a rendezvous with her
son Michael, on terminal leave from the French army. The *Zam Zam*
incident had not prevented his return to the war as an American
Field Service ambulance volunteer driver. Then, in 1943, he joined

the Free French forces, signing on for the duration of the war plus six months. When Kirchwey decided to visit the Middle East, Michael was free to travel with her.

After spending a few days in Cairo, the two continued on to Palestine.[142] During their stay they visited the Hebrew University in Palestine, the offices of the *Palestine Post,* the Dead Sea, Haifa, and a memorial to five boys killed by the Arabs. Kirchwey was impressed by the "incredible job of reclaiming bare rocky hillside." In Tel Aviv she had a good talk with Goldie Meyersohn—later Golda Meir— head of the political department of the Histadrut (Jewish Federation of Labor). She lunched at Rehovoth with Chaim Weizmann, her friend of many years. His beautiful estate overlooked fields and orchards that had been barren before he came to Palestine. Back in Jerusalem, she interviewed Arab leader Aouni Bey Abdul Hadi, whom she described as "fiery, perhaps honest, extremist." An interview with another Arab leader left her still unconvinced of the Arab side. Dr. Husseini Khalidi, former mayor of Jerusalem, "very calm, able, smooth, effective in argument," showed her transcripts of 1939 testimony which proved the British had pledged Arab control over immigration after five years. Kirchwey, unimpressed, reminded him that Britain had broken promises to both sides. Michael Clark remembers that she listened understandingly to Khalidi's eloquent arguments; but it was as if she did not hear him. Her mind was already made up: she was committed to a homeland for the Jews.[143] What really impressed her that day was the marvel of Hadassah Hospital. As she remarked, "Reading is no substitute for seeing." A declared boycott did nothing to dissuade sick Arabs from coming to the hospital, and Kirchwey saw "corridors jammed with Arabs . . . terrible ward of malnourished babies, mostly Arab." British troops and weapons were everywhere in Palestine; "the country is a camp." She was impressed with the way the Jews handled this tense military atmosphere: "How the Jews live and work with such an air of calm confidence I can't imagine. Their temper seems one of mingled courage and fatalism. This, clearly, is their last stop."

Freda Kirchwey was treated like a celebrity. A "former Oxford don," Walter Ettinghausen, and other Jewish Agency people, escorted her. Because she was on a working trip, most days ended at 2 A.M.[144] After the evening meal and lots of conversation, she would go back to her hotel room and work on documents or talk with her contacts until the small hours of the morning. One Saturday Michael and Ettinghausen decided to rest. Freda took a day-long car trip to view some agricultural settlements in the Emek region. Her careful notes record a visit to Ein Hashofed, a kibbutz founded by Americans, which boasted "40 *Nation* readers!"[145]

On her return to Cairo, Kirchwey wrote of the plight of 100,000 Jewish refugees from Europe with no place to go after British Foreign Secretary Ernest Bevin refused to allow them to enter Palestine. She reported Bevin's charge that the United States wanted Britain to open Palestine to 100,000 Jews because "they do not want too many of them in New York." He also suggested that admitting so many Jews would necessitate more British troops in the area. Kirchwey retorted that five weeks of interviews with people of diverse opinions convinced her of Bevin's errors. The problem lay with the British government's "stalling and hedging" and all but openly encouraging an Arab revolt.[146] Her articles reached more than *Nation* readers. Eleanor Roosevelt highlighted an editorial in her nationally syndicated column. In "Crisis for the Jews," she reiterated Kirchwey's plea for resettlement of the 100,000 refugees.[147]

Firsthand reporting in Palestine left Kirchwey even more firmly convinced that the Jews could teach "a lesson in cooperative democracy planning . . . a lesson not for the Jewish people alone, but for the world."[148] She hoped a democratic Jewish state would create stability in the Middle East: "The issue is not simply justice for the Jews, but that justice for the Jews means peace in the Middle East and a more democratic development in that whole area."[149] "I am no mystic, but I must say that the agricultural settlements in Palestine create an atmosphere that is different in its very essence from the atmosphere of a farm community in America: common effort, common faith, and the common fruits of both, give rise to something unique in present-day experience."[150] A homeland for the Jews took precedence over the lessons Palestine could teach. During World War II the *Nation* had painted the stark choice for Jewish refugees: Palestine or death.[151] Kirchwey was frustrated by the opposition to a Jewish homeland: "I am constantly impressed by the collapse of sympathy and the failure of imagination that occur when human beings are not somehow *directly* involved in a tragedy."[152] Filled with the horror of what those refugees had lived through, she demanded land in Palestine to heal them: "Only the combination of sun and open air; of communal living and mutual help and responsibility; of creating and building can wipe out the effects of long years of suffering and mental and physical torture."[153]

Kirchwey fueled the battle for a Jewish homeland with speeches, Nation Associates' studies, and *Nation* articles. In fact the journal was criticized for its overriding coverage of the struggle for a Jewish Palestine at the expense of other news. To Kirchwey, however, special interest in the issue merited the stress, and she continued to keep the Palestine issue alive.

She wanted her son to write an article on Lebanon and the Palestine question. Michael Clark had contributed occasional articles to the *Nation* from France. In one he explained the problems the French were having in Indochina, especially with the Vietnamese. His pro-French explanation of a bloody attack at Hanoi in December 1946 triggered his mother's response. Although she considered his piece "an excellent and able job," it was "a *bit* over-patriotic" for her taste, and she was troubled by Clark's conclusion that negotiations had reached a stalemate with the disappearance of Vietnamese president Ho Chi Minh. "I am temperamentally in need of a solution! You pose the dilemma extremely well, but I can hardly make myself accept the conclusion that no way out exists except continued dismal fighting until some other opportunity of compromise presents itself."[154] She hoped Michael would come home for a visit so she could talk with him about the Indochina situation and Palestine.[155]

That fall Kirchwey suffered a breach between her journal and one of her staunchest allies, Eleanor Roosevelt. In yet another of her extreme moves in support of the establishment of Israel, she let stand some strong words in invitations to a major Nation Associates dinner symposium on Palestine: "There is a gigantic double cross in the offing at the U.N. Our own government seems scheduled to play a stellar role. President Truman is reported as capitulating to the Arabs."[156] Furious, Mrs. Roosevelt refused to attend the dinner and resigned from the Nation Associates, asking that her name be removed from its letterhead. To Kirchwey she explained, "As a representative of the United States government I do not feel I can be affiliated with any group which does such irresponsible things."[157] Kirchwey, "perturbed," wrote that the *Nation* people who sent the letter quite honestly had forgotten Roosevelt's "relationship to the American delegation." Mrs. Roosevelt should have regarded that forgetfulness as a compliment, since at the *Nation* they regarded her as "so much more" than part of a U.S. delegation. Kirchwey defended the attack on President Truman, for "good sources from Washington" said he was going to "yield to the Arabs."[158]

Undaunted, Kirchwey continued pressure to gain support. Her *Nation* pieces often repeated or summarized Associates' studies that were submitted to U.S. government and UN officials. From 1947 to 1954 twelve such publications dealt with the Middle East. Several documented the collaboration between the Nazis and Muhammad Amin Al-Husayni, Mufti of Jerusalem and head of the Arab Higher Committee.[159] Kirchwey made this exposure a major issue. When the *Saturday Evening Post* published an analysis by Kermit Roosevelt defending the Mufti, she wrote a lengthy rebuttal. Roosevelt could have a different point of view about partition, but not about the Mufti: "that there should be two opinions concerning the role of the Mufti in World War II is not tenable." Kirchwey traced the history of the close connection between Hitler and the Mufti and recounted that the Nation Associates had documented the alliance of the Mufti and the Axis powers in a memorandum submitted to the UN as early as May 1947.[160] She documented that Nazi money had financed the Mufti's riots against Jewish Palestine in 1936. German files captured after the war recorded, "only through funds made available by Germany to the Grand Mufti of Jerusalem was it possible to carry out the revolt in Palestine." She noted that the Nazis made the following declaration to the Mufti on 2 November 1943: "that the destruction of the so-called Jewish National Home in Palestine is an immutable part of the policy of the greater German Reich." Page after page documented the collusion between the Mufti and the Axis powers. The Nation Associates' documentation of this link back in 1947 must have had an important influence on the outcome of partition. Historian Abram Leon Sachar points out that pro-Axis dealing had much to do with reversing the White Paper, which had discarded the British mandate and proposed a future independent, primarily Arab, Palestine, with a fixed Jewish population: "Ultimately, however, it was not merely the Jewish war effort, but the pro-Axis record of the Arab states which provided the Zionists with their most telling argument against the White Paper."[161]

As a non-Jewish supporter of a Jewish cause, Freda Kirchwey could reach a broader audience. Furthermore, she had important contacts: "We were familiar with both the American and international scenes and had the necessary influential contacts in both. I mean that literally. These were contacts that permitted us to call an outstanding official in Washington or a Prime Minister on the Pacific Ocean, at one in the morning if necessary."[162] In May, just after Truman's de facto recognition of the state of Israel, Kirchwey wrote that pressure from the *Nation* had had an impact on the decision: Truman "has learned a great deal in recent weeks about British maneuvers in Palestine against partition (the documents published by *The Nation* two weeks ago are known to have opened the eyes of several important Administration officials)."[163]

*

While Freda Kirchwey claimed influence and victory in the Middle East, she had no cause for celebration back in the United States. She was dealing with the ramifications of publishing a series of articles that harshly criticized the Catholic Church. Its author, Paul Blanshard, pointed out that theology had become involved with medicine. "May a Catholic Nurse summon a Non-Catholic Minister?" "May Circumcision by a Jewish Rabbi Be Done in a Catholic Hospital?" What place have questions like these in magazines for priests? Blanshard scathingly attacked the Catholic sexual code by pointing out the severity of the doctrine. The scenario of the rape of a Catholic girl would allow her to "remove the male sperm by mechanical means within the first ten hours and still remain a good Catholic, but she may not, married or unmarried, perform a similar act under any other circumstances without definite risk of hell."[164]

Next he criticized Catholic schools. Since Americans accepted private Catholic schools as substitutes for public education, citizens had a right to ask whether they "teach responsible freedom? Do they teach tolerance and national solidarity?" Blanshard claimed they did not, and he documented poor quality parochial education, lack of intellectual freedom, and efforts to censor education. "The Roman Catholic hierarchy . . . claims the right to censor all general education and to effect this object encourages Catholics to control local boards of education where possible and to place Catholics in key positions as teachers and officials in the public school system."[165]

As soon as the *Nation* published his articles, it felt the influence of the Catholic Church. Readers complained that they were unable to buy the journal at their usual newsstands; many subscribers complained that these particular issues did not arrive in their mailboxes. Kirchwey charged censorship.[166] The superintendent of the New Jersey schools banned the *Nation* from the local high school libraries because of its "virulent, anti-Catholic articles attacking the fundamental religious principles of the Catholic Church in the areas of marriage, birth control and the family."[167]

Such censorship impelled Blanshard to write and the *Nation* to publish yet another set of articles on the Catholic Church.[168] New Jersey's action and the second series of articles pushed the New York Board of Superintendents to ban the *Nation* from the New York City school libraries as of 8 June 1948. This was a serious blow for civil liberties, since "New York is after all a city where civil rights and a lively clash of opinions are old habits."[169] Kirchwey, the perennial optimist, wrote: "*The Nation* will be shut out of the public schools as of July 1, but I dare predict that when they reopen on September 13, it will be back again. Its banning will not be tolerated by the liberal and free-minded citizens of New York."[170] Her estimate was sadly off. It would take until January 1963 to lift the ban, despite actions of many "free-minded citizens of New York" and other states.[171] The fight to reinstate the *Nation* gathered force, as prominent individuals and publishing houses formed an Ad Hoc Committee to Lift the Ban on the *Nation* and demanded a public hearing on censorship.[172]

Henry Steele Commager, Max Lerner, Thomas Mann, Reinhold Niebuhr, Stephen S. Wise, Dorothy Kenyon, and Eleanor Roosevelt are only a few of the people who signed a long statement demanding the end to the censorship. They titled their document, "An Appeal to Reason and Conscience, In Defense of the Right of Freedom of Inquiry in the United States." Published in the October 1948 issue of the *Nation,* it concluded:

> To bar from the schools of New York future issues of one of the country's leading periodicals with a history of responsible journalism since 1865 because a past issue or issues contained paragraphs which one of the many groups which compose this country found objectionable seems to us a violation of the most fundamental principles of American equality. We believe the wrong should be righted at once, not so much in the interest of *The Nation* as in the interest of the people of the United States.[173]

Kirchwey, typically respecting the value of the open forum, printed both sides of the arguments. William Jansen, superintendent of

New York's schools, presented the school board arguments. Supporters of the Appeal addressed his points. Niebuhr challenged the board's principle of allowing "criticism of the public policies of churches but not of religion itself," calling the distinction, "a dangerous one, which has no validity in our American tradition." Albert Einstein opposed the ban: "Young people should have the opportunity to read everything which could help them to form an independent judgment." Virginia Gildersleeve, retired dean of Barnard College, warned: "Even though some of the articles might be obnoxious to Catholics, the total exclusion from our public schools of such a long-established and widely respected periodical . . . sets a dangerous precedent."[174]

Court battles began. In 1949 Kirchwey appealed to her lawyer to absorb some of their costly expenses. "While I do not want to impose too much on your own interest in the public aspects of the case, it is painfully clear that we cannot hope to recompense you on anything like a normal professional basis." By 1950 she acknowledged the tenacity of the forces which continued to keep the *Nation* banned. At the risk of beginning "a religious cold war," she decided to attack clericalism directly, accusing it of "arbitrary influence." The reluctance of liberals to attack any religious group for fear of "infringements on the liberty of any faith" had protected the Roman Catholic Church's pressure groups. Kirchwey documented its censorship in the New York City public school system.[175]

Of her allies and their purpose she stated:

> The Ad Hoc Committee is made up of an impressive collection of educators, ministers, librarians, writers associations, a group which has insisted that the decision against The Nation must be fought, and if possible reversed as arbitrary, and unconstitutional—apart from its concrete effect as a precedent for exercising thought-control throughout the country.
>
> If the decision stands a precedent will be set that threatens freedom of expression everywhere.[176]

8 ‖ *"The Last Battle"*

"I have here in my hand a list of two-hundred and five that were known to the Secretary of State as being members of the Communist Party and who are still working and shaping the policy of the State Department," proclaimed Senator Joseph R. McCarthy to a worried America.[1] Could he be right? The Soviet Union had expanded into Eastern Europe without opposition from the West, and in 1949 the USSR had exploded an atomic bomb. Had that been made possible by traitors in government? McCarthy questioned the loyalty of scientists, writers, and teachers. "McCarthyism" affected the government and professions, marring the reputations and blighting the careers of many Americans. Kirchwey asked:

> How can an innocent person disprove a privileged statement charging him with having unlawfully passed a paper, or having believed in communism? He can only enlist his friends, if he has friends with sufficient courage, to say, "It cannot be true; he is not that sort of man." But words will not give him back his good name . . . This is McCarthyism. This is the means by which a handful of men, disguised as hunters of subversion, cynically subvert the instruments of justice and hold up to contempt the government itself in order to help their own political fortunes.[2]

McCarthyism even threatened the publishing industry with censorship. Freda Kirchwey wrote that a democracy that adopted censorship would cease to be a democracy, as she reminded Americans: "We are still in the stage where we can talk and write about the threats to our freedom to talk and write."[3]

McCarthy capitalized on the fear of communist expansion. The Senator from Wisconsin left his name on a decade of history at a critical time.[4] On 25 June 1950, North Korea invaded South Korea. The absence of the Soviet delegate from the Security Council of the United Nations allowed it to adopt a resolution condemning the invasion and demanding the withdrawal of troops from South Korea. American forces were a major part of the UN army.[5] The *Nation* sanctioned this action because North Korea clearly had violated a treaty separating the two Koreas at the 38th parallel. But behind her public support, Kirchwey worried privately: "Decisive action was called for, that's sure; & when it came the first reaction was a sort of relief, as if a long tension had given way. But now people begin to realize the implications of what we've gotten into."[6]

While war raged in Korea, McCarthyism took a toll at home. A search for traitors was under way. In January 1950 Alger Hiss, former president of the Carnegie Endowment for International Peace, was found guilty of perjury.[7] Some *Nation* writers came under scrutiny during McCarthy's wide sweep, and Kirchwey went to their defense. Maxwell S. Stewart, editor of the Pamphlet Series of the Public Affairs Committee, prepared a long defense of his *Nation* writings, contrasting them with writings of the *New Masses,* and she supported his case.[8] Another former contributor, Arthur Wubnig, economist with the International Bank for Reconstruction and Development, asked for help with his "personal problem—a loyalty investigation, that peculiar creation of our present era." Kirchwey's affidavit stated: "I can say without qualification that the contributions in question showed no pro-Communist or left-wing attitudes or propensities."[9]

Such incidents illustrate the nature of anxiety in the United States, as the war of ideologies hardened between anticommunist and anti-anticommunist liberals. Both sides felt threatened and in need of protecting democracy. Anti-anticommunists like Kirchwey wanted to stop the blanket abridgment of civil liberties that fear of communism provoked. Anticommunists, many of whom were also anti-McCarthy, maintained their vigilance against communist intrusions.

In June 1950 some members of the American Intellectuals for Freedom joined an international gathering of like-minded people in the new Congress for Cultural Freedom and met in West Berlin. Sidney Hook described the creation of "a nucleus for a Western community of intellectuals who will have no truck with 'neutrality' in the struggle for freedom either at home or abroad."[10] Returning participants created the U.S. branch, the American Committee for Cultural Freedom (ACCF), which concerned itself with preserving liberty. The fight against communists broadened. In 1951 the organization of some six hundred included a wide spectrum of opinions, ranging from those of Dwight Macdonald to James Burnham. Many members were anti-McCarthy as well as anticommunist and antifascist.[11]

There was disagreement between the group and other intellectuals as to whether Communist Party members should be permitted to teach in American schools. Sidney Hook explained his viewpoint, which characterized that of other ACCF members, in an important and controversial pamphlet, "Heresy, Yes—Conspiracy, No." He argued that communist ideas were mere heresy and could be espoused; but a teacher's membership in the Communist Party could be intolerable because Communists took an oath of discipline that transcended intellectual integrity. Party membership was a prima facie case for a hearing; it was not an automatic basis for dismissal. Daniel James, managing editor of the *New Leader,* pointed out the interesting questions that Hook's position raised concerning another issue, the separation of ideas from behavior. "Can you prosecute communists without banning their ideas? Is McCarthyism an incubus as dangerous as the matured disease of Communism? Can we arrive at a new theory of freedom that will protect freedom without protecting its enemies?"[12]

Meanwhile Freda Kirchwey continued to argue for greater understanding of the Soviet Union; an open forum between the two superpowers became even more imperative when both possessed atomic weapons. President Truman's authorization for work on the hydrogen bomb in January 1950 made atomic power a timely subject.[13] To discuss the realities of the Atomic Era, the Nation Associates sponsored another meeting, attesting to Kirchwey's belief

that rational discussion informed the public and influenced governmental policy. In late April 1950 twenty-seven participants in the
two-day conference covered a wide variety of issues relating to
atomic power. Harvard historian John K. Fairbank discussed the
Asian policy of the United States; Harrison Brown, University of
Chicago professor of chemistry, advocated world government;
Hans J. Morgenthau of the University of Chicago examined power
politics; MIT professor Norbert Weiner warned of the possible consequences of the abuse of power by a state large enough to manage
the big business of atomic energy. Lord Boyd-Orr of the University
of Glasgow, winner of the Nobel Peace Prize in 1949, spoke of the
basic challenge to the survival of civilization: "The choice before
human society today is total war with total destruction or the adjustment of the international political system to make war obsolete."[14] The consensus of the gathering was the need to discover and
eliminate the causes of the Cold War between the United States and
the Soviet Union.

Kirchwey later described the forum: "the meetings were packed,
the speeches of high quality, and the interest very great"; it was "a
succès d'estime but not a financial triumph."[15] Soon after the conference, she edited several of the speeches for *The Atomic Era,* a
book that she hoped would provide solutions or a guide to the
problems: "If the world is to escape another all-embracing war with
the consequences to civilization guaranteed by the means of destruction now in our hands, it will be through the acceptance, and vigorous application, of the ideas developed in these pages. If no
simple blueprint for peace emerges, one finds at least an informed
guide to the kinds of policy that may check our stumbling, headlong
plunge toward atomic conflict."[16]

*

Coexistence and compromise to avoid war were in the self-
interest of both superpowers, Kirchwey stressed. No nation could
win an atomic war; world survival depended on discussion and negotiation. Kirchwey's quest for survival determined *Nation* attitudes
toward the Soviet Union during the 1950s: "We urged this policy of
detente, not out of trust in Moscow's 'sincerity' but on the grounds
that the ultimate survival of the Soviet Union—like that of the
United States—lay in atomic disarmament all 'round and in a realistic compromise on issues of power. This general attitude informed

our commentary on China, the Berlin blockade, the Korean War, and most of the other international crises as they arose."[17]

For the *Nation's* eighty-fifth anniversary issue Kirchwey chose the theme: "Peace with Russia—Can It Be Negotiated?" She proposed: "Adopting as its premise that peace by agreement need not mean appeasement, the special issue will dig down to the roots of the conflict in Europe, Asia, Africa, the Middle East, and Latin America . . . It will present and analyze the solutions which might be applied to each particular situation and to the overall conflict." In a private note to Eleanor Roosevelt she conveyed the hope that a discussion of peace by negotiation with the Soviet Union could "bring a measure of sanity into a situation which is complicated at the moment by hysteria and panic." She did not think negotiation would be acceptable in a time of fear and suspicion, but she thought that "in the end this view must prevail and liberal spokesmen in this country and abroad must accept the responsibility for promoting it."[18]

Kirchwey and her editors declared in December 1950:

> THE NATION celebrates its Eighty-fifth Anniversary in a sober mood . . . Today only one subject is important—the possibility of averting a general war which would wipe out, impartially, the institutions of civilized life and the forces that threaten them . . . this symposium is presented as a positive contribution to the broadening of the discussion of peace or war in the knowledge that for all nations the issue is survival.[19]

Archibald MacLeish's article, "War or Peace: The Undebated Issue," argued that negotiation becomes "not only *a* realistic means of avoiding war but *the* realistic means." In negotiation, "we shall deserve the responsibility history, if there is to be a history of our time, will let us bear." Isaac Deutscher, an expert on Soviet matters, wrote of the necessity to transcend the confusion of the Cold War and to reach some "negotiated settlement . . . For the alternative . . . to the peaceful coexistence of the two systems is not the victory of one over the other but their mutual destruction."[20] H. Stuart Hughes, Owen Lattimore, Vera Micheles Dean, Claude Bourdet, Harrison S. Brown, Bishop G. Bromley Oxam, Sir Bengal N. Rau, Grenville Clark, and of course Kirchwey, Del Vayo, and Carolus (pseudonym of a West German liberal active in labor and political affairs), also wrote thoughtful and ominous pieces.[21]

During these years the *Nation* became a Cold War battleground. Political differences between Freda Kirchwey and Robert Bendiner increased. Frustrated at being unable to square the journal's position with his own political views, Bendiner stepped down as associate editor, although he stayed on as a contributing editor: "I cannot help feeling that this gradual shift to the outer edges was inevitable as the gap between our points of view became more marked, nor do I see how it could possibly be reversed. While you have been too generous ever to interfere with what I wished to write under my own name, there seems less and less reason for me to confine that writing to The Nation—and still less reason for me to continue as an editor when I have so little to do with the creation of the magazine."[22]

Attitudes toward communism were defining liberals and others in the world of journal publishing as well as in the larger political environment. Long-term friends turned into adversaries. Each side was certain that its position was the right one to preserve freedom. Peter Viereck analyzed the anticommunist liberals: "The honest, non-fellow-traveling liberal must range himself beside the conservative in the inevitable Armageddon between creative, ethical conservatism and destructive, nihilistic Communism. Therefore, in the future, liberalism may vanish as an entity by being torn apart between those who thus gravitate to conservatism and those who unwillingly lend themselves as false-fronts for fellow travelerdom."[23]

In the ideological cold war among political journals, the *Nation* withstood attacks by the *New Leader* and *Commentary*, both of which found its stands unconscionable. Granville Hicks, former Communist turned conservative, specifically attacked Kirchwey and the *Nation* in *Commentary* as "Liberals Who Haven't Learned." Citing articles by Kirchwey, Del Vayo, Carolus, and Deutscher, he denounced the entire eighty-fifth anniversary issue for its "pro-Soviet bias." Appalled by the *Nation*'s symposium, he blamed the participants' views on their personal histories: they were rooted in the liberalism of the twenties, thirties, and forties; they had had unsavory associations with communists in the *New Masses*. Yet he attacked only a few of the twenty-five contributors; and he sometimes quoted their words out of context to prove that the *Nation* issue had an overly conciliatory view of the USSR.[24]

"Very angry at Commentary article" Kirchwey jotted on the copy she kept of a letter to the editor in response to Hicks's charges.

About the "pro-Soviet bias" of her anniversary issue, she said that almost all of the participants were liberals, most anticommunist liberals, with only a few leftists included. There were no communist contributors. She charged *Commentary*'s irresponsible article with breaking a liberal consensus.[25]

The tensions between political journals reflected the ideological dilemmas of the times. A *Commentary* reader, concerned about the charges against the *Nation*, was told by *Commentary* editor Elliot Cohen: "Considering how important and influential a factor the *Nation* has been in American liberalism for many decades, it is a matter of the highest public concern to have a sober discussion of the political character and soundness of the *Nation*'s most recent version of 'liberalism'."[26] Kirchwey's letter to the editor reminded *Commentary* readers that the *Nation* was "a journal with a record of consistent liberalism plus a militant spirit that seems to have largely evaporated from political journalism in this sad post-war world." To prove that the issue met standards acceptable to liberals, she cited people who had approved of the anniversary issue: Attorney General J. Howard McGrath; John Collier; Rabbi Roland B. Gittelsohn; Joseph Short, secretary to the President. In fact, she quoted a letter from Short as saying that President Truman had expressed "appreciation of our effort *after* he saw the issue."[27]

The implication that Truman approved of the *Nation*'s anniversary issue led Sidney Hook to protest to Short and Short to warn Kirchwey not to embarrass the President by attributing more to his "routine" comments than they meant. But Kirchwey felt that more was involved and privately expressed herself:

> Reactionaries of the stripe of McCarthy are today joined by other professional trouble-makers, including certain ex-Trotskyites and ex-Stalinists determined to discredit persons of independent views who, never having shared their sympathies for Communism cannot be coerced into sharing their abhorrence of every suggestion that peace might be sought with the Soviet Union— even though to achieve that peace no sacrifice of democratic principle is implied . . . There are many reactionaries, together with the former leftists I have referred to above, . . . who would like to destroy The Nation precisely because it is both anti-Communist and independent. That is the clear implication of the untruthful statements and insinuations made by Granville Hicks in *Commentary*.

She trusted that Short would not want to participate in that fraud any more than she would want to "embarrass the President." *Nation* editor Willard Shelton tried to smooth things over with his friend Short, explaining that Kirchwey had not tried to "deceive" the public by the statement of "appreciation." Short, however, felt that a White House letter had been misused in a specific controversy. Although one historian considered the affair "a bit silly," even he could see its wider dimensions.[28]

*

Throughout Kirchwey's editorship, the *Nation* had facilitated dialogue in open forum among differing points of view, international as well as domestic. Over the years she had developed a format for airing contrasting opinions, and she had published vehemently anti-communist criticisms in the letters to the editor column, even during the Cold War. Yet Kirchwey found one letter written to her too abusive to print. In it, the *Nation's* former art critic, Clement Greenberg, wrote:

> I find it shocking that any part of your—and our—magazine should consistently act as a vehicle through which the interests of a particular state power are expressed . . .
>
> I would not be shocked if Mr. del Vayo appeared to be just a sympathizer of Soviet policy; but the evidence furnished by his own words would show that his column has become a medium through which arguments remarkably like those which the Stalin regime itself advances are transmitted in a more plausible form to the American public . . .
>
> I could multiply such instances of special and specious pleading on behalf of the U.S.S.R. by the *Nation's* foreign editor, but I would have to go far beyond the limits of a letter.
>
> . . . I protest simply against the fact that the *Nation* permits its columns to be used for the consistent expression of any point of view indistinguishable from that of a given state power. *The Nation* has the right to side with the Stalin regime when it holds itself compelled to by principle (though it does it so often that that constitutes another, if lesser, scandal), but not to put its pages at the regular disposal of one whose words consistently echo the interests of that regime; nor has it the right to make that person its foreign editor.[29]

Furious, the always polite Freda Kirchwey uncharacteristically addressed Greenberg as "Sir": "You charge that *The Nation,* in publishing the writings of J. Alvarez del Vayo, is permitting its columns to be used by a foreign power. This charge is without the slightest foundation in fact and is clearly libelous. Were *The Nation* to print your letter, which is scurrilous and malicious in tone, and defamatory and false in its accusation, it would only be condoning your offense. If the letter is published or circulated anywhere, we will immediately bring suit for libel against you and all others connected with its publication or distribution."[30] She "refused to print it because it was clearly false and defamatory; a periodical has a public as well as a private duty not to spread untrue and malicious statements."[31]

When, two months later, the *New Leader* published Greenberg's letter to her, Kirchwey kept her word, initiating a libel suit against him and the journal. Some on the *Nation* urged her not to sue. Kirchwey explained to one of them, Margaret Marshall, that she underestimated the degree of malice Greenberg held for Kirchwey and the *Nation*. Malice, however, was not the reason for the suit; Kirchwey sued because of "a charge which we simply cannot afford to let stand—that we are serving as spokesmen for the Soviet government."[32] Her integrity and that of the *Nation* were at stake.

There is disagreement about who supported the idea of suing. Carey McWilliams, then associate editor, and those who rely on him as a source, claim that Del Vayo opposed the libel suit. However, at the time, Evans Clark reported to Reinhold Niebuhr that Del Vayo "strongly favored it."[33] A loyal friend, Kirchwey wanted to protect Del Vayo, who, as a political émigré, faced possible deportation if the authorities believed the serious charges directed against him.[34] Also Kirchwey, who opposed prolonged ideological conflict, no doubt objected to the prospect of endless debates that could deflect her journal's attention from more pressing issues.

Once the lawsuit was filed, the *New Leader* charged the *Nation* with censorship, defining the issue as "fundamentally political, and therefore best resolved in the court of public opinion."[35] To Kirchwey, however, the suit upheld freedom of the press. "A time is upon us when frightened men turn with venom to crush those whose views they hate."[36] Clark described their argument:

> The more I have thought about the whole situation the more I have become convinced that the suit is a blow *for* freedom of expression rather than a limitation of it. As you well know, people whose views differ from the majority these days are being driven

to silence by fear of being branded "Communist" and "disloyal." To take false charges of this kind to the courts and to prove their danger and damage—assuming there is some fairness left in the judicial system—should give those who want to express unconventional views a far greater feeling of safety.[37]

Kirchwey saw Greenberg's letter as an attempt to silence her through intimidation. Had it been an attack on the views of Del Vayo or the *Nation,* but not a "libelous letter," she would have printed it and responded. She wrote: "The single point of his letter, as he was frank enough to admit, was to accuse this journal and its foreign editor of acting in behalf of a foreign power—in still plainer words, of being 'committed' to the service of the Soviet government." That kind of accusation was "unquestionably the most damaging that could be leveled, in a time like the present, against any institution or person."[38]

"We have no intention of trying the case in the columns of *The Nation,*" announced Kirchwey.[39] Yet her determination not to dignify the charges by publishing a discussion about them failed when letters on the subject flooded her desk. Loyal *Nation* readers joined in the debate. One writer sympathetically acknowledged the implications of the Greenberg letter, which "represents an increasing tendency to oppose the expression of certain views by appeal to prejudice rather than to reason." However, the reader thought that the *Nation* "would have done much better to slug the question out there." Liberal editor Charles A. Madison applauded:

> I am very much opposed to the so-called liberal who feels the need to prove his liberalism not merely by taking a completely anti-Communist position but also by vilifying those liberals who continue to adhere to the positive principles of democracy rather than the negative doctrines of anti-communism . . . I am, therefore, very grateful to you for making your stand clear and for defending those who have neither the power nor the opportunity to defend their liberalism publicly . . . may you prevail!

The *Nation* printed another opinion: "I am not concerned with the possibly libelous nature of Mr. Greenberg's letter but with *The Nation*'s failure to publish his letter and to give its reasons for deciding that his opinion is false." In a letter Kirchwey did not print, Arthur Schlesinger, Jr., castigated the *Nation* for "betraying its finest traditions . . . when it prints, week after week, *these wretched apologies for*

Soviet despotism." He criticized the *Nation* for refusing to publish Greenberg's letter: "This action deprives *Nation* readers of knowledge—to which they are surely entitled—of the reaction in liberal circles to Del Vayo and to *The Nation* editorials."[40]

Perhaps the most tragic consequence of the episode for Kirchwey was the severing of connections by some old friends and *Nation* contributors. Robert Bendiner and Reinhold Niebuhr asked to be removed from the masthead, and the issue of 12 May 1951 carried neither name.[41] Kirchwey did not comment on the resignations, but she must have considered them defections.

The *New Leader* lawsuit would hold bitter memories for Kirchwey's opponents; it is a tragic memory for her supporters. Strategically the suit was a disaster that did not accomplish what Kirchwey hoped it would, and that cost her emotional agony and money. In the early stages of the conflict Clark wrote Niebuhr, in an attempt to convince him to return to the journal: "The hardest thing for her [Freda] to bear has been the desertion of a few of *The Nation*'s good friends through a complete misunderstanding of the entire situation."[42]

Freda Kirchwey had come to view J. Alvarez del Vayo as a living symbol of good: "He represents something very profound in our tradition of independent radicalism, and in our individual consciences. He is a declaration of faith."[43] This extravagant opinion influenced her decision to sue—a tactical error that alienated many friends and colleagues and allowed others to ridicule her.

Kirchwey discounted her friends' warnings. When she first considered Marshall's argument about "the kind of capital that can be made out of the suit by reactionaries or the anti-Communist fanatics around *The New Leader*," she told her: "the contrary is the case . . . newspapers and magazines are likely to pipe down about the whole affair if only because any repetition of the libel is itself libelous."[44]

Kirchwey was sadly wrong. The attacks continued. "Sermons of Self-Destruction" by Peter Viereck appeared in the August 1951 *Saturday Review of Literature*. In it he defined "the non-Communist dupes of Communism" as "Lumpen-intellectuals," those "highbrows near the top of the literary and journalistic world . . . He signs Soviet 'peace' petitions against atomic war and flocks to fake 'peace' conferences."[45] The *Nation* was the chief American organ of "softness" toward the Soviet Union. Viereck considered the libel suit served on the *New Leader* as symptomatic of this controversy, which he defined as a choice "between all-out anti-Stalinism and a new 'treason of the clerks.'" He acknowledged the fear of "witch-hunt hysteria," but was concerned about the other hysteria: "the present witch-hunt against witch-hunts." He worried about the *Nation*'s role because, despite its small circulation, the journal was a major influence in establishing a "climate of opinion": "The influence of intellectual journals can never be measured by quantitative circulation."[46]

Reviewing the libel suit, Viereck quoted in its entirety the letter from Arthur Schlesinger, Jr., which the *Nation* had not printed in its representative letters to the editor about the controversy. He used Niebuhr's and Bendiner's resignations as ammunition to attack the *Nation*'s attitude toward the Soviet Union and its decision to sue the *New Leader*. Viereck appealed to the editors of the *Nation* to recognize the critical problem of the times: "Today the savage armies of Soviet fascism are the gravest single menace to mankind." He begged intellectuals to consider the words of [Oliver] Cromwell: "I beseech you in the bowels of Christ, think it possible that you may be mistaken."[47]

Kirchwey sought legal counsel on how to phrase a response to Viereck. Her attorney advised her to wait until letters raised the issue in the *Saturday Review* and then to give an answer that explained the "tactics and strategy in the libel suit." "The answer should make crystal clear the issue of principle which compels *The Nation*, as a liberal publication, to sue, viz: the right to discuss in a free democracy all controversial questions, including Russia, war and peace, without criminal and penal calumnification as a Soviet agent." The *Saturday Review* received so many letters during the next couple of months that it observed: "Few articles published in SRL have occasioned more comment pro and con, than Peter Viereck's 'Sermons of Self-Destruction.'"[48]

In that same issue Viereck responded to the letters by sharpening his attack: "Enemies of *The Nation* would confine themselves to pointing out that it is no longer the 'great old liberal institution' which all liberals must defend against attack but it is a mere *rump remnant* of left-overs after most of its leading liberal editors—Niebuhr, Bendiner, Greenberg, etc.,—felt forced to resign by its appeasement policy." Other attacks were so determined that one liberal wrote that it seemed as though a small group was trying to destroy the journal. Illinois Unitarian minister Homer A. Jack wrote: "Although *The Nation* has made plenty of editorial mistakes, I condemn the current studied efforts by a small coterie of men to drive it out of existence."[49]

Kirchwey's response was confined to Viereck's remark about the *"rump remnant* of left-overs." She clarified the nature of the relations to the *Nation* of the editors who had left and then addressed herself to Viereck's concluding comments about name-calling. He had said: "Cannot writers, intellectuals, and upholders of academic freedom drop this mutual name-calling? It was not begun by us anti-Communists. It was begun by *The Nation*'s attempt to silence a less affluent and more anti-Communist magazine through an expensive libel suit and by endless hysterical diatribes of the non-Communist Lumpen-intellectuals." Kirchwey denounced the statement as "at least astonishing." "We had thought the name-calling preceded the libel suit; or was it the other way around—did we sue first and Mr. Greenberg *afterward* accuse *The Nation* of being committed to the interests of the Soviet Government?"[50] Not all *Nation* supporters agreed with her analysis. Paul Blanshard, who criticized Viereck's attack, also criticized Kirchwey, who retorted: "I did not undertake this costly and difficult fight either for fun or for money."[51]

The controversy festered for four years before an out-of-court settlement ended it. Neither side won. The week of 17 September 1955, the *Nation* and the *New Leader* published an identical statement. It restated the position of each and then declared:

> WHEREAS the parties to the litigation desire to compose the issue which has arisen between them; now
> IT IS HEREBY STIPULATED AND AGREED, by and between the parties hereto, that the above-entitled action be and the same hereby is settled and discontinued without costs to any party as against any other party.[52]

*

Growing McCarthyism and its repercussions led Kirchwey to sponsor a special issue on civil liberties. "How Free Is Free?" she asked in the lead article, which gave a name to the 28 June 1952 issue. The *Nation* rarely devoted an entire issue to one theme, and the size of the issue was doubled, "with an eye to the overriding importance of the problem and to the critical need for an early solution." The several essays shared the theme of fear, and Freda Kirchwey quoted Eleanor Roosevelt as recently having said: "I am tired of being afraid."[53] Roosevelt's sentiment seemed to capture the feelings of many liberals, and Kirchwey's purpose was to make that fear unnecessary; she longed for "the restoration of democratic safeguards and procedures." "This special issue of *The Nation* is designed for one primary purpose: to provide an arsenal of facts and ideas for all Americans who are ready to take up this fight." Kirchwey manifested her "militant liberalism" by advocating an attack on the abridgment of civil liberties that was occurring in the early 1950s. "To try to pin the trouble on Stalin is a temptation." Yet a much broader world revolution was upsetting the balance, and Kirchwey urged the United States and its allies to come to terms with it.[54] She placed fear of communism in the perspective of world revolution.

The special issue included articles by prominent specialists in the many fields where a loss of civil liberties was particularly prevalent: academia, science, government, entertainment, law, and organized labor. Zechariah Chafee, Jr., Harvard Law School professor, wrote: "I am disturbed by the growing inclination to turn spies into heroes." (He was speaking of those, like Whittaker Chambers, who gained in status after testifying against persons accused of being communists.) In "The Battle of the Books," Matthew Josephson discussed the case of Angus Cameron, vice-president and editor-in-chief of Little, Brown. In January 1951 the *American Legion Magazine* criticized Cameron (a Wallace supporter in 1948) for publishing communist novelist Howard Fast. In August the anticommunist weekly *Counterattack* escalated the attack, accusing both Cameron and Little, Brown of publishing some thirty-one authors who were either avowed or secret communists. Little, Brown denied the allegations; Cameron was forced to resign. Josephson described the risk inherent in refusing to publish noncomformist views: not printing the views of Edgar Snow or Owen Lattimore would "leave us in danger of flying blind." We would not have the knowledge we need to make responsible decisions about urgent critical issues in the world.[55]

A few months earlier the *Nation* had withstood another attack. In an article in *Commentary,* "'Civil Liberties,' 1952—A Study in Confusion," Irving Kristol, the journal's managing editor, asked, "Do We Defend Our Rights by Protecting Communists?" The essay served to polarize those who equated communism with fascism, and those who did not, including Kirchwey. Kristol argued that the confusion of the anti-anticommunist liberals (whom he referred to simply as "liberals") came from their regarding communism as "left" and therefore different from the fascist "right." "This notion of Communism as 'left' and therefore at an opposite pole from fascism, which is 'right,' appears to have become intrinsic to the liberal outlook."

Kristol claimed that there was a tie between communism and fascism. He explained to confused liberals that the former was more than an idea. Soviet Communism and official Communist parties demanded the overthrow of any opposing social or political order. Communism was not merely a differing viewpoint that needed to be protected as "merely another form of 'dissent,'" but a "movement guided by conspiracy and aiming at totalitarianism." Those liberals who refused to see this "true" nature of communism and mistakenly defended the civil liberties of communists were abetting subversion against American democracy.[56] William O'Neill has pointed out that Kristol's essay "has been held against him" since 1952. James Nuechterlein, a political philosopher, in a review of Kristol's memoirs, *Reflections of a Neoconservative,* said of the 1952 article: "Kristol started an argument so fierce that it still remains alive more than three decades later." In his essay Kristol stigmatized the liberal: "if a liberal wishes to defend the civil liberties of Communists or of Communist fellow-travelers, he must enter the court of American opinion with clean hands and a clear mind. He must show that he knows the existence of an organized subversive movement such as Communism is a threat to the consensus on which civil society and civil liberties are based . . . He must speak as one of *us,* defending *their* liberties. To the extent he insists that they are on our side, that we can defend our liberties only by uncritically defending theirs, he will be taken as speaking as one of them."[57]

According to the Kristol argument, the *Nation*'s advocacy of communists' civil liberties made the journal suspect of being in the communist camp. When, in April, invitations for a May Nation Associates forum on the Middle East were issued, the charge of "Communist infiltration" emerged. The invitation contained the names of 158 sponsors and several distinguished speakers. "Big Names Deny Any Part in Forum Run by The Nation," charged Frederick Woltman in the *New York World-Telegram and Sun,* reporting that several sponsors and speakers denied that they had agreed to support the conference. *Counterattack* claimed that the *Nation* was using the names to "revive the united front" and advised any anticommunists on the list of sponsors to resign and to put pressure on the speakers to withdraw. The *New Leader* joined the attack: "Wedged in among many respectable sponsors of this affair" were some "dubious 'liberals.'" That journal was confident, however, that when presidential candidate Senator Estes Kefauver and Maryland governor Theodore R. McKeldin saw the complete list, they would withdraw as speakers and repudiate "the assorted Stalinoids and 'muddleheads'" among the sponsors.[58]

To some degree this tactic worked. Kirchwey commented: "The whole experience . . . has been a horrifying one as it is a clear expression of the power of the McCarthyites and the vigilante groups which they are able to summon at will." American Federation of Labor president William Green, one of the dinner's four co-chairmen, resigned, as did New York Senator Jacob K. Javits, who reluctantly removed his name from the list of sponsors. Kefauver arranged to have his speech delivered by the head of his New York State Committee, but Hernán Santa Cruz, Chilean delegate to the United Nations Security Council, succumbed to pressure and withdrew as a speaker the day before the conference, explaining: "I feel that I cannot because of a personal action on my part, expose my country or my government to any kind of controversy, notwithstanding how great an interest I may have in the matter. And I am sure that these attacks would come, because of the innumerable amount of letters I have received during the past few weeks."[59]

The conference was in jeopardy. Freda Kirchwey decided to rally a counterattack by invoking a powerful voice of liberalism, Eleanor Roosevelt. She had other commitments that evening and had declined to attend. As a rule, Kirchwey asked influential people for favors for herself or her journal only when she deemed help crucial. This was one of those times. She needed the presence of Eleanor Roosevelt as a symbol of support and courage and begged her to reconsider. When the former First Lady agreed, Kirchwey was overcome:

> My all-too-evident emotion was testimony enough; indeed I even feel I should apologize for allowing it to be so evident. But the nightmare we have been going through is perhaps excuse enough for so understanding a person as you! And please don't think we are unaware of the extra burden the occasion will place on you who are already too heavily burdened. Again our only excuse for throwing ourselves upon your generosity and strength is the sinister nature of the assault and the fact that if it succeeds

a victory will be chalked up for the very worst elements in the "counter-attack" of intimidation against, not communism, but the whole range of liberal opinion and action in this country.

Kirchwey assured Mrs. Roosevelt that by her decision she "defended a free and liberal institution" and "helped defeat a particularly vicious form of un-Americanism and encouraged others more timid to stand up to the fight for the freedoms of our country."[60]

Roosevelt's surprise appearance and brief prefatory remarks stressed the right of dissenters to be heard:

> I thought that I could not be with you tonight because I had so many things that I had set out to do today. But I decided that it would be wise to come since I understood that there had been some attacks made. And I believe that it is a great mistake not to stand up for people, even when you differ with them, if you feel that they are trying to do things that will help in our country.
>
> I think we have become a little too afraid of what certain groups may say. It is true that sometimes we may make mistakes; sometimes people nowadays have to think more carefully than they used to. I can remember a time when you didn't really have to worry very much about the people you happened to meet. You do now, apparently. But I don't like that.
>
> I think we should try not to make mistakes. Having tried to avoid mistakes, if we decide to do something which certain groups may attack us for, the attack should not be accepted without proof. This is one of the things that I think we are suffering from in these days—accusations which do their harm before they can be disproved.
>
> One of the things we must be concerned about today is to preserve our own freedom. I think that it is essential to learn that while we have to fight against things that we consider wrong, we should not do it through fear. We should do it through intelligent education.

Kirchwey, relieved, thanked Roosevelt: "I am so glad you came to the dinner! . . . your presence there, together with what you said, was a better rebuttal to the *Counterattack* slanders than a dozen Santa Cruzes."[61]

That May victory could not erase memories of February when the consequences of being suspected of communism were brought home forcefully to Freda. The Alvarez del Vayos, returning to the United States from Europe, reentry papers in hand, were detained at Ellis Island under the McCarran Act. Although Del Vayo swore that he was not and never had been a Communist, he and his wife, Luisi, were detained for several days and permitted only limited communication with Freda Kirchwey. Using their contacts in government, Kirchwey and Clark spent a frantic couple of days of phone calls and telegrams to effect the release of their friends.[62] As Evans Clark wrote Michael: "F & I spent every minute of Friday afternoon, Sat. and Sun. and Mon. pulling every wire we could to get the Vayos released. Finally, through direct intervention by the White House, they were freed on parole." Freda added, "Whatever you may think of V's ideas you will agree I am sure that this is a nasty business."[63] "ELEMENTARY CONSIDERATIONS, JUSTICE AND HUMANITY AS WELL AS INEVITABLE UNFAVORABLE REACTION DEMOCRATIC LEADERS THROUGHOUT WORLD, ESPECIALLY EUROPE AND LATIN AMERICA, DEMAND IMMEDIATE RELEASE," read Freda Kirchwey's telegram to President Truman, and she urged him to intercede before the news media publicized the situation.[64]

Meanwhile, she got newspaper assurances to keep the story quiet while she was negotiating for the release. The Del Vayos, released on parole in February, were formally cleared in August 1952. The incident illustrates one abridgment of civil liberties during the McCarthy period. Kirchwey and Clark harbored bitter resentment against the anticommunist liberals, for they believed the charges against the Del Vayos originated with "one of the New Leader crowd." So did Carey McWilliams, who said: "I thought then and think now that *The Nation's* liberal critics who disagreed with its stand on the Cold War instigated this action."[65]

*

In January 1953 Freda Kirchwey fired Margaret Marshall. This action virtually severed her relations with the anticommunist liberals who had continued to review books for the *Nation*. Faced with a $90,000 deficit, Kirchwey and Clark signed for an enormous bank loan for the *Nation* and also assumed a *Nation* debt for $12,000.[66] The desperate financial straits forced Kirchwey to hire a consultant, George Braziller, who recommended "an austerity program of awful dimensions: Four people fired, including Hugo [Van Arx] and Peggy M[arshall]!; Paper reduced to 24 pp. weekly. . . And soon moving to smaller and cheaper quarters."[67]

Freda, detailing these facts in a letter to "Peggy dear," reported the decision to reduce the book department to "a single long review supplemented by briefs, as in the *New Yorker;*" the managing editor could oversee the work of the literary department. After spelling out the "elimination" of Marshall's job, Kirchwey offered her the opportunity to remain at the *Nation* as the drama critic, at the much lower weekly rate.[68] Marshall felt "deep regret" and "equally deep disgust that the editors-in-power of The Nation, of all magazines, should have decided that the book section, small though it was, must bear the brunt of the cuts which (I have no doubt) must be made. I consider this decision stupid as well as sad." Further, she did not accept that the cuts made were a "simple case of reducing a department and eliminating an editor for reasons of economy," but claimed that she was "singled out for elimination"—the editor "'out of line' with the rest of the paper."[69]

Angry words were exchanged. Apologizing for raising her voice, Marshall acknowledged the difficulty of the decision for Kirchwey: "Believe me, I know how painful it must have been for you to discharge me after all these years. It was less painful, apparently, than it would have been to discharge some other editor; still it was sufficiently painful to make you miserable. I recognize that." Nevertheless, "the elimination of me and of the book section as I conducted it was not *simply* a matter of economy."[70] Kirchwey could understand Marshall's unhappiness and bitterness, but, equally insistent, she argued: "there are no plots or ulterior motives—nothing but high costs, too little income, and a determination to keep the paper alive even with a reduced staff and other economies. I wish you could believe that."[71]

The formal notification to *Nation* readers outlined several changes "to produce a more effective journal, as well as a more economical one." The list of contributing editors would be broadened to include: H. H. Wilson, associate professor of political science at Princeton; W. Macmahon Ball, professor of political science at the University of Melbourne; Max Geismar, author and critic; and Bruce Catton, historian and journalist. Kirchwey then announced the big change in the book section: a major article on one book and brief comments on other books would cut down space and allow for personnel "economies necessitated by the inflationary rise in production costs." The change would mean that "Margaret Marshall will no longer serve as Literary Editor." The tribute to Marshall was friendly enough. Kirchwey spoke of her fifteen years as literary editor and twenty-four years on the journal: "Herself an able writer and discerning critic, she has been responsible for the integrity and high standards maintained by the book section. It is the firm intention of the Editors to preserve those standards."[72]

"Dissenter Eliminated," *Time* headlined under a handsome picture of Marshall, with the caption: "And then there were none." It did not accept the economic arguments for the change. A concerned reader wrote the *Nation* that the dismissal of Marshall "raised certain doubts in some of your readers' minds and the reference to these changes in the January 19 issue of *Time*—however distorted it may prove to be—converted these doubts into suspicions." The editors responded that *Time* distorted the reasons and "played up the untrue implication that Miss Marshall was dropped because of political differences. The single motive behind the staff reductions was a need with which we could no longer temporize, to cut costs; politics had nothing to do with the case, as we hope to prove week by week."[73] But Marshall was convinced otherwise: "It took a great deal of nerve for the editors of *The Nation* to make the statement, in the issue of January 31, that politics had nothing to do with my elimination." She pointed out that the book department was under the absolute control of the "editors-in-power," and she said she would be very happy if she were proved wrong about what they were going to do with that power.[74] Freda Kirchwey and Margaret Marshall never renewed their friendship.

Kirchwey, intent on proving that the change lacked political motivation, sent former *Nation* editor Joseph Krutch all the financial details, with her assurance that economics was the cause: "I want to tell you all this very explicitly because I recall that you were disturbed about the Greenberg affair and might otherwise be inclined to suspect this was a sequel to it."[75] She continued to insist that the abolition of the literary section was not political and that the financial strain was real. (Inflation, the cost of the libel suit, and the expense of attempting to break the *Nation* ban were important factors.) McWilliams said: "In retrospect I find it nothing short of miraculous that we were able to keep bringing out *The Nation* week after week in those years of perpetual crisis from 1951 to 1955." Marshall and Del Vayo had received identical highest salaries for *Nation* union members in 1952; cutting Marshall would result in a large savings.[76] It is clear from many sources that Kirchwey believed this to be a financial decision, but there is no way of knowing her unconscious motivation. Why Marshall and not Del Vayo? Perhaps the arrest of the Del Vayos gave the final impetus for abolishing the anticommunist literary section. Kirchwey had time to think about this and to consider the advisability of strengthening the anticommunist liberal faction by continuing to publish such a section.

The 21 February 1953 *Nation* included the promised "new look": a new cover; some use of three columns instead of the previous two-column space; a major book review and a "books in brief" section.[77] The panel of reviewers that replaced Marshall was more anti-anticommunist. Kirchwey wrote some brief reviews, as did Carey McWilliams and H. H. Wilson. Theirs were familiar names urging safeguards on civil liberties. Mark Gayn, a specialist on the Soviet Union who had spent much time in the Far East, did feature reviews of the Soviet Union and the Far East. His opinions reflected great sympathy for the Soviet Union and other communist countries. Edgar Snow, criticized in anticommunist circles, reviewed books on China for the *Nation*.[78]

It is interesting to note, however, that in the *Nation*'s 1953–1955 period an attempt was made to include former as well as new reviewers. Joseph Wood Krutch continued to write many reviews. Richard Hofstadter, on the other hand, expressed his disgust: "I need hardly add that I won't write for the Nation under the new dispensation—ever." H. Stuart Hughes wrote to Margaret Marshall: "My only real link with the magazine was through you—as you know, I felt exactly as you did about its general editorial line—and I wrote reviews for it only through my personal regard for you and admiration for the fashion in which you ran the section. So there will be no question of my continuing to write now that you have gone."[79] With these disappearances, along with others such as Rolfe Humphries, Irving Howe, and Marshall herself, the back of the *Nation* looked more like the front, despite some attempt to include a differing viewpoint.

More than the *Nation*'s format and the concurrence between front and back changed; Kirchwey also changed her own kind of writing. Shorter editorial paragraphs and brief book reviews outnumbered her familiar long editorials. She kept her eye on Korea, the Middle East, civil liberties, and the atomic era—all earlier concerns.

Freda Kirchwey wrote less as she spent more time raising money. The *Nation* fought an increasing deficit from 1946 on, despite Lillie Shultz's efforts to raise money through the Nation Associates.

Kirchwey labeled her share of the financial struggle, "The Last Battle." She saw it as "a personal struggle, for it inevitably deflected" her "from her normal role of editor and publisher."[80]

*

During these financially trying times Kirchwey had secured the assistance of Carey McWilliams. As early as 1951 she had urged the contributing journalist from California to move East to increase his responsibilities at the *Nation*'s New York office: "There are so few people who combine the right point of view, a fertile and creative mind, passionate interest in the jobs that need to be done, and first-rate writing ability. You can understand, therefore, why I am loath to give up the idea of having you here at 'headquarters.'"[81] Mc-Williams agreed to stay only a few months, and Kirchwey assured him that she would not urge him to relocate permanently: "You can be sure that you will be put under no pressure whatsoever—not so much as the weight of a feather—to subordinate your conviction to our wishes. That's a promise, as far as I am concerned! Politically I may be a Socialist of sorts, but in these matters I am laissez faire to the limit."[82]

Within a year McWilliams moved to New York. Whether pressured or not, years later he recounted his initial reluctance to leave California and his relocation to New York: "the thought of leaving California even for six months or a year did not appeal to me . . . I did agree to return to New York for a short time. I have stayed, to date, fourteen years."[83] Kirchwey delegated increasing responsibility to him, though she monitored her enthusiastic assistant and curbed some of his more spectacular plans when they conflicted with her editorial judgment. Early in 1952, when McWilliams wanted the *Nation* to publish several special issues and several special articles, she would not approve:

> While I recognize the value of occasional special issues, both for promotion purposes and to advance some particular editorial policy, I think too many coming too close together are journalistically bad.
> Basically my objection to them is that they tend to take the place of well-rounded, varied issues which keep abreast of events in the very areas a special issue would cover.
> . . . Much of what I have said goes for [series] of articles too. One plans and starts them with enthusiasm and gets to hate them before they are finished up. I suspect the reader does the same.[84]

McWilliams helped as editor, Evans Clark wrote, while Kirchwey bore the *Nation*'s financial burdens: "she has been under such terrific pressure trying to keep 'The Nation' afloat that she hasn't had time for anything else—not even editing the paper. Luckily Carey McWilliams is proving to be a very capable next-in-command."[85]

Although Kirchwey did not write as many editorials, she decided what should be written. "Why the Jews?" she questioned, noting the spread of "Communist-inspired anti-Semitism" with which Kremlin leaders denounced nine Jewish doctors. "Since no informed person believes that Zionists or representatives of the [American] Joint Distribution Committee [JDC] as such, are degenerates, murderers, or spies, the labels only exposed the anti-Semitism behind the attacks." The rise of Soviet anti-Semitism was cause for alarm: "We remember with horror how the world refused to believe the first reports of Hitler's extermination program, and how hesitation and doubt delayed rescue until the war made it impossible. We are determined that the civilized world should today make an effort to prevent a new possibility of genocide while there is yet time."[86]

The appeal of the American Committee for Cultural Freedom to the Secretary General of the United Nations in December 1952 condemning anti-Semitism in Prague sounded similar to the *Nation*'s warning:

> The introduction of "Zionism" as an issue in the Prague trial, and the insinuation that international Jewry and the new state of Israel is seeking to provoke conflicts among nations, is a charge so close to that incitement to racial genocide for which a number of leaders of National Socialism were sentenced to death at Nuremberg that the Government of Prague and those who instigated that Government's action already stand convicted before the bar of world public opinion of similar crimes for a similar purpose, namely to divert public attention from their own misdeeds.[87]

During the 1950s even this shared concern—fear of anti-Semitism—could not bridge the tremendous gap between American anticommunists and the anti-anticommunists. They issued separate pleas. Freda Kirchwey and the Nation Associates appealed to other influential Americans to seek President Eisenhower's attention. They feared that the Soviet Union's anti-Semitic campaign threatened to spread, leading to "a new epidemic of pogroms in countries where anti-Jewish feeling is overt or latent. Such countries include not only those in the Soviet bloc, but Germany, East and West, the Arab states and North Africa as well." Seeking support, they wrote:

> The recent manifestations of Soviet anti-Semitism are a source of profound disturbance to all decent people . . . Some 3,000,000 Jews may become, for the second time in our generation, the victims of a blood purge . . .
>
> Remembering how unbelievable Hitler's threat of Jewish extermination seemed to the civilized world, and how hesitation and delay prevented effective action until war made it impossible, we are concerned that an attempt should be made now, while there is yet time, to halt the new anti-Semitic threat before it leads to genocide. For this reason we have prepared the enclosed draft of a communication to the President asking action by him in the form of a warning, both as a means of preventing disaster for the Jewish people and the acceleration of the cold war.[88]

Forty-nine individuals, including Freda Kirchwey, Roger N. Baldwin, Eleanor Roosevelt, and Edith Wilk (Mrs. Wendell) Wilkie, urged President Eisenhower to demand UN action against Soviet Union anti-Semitism. Their appeal was front-page news in the *New York Times,* which endorsed it.[89]

Kirchwey's criticism of Soviet anti-Semitism did not placate those who still considered the *Nation* too uncritical of communism. Her editorial urging clemency for convicted spies Julius and Ethel Rosenberg did nothing to dissuade them. Nor did her plea that the United States be receptive to the "peace aims" of the new Soviet leader, Georgi Malenkov, following Stalin's death in March 1953. Her publication of Frank J. Donner's "The Informer," a huge exposé of all aspects of the Department of Justice's encouragement of informers, did little to halt criticism of the *Nation.*[90] When Harvey M. Matusow confessed to the lies that he, as an informer, had told the Department of Justice, Attorney General Brownell feared others might do the same and decided to make an example of him. Matusow was indicted on six counts of perjury by a Department of Justice federal grand jury. His confession to perjury as an informer for the Department of Justice brought his own indictment. It also brought indictments against three people associated with the *Nation*: R. Lawrence Siegel, Hadassah Shapiro, and Martin Solow.[91]

Siegel, the *Nation*'s attorney, while lunching in a New York restaurant with a client, Gloria Swanson, chanced to meet Matusow there. In an attempt to avoid embarrassing the famous movie star, he failed to acknowledge the meeting to the grand jury. His associate, attorney Hadassah Shapiro, protected him by denying it also.[92] At about this time, the *Nation*'s business manager, Martin Solow, fearing that correspondence concerning Matusow might incriminate him, destroyed some letters. Kirchwey termed his action "idiotic," but, against the legal counsel of attorney Telford Taylor, decided not to dismiss him. As she explained to Solow, "were I to dismiss you for unauthorized and foolish acts as a *Nation* employee, it would almost certainly give the impression that I regarded the letters themselves as politically or legally improper and so play into the hands of the Department of Justice." Nevertheless, as she wrote him, she deplored his "lack of responsibility in regard to The Nation."[93]

The *Nation* issued a statement repudiating the allegations:

> *The Nation* is fully aware of the fact that one of the purposes of the indictments against Mr. Siegel, Miss Shapiro and Mr. Solow is to punish, and if possible silence, this publication for the political sin—and it is that in Mr. Brownell's book—of having repeatedly, consistently, and from the outset, denounced the unjust and incompetent administration of the Department of Justice under his direction.[94]

The grand jury hearings continued for some time. As McWilliams remembered, "for several months Freda, Lillie Shultz, and I were preoccupied days, nights, and weekends with this weird tangle of events . . . The courage and loyalty Freda displayed throughout this ordeal were beyond praise."[95] Meanwhile the editors planned a large anniversary issue and warned the Justice Department: "*The Nation* has been aroused [around] for a long time, much longer than Mr. Brownell, and we have no intention, in celebrating this year our ninetieth anniversary, of surrendering our independence under pressure of his vindictive bullying."[96]

To celebrate the *Nation*'s ninetieth anniversary, Kirchwey decided to feature Atoms for Peace, "to show the world that the threat of destruction by the atom could be more than balanced by its promise of abundance in a world of peace."[97] She consulted renowned scientist J. Robert Oppenheimer, who felt that the theme of atomic power was important, but only one aspect "in a much greater technological revolution." Kirchwey reported to Shultz: "Therefore he considers our plan for both issue and forum as lopsided and superficial. On the one hand we pay no attention to other technological advances—electronics, automation, etc., etc.—and on the other we pin greater hopes to the use of the atom than he considers justified by the public facts." Despite Oppenheimer's "rather fundamental criticism," Kirchwey decided to modify her original theme only slightly.[98]

For what would be her final forum as editor and publisher, Kirchwey focused on the atom and its potential for "limitless good and limitless evil . . . mass destruction or a braver and newer world than man has ever known." She expressed a belief she had held throughout her long career in journalism, that education and reason can solve the world's problems. She announced the forum: "so far as the atom is concerned, mass instruction is the only alternative to mass destruction . . . the great forces of change can be harnessed and used for the enlightenment of people's lives only if their very impact is understood and dealt with in its own terms."[99]

The Atoms for Peace forum undertook that challenge, featuring Bertrand Russell, who presented the familiar theme "Coexistence or No Existence." It was concerned also about peaceful uses of atomic power, for example, for irrigation in the Negev or for research in medicine. And there was a lengthy chronology of the history of the bomb up to 1955.[100]

Kirchwey's own contribution focused on the impact of the atomic age on journalism. The free press needed to meet the challenges of dramatic changes: "*new* changes so overpowering in what they promise or threaten." The free press must meet these dramatic changes with "every element of strength and imagination, of adaptability and penetration, and particularly of courage and candor that a free press can possibly muster."[101] She had argued the need for independent liberal expression since the beginning of her writing career in 1918. Now, in 1955, the powers and dangers of the new atomic age, increasing publishing costs, and pressures on the media to conform made the need for a free press even more imperative. At this ninetieth anniversary Kirchwey declared that the *Nation* had "no hard-and-fast program for the atomic age." She looked to the possibilities: "Out of it *could* come, in place of freedom, the tightest garrison state the world has ever seen. Out of it could come a global cartel of atomic-energy-controlling powers. Out of it could come a World Government." She did not pretend that the journal would provide a solution to such an immense problem, but she promised that the *Nation* would "see to it that the full facts of its progress are made public; that they are interpreted in terms of the peoples' interests."[102]

*

Kirchwey did not tell the patrons of the Atoms for Peace dinner that she would not continue to direct the *Nation* in this effort. Yet long before, she had chosen Carey McWilliams to succeed her as editor of the *Nation*. Physical and emotional exhaustion played a part in her decision to retire. The strain of raising money for the *Nation*'s survival had left her "enslaved to permanent insolvency."[103] As Evans Clark reported to Michael, the two of them needed a vacation: "Freda is really exhausted and must get out from under the terrific pressures and burdens of the last few months, not to mention years."[104] Later, writing from a cruise ship, Freda promised to limit her "work and responsibility at the N. when I get back . . . Of course this idyllic picture assumes a *Nation* with enough financial underpinning to survive—or at least to find needed capital without the agony of worry and frustration that have all but finished me— and Lillie [Shultz], too, but she doesn't know it."[105]

In order to accept the transfer of editorship, McWilliams needed financial support.[106] To a backer, Mary Dreier, he explained his sixty-day-option from Kirchwey and his perception of the cause for the changeover: "For a variety of reasons—principally having to do with accumulated psychological fatigue—she wants to pass on the major responsibility for the paper to me." But he could not accept financial responsibility for the journal unless he could raise enough money to operate on at least a "bedrock budget." If enough money could not be raised to satisfy his financial qualms, and Freda had to sell the *Nation*, he thought "it would be sold to a rival publication and liquidated."[107] By late June, McWilliams had already acquired approximately $55,250 of an estimated $80,000–$90,000 needed. To help raise the rest of the money required to meet Kirchwey's terms for liquidating the journal's debt and guaranteeing continued publication for two more years, he sought a publisher who would contribute financially. In George G. Kirstein, he found a man with executive skills, values which complemented the journal, and money. Kirstein, an expert on labor relations, then served as executive vice president of the Health Insurance Plan of Greater New York.[108]

Negotiations ensued during the summer of 1955. Kirchwey stated her terms of retirement straightforwardly. She was somewhat irritated by Kirstein's warnings against her future involvement in *Nation* policy. She had no intention of meddling with the new regime, remembering only too well how she had suffered from "the pressures, criticism, and interventions" of the retired Villard.[109] Before she left her post, however, and despite reassurances of noninterference, Kirchwey wrote a strong directive concerning the status of Del Vayo, whom the new board wanted to terminate as foreign editor. She told McWilliams: "I am more troubled by this question than anything else in the prospective change-over. In fact it is the one thing I find difficult to swallow."

> Vayo has been, for *The Nation* both a banner and a hair-shirt . . . and also a continuing sign that we are not willing to be politically coerced. He has been a full editor for eleven years and can't be shunted into a lesser position or offered financial terms he can't accept, without its creating a bad impression among the people and groups who are closest to us, politically and humanly, or without giving immense satisfaction to all the assorted New Leaderites, from Greenberg to Rovere and the press editor of *Time*. In other words this can't be merely an inside financial arrangement; it becomes a political act.[110]

For the time being, Del Vayo remained.

Freda Kirchwey's last words to *Nation* readers as editor and publisher appeared in the 17 September 1955 issue. Explaining that the change of control was of her own doing, she mentioned the financial difficulty that made it timely. She guaranteed that the journal would be "as firm in its liberal position and as rigorous in its journalistic standards as ever before, but stabler and with more vitality." Confident in those who had assumed control, she asked readers to give them "loyal support." "Kirchwey Regime Quits The Nation," read the *New York Times*.[111]

Michael Clark's letter to his mother shows an almost ironic insight into her decision: "It was a great relief to learn that the Nation deal was finally consummated. I know that you, Mother, must have mixed feelings about relinquishing control of the paper, but I trust your regrets will be greatly outweighed by your release from so many frightful burdens. And in writing more and worrying less, will you not find final satisfactions that have been denied to you in the past?"[112]

Evans Clark described Freda's "overwhelming relief" with the firm agreement for a changeover but also her difficulty in readjusting to life without work. Still she could continue writing for the journal and, he reminded Michael, "as I think she has told you, [she] wants to get ahead with a book she has long had in mind—a biography of the Nation during those years she has been so involved with it."[113]

Freda Kirchwey intended her book to end with "The Last Battle," the past decade's struggle for the survival of the journal.[114] During that decade she wrote the truth as she saw it, holding to her commitment to people and beliefs she considered important, even if it cost subscribers or bitter criticism. She continued to champion causes she had adopted early in her career. Her support for the Jews never slackened, nor her affirmation of civil liberties. She continued her crusade for peace in an increasingly volatile atomic age, working unselfishly to make the world a better place. Earlier, in the heat of battle, she had taken rigid stands, such as her support of the "court-packing" plan and her call to "purge the fascist press." But these were exceptions to a consistent editorial policy of fighting for her ideas within a context of dialogue. Typical of her commitment to an open discussion was her response to criticism she received for printing Loyalist critics in her journal during the Spanish Civil War. Other viewpoints had to be expressed: "To say otherwise is to say *The Nation* ought to be a party organ. The whole value of its function is to be analytical and critical and free to present varying views without any inhibitions resulting from partisan control or even rigid ideological limits."[115] Those words, written in 1937, would have fallen on deaf ears during Kirchwey's last few years of editorship. Her positions against her enemies hardened until she evoked a quality she had disparaged in others so often and so early on. She became dogmatic.

The political climate of the 1950s and Kirchwey's uncompromising positions compounded the *Nation*'s financial problems. That Kirstein would financially sustain the journal and continue its "militant liberalism" "did a lot to offset my feeling of loss and defeat," Kirchwey wrote. "*The Nation,* in other hands, is still *The Nation.*" Yet would it be? And would Freda Kirchwey be Freda Kirchwey without daily responsibility for that journal? She had invested too much of herself in the *Nation* to write about her years with it. She seemed to have lost that "Last Battle."[116]

Epilogue

The year Freda Kirchwey retired as editor and publisher of the *Nation* marked the end of an era. As John P. Diggins points out in *Up from Communism*, 1955 serves as an interesting departure point in the history of American ideas. Louis Hartz published *The Liberal Tradition in America*, which signified a consensus among leading intellectuals that led to a celebration of American nationalism and, later, a conservative revival of old values. That same year William F. Buckley inaugurated the *National Review*, a voice of the new conservatism.[1] At least part of the fervor of the new intellectual right stemmed from disillusionment with, and in some cases disdain for, the performance of liberalism. The particular brand of the *Nation*'s liberalism also changed in 1955. Despite Kirchwey's reassurances to her readers that the magazine she turned over to McWilliams and Kirstein was "still *The Nation*," the weekly would soon undergo a substantial transformation.[2]

Carey McWilliams called that fateful year the "logical time" for the transfer. As a decade of the Cold War drew to an end, major social, cultural, and technological changes in America pulled his attention away from foreign issues. Although the *Nation* continued to cover foreign events such as tension in Spain, the growing war in Vietnam, and unrest in Cuba, McWilliams instituted investigative reports mostly on domestic issues. Such attention, using the method of reports, was not new to the *Nation,* but the number of special issues that had a domestic focus and the decrease in attention to foreign policy coverage changed the tone of the journal quite significantly. McWilliams considered these special series in "the muckraking tradition."[3] The *Nation* covered the growth of the military-industrial complex that Eisenhower had warned against in his farewell speech as President. A series on civil rights declared it was "Time To Kill Jim Crow." With McWilliams' support, consumer advocate Ralph Nader got his start when the *Nation* published his first disclosures. There was also a series of reports that linked cancer to certain occupations.[4]

Not only did the journal's subject matter change, so did its cast of characters. Perhaps most important, McWilliams abolished J. Alvarez del Vayo's position of foreign editor, keeping him on the masthead as European correspondent; the former mainstay of the journal wrote only infrequent articles. Another former *Nation* writer, Andrew Roth, complained to Kirchwey that the *Nation* refused to publish many of the old-timers, including him. Blaming the conservatism of Kirstein, he wrote, "at least I understood why all the radical 'Kirchweyites' had been given the cold shoulder."[5]

Kirchwey too disappeared from the *Nation,* though this seemed to be her own doing rather than that of the new regime. She had planned to continue writing for the *Nation,* but a few months after her retirement she traveled to Algiers to witness Michael's marriage to a French woman, Edmée Janier. She "postponed her writing." With the exception of a short book review in 1961 and a reminiscent piece about her early years on the weekly for the *Nation*'s one-hundredth anniversary issue, she wrote almost nothing for it from her retirement in 1955 until her death in 1976.[6]

She did write some for the *Gazette and Daily* (York, Pennsylvania) as its United Nations correspondent. Observing the UN General Assembly, she wrote about the emergent African nations with much interest and support. But she found the assignment difficult; as she explained to her editors: "I must admit I've found it harder than I dreamed to get my bearings in that many-ringed circus—even the geography of the U.N. still baffles me . . . if you really want prompt and regular service you must feel free to get stories from other, more efficient correspondents."[7]

Kirchwey had another reason to attend United Nations sessions. A long-term active member of the Women's International League for Peace and Freedom (WILPF), in the 1950s she became its UN delegate. The WILPF hoped that the United Nations would achieve peace and strongly endorsed its Universal Declaration of Human Rights, which stated: "the inherent dignity of inalienable rights of all members of the human family is the foundation of freedom, justice, and peace in the world."[8] Along with René Cassin of France, Eleanor Roosevelt, the U.S. delegate to the United Nations, was one of the chief architects of the 1948 document, which Roosevelt called an agreement of "very great intrinsic worth." When celebrations marked the Declaration's tenth anniversary, Kirchwey wrote the WILPF statement, calling the Declaration "a model document," one that had influenced the constitutions in some twenty nations that came into being after World War II. Although she was aware that constitutional guarantees were not automatic, "at least the rights are recognized in law and all citizens are acknowledged as possessing them." The document gave strength to the forces trying to carry out its ideals and became a "yard-stick with which to measure progress" and "a symbol of hope and inspiration."[9] As in earlier years, Kirchwey retained an unshakable belief in the power of the written word. She held to declarations of principles, despite situations that mocked them—such as the Soviets' crushing of the Hungarian uprising and the South African apartheid policy. As the WILPF representative to the UN for the United States, Kirchwey urged several American delegates to oppose the arms race and to advocate action to bridge economic gaps between nations.[10]

Not all WILPF action was critical of U.S. policy. President John F. Kennedy's decision not to invade Cuba during the missile crisis in October 1962 gained him immediate WILPF public praise.[11] Just as quickly, a month later, when Kennedy bypassed the UN and imposed a quarantine around Cuba, the WILPF issued protest telegrams to the President and to Senator J. William Fulbright, chairman of the Senate Committee on Foreign Relations: "You must urge the President to accept U Thant's proposal for moratorium and negotiations immediately and without qualification." In early 1959 Kirchwey retired from her active service with WILPF. She said that one representative could not do a conscientious job at the UN and alluded to her own exhaustion. At least two people were needed, she wrote: "Such a change may not be feasible; possibly the idea merely reflects my own rather depleted state."[12]

By the early 1960s Freda Kirchwey and Evans Clark were in ill health. Insomnia was the long-time nemesis of Freda, who also suffered from debilitating migraine headaches. More important, both husband and wife began to pay much more attention to their ailments. Freda was "what used to be called 'peaked'—just below par in every department—blood count, temperature, blood pressure, etc.," and her doctor urged that she give up "at least one major 'job.'" Her decision to drop the WILPF post meant relinquishing status at the UN and the covering of issues that interested her, but she hoped to regain for Evans and herself, "all the health and energy we can reasonably hope for." Yet even as she agreed to give up the post, she mentioned some remaining "minor obligations," which she would "cling to."[13]

It was time for Freda to "tackle" her book about the *Nation*. Her attempt to sort through her numerous *Nation* files was stressful. After twenty years the Kirchwey-Clarks were preparing to move from their Washington Square West apartment, and that too was a burden. "I'm drowning in all my papers," she admitted to a friend who offered to "rescue" her; but she did not accept the offer.[14] After moving to an apartment building on the East Side, she still "felt like a piece of tissue paper." Nothing specific could be diagnosed: "I really find myself wishing for an acute easily disposed ailment that could be dosed or operated on—& done with!"[15]

In the hope that travel might help, she planned a trip to her beloved Israel, about which—to paraphrase a remark by Carey Mc-Williams—she knew a great deal more than Indiana. She visited Israel in 1956 and again in 1965, the latter visit marred by "a very aggressive Israeli bug, or perhaps it was an Arab one!"[16]

Kirchwey's illness cut short a rather formidable itinerary she and Evans had planned for a three-week Israel sojourn. But she saw enough to remain a staunch partisan: "It is one of the few fine and hopeful places in this grim world of ours and what has been accomplished in the last 15—no 17 years is almost unbelievable." That summer ended with a trip to Nyon, Switzerland, to visit Michael and his family, which now included two grandchildren, Philip and Marie-Gabrielle, nicknamed Maïe. "My insides are okay now," Freda wrote her friend and former copy editor, Marion Hess, "so I have nothing really to grouse about." And, "the kids are dears."[17] She and Evans visited them a summer later, after a trip to Puerto Rico failed to provide the salutary effects she had hoped for: "Somehow my state of being is rather low. Nothing serious and nothing new.

Just the old troubles of little or no sleep at night . . . I've had less acute nerve-'joint'-muscle aches, but still enough to be tiring and to encourage lazyness. It's all unserious but a bore."[18]

Despite persistent debilitating health problems during her retirement years, Kirchwey devoted what energy she had to various attempts to loosen Franco's grip on Spain. In 1960 she helped organize a committee to generate support for Franco's enemies, but times were difficult for recruitment to what would become the Committee for a Democratic Spain. The response of C. Wright Mills, who wrote that time constraints prohibited his support, made Kirchwey wonder whether other reasons restrained liberals from joining the organization. "Here it is hard to get the name of even so brave and liberal a person as Eleanor Roosevelt. Whether this all stems from a lack of interest and lack of hope, or whether it is part of the aftermath of McCarthyism I can't say." Recruiting author William L. Shirer, she wrote of the venture: "I am again involved— don't weep, or laugh! in a committee for Spain."[19]

"Franco Foes Organize" read the *New York Times*'s coverage of the organizational meeting of the new Committee for a Democratic Spain (CDS), which Kirchwey and other Americans launched. Waldo Frank chaired the committee, with Freda Kirchwey and Otto Nathan (economist and executor of Einstein's estate) as vice-chairmen. In her work for CDS, Kirchwey maintained her belief in the power of reasonable arguments presented to reasonable people to affect policy changes. She appealed to Lawrence Fernsworth, expert on Spain, to help draft a document that detailed the plight inside Spain and showed why the United States should reverse its policy and cease supporting Franco: "In short, what we need is a basic document presenting the facts which should convince reasonable people that the United States is not only backing a brutal tyranny but is artificially keeping alive a crumbling, corrupt and inefficient governmental structure—unsuited in every way to the role of ally or friend."[20]

Russell Nixon, Washington representative of the United Electrical, Radio & Machine Workers of America, suggested that the CDS should testify before the Senate Foreign Relations Committee,[21] and in the summer of 1961 Freda Kirchwey appeared there as the CDS representative. She pleaded the case for withdrawing funds from Spain. Although the CDS agreed about the importance of aiding underdeveloped countries, such aid could not be given indiscriminately. Past examples of American aid had had counterproductive effects in Korea, Turkey, and Iraq. Such aid often: "subsidized social injustice, failed to prevent the waste and corruption that foster economic chaos, and promoted rather than forestalled the kind of revolt born of despair, and in the end have made the United States hated instead of loved by the people suffering under reactionary rulers, rulers who so greedily take our money."

Kirchwey argued that such was the case in Spain. Reminding the Senate Committee that Franco's rise to power had been made possible by the support and collaboration of Hitler and Mussolini, she traced the history of recent relations. She detailed the UN boycott of Spain in 1946, the reversal of policy and admission of Spain to the UN in 1950, and the U.S. change of policy from boycott to a resumption of aid to Spain in 1953. Documenting the current economic hardships of the Spanish people and political unrest in Spain, she inserted a 1961 article from the *Reporter* and stories about Spain from various foreign correspondents into the Committee's record to substantiate her points. Opposing continued aid, she emphasized: "It is our view that by ending economic aid, this country will not hurt the people of Spain. It will only weaken the dictatorship that oppresses them, and open the way for democratic elements to take control in a land that has suffered too much and too long."

Ohio Senator Frank Lausche challenged Kirchwey to compare her committee's stand against aid to Spain with a position toward aid to Poland and Yugoslavia. She admitted, "I certainly would not give aid to Poland if I thought it was going to be used to perpetuate the dictatorship over the Polish people." But in her defense of aid to Yugoslavia, Kirchwey reiterated her belief in the difference between dictatorships of the left and the right. She did not like either, but she saw a qualitative difference between Yugoslavia's regime and that of Spain: "We believe that an effort is being made to develop the economy of the country rather than to pour money into the pockets of the henchmen of the regime . . . the actual condition of a very poor people had probably been improved by it . . . I think it would be impossible to claim that in Spain. I think it has gone exactly the opposite way. People are more miserable than when they began to give money to Spain." Spain under Franco could never shed its ugly skin as "the last hateful remnant of Nazi-Fascist power in Europe."[22] Kirchwey and the CDS efforts did not prevail; Spain was included in the U.S. aid package put together that September.[23]

The Committee for a Democratic Spain continued to try to persuade senators and congressmen to change their minds. Writing to Wisconsin representative Clement J. Zablocki, and others who had eulogized Franco on the occasion of the twenty-fifth anniversary of the start of the civil war in Spain, Kirchwey wrote: "We strongly urge that you consider whether it is not in the best interests of the American people that our Congress align itself with those who seek to end the enslavement of the Spanish people—now, before it may be too late."[24] The CDS also held meetings, gave speeches, and published a newsletter, *Spain Today*. First published in 1961, *Spain Today* carried inside information about Spain that was censored by Franco. It publicized protests against the regime and "the economic misery" of the Spanish people.[25] Kirchwey became the unofficial editor of the newsletter; this was the only journalistic venture of her declining years. Two years after retiring from the *Nation,* she had considered creating a sixteen-page, fortnightly foreign policy journal: "Analytical, behind the news (exposé when possible), with a clear left-liberal p[oint] of v[iew] and policy of advocacy and attack as well as interpretation and criticism." She would edit it gratis, with the help of three paid staff. She would have regular contributors from the UN and Washington, D.C., and irregular contributors from other important spots around the world. The project never materialized beyond the budgeting stage.[26]

*

Freda Kirchwey's final journalistic project—a book about her years at the *Nation*—remained unfinished. No matter how hard she tried, she could not write it. She decided to publish the book with Stanley Rinehart, but she had difficulty composing even a brief outline. Writing an old friend about the "still non-existent book," she remarked: "I haven't done it yet, but I will soon. I really will. (Why have I such reluctance about this venture? Just lazy probably!)" The next month, still unable to finish the description, she wrote Rinehart, "Don't despair of me yet!" She produced the sketch a few months later, blaming the delays on "urgent claims of some family crises." By October she wrote to her former secretary that she could not write before she got a contract: "I've agreed to do the *Nation* book for Rinehart. No contract, yet, however, and I can't seem to make myself put pencil to paper until I get one." Nevertheless, the contract arrived a few days later, and there was still no work on the book. About a year later Kirchwey's comments to Barbara Tuchman revealed her inability to get on with the project: "I do so much admire your ability to combine an immense job of this kind with the complications of children and social life and all the rest. Admire and envy you because I have been trying to get myself to work on a book about *The Nation* and, after a year, have found myself bogged down almost beyond help."[27]

Kirchwey became preoccupied with what she came to regard as a momentous task of completing her book. She compared Del Vayo's busy schedule with her own inactivity: "You have loaded yourself up with so much writing that I don't see how you will be able to swing all you have to do (Esp. since I can't write even *one* book!)" Carey McWilliams urged her on: "If I didn't hold you in such reverence I would say that you should have a brisk and vigorous spanking if you abandon the book project. I read the outline with the greatest interest, and if I ever saw a complete outline for a book this is it. For the life of me I don't know why you are throwing in the towel." By 1962 she seemed to have given up the project and admitted completing "an outline of a book I probably shall never write." A couple of years later she still agonized over it: "I'm still struggling with my Spanish committee; no money, not much help . . . I'm also doing several other things—but not my book! To settle down to that grind, I'm afraid is beyond me."[28]

In 1964 even the brief piece about her early *Nation* years for the journal's hundredth anniversary issue seemed too much. She accumulated research for the "opus," but was overwhelmed by the magnitude of the task.[29] Why did a woman who had not been daunted by the enormity of Hitler, war, and the atomic bomb have such resistance to writing about her years with the *Nation*? Procrastination may have been a factor. During her long career Kirchwey produced scores of editorials, each under the prodding of an imminent deadline. But though she edited two books, she never attempted the kind of sustained concentration that a book on the *Nation* would have required. Carey McWilliams hypothesized that she never wrote it because of "an innate reluctance to talk about herself."[30] She wanted the book to be a personal account but "to avoid the subjective, self-focused emphasis of an autobiography"; it should be "a biography of the paper itself."[31] Kirchwey could never write that book, for there was no way that she could write the *Nation*'s history without writing her own. Perhaps something even deeper lay beneath a reluctance to complete the task. In 1932, when Kirchwey returned to the *Nation* after mourning the death of her son in seclusion, she seems to have merged herself into the journal; she and the journal became one. When she retired in 1955, she lost her raison d'être.

✳

The once public Freda Kirchwey spent her remaining years in relative obscurity. By 1970 Evans' health demanded all her attention: "My own job is the only one I now care about: keeping E. as happy as conditions permit and being with him constantly, so he can suffer no moments of dread. As you can imagine he is an *angel* of patience and fortitude. Pray that I may have all that is needed to sustain and comfort him. Since things became so difficult, I have not been an hour away from him. (Just once I had a hair-do across First Ave.— and he was there with me!)" She described a very frail man whose mind was slipping: "His speech—it is perfectly cogent in rather broad terms. But he will lose the single word he is fishing for, and then obviously feel confused and helpless . . . I, of course, do all I can to bridge these hiatuses, without seeming to keep correcting or rescuing him."[32] Evans' condition deteriorated further. By summer Freda wrote, "My time is totally absorbed in trying to bring my dear Evans back to a nearly normal state of health and mind."[33]

Later that summer of 1970 Freda and Evans returned to Nyon to be near Michael and his family. There on a sunny August day, as the two of them sat peacefully on the balcony of their hotel room overlooking Lake Geneva and the Alps he had so loved, Evans quietly died. Freda was so distraught by his death that she could not even attend the funeral. Caroline Whiting, whose desk was next to Freda's at the *Nation* for more than twenty years, said that even she had never realized how much Freda depended upon her husband.[34] From the time Evans died to her own death six years later Freda was never the same.

Early in 1971 Michael accompanied a "weak and shaky" Freda back to Switzerland and settled her in an apartment above that of his family. He worried about his mother, who seemed "unusually unsettled and disoriented (for instance: constantly getting lost between our apt. and hers)." Her insomnia worsened and she had "horrible dreams." Freda hoped that "this dear sunshine—even with the cold air of the mountains will gradually make me over," but she found life in Nyon "rather hard to adjust to" and felt out of her "natural orbit." The language barrier exacerbated her feelings of isolation: "Much as I love my family here, I'm desperately tired of the whole place and eager to get away. We'll see what next. (Perhaps the main trouble is my total lack of French—which is the common tongue of the whole family and even those who are perfectly fluent in English (Mike, at least) stick to F[rench] almost totally. Too bad I'm such an ignoramus but since its a fact of life I'd better cope which means a holiday from the *whole* tribe."[35]

The thought of living permanently in Switzerland frightened Freda, and she begged her sister to come and take her away: "Dotty I doubt if my remaining years could be happily spent in Nyon. What seems most possible is that I can mull along here till you are ready to rescue me!"[36] Yet her friend and lawyer, Irwin Miness, vetoed Dorothy's suggestion that Freda return to live alone in her New York apartment, reminding her of the time Freda forgot to turn off the stove and could not discover the reason for her overheated apartment. He worried about the serious harm Freda could cause herself without constant supervision.[37] Although Freda's deteriorating condition precluded a return to her apartment, her sister, doctor, and lawyer decided that breaking it up so soon after Evans' death would be too traumatic. For some time Dorothy paid for the rental and upkeep of the New York apartment to shield her sister from the reality that she could never come home again.[38]

Freda continued to beg Dorothy for help: "I'm worried. Things are going on as usual here, everybody nice and affectionate to me. But still I have worries that I can't easily brush off. I don't feel very well for one thing (no energy). I don't sleep well except with pills—cautiously used." "One of these days," she told her sister, "I'm going to want to go home! Where is home? Well, it's where books and prints and the high-boy and other familiar domestic friends reside—not to mention a few real live ones—first among them being Dottie!"[39]

Meanwhile, she hoped that some editing would make her feel better and asked Dorothy to send along the diaries of her husband, Larry Brown, who had died in April 1969. Freda wanted to edit them for publication, but when they came, she agonized over the difficulty. It took days to get through twenty-three pages. The arrival of a second installment so overwhelmed her, that she sent the entire collection back: "Dottie, I had no idea I would find the work (a familiar kind of work) so difficult, or my powers so feeble! Even before you sent the recent huge batch of copy I was getting scared.

It's (sic.) arrival seemed to seal my fate!" She lamented her inability to complete it: "my failure as an editor of dear Larry's diaries is a burden I can't ever shake off."[40]

Freda's depression continued and she found herself in a "quite depleted state." Finally, in June 1971, Dorothy arranged for her departure from Switzerland. Freda and her grandson, Philip, traveled to America, he to attend the Phillips Exeter Academy summer school, and she to live with Dorothy in Boston. That worked for a while. Dorothy, though six years older, was in fairly good health. She hired a male nurse, George Holley, to help care for Freda in a comfortable apartment on the corner of Charles and Beacon streets that the sisters shared. Freda cheered up a bit, but still wrote about "a state of exhaustion that I can't seem to get rid of."[41] She also confessed "I miss horrid old N.Y. in spite of its sins!" She continued her walks in the Boston Common and Public Garden, but "strangely the tiredness nags at me even on good and sunny days—like today!" Once again she wanted to try editing and suggested to Otto Nathan that she help him edit the Einstein papers: "I'm a pretty good editor and I love my trade."[42] Freda, recalling her father's memory lapses during his final years, once said, "I hope I never get to that point." Yet increasingly she did. At a party for the Del Vayos, she agonized, "It's awful. I don't remember anything and anybody's name. I shouldn't come to these dinners."[43]

Late in 1972 Freda took Holley's puppy for a walk in the Boston cold, tripped over the dog, and broke her hip. Although she survived an operation, she never fully recovered, and mentally she deteriorated so badly that she required more comprehensive care. Dorothy selected a private nursing home in New Brunswick, Canada. From there Freda was transferred to Saint Petersburg, Florida—the same state in which she had felt such alienation years before, when she tried to nurse Jeffrey back to health.

When Michael Clark visited his mother just after Christmas 1975, she no longer recognized him. As she lay dying, on 3 January 1976, Freda Kirchwey's last words were about the *Nation*.[44]

Bibliographical Note

The Freda Kirchwey manuscript collection is cited as Freda Kirchwey papers, Schlesinger Library, Radcliffe College, MC 280; hereafter cited as FK MSS. References to processed collections in the Schlesinger Library holdings include file unit numbers. The Kirchwey papers were deposited in Schlesinger Library by Freda Kirchwey's sister, Dorothy Kirchwey Brown, from December 1969 through August 1977. During that time I received special permission from Mrs. Brown to use this collection in its uncatalogued state; file unit numbers were not then available. In March 1979 the Kirchwey papers were processed. Notes resulting from research conducted after 1979 include file unit numbers. Although I had access to personal papers prior to processing and was granted special access while completing this book, FK's personal papers (#1–100 and 384–397) have been closed to researchers since 1979.

Several citations that appear frequently include Kirchwey's book manuscript outline (#363) and her scrapbook writings for the New York *Morning Telegraph* and for *Every Week* (microfilm #M–28). Some clippings appear in oversized folders marked with a °.

The location of frequently cited Freda Kirchwey and Evans Clark diaries are:

FK	10 December 1909–December 1911	69v
FK	January–February 1918	70v
FK	January–March 1930	71v
FK	June–November 1935	72v
Evans Clark, 1928–1929		73v
Evans Clark, 1933		74v

Several notes refer to Memoranda pages of the diaries.

Unsigned articles and editorials attributed to Kirchwey have been verified by checking the annotated set of *The Nation* deposited by Oswald Garrison Villard in the New York Public Library. (Most, but not all of those years are annotated.) Freda Kirchwey's unsigned articles and editorials are designated by her name in brackets. Other unsigned articles and editorial paragraphs appear with periodical citations.

Materials from Freda Kirchwey's high school years are found in the *Horace Mannikin* and *Horace Mann Bulletin* in Horace Mann Archives, Horace Mann Barnard School, Bronx, N.Y. For her college years, consult appropriate issues of the *Barnard Bear* and *Mortarboard* at Barnard College Archives, Barnard College, New York, N.Y.

Michael Clark's private collection, hereafter cited as MC private collection, consists of vast papers and diaries, his own and those of his parents, Freda Kirchwey and Evans Clark. In addition, Clark holds two separate FBI files on Kirchwey. I have designated FBI file #100–40612–7 as FK FBI f. 1 and #100–36197 as FK FBI f.2.

Additional materials were used from the private collections of Sara Alpern, hereafter cited as Alpern private collection; Marion Hess, hereafter cited as Marion Hess private collection; Otto Nathan, hereafter cited as Otto Nathan private collection; Michael Wreszin, hereafter cited as Michael Wreszin private collection. Evans Clark's papers appear in Amherst College Archives, Amherst College, Amherst, Massachusetts, hereafter cited as EC MSS.

The Dorothy Kirchwey Brown Papers appear in two unprocessed collections: Dorothy Kirchwey Brown Papers, Schlesinger Library, Radcliffe College, Cambridge, Mass., hereafter cited as DKB addenda, 70s; Dorothy Kirchwey Brown Papers, Schlesinger Library, Radcliffe College, Cambridge, Mass., hereafter cited as DKB addenda, 81. Details of the birth of Evans Clark, Brewster Clark and Michael Clark are located in *The Mother's Register*, 27v, DKB addenda, 70s.

The Oswald Garrison Villard Papers, Houghton Library, Harvard University, Cambridge, Mass., hereafter cited as OGV MSS, contain separate folder numbers for several *Nation* correspondents. Other manuscripts are located in two additional boxes: 106 and 107.

*

The following additional manuscripts were consulted for this book. Specific collections are listed alphabetically under their respective libraries; those that are cited in the book are abbreviated as used in the notes.

Special Collection Archives, Franklin Trask Library, Andover Newton Theological School, Newton Centre, Mass.; hereafter cited as Andover Newton Archives.
Beinecke Library, Yale University, New Haven, Conn.: Margaret Marshall Papers; hereafter cited as MM MSS.
Columbia University Oral History Project, Columbia University, New York, N.Y.
Franklin Delano Roosevelt Library, Hyde Park, N.Y.:
  Franklin Delano Roosevelt Papers; hereafter cited as FDR MSS.
  President's Personal File; hereafter cited as PPF.
  Eleanor Roosevelt Papers; hereafter cited as ER MSS.
  Louis Fischer Papers; hereafter cited as LF/FDR MSS.
Houghton Library, Harvard University, Cambridge, Mass.:
  American Fund for Public Service Papers.
  Samuel June Barrows Papers; hereafter cited as Barrows MSS.
  Lewis Stiles Gannett Papers; hereafter cited as LSG MSS.
  Trotskii Exile Papers; hereafter cited as Trotskii MSS.
Manuscript Division, Library of Congress, Washington, D.C.:
  Jo Davidson Papers.
  Felix Frankfurter Papers; hereafter cited as FF MSS.
  Harold L. Ickes Papers.
  Joseph Wood Krutch Papers; hereafter cited as JWK MSS.
  Reinhold Niebuhr Papers; hereafter cited as RN MSS.
  William Allen White Papers; hereafter cited as WAW MSS.
Rare Books and Manuscripts Division, The New York Public Library, Astor, Lenox and Tilden Foundations, New York, N.Y.:
  American Fund for Public Service Papers; hereafter cited as AFPS MSS.
  Norman Thomas Papers; hereafter cited as NT MSS.
Princeton University Library, Princeton, N.J.:
  American Civil Liberties Union Papers.
  Louis Fischer Papers; hereafter cited as LF MSS.
Schlesinger Library, Radcliffe College, Cambridge, Mass.:

Vera Micheles Dean Papers, A–17; hereafter cited as VMD MSS.
Mary Elisabeth Dreier Papers, MC 309; hereafter cited as Dreier MSS.
Inez Haynes Irwin Papers, A–25; hereafter cited as Irwin MSS.
Leon Malmed and Emma Goldman Papers, MC 332; hereafter cited as Malmed/Goldman MSS.
Mary Melinda Kingsbury Simkhovitch Papers, A–97.
Miriam Van Waters Papers, A–71; hereafter cited as MVW MSS.
Social Welfare History Archives, University of Minnesota, Minneapolis, Minn.:
Paul U. Kellogg Papers; hereafter cited as PUK MSS.
Survey Associates Papers; hereafter cited as Survey MSS.
Department of Special Collections, Stanford University Library, Stanford, Calif.: Bruce Bliven Papers.
Sterling Memorial Library, Yale University, New Haven, Conn.:
Jerome N. Frank Papers.
Max Lerner Papers; hereafter cited as ML MSS.
Walter Lippmann Papers.
Dwight Macdonald Papers; hereafter cited as DMcD MSS.
Henry L. Stimson Papers; hereafter cited as Stimson MSS.
Swarthmore College Peace Collection, Swarthmore, Pa.: Women's International League for Peace and Freedom Papers; hereafter cited as WILPF MSS.
Tamiment Library, New York University, New York, N.Y.: American Committee for Cultural Freedom Papers; hereafter cited as ACCF MSS.
Zionist Archives and Library, New York, N.Y.

*

The following are names and dates of interviews conducted for this book. I take this opportunity to thank those listed below for their time and for their recollections.

Alexander, Philip R., M.D. Bryan, Tex., 8 February 1985.
Bell, Daniel. Telephone interview, 18 July 1983.
Bendiner, Robert. New York, N.Y., 16 April 1976.
———— Huntington, N.Y., 4 January 1980.
Bernstein, Selma. New Milford, Conn., 10 July 1983.
Bernstein, Victor. New Milford, Conn., 10 July 1983.
Brown, Dorothy Kirchwey (deceased). Boston, Mass., 16 August 1974.
———— Boston, Mass., 15 October 1974.
Clark, Michael. Cambridge, Mass., 6 September 1974.
———— Interview form, February, 1984.

——— Boston, Mass., 12 May 1984.
——— Boston, Mass., 13 May 1984.
——— Nova Scotia, Canada, 27 July 1984.
——— Nova Scotia, Canada, 28 July 1984.
——— Nova Scotia, Canada, 29 July 1984.
——— Nova Scotia, Canada, 30 July 1984.
——— Telephone interview, 3 January 1986.
——— Telephone interview, 26 January 1986.
——— Telephone interview, 15 March 1986.
Del Vayo, Diego. New York, N.Y., 30 June 1983.
Elkin, Lillian. New York, N.Y., 20 June 1983.
Epstein, Grace. Scarsdale, N.Y., 16 April 1976.
Gannett, Michael R. Telephone interview, 27 January 1986.
Hess, Marion. New York, N.Y., 13 April 1976.
——— New York, N.Y., 5 January 1980.
——— San Diego, Calif., 12 August 1985.
Hook, Sidney. South Wardsboro, Vt., 19 July 1983.
Howe, Irving. Telephone interview, 21 June 1983.
Hutchinson, Keith. Southbury, Conn., 9 July 1983.
Hutschnecker, Dr. Arnold A. New York, N.Y., 20 June 1983.
Kirchwey, George W. III. Telephone interview, 6 January 1986.
MacKenzie, Mary, Lake Placid Historian. Telephone interview, 26 January 1984.
McWilliams, Carey (deceased). New York, N.Y., 13 April 1976.
——— New York, N.Y., 14 April 1976.
McWilliams, Iris. New York, N.Y., 14 April 1976.
Miness, Irwin. New York, N.Y., 15 April 1976.
——— New York, N.Y., 23 June 1983.
Miness, Nina. New York, N.Y., 15 April, 1976.
——— New York, N.Y., 23 June 1983.
Moroch, Dorothy Conigliaro, editor, *Horace Mann–Barnard Alumni Magazine*. Telephone interview, 10 April 1986.
Nathan, Otto. New York, N.Y., 14 April 1976.
Negrin, Dr. Juan. New York, N.Y., 1 July 1983.
Schlesinger, Arthur M., Jr. New York, N.Y., 22 June 1983.
Shirer, William L. Lenox, Mass., 19 July 1983.
Stone, I. F. Washington, D.C., 21 July 1980.
——— Washington, D.C., 22 July 1980.
Straight, Michael. Interview form. 2 November 1983.
Trilling, Diana. New York, N.Y., 21 June 1983.
Tuchman, Barbara. Cos Cob, Conn., 21 July 1983.
Van Doren, Dorothy. Interview form, n.d., 1983.

Voss, Carl Hermann. Telephone interview, 28 October 1983.
Whiting, Caroline (Mrs. Robert A. Nash). Winsted, Conn., 10 July
    1983.
———— Winsted, Conn., 11 July 1983.
———— Winsted, Conn., 12 July 1983.

Notes

In addition to the abbreviations of archival materials given in the Bibliographical Note, the following abbreviations are used:

INDIVIDUALS

Freda Kirchwey	FK
Evans Clark	EC
Michael Clark	MC
Dorothy Kirchwey Brown	DKB
Dora Wendell Kirchwey	DWK
George Washington Kirchwey	GWK
Carey McWilliams	CMcW
Oswald Garrison Villard	OGV

TITLES

International Relations Section	IRS
The Morning Telegraph	*TMT*
New York Times	*NYT*

1. The Proper Rebel

1. Quote from Maude (Howe) Elliott, ed., *Art and Handicraft in the Woman's Building of the World's Columbian Exposition, Chicago, 1893* (Paris, France: Goupil, 1893), preface.

2. Dora Child Wendell Kirchwey, "Summers," n.d. #26, DKB addenda, 81. Telephone interview with Mary MacKenzie, Lake Placid Historian, 26 January 1984; FK 1910 diary, 26 September 1910; interview with DKB, 15 October 1974; *The National Cyclopaedia,* 1927 ed., s.v. Kirchwey, George Washington; Warner Oliver, "Oh, Stop That, Freda!" *Saturday Evening Post* 219 (9 February 1946): 21–22; interview with Grace Epstein, 16 April 1976.

3. GWK's father may have come from Kirchentellinsfurt (West Germany). Telephone interview with George Kirchwey, Jr., 6 January 1986; "George Washington Kirchwey," *A History of the Class of '79, Yale College* (New Haven: Yale, 1906), pp. 257–258; *A History of the School of Law, Columbia University,* by the Staff of the Foundation on Research in Legal History, Under the Direction of Julius Goebel (New York: Columbia, 1955), p. 212; "Obituary of George Washington Kirchwey," *NYT,* 5 March 1942, p. 3; *National Cyclopaedia,* Kirchwey, George Washington; *NYT,* 5 October 1901, p. 5, "Portrait," *The Green Bag* 2 (April 1890): 159; Maurice I. Wormser, ed., *Kirchwey's Cases on the Law of Mortgage,* 2nd ed. (New York: Baker, Voorhis, 1921), p. v; Junius P. Lewis to Henry L. Stimson, 18 February 1926, Stimson I, Box 90 f. 10, Stimson MSS; George A. Finch to DKB, 13 August 1942, #40, DKB addenda, 81.

4. GWK, "The Columbia Law School of To-day," *The Green Bag* 10 (May 1898): 203; "Crime Waves and Remedies," *The Nation* 112 (9 February 1921): 207–208; Lawrence J. Friedman, *A History of American Law* (New York: Simon & Schuster, 1974), 530–536, 591, 592, 563.

5. *NYT,* 22 October 1902, p. 9; 6 October 1901, p. 5; Richard Hofstadter, *Age of Reform, From Bryan to F.D.R.* (New York: Alfred A. Knopf, 1955), pp. 155–164; GWK, "Respect for Law in the United States," *Annals of the American Academy of Political and Social Science* 36 (July 1910): 217; "The Education of the American Lawyer," *American Law School Review* 6 (October 1905): 269.

6. GWK, "Respect for Law," p. 270; James Gilbert, *Designing the Industrial State: The Intellectual Pursuit of Collectivism in America* (Chicago: Quadrangle, 1972), pp. 7–8, 31–33; *NYT,* 14 May 1911, p. 16; GWK, "Crime and Punishment," *Journal of Criminal Law and Criminology* 6 (January 1911): 732; GWK, "Ending the Reign of Terror," *Survey* 25 (5 November 1910): 186; "The Future Attitude toward Crime," *Journal of Criminal Law and Criminology* 2 (November 1911): 501–504; *NYT,* 1 January 1916, p. 4.

7. *New York Post,* 18 February 1944, #40, DKB addenda, 81; GWK to FK, 18 July 1913, p. 1, 2, #392, FK MSS; *History Columbia Law,* p. 248; Mrs. Mabel S. Call to DKB, 25 August 1942, #40, DKB addenda, 81. C. Roland Marchand, *The American Peace Movement and Social Reform, 1898–1918* (Princeton: Princeton University Press, 1974), pp. 74–98.

8. FK 1911 diary, 5 February 1911; FK 1910 diary, 19 February, 12 June 1910; FK 1911 diary, 5 February, 10 December 1911; DWK to FK, 24 May 1911, #389, p. 4; all FK MSS.

9. *Private Independent Schools,* 33rd ed., s.v. Horace Mann School; *The Handbook of Private Schools: An Annual Descriptive Survey of Independent Education,* 61st ed., s.v. Horace Mann School; obituary, Clara B. Kirchwey, *NYT,* 24 June 1936, p. 23; obituary, Mary Frederika Kirchwey, *NYT,* 26 March 1942, p. 23; John Palmer Gavit to FK, 26 July 1937, FK MSS.

10. FK 1910 diary, 16 January, 25 January, 8 May, 10 June, 15 June, 23 June, 24

June 1910; FK 1911 diary, 6 June 1911; FK 1910 diary, 18 June 1910; FK 1911 diary, 9 June 1911; all FK MSS.

11. FK 1910 diary, 16 January 1910; *The Horace Mannikin* 8 (New York: The Senior Class of Horace Mann High School, 1911): 24, 89, 61, 16; interview with DKB, Boston, Mass., 15 October 1974.

12. FK, "The Flanigans," *Horace Mann Bulletin*, April 1909, p. 9; FK, "Mr. Spofford Fitch," *Horace Mann Bulletin*, March 1910, pp. 12–13.

13. FK, "A Private Letter to H. G. Wells," *The Nation* 125 (2 November 1927): 574. About the same time, a contemporary political writer, Rebecca West, also wrote about Wells's, Galsworthy's and Shaw's influence on herself. She recalled: "All our youth they hung about the house of our minds like Uncles." Rebecca West, *The Strange Necessity* (New York: Doubleday, 1928), p. 215.

14. FK, "A Trip to Gooseland," *Horace Mann Bulletin*, June 1908, pp. 23–25; italics in original.

15. Oliver, "Oh, Stop That, Freda!" p. 22; see Dorothy Canfield Fisher to Lillie Shultz, 8 June 1944, #418, FK MSS for Fisher's description of the incident.

16. Eugene Wambaugh to GWK, poem, 18 May 1905, #33, DKB addenda, 81; "George Washington Kirchwey," *History of Class of '79*, p. 261.

17. FK 1911 diary, 21 March 1911; FK 1910 diary, 30 March 1910; FK 1911 diary, memoranda, p. 14; *The Horace Mannikin* 8, p. 24.

18. FK to DKB, 14 February 1913, #22, DKB addenda, 70s; FK to DKB, 12 March 1911, p. 1, #45, DKB addenda, 81. The Girls' League was a civic organization which did charity work. Telephone interview with Dorothy Conigliaro Moroch, editor, *Horace Mann-Barnard Alumni Magazine*, 10 April 1986.

19. Rufus Wendell to DWK, 26 May 1898, p. 2, #26; DWK to DKB, n.d. #27, both DKB addenda, 81. In this letter Rufus Wendell called himself an "Adventist," but he was known as a Methodist minister. Telephone interview with MC, 3 January 1986.

20. DWK to FK, n.d. [1911], # 389, FK MSS; where Lawrence's early heroes yearned for a new consciousness in nature that would join or balance conflicting claims of self, Mary rejoices in the freedom and aliveness of the natural world. Paul's rebellion is against the narrow life of a mining village in the Midlands; Mary rebels against a superficial upper-middle-class background. D. H. Lawrence, *Sons and Lovers* (New York: Viking, 1958); FK, "Afternoon of a Nymph," unpublished manuscript, n.d., pp. 1–29, #5, FK MSS.

21. FK, unpublished manuscript, 18 February 1913, #22, DKB addenda, 70s.

22. FK, review of *Living My Life* by Emma Goldman, *The Nation* 133 (2 December 1931): 612–613.

23. FK to DKB, 20 August 1912, p. 5, #45, DKB addenda, 81; FK, "Feet of Clay," n.d., FK MSS.

24. Jane Marcus, ed., *The Young Rebecca: Writings of Rebecca West, 1911–1917*, (New York: Viking, 1982), p. 64. See also text and n. 13.

25. Ibid., pp. 146, 39, 119, 124.

26. FK, "On Reviewing Books for Children," *The Nation* 127 (21 November 1928): 547; FK, 28 February 1913, #22, DKB addenda, 70s; see other stories there.

27. FK's Barnard transcripts.

28. FK's Barnard transcripts; Columbia University Bulletin of Information, Barnard College announcement, 1914–1915; FK to DKB, 20 August 1912, p. 3, #45, DKB addenda, 81.

29. [FK], "Spring Realism," *The Nation* 118 (16 April 1924): 417.

30. FK, Story, 26 March 1913, #22, DKB addenda, 70s; clippings, 17 January 1913; additional clippings, n.d., #430, FK MSS.

31. Clipping, n.d., #430, FK MSS.

32. FK, "College Life," *Barnard Bear* 10 (October 1914): 4–7; FK 1911 diary, 13, 27 November 1911.

33. Emily M. Pierson, M.D., to FK, 19 October 1961, FK MSS; FK, "Peddling the Gospel," *Barnard Bear* 8 (December 1912): 5–8; FK to DKB, n.d., p. 1, #121, DKB addenda, 81.

34. DWK to FK, 17 April 1913, #389, FK MSS. As a young reporter, FK would say of the head probation officer of the Domestic Relations Court: "Miss McQuade had that most valuable of all human assets, a 'way' with people"; FK, scrapbook, 16 September 1915.

35. FK, "Fraternities versus Democracy," *Barnard Bear* 8 (October 1912), 3–6.

36. *NYT,* 8 June 1913, sec. v, p. 10; FK also opposed the idea of an all-Jewish Menorah Society as proposed by some Jewish women at Barnard. See FK, "Religious Organizations in Barnard," *Barnard Bear* 9 (March 1914): 3–4.

37. DWK to FK, 30 March 1913, #389, FK MSS.

38. FK to DKB, 20 March 1914, pp. 1, 2, #17, DKB addenda, 70s; interview with Grace Epstein, 16 April 1976.

39. *Columbia University Alumnae Register, 1754–1931* (New York: Columbia University Press, 1932), p. 156; Princeton University catalogue, 1914–1915, pp. 123–125; MC, written interview form, February 1984, Alpern's private collection; *Who's Who in America,* 1950–51 ed, s.v. Clark, Evans.

40. FK to DKB, 20 March 1914, p. 2, #17, DKB addenda, 70s, *The Mortarboard* 21 (New York: The Junior Class of Barnard College, 1915): 138.

41. Interview with Grace Epstein, 16 April 1976; FK 1910 diary, 10 February 1910; memorandum, p. 12; EC to FK, 10 August n.d., #388, FK MSS.

42. GWK to FK, 11 March 1915, pp. 1–2, #392, FK MSS.

43. Interview with Nina Miness, 23 June 1983.

44. DWK to DKB, 15 March 1915, pp. 2b, 3b, 4a, #17, DKB addenda, 81.

45. *NYT,* 17 March 1915, p. 11; W. E. Lewis to FK, [1915]; Bail [?] to Fritz, [1915]; John Temple Graves, Jr., to FK, n.d. [March 1915]; last three, #396, FK MSS.

46. FK to DKB, n.d.; EC to DKB, n.d., both #45, DKB addenda, 81.

47. Columbia University Bulletin of Information, Barnard College Announcement, 1914–1915; Freda Kirchwey sketch, 2 June 1965, #385, FK MSS; FK to DKB, 26 June [1935], #127, DKB addenda, 81.

48. GWK to FK, July 1914, pp. 3, 4, #392, FK MSS; FK to DKB, 9 April 1925, #46, DKB addenda, 81.

49. FK, "Valedictory 1915," *Barnard Bear* 11 (October 1915): 1–4; FK, "The New Heresy," *Barnard Bear* 10 (May 1915): 10; FK, "College Life," p. 5; *NYT,* 11 June 1915, p. 1.

50. FK, "Valedictory," pp. 2, 3, 4.

51. FK, review of *Why Women Are So* by Mary Roberts Coolidge, *Barnard Bear* 8 (March 1913): 29.

52. Interview with DKB, 15 October 1974; Oliver, "Oh, Stop That, Freda!" p. 22.

53. *NYT,* 30 September 1915, p. 7; 16 March 1916, p. 12; 28 May 1916, sec. 1, p. 19; 18 June 1916, sec. 1, p. 6; 24 June 1916, p. 4; 7 July 1916, p. 22; 17 July 1916, p. 1; 1 January 1916, p. 4.

54. FK, "Interviewing Sing Sing's New Warden," *Mutual Welfare League Bulletin,* 28 February 1916, pp. 1–3, #353, FK MSS.

55. FK, "Just 'Tom Brown,' The Story of a Great Experiment," *Mutual Welfare League Bulletin,* p. 5, #353, FK MSS.

56. "The Motion Picture vs. Crime" in *National Board of Review Magazine,* p. 29, #40, DKB addenda, 81. Years later ex-convicts came to him for help getting back on their feet after prison. After his death they came to his daughter at the *Nation* office where Freda's secretary, Caroline Whiting (without Freda's knowledge), gave them whatever money she could spare to send them on their way without bothering Freda. Interview with Caroline Whiting Nash, 11 July 1983.

57. FK, "Laurence Housman—Propagandist, Fighter, and Dramatist," *TMT,* 26 March 1916, scrapbook, p. 127; *NYT,* 14 April 1916, p. 5.

58. EC to FK, n.d. [1915], pp. 2, 4; n.d. [1915], p. 2; [1915], p. 2; all #388, FK MSS.

59. EC to FK, [15 August 1915], pp. 2, 3, 7, 8, #388; [FK], "Song," n.d., #5, both FK MSS.

60. Harold I. Weston to EC, 30 March 1915, p. 2, #396; [FK], "Comradeship," #5; EC to FK, 15 September 1915, p. 2, # 388; all FK MSS.

61. EC to FK, n.d. [1915], p. 5, #388, FK MSS; interview with MC, 12 May 1984. The faculty minutes of Andover Newton Theological School, 28 September 1910, show EC admitted to the junior class (first year). No mention is made of his withdrawal, so presumably he completed the year. At this time, 1910, it was called Andover Theological Seminary, located in Cambridge, Mass., and associated with Harvard. In 1931 it became affiliated with Newton Theological Institution in Newton Centre to form Andover Newton Theological School. Andover Newton Archives.

62. EC to FK, n.d. [Summer 1915], p. 5, #388, FK MSS; FK, "Three Prayers to Ceres," *The Independent* 77 (23 February 1914): 265, #23, DKB addenda, 70s; EC to FK, n.d. [1915], p. 3, #388, FK MSS.

63. EC to FK, 2 November [1915], p. 1, #388, FK MSS; H. G. Wells, *The World Set Free* (New York: Dutton, 1914), p. 299.

64. Clipping, n.d., #385, FK MSS.

65. Interview with Grace Epstein, 16 April 1976; list, #124, DKB addenda, 81; *NYT,* 24 November 1915, p. 13.

66. Oliver, "Oh, Stop That, Freda!" pp. 22–23; interview with Grace Epstein, 16 April 1976; June Sochen, ed., *The New Feminism in Twentieth-Century America* (Lexington, Mass.: Heath, 1971).

67. June Sochen, *Movers and Shakers: American Women Thinkers and Activists, 1900–1970* (New York: Quadrangle, 1973), p. 10.

68. Works to consult on woman suffrage include: Lois W. Banner, *Women in Modern America: A Brief History* (New York: Harcourt Brace Jovanovich, 1974); Mari Jo Buhle and Paul Buhle, eds., *The Concise History of Woman Suffrage: Selections from the Classic Work of Stanton, Anthony, Gage, and Harper* (Urbana:

University of Illinois Press, 1978); Ellen Carol DuBois, *Feminism and Suffrage: The Emergence of an Independent Women's Movement in America, 1848–1869* (Ithaca, N.Y.: Cornell University Press, 1978); Eleanor Flexner, *Century of Struggle: The Woman's Rights Movement in the United States* (Cambridge, Mass.: The Belknap Press of Harvard University Press, 1959; rev. ed., 1975); Aileen S. Kraditor, *The Ideas of the Woman Suffrage Movement 1880–1920* (New York: Columbia University Press, 1965; Garden City, N.Y.: Doubleday, 1971); William L. O'Neill, *Everyone Was Brave: The Rise and Fall of Feminism in America* (Chicago: Quadrangle, 1969); William L. O'Neill, *The Woman Movement: Feminism in the United States and England* (New York: Barnes & Noble, 1969).

69. Interview with DKB, 15 October 1974; Oliver, "Oh, Stop That, Freda!" p. 22; *TMT,* 14 June 1915, scrapbook, p. 1; *TMT,* n.d., scrapbook, p. 8.

70. FK, "A Suffrage Swim," *TMT,* 12 September 1915, scrapbook, p. 27.

71. FK, "A Suffrage Courtship," *TMT,* 17 October 1915, scrapbook, p. 65.

72. FK, "Suffrage Strategy," *TMT,* 26 September 1916, scrapbook, p. 45.

73. Ibid.

74. FK, "How To Make A Suffragist," *TMT,* 5 September 1915, scrapbook, p. 21.

75. FK, "Interviewing a Volcano," *TMT,* 27 February 1916, scrapbook, p. 119; "How To Make A Suffragist," p. 21.

76. *TMT,* 30 October 1915, scrapbook, p. 73.

77. *TMT,* n.d., scrapbook, p. 79.

78. FK, "A Suffrage Swim."

79. *TMT,* 26 October 1915, scrapbook, p. 67.

80. Ibid., 3 November 1915, scrapbook, p. 73.

81. Ibid., 5 September 1915, scrapbook, p. 23.

82. Ibid., 14 August 1915, scrapbook, p. 5.

83. FK, "The 'Weaker Sex' from Another Angle," *TMT,* 31 October 1915, scrapbook, p. 71.

84. *TMT,* "Girls Should Tote Guns Says Woman Professor," 18 October 1915, scrapbook, p. 57.

85. FK, "The Personal Note: Memoirs of NATION Publishers and Editors," *The Nation* 201 (20 September 1965): 28.

86. Evidently streptococcal septicemia (a blood-born disease) had proved fatal. [FK], notes, n.d., p. 3, MC private collection; Philip R. Alexander, M.D., the internist I consulted for more information on possible causes of Brewster's death, postulates that the baby may have been born with a congenital gastrointestinal malformation. From Freda's records of Brewster's frequent vomiting and diarrhea, he thinks the child may have suffered from gastrointestinal infections or bad food allergies. The former appears more likely, based on a family history of gastrointestinal problems. The maternal grandmother suffered years of ill health from what appeared to be primarily gastrointestinal disorders. The Kirchwey-Clarks' third child, Jeffrey, was born with a congenital malformation of the heart. Evans Clark's baby book, DKB addenda, 70s; autopsy report of Jeffrey Clark, #15, FK MSS; interview with Philip R. Alexander, M.D., 8 February 1985.

87. Notes, n.d., pp. 2, 3, MC private collection; William E. Caldwell to DKB, 14 September 1917, #19, DKB addenda, 70s.

88. Birth announcement, 1 August 1917, #92; FK to DKB, 1 August 1917, #45; both DKB addenda, 81.

89. FK to DKB, 16 September 1917, p. 1, #45, DKB addenda, 81; notes, n.d., pp. 3, 4, 5, MC private collection; Evans Clark, biographical notes, EC MSS; FK, "Memoirs of *Nation*," p. 28; *Every Week*, 22 June 1918, n.p.; *Every Week*, n.d., n.p., scrapbook.

90. FK, Leon Trotsky, "When Trotsky Lived in New York," n.d., #427, FK MSS; FK 1918 diary, 9 February 1918; Leon Trotsky, "Moving Jaws" (a copy of which is in #427, FK MSS); [FK], *The Nation* 117 (7 November 1923): 501.

91. Bruce Barton, *The Man Nobody Knows* (New York: Bobbs-Merrill, 1925).

92. EC's 1918 memo book, 24 August 1918, MC private collection; FK to Henry Mussey, 21 August 1918, f. 2073, OGV MSS. Her letter requesting consideration for the *Nation* position predated the notification from the *Tribune* by three days.

93. FK "Memoirs of *Nation*," p. 28; FK to Henry Mussey, 21 August 1918, f. 2073, OGV MSS; OGV to FK, 23 August 1918, #135, FK MSS; EC 1918 memo book, 27 August, 28 August 1918, MC private collection.

94. Freda Kirchwey, "Memoirs of *Nation*," p. 28.

95. FK to Maurice Wertheim, 17 October 1935, p. 2, FK MSS; Michael Wreszin, *Oswald Garrison Villard: Pacifist at War* (Bloomington: Indiana University Press, 1965), pp. 208–231, 247–274; William E. Leuchtenburg, review of *Oswald Garrison Villard: Liberal of the 1920's* by D. Joy Humes, *NYT Book Review*, 1 January 1961, p. 6.

2. From Apprentice to Journalist

1. FK to DKB, 16 September 1918, #45, DKB addenda, 81; FK, "Memoirs of *Nation*," p. 29.

2. FK, "Memoirs of *Nation*," pp. 27–35; Emily Greene Balch won the Nobel Peace Prize for her work in the Women's International League for Peace and Freedom in 1946. Mercedes M. Randall, *Improper Bostonian: Emily Greene Balch* (New York: Twayne, 1964).

3. FK, "Zionism and Democracy," in Meyer W. Weisgal, ed., *Chaim Weizmann: Statesman, Scientist, Builder of the Jewish Commonwealth* (New York: Dial, 1944), pp. 70, 71, 74.

4. FK, "Memoirs of *Nation*," p. 29.

5. FK to DKB, 3 November 1918, pp. 2, 1, # 45, DKB addenda, 81; Lewis S. Gannett, "Villard's *Nation*," in Henry M. Christman, ed., *One Hundred Years of The Nation* (New York: Capricorn, 1972), pp. 35–40; FK, "Memoirs of *Nation*," p. 29; *The Nation* 108 (21 June 1919): 969; William MacDonald, "A Conference Unrepentant," p. 978.

6. Wreszin, *Oswald Garrison Villard*, pp. 86–90; I. F. Stone, "Free Inquiry and Free Endeavor," in Christman, ed., *One Hundred Years*, p. 41; original prospectus in ibid., pp. 27–28.

7. *Encyclopaedia of the Social Sciences*, 1933 ed., s.v. "Liberalism," by Guido de Ruggiero, pp. 435–441; *Encyclopaedia of the Social Sciences*, 1968 ed., s.v. "Liberalism," by David G. Smith, pp. 276–282; Theodore F. Lowi, "The Public

Philosophy: Interest-Group Liberalism—Liberal Economics, Corporate Capitalism and Foreign Policy," in Jerome M. Mileur, ed., *The Liberal Tradition and Crisis: American Politics in the Sixties* (Lexington, Mass.: Heath, 1974), pp. 98–127; Stone, "Free Inquiry," p. 43.

8. Wreszin, *Oswald Garrison Villard*, p. 90; Stone, "Free Inquiry," p. 43; announcement, *The Nation* 107 (10 August 1918); J. B. Moore, "The International Situation," *The Nation* 107 (5 October 1918): 383–385; Thomas G. Masaryk, "The Czecho-Slovak Nation," *The Nation* 107 (5 October 1918): 386–388; "General Smuts's Plan for the League of Nations," *The Nation* 108 (8 February 1919): 225–237. *The Nation* actually endorsed U.S. rejection of the League of Nations. "The Madness at Versailles," an editorial often attributed to Villard, but actually written by William MacDonald, was a devastating critique of the treaty and the League. Both represented to many on *The Nation* reactionary resistance against the popular forces of the world. [William MacDonald], "The Madness at Versailles," *The Nation* 108 (17 March 1919): 778–780; "A Spartacan Manifesto," *The Nation* 108 (8 March 1919): 373–374; IRS, *The Nation* 108 (4 Jaunary 1919): 8–12.

9. [FK], *The Nation* 107 (23 November 1918): 612.

10. FK, IRS, *The Nation* 108 (16 November 1918): 609–610; [FK], "The Allies' New War," *The Nation* 110 (22 May 1920): 672.

11. EC diary, 10 April, 16 April 1919, MC private collection; *NYT*, 25 January 1919, p. 4; 19 December 1919, p. 1; EC, "Americanism and the Soviet Union," *The Nation* 108 (22 March 1919): 423; EC, "The Diplomatic Balance Sheet in Russia," *The Nation* 109 (6 December 1919): 725. See also [FK], *The Nation* 111 (29 December 1920): 764.

12. *NYT*, 25 January 1919, pp. 1, 4; EC, biographical notes, n.d., p. 1, EC MSS; *NYT*, 19 December 1919, p. 1; 28 February 1920, p. 1.

13. Ludwig Martens to EC, 21 April 1920; 19 January 1921, MC private collection; [FK], *The Nation* 111 (29 December 1920): 764–765.

14. [FK], *The Nation* 111 (29 December 1920): 764; *The Nation* 111 (10 July 1920): 30; in addition to the Soviet Union, struggles in Haiti, Santo Domingo, and Ireland received substantial coverage by *The Nation;* [FK], "Recognize Russia!" *The Nation* 112 (30 March 1921): 468; William E. Leuchtenburg, *Franklin D. Roosevelt and The New Deal, 1932–1940* (New York: Harper & Row, 1963): 206; [FK], "Strangling Business," *The Nation* 110 (12 June 1920): 786; *The Nation* 111 (1 December 1920): 606; *The Nation* 112 (2 February 1921): 162; *The Nation* 111 (1 December 1920): 606.

15. Quoted in Beulah Amidon, "*The Nation* and *The New Republic*," *Survey Graphic* 29 (January 1940): 26; *The Nation* 110 (15 May 1920): 635; FK, "Memoirs of *Nation*," pp. 30–31.

16. [FK], *The Nation* 115 (22 November 1922): 538; [FK], *The Nation* 122 (24 March 1926): 305; [FK], "Home and Highwaywomen," *The Nation* 112 (2 February 1921): 167; [FK], *The Nation* 117 (14 November 1923): 543; clipping, 18 June 1937, f. 2073, OGV MSS.

17. Oliver, "Oh, Stop That, Freda!" p. 100; Mary Morris, "The Editor of *The Nation*," clipping, #435°, FK MSS. Villard also paid her full salary during the period after Michael's birth. Notes, n.d., #432, FK MSS.

18. EC to Anne [?], 27 June 1919, p. 1, #29, FK MSS; *The Mother's Register.*

Michael's full name was Michael Kirchwey Clark; later in life he shortened it to Michael Clark for convenience. FK to OGV, 11 July 1919, 19 August 1919, n.d., Monday [1923], p. 6, f. 2073, OGV MSS.

19. FK to OGV, 11 July 1919, OGV MSS; Michael Wreszin, *The Superfluous Anarchist: Albert Jay Nock* (Providence: Brown University Press, 1971).

20. FK to OGV, 19 August 1919, p. 2, f. 2073, OGV MSS; Morris, "Editor of *Nation*"; telephone interview with Michael Clark, 3 January 1986.

21. FK to OGV 19 August 1919, f. 2073, OGV MSS; FK to DKB, 13 September 1922, #45, DKB addenda, 81; EC, "Coal Strike Battle Lines Tense and Firm," *NYT*, 15 November 1925, sec. 9, p. 4.

22. *World* clipping, [1922], #429, FK MSS.

23. FK, "Miners' Wives in the Coal Strike," *Century* 105 (November 1922): 83–90; quotations on pp. 83, 84.

24. FK to EC, 1 February [1930], p. 4, #19, FK MSS.

25. FK Wyoming diary, 4 August [1921], #48, FK MSS.

26. Ibid., 6 August [1921]. Figuring things out through the use of dialogue was typical of FK.

27. FK Wyoming diary, 11 August [1921] #48, FK MSS; *NYT*, 4 June 1919, p. 3; 5 January 1921, p. 2; 5 April 1921, p. 21; FK, "The Menace of Americanism," *The Nation* 113 (21 September 1921): 312. For FK's coverage of the original ousting, see [FK], "Minority Rights at Albany," *The Nation* 110 (6 March 1920): 288; (24 April 1920): 536.

28. DWK to DKB, 10 October 1920, #27, DKB addenda, 81; see Dorothy Canfield Fisher, "A Square Deal for the Nameless Child," *Pictorial Review*, October 1920, pp. 5, 78, 81, 82.

29. DKB, "The Case for Acceptance of the Sheppard-Towner Act, 1920–1922," #52, DKB addenda, 70s; DWK to DKB, 2 December 1920, #27, DKB addenda, 81; [FK], "Women and Children First," *The Nation* 111 (22 December 1920): 724. See also [FK], "Nobody's Children," *The Nation* 119 (6 August 1924): 135.

30. Karl Kirchwey to DKB, 14 February 1920, #96; EC to DKB, 15 February 1920, #96; DWK wrote to DKB: "Time blurs details inevitably and those memories are too precious not to preserve accurately . . . May a faith in the life unending come to you through this experience, which nothing in the future can ever disturb." DWK to DKB, [1920], #95; all DKB addenda, 81; [FK], *The Nation* 112 (15 June 1921): 835.

31. FK, *Every Week*, 19 January 1918, scrapbook, p. 137; response to Women's Charter, 5 January 1937, p. 1, FK MSS.

32. See, for example, FK, "The Pan-American Conference of Women," *The Nation* 114 (10 May 1922): 565; FK, "Alice Paul Pulls the Strings," *The Nation* 112 (2 March 1922): 332–333; FK, speech to AAUW, 1945, p. 2, FK MSS.

33. [FK], *The Nation* 113 (21 December 1921): 717. Though Margaret Sanger disseminated birth-control information through her New York clinic after 1916, she was always skirting the law.

34. [FK], *The Nation* 118 (9 April 1924): 384; *The Nation* 116 (14 February 1923): 163; *The Nation* 118 (14 May 1924): 547.

35. FK, "Pan-American Conference," p. 565; "Out of Bondage," *The Nation* 127 (12 December 1928): 661.

36. William Henry Chafe, *The American Woman: Her Changing Social, Economic and Political Role, 1920–1970* (New York: Oxford University Press, 1972), p. 89.

37. For background about American women in journalism, see Madelon Golden Schilpp and Sharon M. Murphy, *Great Women of the Press* (Carbondale, Ill.: Southern Illinois University Press, 1983); Marion Marzolf, *Up from the Footnote* (New York: Hastings House, 1977); Ishbel Ross, *Ladies of the Press* (New York: Harper & Row, 1936); and Edward T. James, et al., eds., *Notable American Women* (Cambridge, Mass.: Harvard University Press, 1971); FK 1917 diary, 6 January, 20 January 1918.

38. Elizabeth Gurley Flynn to Marie Jenny Howe, 25 December 1920, Irwin MSS.

39. Dorothy Dunbar Bromley, "Feminist—New Style," *Harper's Magazine* 155 (October 1927): 552–560.

40. [FK], *The Nation* 113 (5 October 1921): 363; [FK], *The Nation* 116 (21 March 1923): 325; [FK], *The Nation* 117 (8 August 1923): 128–129. For similar position, see [FK], *The Nation* 114 (2 January 1937); for different *Nation* viewpoint, see *The Nation* 142 (10 June 1936): 726. See also Alice Kessler Harris, *Out to Work: A History of Wage-Earning Women in the United States* (New York: Oxford University Press, 1982), pp. 206–210.

41. [FK] , "Are Women a Menace?" *The Nation* 112 (9 February 1921): 198; [FK], "A Women's Bloc," *The Nation* 119 (3 September 1924): 230–231.

42. [FK], "A Women's Bloc." See also FK, "Alice Paul Pulls the Strings," *The Nation* 112 (2 March 1921): 332. For analysis of the National Woman's Party, see Nancy Cott, "Feminist Politics in the 1920s: The National Woman's Party," *Journal of American History* 71 (June 1984): 43–68.

43. "No Sex Line Up," *Woman Citizen* 7 (3 June 1922): 13; Elizabeth Green, "I Resign From Female Politics," *New Republic* 42 (22 April 1925): 233–235; Grace Abbott, "What Have They Done?" *The Independent* 115 (24 October 1925): 475–478; Emily Newell Blair, "Are Women a Failure in Politics?" *Harper's Magazine* 151 (October 1925): 513–522; Anne Martin, "Feminists and Future Political Action," *The Nation* 120 (3 February 1925): 185–186; "Woman's Inferiority Complex," *New Republic* 27 (20 July 1921): 210; Emily Newell Blair, "Why I Am Discouraged About Women in Politics," *Woman's Journal* 16 (January 1931): 20–22, 44–45. See also Sara Alpern and Dale Baum, "Female Ballots: The Impact of the Nineteenth Amendment," *Journal of Interdisciplinary History* 16 (Summer 1985): 43–67.

44. FK, "A Women's Bloc"; Crystal Eastman, "Feminists Must Fight," correspondence, *The Nation* 119 (12 November 1924): 523.

45. For a similar thesis, see Estelle Freedman, "Separatism as Strategy: Female Institution Building and American Feminism, 1870–1930," *Feminist Studies* 5 (Fall 1979): 514–515; 521, 524–525, 515.

46. [FK], "Girls Will Be Ladies," *The Nation* 116 (20 June 1923): 712; "The Languid Generation," *The Nation* 117 (21 November 1923): 572.

47. FK to DKB, 31 March 1925, #46, DKB addenda, 81; FK, "Too Many College Girls? III. Good College Material," *The Nation* 120 (10 June 1925): 647, 648.

48. OGV to Herbert J. Friedman, 11 August 1922, p. 1, and Norman Thomas to OGV, 31 May 1922, p. 1, box 107, OGV MSS; FK to DKB, 13 September

1922, #45, DKB addenda, 81; OGV to Norman Thomas, 3 October 1922, box 107, OGV MSS. OGV refers to Dorothy Graffe, another *Nation* editor.

49. *The Nation* 115 (8 November 1922): 487. When Freda became managing editor, Gruening became associate editor. FK memorandum on staff organization, 12 September 1945, p. 6, FK MSS; FK to OGV, 19 September [1925], pp. 1, 2, 3, f. 2073, OGV MSS; DWK to DKB, 8 May 1923; FK to DKB, 4 May 1923, #45; both DKB addenda, 81.

50. FK to OGV, Monday [1923], pp. 2–3, 6, f. 2073, OGV MSS.

51. FK to DKB, Monday, June 1923, p. 3, #45, DKB addenda, 81.

52. FK to OGV, n.d. November [1923], p. 1, box 106, OGV MSS; [FK], *The Nation* 117 (7 November 1923): 501; Donald W. Treadgold, *Twentieth Century Russia*, 5th ed. (Boston: Houghton Mifflin, 1981), pp. 176–195.

53. FK to OGV, November [1923], p. 1, box 106, OGV MSS.

54. The contributors included: Jessica Smith, American Friends Service Committee; Dorothy Brewster, Columbia University English professor; Max Eastman, American radical; Isaiah J. Hoorgin, Soviet economic expert; L. Talmy, editor of the American Jewish publication *Reconstruction*. Jessica Smith, "In the House of the Sugar King," *The Nation* 117 (7 November 1923): 518–519; Dorothy Brewster, "Lenin, and the Prize Pig," *The Nation* 117 (7 November 1923): 510–511; Max Eastman, "The Land of Leisure," *The Nation* 117 (7 November 1923): 515; Isaiah J. Hoorgin, "Russia's Era of Revival," *The Nation* 117 (7 November 1923): 516–518; L. Talmy, "The Soviet Press," *The Nation* 117 (7 November 1923): 519–520; Magdeleine Marx, "The New Russian Women, I. The Working Woman," *The Nation* 117 (7 November 1923): 508–510. DWK's interest in Magdeleine Marx's philosophy was evident in FK's inclusion of Marx's several-part series on Russian women.

55. In Isaiah J. Hoorgin, "Russia's Era of Revival," *The Nation* 117 (7 November 1923): 516–518. Other cartoons by Hugo Gellert, Käthe Kollwitz, and Art Young followed in *The Nation*. Hugo Gellert, "In the Steel Country, A Diary with Drawings, I." *The Nation* 117 (28 November 1923): 604–605; "In the Steel Country, A Diary with Drawings, II." *The Nation* 117 (5 December 1923): 623–633; Edith Van Hook, "Starving the New Generation in Germany," *The Nation* 118 (19 March 1924): 304. In OGV, "The Convention of the Fit to Rule," *The Nation* 118 (25 June 1924): 730–732; FK to OGV, November [1923], p. 1, box 106, OGV MSS; the Kirchwey-Clarks moved to 27 Vandam Street in lower Manhattan, notes, n.d., p. 9, MC private collection.

56. Notes, #144, FK MSS; Beatrice M. Hinkle, "Women and the New Morality," in FK, ed., *Our Changing Morality* (New York: Albert & Charles Boni, 1924; rpt. New York: Arno & New York Times, 1972), p. 235; FK, *TMT*, 5 October 1915, scrapbook, p. 49.

57. FK to OGV, 7 September 1923, pp. 1, 2, box 106, OGV MSS.

58. [FK],"Are We Better Than Starfish?" *The Nation* 118 (23 April 1924): 470; Bertrand Russell, "Styles in Ethics," *The Nation* 118 (30 April 1924): 497; FK to DKB, 9 May 1924, #47, DKB addenda, 81.

59. Florence Guy Seabury, "Stereotypes," in FK, ed., *Our Changing Morality*, p. 231.

60. Isabel Leavenworth, "Virtue and Women," in ibid., p. 97.

61. Elsie Clews Parsons, "Changes in Sex Relations," in ibid., pp. 45–46; Arthur Garfield Hays, "Modern Marriage," in ibid., pp. 28, 32–33.

62. Parsons, "Changes in Sex Relations," in ibid., p. 41.

63. Floyd Dell, "Can Men and Women Be Friends?" in ibid., pp. 183, 184, 185.

64. Hinkle, "Women and the New Morality," in ibid., pp. 236, 243, 246, 248.

65. EC to DKB, 24 July 1924, #47, DKB addenda, 81; EC, *NYT*, 28 September 1924, p. 20. Clark's interview with Hinkle may have convinced him to enter analysis; his diary entry for April 22 read: "Dr. Hinkle. Think I'll be analyzed." He started twice a week sessions with Hinkle on May 7. On May 9, he recorded: "Grand session; dope on causes and symptoms and fire fad." Reared by a doting but rigid mother, EC, a passionate man, must have suffered from the restraints put on him. His love of chasing fires may have been a safe way to unleash pent-up passion. He also may have had difficulty sharing his wife with their two children and with her busy career, which spilled over into business-related visits at night. His diary entry for "Memoranda" for October 1924 read: "9 evenings at home without company"; the next month he recorded: "7 evenings without company." EC 1924 diary, October Memoranda; November Memoranda 1924, MC private collection.

66. FK, ed., *Our Changing Morality*, pp. v–ix.

3. A Search for Certainty

1. [FK], 14 November 1923, *The Nation* 117, p. 546; FK to DKB, 1 September 1924, #47, and 5 October 1924, p. 3, #28, DKB addenda, 81.

2. EC to DKB, 17 December 1924, #47, and DWK to DKB, 17 December 1924, #30, DKB addenda, 81; interview with Nina Miness, 23 June 1983.

3. *The Nation* 120 (7 January 1925): iii; FK, "Memoirs of *Nation*," p. 32.

4. EC to DKB, [January 1925], #47, and DWK to DKB, [January 1925], #30, DKB addenda, 81.

5. FK to OGV, 21 August 1925, f. 2073, OGV MSS; Robert L. Wolf, "Loony: A Modern Movie," *The Nation* 121 (9 September 1925): 270–276; FK to OGV, 19 September 1925, p. 1, and OGV to FK, 21 September 1925; both f. 2073, OGV MSS.

6. FK to OGV, n.d., p. 3, f. 2073, OGV MSS; GWK to DWK, 27 December 1925, #35, DKB addenda, 81; FK to OGV, n.d., p. 3, f. 2073, OGV MSS.

7. DWK to DKB, 6 September 1924, #28, DKB addenda, 81; DWK, review of *Colonial Women of Affairs* by Elizabeth Anthony Dexter, *The Nation* 121 (2 September 1925): 260. This book review appeared in the same issue as a printed letter from Adolf Hitler, objecting to an error in a Louis Fischer *Nation* article about the length of a prison sentence he had served. FK, commenting on the fate of the letter, remembered that the original was discarded after being printed; in 1925 no one could imagine the import of Hitler in the years to come. See Louis Fischer, "Class Justice in Germany," *The Nation* 120 (3 June 1925): 624–625; Adolf Hitler, correspondence, *The Nation* 121 (2 September 1925): 256.

8. DWK to DKB, 4 December 1925, #30; GWK to DWK, 27 December 1925, #35; DWK to DKB, 30 December 1925, #31; GWK to DKB, 25 April 1926, #35; 28 April 1926, #36, all DKB addenda, 81; FK to Mabel J. B. Mussey, [1920], Barrows MSS.

9. DWK to DKB, 24 January 1926, #31, DKB addenda, 81; telephone interview with George W. Kirchwey III, 6 January 1986.

10. DWK to DKB, 29 January, 24 January 1926, #31, DKB addenda, 81.

11. DWK to DKB, 5 February 1926, #31, DKB addenda, 81; advertisement, "Wages for Wives," *The Nation* 122 (13 January 1926). Clarence Darrow was a noted lawyer; S. K. Ratcliffe, a British liberal, was a journalist and lecturer.

12. GWK to DKB, 7 May 1926, #35, DKB addenda, 81.

13. Notes [30 June 1926], #32, DKB addenda, 81; obituary, Dora Wendell Kirchwey, *NYT,* 1 July 1926, p. 23; interview with MC, 12 May 1984. Dora may have died of an upper-gastrointestinal malignancy, a stomach or pancreatic tumor. In its final stages, the disease could have spread to her head, causing the headaches, depression, and paralysis she suffered; interview with Philip R. Alexander, M.D., 8 February 1985.

14. "Dr. Nancy" Jenison to DKB, 1 July 1926; Samuel A. Eliot to GWK, 20 July 1926, both #32, DKB addenda, 81.

15. GWK to DKB, 25 August 1926, pp. 2, 3, #36, DKB addenda, 81; FK to Otto Nathan, 10 February 1961; Otto Nathan private collection.

16. FK to OGV, "The Nation," box 106, OGV MSS.

17. FK to EC, 1 February [1930], pp. 4, 5, #19, FK MSS.

18. EC was in psychoanalysis before 1926 and in 1930; it is not known if he was during the years between. FK to EC, 1 February [1930], p. 6, #19, FK MSS.

19. Ibid., pp. 6, 7; EC, 1928–29 diary, 15 August, 29 October, 15 December 1928.

20. FK to EC, 1 February [1930], p. 7, #19, FK MSS.

21. FK to OGV, [1926], pp. 1, 2, box 106, OGV MSS.

22. FK to DKB, 2 August 1926, p. 5, #46, DKB addenda, 81; FK to OGV, 27 August 1926, pp. 1, 2, box 106, OGV MSS; MC to Sara Alpern, 11 May 1985, p. 1, Alpern private collection.

23. FK to DKB, 15 September 1926, #46; FK to DKB, 15 September 1926, p. 3, #46; GWK to DKB, 28 September 1926, p. 3, #36; all DKB addenda, 81.

24. FK, "Millions of Words," *The Nation* 128 (12 June 1929): 711; [FK], caption under "Why I Earn My Own Living," *The Nation* 123 (8 December 1926): 579.

25. [FK], *The Nation* 124 (16 March 1927): 275.

26. [FK], *The Nation* 123 (22 December 1926): 653.

27. Advertisement, *The Nation* 124 (16 February 1927): 172; GWK to DKB, 18 February 1927, #35, DKB addenda, 81.

28. [Inez Haynes Irwin], "The Making of a Militant," *The Nation* 123 (1 December 1926): 553.

29. [Elizabeth Stuyvesant], "Staying Free," *The Nation* 124 (30 March 1927): 341; [Wanda Gág], "A Hotbed of Feminists," *The Nation* 124 (22 June 1927): 693.

30. [Genevieve Taggard], "Poet Out of Pioneer," *The Nation* 124 (19 January 1927): 65; [Sue Shelton White], "Mother's Daughter," *The Nation* 123 (15 December 1926): 633; [Phyllis Blanchard], "The Long Journey," *The Nation* 124 (27April 1927): 473; [Lou Rogers], "Lightning Speed Through Life," *The Nation* 124 (13 April 1927): 397; [Kate L. Gregg], "One Way to Freedom," *The Nation* 124 (16 February 1927): 167.

31. I am using the phrase from Caroline Bird's book of the same name: Car-

oline Bird, *Born Female* (New York: David McKay, 1968); [White], "Mother's Daughter," p. 634.

32. [Lorine Pruette], "The Evolution of Disenchantment," *The Nation* 124 (2 February 1927): 114; [Mary Alden Hopkins], "Why I Earn My Own Living," *The Nation* 123 (8 December 1926): 580.

33. The stress on psychology and personal factors also reflects the 1920s culture; infrequent use of political or social explanations may indicate a reaction against progressivism.

34. Caption in [Ruth Pickering], "A Deflated Rebel," *The Nation* 124 (5 January 1927): 11; caption, [Gág], "A Hotbed of Feminists," p. 691.

35. John B. Watson, "The Weakness of Women," *The Nation* 125 (6 July 1927): 9–10; Joseph Collins, "Half-Confessed," *The Nation* 125 (6 July 1927): 10–11.

36. Watson, "The Weakness of Women," p. 10. Another interpretation of Watson's analysis could be a suggestion that women's search for freedom and their militancy came from their abnormality.

37. Ibid.

38. Collins, "Half-Confessed," pp. 10, 11. FK probably anticipated Collins' and Watson's extremely negative judgments of feminists, but chose them because of their prominence in their respective fields of medical psychology and behaviorist psychology.

39. Beatrice M. Hinkle, "Why Feminism?" *The Nation* 125 (6 July 1927): 9.

40. Ibid.

41. Ibid.

42. Dorothy Dunbar Bromley, "Feminist—New Style," *Harper's Magazine* 155 (October 1927): 552–560; Ann D. Gordon, Mari Jo Buhle, Nancy E. Schrom, "Women in American Society: An Historical Contribution," *Radical America* V (1973): 48; Elaine Showalter, ed., *These Modern Women: Autobiographical Essays from the Twenties* (Old Westbury, N.Y.: Feminist Press, 1978), pp. 16–17; Estelle Freedman, "Separatism as Strategy: Female Institution Building and American Feminism, 1870–1930," *Feminist Studies* 5 (Fall 1979): 514–525.

43. FK, "The Law and Mr. Dies," *The Nation* 149 (4 November 1939): 486.

44. FK to Louis Fischer, 20 December 1934, FK MSS.

45. FK to EC, 7 February [1930], p. 2, #19, FK MSS.

46. FK to EC, 30 January [1930], #19, FK MSS; FK 1935 diary, 24 June 1935.

47. FK, Memorandum, 5 August [1943], p. 16, #344, FK MSS.

48. FK to EC, 8 February [1930], p. 3, #19, FK MSS.

49. Sketch, "Dr. Schubiger" [back of 1949 letter], #350, FK MSS.

50. FK, untitled poem, n.d., FK MSS; MC verified that this poem was in FK's handwriting; MC to Sara Alpern, 23 May 1985, p. 2, Alpern private collection.

51. GWK to DKB, 15 December 1927, #38, DKB addenda, 81; Mary Morris, "*Nation* editor," FK MSS; EC, "Screech of Fire Sirens Is Music to Fire Buffs," *NYT,* 15 April 1925, p. 10.

52. EC, "Rearing of Children Becoming a Science," *NYT,* 18 November 1925, sec. 9, p. 10.

53. Interview with MC, 6 September 1974; interview with MC, 13 May 1984. Although MC apparently recalled such childhood details, this particular information may have been handed down from his aunt, DKB, who indicated in an

interview with me, 15 October 1974, that she believed FK should have chosen between a career and a family.

54. Interview with MC, 6 September 1974.

55. MC to FK and EC, 8 April 1952, p. 7, FK MSS.

56. EC, "Rearing of Children," p. 10; John B. Watson, "Psychological Care of Infant and Child," in Robert Sklar, ed., *The Plastic Age* (New York: Braziller, 1970), p. 315. See also John B. Watson, *Psychological Care of Infant and Child* (New York: Norton, 1928), and Paula Fass, "The Family Redivivus: 1880–1900," in *The Damned and the Beautiful* (New York: Oxford University Press, 1977), on Watson and his contemporaries.

57. Interview with MC, 6 September 1974.

58. EC, review of *Our Enemy the Child* by Agnes de Lima, *New York Tribune*, 3 January 1926, p. 20.

59. FK, "Millions of Words," *The Nation* 128 (12 June 1929): 711.

60. FK, untitled unpublished manuscript [1930s], pp. 1, 2, 3, FK MSS.

61. [FK], "The Seas of Democracy," *The Nation* 117 (19 December 1923): 704.

62. MC to FK and EC, 8 April 1952, pp. 1, 6, 8, FK MSS; interview with MC, 28 July 1984.

63. [FK], "Parents: Gods, Policemen or Friends," *The Nation* 117 (29 August 1923): 210; FK to DKB, n.d., #47, DKB addenda, 81.

64. FK to DKB, 21 April 1927, #47, DKB addenda, 81.

65. FK to DKB, n.d., p. 7, #47, DKB addenda, 81. At an earlier time she had asked her sister to "adopt" her "offspring for the summer" for the same reason: "we are solemnly determined not to send them to N. S.—not, at least, without an armed bodyguard to protect their natural liberties." FK to DKB, [1925 or earlier], #46, p. 1, DKB addenda, 81.

66. FK to OGV, 26 August [1927], f. 2073, OGV MSS; interview with MC, 28 July 1984.

67. FK to DKB, 23 June [1927], pp. 4, 5, #46, DKB addenda, 81; FK, "England—Too Bitter to Compromise?" *The Nation* 125 (3 August 1927): 103, 104.

68. FK, "England—Too Bitter," p. 104.

69. EC, "British Labor Storms the Baldwin Citadel," *NYT*, 21 August 1927, sec. 8, p. 12.

70. FK to OGV, 26 July [1927], f. 2073, OGV MSS.

71. FK, "Some Mass Demonstrations," *The Nation* 125 (5 October 1927): 337, 338.

72. Ibid.

73. FK to OGV, 26 August [1927], f. 2073, OGV MSS; GWK, "Sacco-Vanzetti," *The Nation* 124 (20 April 1927): 415–416; [OGV], "Massachusetts the Murderer," *The Nation* 125 (28 August 1927): 192.

74. FK to OGV, 26 July [1927], p. 1, f. 2073, OGV MSS; [Crystal Eastman], "Mother-Worship," *The Nation* 124 (16 March 1927): 284. On the basis of correspondence between FK and OGV and my research with Blanche Cook, editor of *Toward the Great Change*, a collection of Eastman pieces, this concluding paragraph is apparently the one to which she objected. FK to OGV, 26 August [1927], pp. 2–3, f. 2073, OGV MSS. It evoked an almost story-book ending: "I have lived my life according to the plan. I have had the 'career' and the children and, except for an occasional hiatus due to illness or some other circumstance

over which I had no control, I have earned my own living. I have even made a certain name for myself. If I have not fulfilled the promise of my youth, either as a homemaker or as a professional woman, I have never wavered in my feminist faith. My mother has always been a beacon to me, and if today I sometimes feel a sense of failure it may be partly because I have always lived in the glow of her example. In their early struggle for survival against narrow-minded and prejudiced parents some of my contemporaries seem to have won more of the iron needed in the struggle of life than I got from my almost-perfect parents."

75. FK to DKB, 28 June [1927], #46, DKB addenda, 81; FK to OGV, 26 July [1927], p. 3; 26 August [1927]; both f. 2073, OGV MSS.

76. FK to OGV, 26 July [1927], p. 2, f. 2073, OGV MSS; FK to DKB, n.d. [1925 or earlier], #46, DKB addenda, 81.

77. EC, "Economic Conditions in Europe," *NYT,* 25 September 1927, sec. 9, p. 1; "Industrial Recovery in Europe," *NYT,* 18 September 1927, sec. 8, p. 1; FK, "Some Mass Demonstrations," pp. 337, 338; GWK to DKB, 4 September 1927, pp. 2, 3, #37, DKB addenda, 81.

78. FK to DKB, 12 December 1927, #47, DKB addenda, 81.

79. "*Nation* 10th Anniversary," pp. 61, 11, 1, box 106, OGV MSS; GWK to DKB, 14 March 1928, #38, DKB addenda, 81.

80. "*Nation* 10th Anniversary," p. 65, pp. 62–66, box 106, OGV MSS.

81. EC 1928–29 diary, 13 March 1928; Adolph A. Berle, *Leaning Against the Dawn* (New York: Twentieth Century Fund, 1969); EC, Alfred L. Bernheim, J. Frederic Dewhurst, Margaret Grant Schneider, eds., *Stock Market Control* (New York: Twentieth Century Fund, 1934): Alfred L. Bernheim, Margaret Grant Schneider, eds., *Labor and the Government* (New York: Twentieth Century Fund, 1935); press release of Twentieth Century Fund report "American Foundations and Their Fields," 27 December 1932, p. 2, f. 43, Survey MSS; *NYT,* 27 June 1931, pp. 11, 18.

82. Interview with MC, 12 May 1984; *NYT,* 25 January 1919, p. 4.

83. "Members of Sub-Committees" Lewis Stiles Gannett, American Fund for Public Service, Inc., f. 1 (1922), LSG MSS; Dick Cowen, "Charles Garland: Catalyst for Social Change," *Allentown Call-Chronicle,* 18 May 1975, sec. F, pp. 1, 8; Roger Baldwin to Friends, "Letters to Members of Board of Directors," 4 October 1922, American Fund for Public Service, Inc., f. 1, 2, LSG MSS; FK served on its board of directors, beginning in 1924, the same year that Elizabeth Gurley Flynn joined the board. When FK joined, she accepted the position with the hope that she had "the varied contacts and connections necessary" to make her "useful." Roger Baldwin to FK, 10 June 1924; FK to Roger Baldwin, 13 June 1924; both correspondence with Board of Directors, 1923–1933, AFPS MSS.

84. GWK to DKB, 14 March 1928, #38, DKB addenda, 81.

85. EC 1928–29 diary, 29 April 1928.

86. Ibid.; OGV to Ernest Gruening, 5 April 1928; Ernest Gruening to OGV, 6 April 1928, both f. 1424, OGV MSS; OGV to Joseph Wood Krutch, 25 April 1928, f. 2138, OGV MSS; OGV to Ernest Gruening, 24 April 1928; Ernest Gruening to OGV, 25 April 1928; both f. 1424, OGV MSS; EC 1928–29 diary, 26 April 1928; OGV to Joseph Wood Krutch, 20 May 1928, f. 2138, OGV MSS. The first *Nation* masthead with new title was 127 (3 October 1928): 307.

87. OGV to Joseph Wood Krutch, 3 July 1928; Joseph Wood Krutch to OGV, 24 June 1928; both f. 2138, OGV MSS.

88. William Allen White to FK, telegram, 15 May 1928, General Correspondence 1928 series C, WAW MSS; Heywood Broun, "It Seems to Heywood Broun," *The Nation* 126 (9 May 1928): 446; FK to William Allen White, 18 May 1928; 10 May 1928, General Correspondence 1928 series C, WAW MSS; "Heywood Broun," *The Nation* 126 (9 May 1928): 553.

89. [FK], "Henrietta Spills the Beans," *The Nation* 120 (22 April 1925): 456; FK to DKB, 20 April 1928, #47, DKB addenda, 81; [FK], "The Blacklist Party," *The Nation* 126 (9 May 1928): 580.

90. [FK], "Crystal Eastman," *The Nation* 127 (8 August 1928): 123–124.

91. FK, review of *Coming of Age in Samoa* by Margaret Mead, *The Nation* 127 (24 October 1928): 427.

92. Henry Mussey to OGV, 6 September 1928, f. 2738, OGV MSS; FK, "The Good Fanatic," review of *Susan B. Anthony* by Rheta Childe Dorr, *The Nation* 127 (31 October 1928); 455; Henry Mussey to OGV, 7 November 1928, pp. 2, 3; OGV to Henry Mussey, 12 November 1928; both f. 2738, OGV MSS.

93. FK, review of *Mr. Bletsworthy of Rampole Island* by H. G. Wells, *The Nation* 127 (28 November 1928): 576.

94. FK, review of *Motherhood in Bondage* by Margaret Sanger, *The Nation* 127 (12 December 1928), 660–661; program, National Conference of Social Work (26 June–3 July 1929): 60, #581, MVW MSS.

95. FK to GWK, 7 July [1929], #47, DKB addenda, 81; interview with MC, 12 May 1984.

96. Interview with MC, 12 May 1984.

97. DWK to DKB, 25 November 1924, #28, DKB addenda, 81; FK, "Millions of Words."

98. FK to DKB, n.d., #47, DKB addenda, 81; interview with MC, 12 May 1984.

99. GWK to DKB, 11 December 1929, #38, DKB addenda, 81.

100. *NYT,* 10 January 1930, p. 1; FK to EC, 10 January [1930], p. 1; 11 January [1930], p. 1; FK to EC, 10 January [1930]; all #19, FK MSS.

101. FK to EC, 10 January [1930]; 11 January [1930]; both #19, FK MSS.

102. FK to EC, 11 January [1930], p. 2, f. 19, FK MSS.

103. FK to Lewis Gannett, 31 January [1930], p. 1, f. 645, LSG MSS.

104. Advertisement, *Sarasota Advertisors' Directory*, 1927–28, p. 9; FK to Lewis Gannett, 31 January [1930], p. 1, f. 645, LSG MSS.

4. *The Missing Years, 1930–1932*

1. FK to EC, 13 January [1930], p. 4, #19, FK MSS.

2. FK to EC, 14 January [1930], p. 5, #19, FK MSS.

3. FK to EC, 17 January [1930], p. 2, #19, FK MSS.

4. J. A. Miller to FK, hand copied, n.d.; FK to EC, 27 January [1930], p. 2; 29 January [1930], p. 3; all #19, FK MSS.

5. FK to EC, 27 January [1930], p. 6; 18 January [1930], p. 2; both #19, FK MSS.

6. FK to EC, 1 February [1930], pp. 7, 8, #19, FK MSS.

7. Ibid., pp. 8, 9.

8. Ibid., p. 3.

9. Ibid., pp. 8, 9, 3, 10, 3. Quite possibly FK also began psychoanalysis with Hinkle by late 1929, for EC recorded a joint session with the psychoanalyst and noted that "F. had 1½ hrs. re her analysis." EC 1928–29 diary, 19 October 1929; FK to EC, 8 February [1930], p. 3, #19, FK MSS.

10. FK to EC, 13 February [1930], p. 2, 16 February [1930], pp. 2, 3; both #19, FK MSS.

11. FK to EC, 11 March [1930], p. 3, #19, FK MSS.

12. FK to EC, 23 January [1930], p. 4, #19, FK MSS. That same day she remarked that she had "abandoned" him to the mother of a little girl he played with; such delegation of responsibility for Jeffrey was rare. In fact, in February FK wrote EC that she felt shackled to Jeffrey, yet was reluctant to delegate even the responsibilities for decisions like how much sun he should get; FK to EC, 19 February [1930], p. 4, #19, FK MSS.

13. FK to EC, 19 February [1930], p. 4, #19, FK MSS.

14. FK to EC, 27 January [1930], p. 5, #19, FK MSS.

15. FK, "Life on Sarasota Beach," n.d.; FK to EC, 16 February [1930], p. 3; both #19, FK MSS.

16. FK to EC, 21 January [1930], p. 3, #19, FK MSS.

17. FK to EC, 22 January [1930], p. 5, #19, FK MSS.

18. FK to OGV, 29 January 1930, p. 3, f. 2073, OGV MSS.

19. FK 1930 diary, 18 January 1930.

20. OGV to FK, 22 January 1930, p. 1; FK to OGV, 29 January 1930, p. 1, both f. 2073, OGV MSS; FK to EC, 2 February [1930], p. 3, #19, FK MSS.

21. FK to EC, 31 January [1930], p. 2, #19, FK MSS.

22. FK to EC, 4 February [1930], p. 4, #19, FK MSS.

23. Jeffrey Kirchwey Clark to EC, 23 February [1930], pp. 3, 4; Jeffrey Kirchwey Clark to EC, 26 February [1930], p. 1; both #19, FK MSS.

24. FK 1930 diary, 1 March 1930.

25. Ibid., 2 March 1930; EC visited from March 2–8, 1930.

26. GWK to DKB, 4 March 1930, p. 4, #38, DKB addenda, 81.

27. GWK to DKB, 12 March 1930, pp. 3, 4, #38, DKB addenda, 81.

28. FK to EC, 15 March [1930], pp. 1, 3, #19, FK MSS.

29. FK to EC, 17 March [1930], p. 1, #19, FK MSS.

30. FK to OGV, n.d. [March 1930], f. 2073, OGV MSS. In this note FK probably enclosed a clipping from the Florida press which had published an abundance of snake stories. The resulting *Nation* story involved the fate of a snake that had climbed a telephone pole. Drifter, "In the Driftway," *The Nation* 130 (26 March 1930): 362.

31. FK to Miriam D. Dole, telegram draft, n.d. [1930], FK MSS; FK 1930 diary, 27 March 1930.

32. Jeffrey Clark autopsy, 10, 421, #15, FK MSS.

33. FK to DKB, 5 April [1930], pp. 3, 4, #48, DKB addenda, 81; DKB to FK, 30 March 1930, pp. 1–2, #13, FK MSS. Consultation with Philip R. Alexander, M.D., revealed that, even without tuberculosis, Jeffrey would not have lived beyond the age of twenty-five because of a congenital heart malformation. The doctors who treated him for tuberculosis used the medical knowledge of the time. In 1929 treatment for tuberculosis, in order of importance, included: rest;

food; fresh air; heliotherapy (sun); occupational therapy; lung collapse (Russell Cecil, *Textbook of Medicine* [Philadelphia: Saunders, 1929], pp. 236–241). As late as 1946 treatment for tuberculosis, in order of importance, included: isolation from others; collapse therapy; heliotherapy; x-ray treatment; diet, including cod liver oil; insulin; salt-free diet; cod liver oil topical treatment. Therapeutic chemotherapeutic treatment was in experimental stages; there were no cures yet (Harry Beckman, *Treatment in General Practice* [Philadelphia: Saunders, 1946], pp. 318–323).

34. FK to DKB, 5 April [1930], pp. 6, 7, #48, DKB addenda, 81; FK to OGV, n.d., Monday [1923], p. 6; FK to OGV, n.d., November [1923], p. 3; both f. 2073, OGV MSS. Jeffrey may have been FK's favorite child. At birth she recorded her delight in him: "I can see now that he will soon be able to wipe off the map all possible Michaels!" Even after FK resumed working, the loss weighed on her, though she did not talk about it. Some twenty-eight years later she unburdened herself to her friend Nina Miness. FK talked about Jeff and cried a whole evening. On another occasion, in the early 1960s, an acquaintance, Lillian Elkin, was distraught over her son. Uncharacteristically, FK started to talk of the loss of her "dear bright" child, and the tears surfaced. Interview with Nina Miness, 23 June 1983; interview with Lillian Elkin, 20 June 1983.

35. Florence Martin to FK, 16 April 1930, FK MSS; FK, untitled poem, n.d., #5, FK MSS.

36. Arthur Warner to FK and EC, 5 April 1930; Norman Thomas to FK, 13 April 1930; both #14, FK MSS; Edwin Markham to GWK, 20 March 1930, #33, DKB addenda, 81; FK to DKB, 5 April [1930], p. 2, #48, DKB addenda, 81.

37. FK to DKB, 5 April [1930], p. 5, #48, DKB addenda, 81; interview with MC, 12 May 1984.

38. FK to Louis Fischer, 10 May 1935, FK MSS.

39. FK to OGV, 7 April n.d., pp. 1–2, f. 2073, OGV MSS.

40. FK to DKB, 12 June [1930], p. 2, #47, DKB addenda, 81; MC to Sara Alpern, 13 May 1985, Alpern private collection; telephone interview with Michael R. Gannett, 27 January 1986.

41. EC, "'Mass Financing' Comes To Aid Mass Production," *NYT,* 27 April 1930, sec. 10, p. 4.

42. EC, "Our Foundations For Giving Have a Billion of Capital," *NYT,* 20 July 1930, sec. 9, p. 3.

43. FK to DKB, 12 June [1930], p. 3, #47, DKB addenda, 81; FK to OGV, 29 June [1930], f. 2073, OGV MSS.

44. FK to DKB, 12 June [1930], p. 2, #47, DKB addenda, 81; OGV to Joseph Wood Krutch, 26 August 1930, pp. 2, 3, f. 2138, OGV MSS. She found her sessions with Dr. Hinkle "very interesting and often illuminating." Years later she experienced some similar behavior: "I put off things—the few things I should do, from day to day" and labeled her feelings "not an obvious depression—but an inability—or an unwillingness to come to grips with anything." Her state of mind reminded her of her reaction to Jeff's death: "I had it a lot in those years after J. died and then, too, I might have overcome it better by forcing myself to do a real job of some sort." FK to EC, n.d., #26, FK MSS.

45. FK to DKB, 29 August [1930], #47, DKB addenda, 81; Freda liked to

describe the time her father tried to telephone her at a hotel. The desk clerk could not find Freda Kirchwey, no matter how many ways he spelled the name. Finally GWK said, "Try Mrs. Evans Clark." When FK picked up the phone, GWK reproached her: "Freda, you are listed as Mrs. Evans Clark. What has happened to your principles?" She answered: "Father, how many times do I have to tell you? At maternity wards and hotels I am *always* Mrs. Evans Clark" (interview with DKB, 16 August 1974).

46. GWK to DKB, 18 August 1930, pp. 2, 3, #38, DKB addenda, 81; Dorothy Van Doren to OGV, 8 December 1930, p. 2, f. 3960, OGV MSS.

47. New School for Social Research Announcement, winter term 1931 (New York: New School for Social Research, 1930), p. 14.

48. Interview by Dorothy Woolf, "Projections," Barnard *Alumnae Monthly,* p. 9, #23, DKB addenda, 70s; New School Announcement, p. 13.

49. *The Nation* 130 (1 January 1930): 1; *The Nation* 131 (8 October 1930): 361, 363; *The Nation* 132 (21 January 1931): 57; FK, "A Duchess and a Dancer," *The Nation* 132 (2 February 1931): 190.

50. EC to DKB, 27 March [1931], #48, DKB addenda, 81.

51. FK to DKB, 23 June 1931, #48, DKB addenda, 81.

52. Interview with Grace Epstein, 16 April 1976.

53. FK to DKB, 28 September 1931, p. 2, #48, DKB addenda, 81.

54. EC to DKB, 2 November 1931, p. 3; FK to DKB, 9 November 1931; both #48, DKB addenda, 81.

55. FK to DKB, 2 March 1932, p. 4, #48, DKB addenda, 81.

56. FK, review of *Living My Life* by Emma Goldman, *The Nation* 133 (2 December 1931): 614.

57. Emma Goldman to Evelyn Scott, 2 February 1932, #59, Malmed/Goldman MSS.

58. OGV to FK, 7 June 1932; FK to OGV, 14 June 1932; 27 August 1932; all f. 2073, OGV MSS.

59. FK to GWK and DKB, 20 August 1932, p. 3, #48, DKB addenda, 81.

60. *New York World-Telegram* clipping, n.d. [1932], FK MSS.

61. Interview by Woolf, *Projections,* p. 9.

62. *New York World-Telegram* clipping, n.d. [1932], FK MSS.

5. A Desk with a View

1. FK listed on the masthead as associate editor: *The Nation* 135 (24 August 1932): 153; "Memorandum Setting Forth Proposal for Management of The Nation," n.d. [1932], f. 2138, OGV MSS; OGV to Joseph Wood Krutch, 22 August 1932, f. 2138, OGV MSS; *The Nation* 136 (4 January 1933): 1; FK, Joseph Wood Krutch, Ernest Gruening, and Henry Hazlitt are listed as board of editors. OGV is listed as the sole contributing editor; Carl Van Doren to OGV, 4 January 1933, f. 3959, OGV MSS. FK, book manuscript outline, p. 5; FK to Maurice Wertheim, 17 October 1935, p. 2, #137; both FK MSS.

2. Interview with Caroline Whiting Nash, 11 July 1983; FK to Maurice Wertheim, 17 October 1935, p. 2, #137, FK MSS.

3. Speech, 30 August 1939, pp. 1, 2, #324, FK MSS.

4. FK, speech, 14 July 1944, pp. 2, 3, #324, FK MSS.

5. Ibid., p. 4.

6. FK, speech, 30 August 1939, p. 2, #324, FK MSS.

7. Interview with MC, 28 July 1984; *Nation* deadlines varied over the years, moving between Monday and Tuesday; telephone interview with Caroline Whiting Nash, 6 January 1986.

8. "I Married a Printer's Devil," unpublished manuscript, n.d., pp. 1–4, #8, FK MSS; Caroline Whiting Nash says this spoof was written by Bennett Epstein; interview with Caroline Whiting Nash, 11 July 1983.

9. EC to FK, n.d., #22, FK MSS.

10. FK to Hugo Van Arx, 18 March 1938, #108, FK MSS.

11. FK, "Old Liberties for a New World," *The Nation* 150 (10 February 1940): 146.

12. *The Nation* 139 (29 August 1934): 227; *The Nation* 139 (28 November 1934): 603.

13. Raymond Gram Swing, "Father Coughlin. I. The Wonder of Self-Discovery," *The Nation* 139 (26 December 1934): 730, 731.

14. "Father Coughlin in the Garden," *The Nation* 140 (5 June 1935): 644; *The Nation* 141 (27 November 1935): 607.

15. Raymond Gram Swing, "The Build-Up of Long and Coughlin," *The Nation* 140 (20 March 1935): 325, 326.

16. FK, "A Plea for Democracy," *Journal of the American Association of University Women* 36 (October 1935): 4, 5, 8, #353, FK MSS.

17. Ibid., p. 3.

18. *The Nation* 132 (28 January 1931): 85; Robert A. LaFollette, "President Hoover's Record, IV. The President and Unemployment," *The Nation* 133 (15 July 1931): 61–63.

19. "Mr. Hoover Praises Mr. Hoover," *The Nation* 135 (19 October 1932): 342.

20. "The Faith of Roosevelt," *The Nation* 136 (15 March 1933): 278.

21. *The Nation* 136 (4 January 1933): 1; OGV, "Issues and Men," *The Nation* 136 (11 January 1933): 34; [FK], *The Nation* 136 (22 March 1933): 301.

22. FK, book manuscript outline, p. 10.

23. See, e.g., Ronald Radosh, "The Myth and the New Deal," in Ronald Radosh and Murray Rothbard, eds., *A New History of Leviathon Essays on the Rise of the American Corporate State* (New York: Dutton, 1972); Paul K. Conkin, *The New Deal,* 2nd ed. (Arlington Heights, Ill.: AHM, 1975).

24. Arthur A. Ekrich, Jr., *Ideologies and Utopias, The Impact of the New Deal on American Thought* (Chicago: Quadrangle, 1969), pp. 94, 93; "Mr. Roosevelt Must Lead," *The Nation* 136 (8 February 1933): 137.

25. Arthur M. Schlesinger, Jr., *The Age of Roosevelt* (Boston: Houghton Mifflin, 1957–1960); *The Crisis of the Old Order* (Boston: Houghton Mifflin, 1957); *The Coming of the New Deal* (Boston: Houghton Mifflin, 1959); *The Politics of Upheaval* (Boston: Houghton Mifflin, 1960); Leuchtenburg, *Franklin D. Roosevelt and the New Deal;* Conkin, *The New Deal;* Barton J. Bernstein, "The New Deal: The Conservative Achievements of Liberal Reform," in Bernstein, ed., *Toward a New Past* (New York: Pantheon, 1968); Frank Freidel, ed., *The New Deal and the American People* (Englewood Cliffs, N.J.: Prentice-Hall, 1964); James MacGregor Burns, *Roosevelt: The Lion and the Fox* (New York: Harcourt, Brace, and World, 1956); John W. Allswang, *The New Deal and American Politics: A Study in Political Change* (New York: Wiley, 1978).

26. [FK], "Circuses Without Bread," *The Nation* 136 (3 May 1933): 488. [FK], "Can Controlled Capitalism Save Us?" *The Nation* 136 (7 June 1933): 630.

27. [FK], "Can Controlled Capitalism Save Us?" p. 630; "Mr. Roosevelt— So Far," *The Nation* 136 (28 June 1933): 711.

28. [FK], "Business Hops Aboard," *The Nation* 136 (28 June 1933): 713; for EC, see, e.g., EC, "Says Labor Has Failed to Share Full Gains in Industry and Business," *NYT,* 7 June 1931, sec. 2, p. 18.

29. [FK], "Roosevelt in Review," *The Nation* 137 (20 December 1933): 695.

30. *NYT,* 6 February 1935, p. 15.

31. "Where Is Security, Mr. Roosevelt?" *The Nation* 140 (30 January 1935): 116; "Defeat the Wagner-Lewis Bill!" *The Nation* 140 (17 April 1935): 433; *The Nation* 141 (3 July 1935): 3.

32. Abraham Epstein, "'Social Security' Under the New Deal," *The Nation* 141 (4 September 1935): 261–263; *NYT,* 2 October 1936, p. 3; see also *NYT,* 2 October 1936, p. 7; 1 October 1936, p. 18. Committee on Old Age Security of the Twentieth Century Fund, *The Townsend Crusade* (New York: Twentieth Century Fund, 1936); Committee on Old-Age Security of the Twentieth Century Fund, *More Security for Old Age* (New York: Twentieth Century Fund, 1937).

33. *The Nation* 142 (15 April 1936): 466; Paul Ward, "Planning Future Slums," *The Nation* 142 (20 May 1936): 635–636; "Just Before the Battle," *The Nation* 142 (17 June 1936): 763–764; EC, address at Mr. Eustace Seligman's Luncheon, Bankers Club, 28 May 1936, pp. 1–10, 3, f. 432, Survey MSS.

34. See Leuchtenburg, *Roosevelt and the New Deal,* p. 151; "A National Labor Law," *The Nation* 140 (6 March 1935): 265; "Strengthening the Wagner Bill," *The Nation* 140 (20 March 1935): 322.

35. "Can Labor Enforce the Wagner Bill?" *The Nation* 141 (10 July 1935): 32; "The Wagner Bill and the NRA," *The Nation* 140 (29 May 1935): 616.

36. Paul Ward, "Roosevelt's Hollow Triumph," *The Nation* 141 (11 September 1935): 293; see also "The President Completes the Record," *The Nation* 141 (18 September 1935): 313; Ward, "Hollow Triumph," p. 294.

37. *The Nation* 141 (6 November 1935): 521; "The New Deal Ends," *The Nation* 141 (27 November 1935): 609.

38. "1940 Is Just Around the Corner," *The Nation* 142 (10 July 1936): 729, 730; *The Nation* 141 (17 July 1935): 57; "Mr. Roosevelt Holds Fast," *The Nation* 143 (4 July 1936): 3–5.

39. "Mr. Roosevelt Holds Fast," p. 5; EC to MC, 5 November 1936, MC private collection.

40. Stuart Chase, "Elegy for the Elite," *The Nation* 143 (21 November 1936): 600.

41. Heywood Broun, "Betrayal in a Garden," *The Nation* 140 (5 June 1935): 659–660; *The Nation* 140 (12 June 1935): 660–670; "A Constitutional Plutocracy," *The Nation* 140 (12 June 1935): 672–673; "What Does the Supreme Court Mean?" blustered an editorial which analyzed the deletion of a section of the NRA case. "The Supreme Court Swings the Ax" read another editorial which recounted the doomed Agricultural Adjustment Act. "What Does the Supreme Court Mean?" *The Nation* 140 (23 January 1935): 87–88; "The Supreme Court Swings the Ax," *The Nation* 142 (15 January 1936): 61.

42. Max Lerner, "The Riddle of the Supreme Court, I. The Divine Right of Judges," *The Nation* 142 (29 January 1936): 121–123.

43. "A Constitutional Plutocracy," *The Nation* 140 (12 June 1935): 673; *The Nation* 140 (12 June 1935): 669–670, 669.

44. "Purging the Supreme Court," *The Nation* 144 (13 February 1937): 173–174.

45. Ibid., p. 173.

46. See William E. Leuchtenburg, "Franklin D. Roosevelt's Court Packing Plan," in *Essays on the New Deal* (Austin: University of Texas, 1969), p. 91. The *New York Times* is filled with news about the reorganization plan from the time FDR proposed it on 6 February 1937, until it was defeated on 9 April 1938. See *NYT,* 6 February 1937, pp. 1, 8; 9 April 1938, p. 1, and through the summer of 1938.

47. "The Court and Fascism," *The Nation* 144 (20 January 1937): 200–201; "Purging the Supreme Court," pp. 173–174.

48. John Haynes Holmes, quoted in Wreszin, *Oswald Garrison Villard,* p. 252; William A. White to FK, 9 June 1937, WAW MSS; OGV, "What Is *The Nation* Coming To?" *The Nation* 144 (27 March 1937): 352; Maurice Wertheim, "*The Nation* and the Court," *The Nation* 144 (10 April 1937): 145.

49. Hugo Van Arx to FK, 25 August 1936, p. 1, FK MSS. Wertheim, an investment banker, formerly on the *Nation*'s board of directors, had bought the journal from Villard in 1935.

50. FK to Maurice Wertheim, 17 October 1935, p. 4, #137, FK MSS.

51. FK book manuscript outline, p. 6; memorandum from the Editors to Maurice Wertheim, 10 June 1936, p. 1, FK MSS.

52. EC to FK, 21 August 1936, p. 3; EC to FK, 20 August 1936, p. 1; Joseph Krutch to FK, Tuesday [August 1936?], p. 2; Hugo Van Arx to FK, 25 August 1936, pp. 1–2; all FK MSS.

53. FK, book manuscript outline, p. 7; FK to Maurice Wertheim, 22 June 1937, #101, FK MSS.

54. FK, book manuscript outline, p. 7; Karl Kirchwey to EC, memorandum on sale, 22 April 1937, #101; FK, book manuscript outline, p. 7; all FK MSS.

55. Maurice Wertheim, announcement [1937], pp. 1, 2, #101, FK MSS; FK, book manuscript outline, p. 7; *NYT,* 4 June 1937, p. 21. Maurice Wertheim, announcement, p. 2.

56. [FK], "*The Nation*'s Future," *The Nation* 144 (19 June 1937): 695.

57. EC, correspondence, *The Nation* 134 (22 June 1932): 703; editor, correspondence, *The Nation* 134 (22 June 1932): 703.

58. [EC and FK], "Can Italy Defy Sanctions?" *The Nation* 141 (11 September 1935): 283.

59. [FK], "Back the League!" *The Nation* 136 (1 March 1933): 221; [FK], *The Nation* 137 (29 November 1933): 605.

60. [FK], *The Nation* 136 (22 March 1933): 302; "Hitler in Power," *The Nation* 136 (8 February 1933): 137; *The Nation* 136 (15 February 1933): 163; "Hitler Wins," *The Nation* 136 (15 March 1933): 277; [FK], *The Nation* 136 (22 March 1933): 303.

61. [FK], "Our New Role in Europe," *The Nation* 136 (24 May 1933): 573.

62. [FK], *The Nation* 137 (13 September 1933): 281; Ludwig Lore, "What Are American Nazis Doing?" *The Nation* 144 (5 June 1937): 636–637.

63. "The Nazi Hexenkessel, A Personal Letter," *The Nation* 137 (6 September 1933): 269–270.

64. [FK], *The Nation* 142 (29 April 1936): 535.

65. FK, speech, 30 August 1939, pp. 1, 2; FK, 14 July 1944, p. 3; both #324, FK MSS; [FK], "War Against the Jews," *The Nation* 147 (19 November 1938): 525.

66. Robert Dell, "Hitler Over Europe," *The Nation* 136 (3 May 1933): 498, 497.

67. See Dr. Naomi Weisstein, "'Kinder, Kuche, Kirche,' as Scientific Law: Psychology Constructs the Female," in Robin Morgan, ed., *Sisterhood Is Powerful* (New York: Vintage, 1970), pp. 205–220; [FK], "Nazi Women Speak Out," *The Nation* 139 (12 September 1934): 286. This underlying attitude continued even during the period in World War II when Nazis needed to recruit women for war-related industries. See Leila Rupp, "Women's Place Is in the War," in Leila Rupp, *Mobilizing Women for War: German and American Propaganda, 1939–1945* (Princeton: Princeton University Press, 1980); [FK], *The Nation* 137 (16 August 1933): 170, 171.

68. [FK], "Birth Control Today," *The Nation* 144 (9 January 1937): 34; Hannah M. Stone, "Birth Control Wins," *The Nation* 144 (16 January 1937): 70–71.

69. FK, "The Role of the College Woman in a Shaken World," speech at Hunter College, New York, N.Y., 11 October 1940, p. 11, #324, FK MSS.

70. Ibid., pp. 3, 1.

71. FK, "Conversation with Myself," unpublished manuscript, FK dated it "February 1939?", pp. 1–16, quotations on pp. 1, 2, 3, 8, 9, 12, #7, FK MSS.

72. "Can Hitler Be Trusted?" *The Nation* 140 (5 June 1935): 645; see also "Europe Must Choose," *The Nation* 140 (3 April 1935): 376; John Gunther, "The Rhineland Crisis," *The Nation* 142 (1 April 1936): 407–408; [FK], *The Nation* 142 (29 April 1936): 535.

73. [FK], "Moscow Offers an Olive Branch," *The Nation* 141 (7 August 1935): 145.

74. [FK], *The Nation* 139 (19 December 1934): 696; *The Nation* 144 (19 June 1937): 691; Louis Fischer to Max Lerner, 12 September 1936, box 1, LF MSS. For a different view, see *New Republic*, "The Purge Goes On," *The New Republic* 93 (5 January 1938): 240–241.

75. [FK], "Russia and the World," *The Nation* 145 (13 November 1937): 521.

76. FK to George Novack, 9 February 1937, pp. 1, 2, Trotskii MSS.

77. FK to MC, 10 February 1937, MC private collection, p. 2; the results of the Trotsky Commission left her in a state of "uncomfortable agnosticism"; [FK], "The Trotsky Commission," *The Nation* 144 (1 May 1937): 496.

78. "Spain Is the Key," *The Nation* 144 (13 February 1937): 172; the Soviet Union later withdrew support.

79. FK to Vera Micheles Dean, 17 December 1936, #8, VMD MSS; "A Challenge to Pacifists," *The Nation* 144 (6 February 1937): 148–150; [FK], "The Little World War Begins to Grow," *The Nation* 143 (28 November 1936): 620–621.

80. [FK], *The Nation* 144 (30 January 1937): 114. Although other brigades made up of Americans saw action in Spain, the Eugene V. Debs group did not. See Robert A. Rosenstone, *Crusade of the Left* (New York: Pegasus, 1969).

81. [FK], *The Nation* 148 (11 February 1939): 161.

82. [FK], *The Nation* 148 (25 February 1939): 217.

83. [FK], *The Nation* 148 (11 March 1939): 279.

84. FK, "'Peace' in Spain," *The Nation* 148 (8 April 1939): 393–394.

85. During the complex struggle among the various Spanish groups that fought the fascists, Kirchwey consistently supported the Loyalists. FK to Louis Fischer, 9 September 1937, p. 1, box 2, LF MSS.

86. Louis Fischer to FK, 17 October 1937, #170, FK MSS; FK to Dwight Macdonald, 13 January 1938, p. 2, Y series I, box 26, f. 670, DMcD MSS; FK to Louis Fischer, 22 November 1937, #170, FK MSS.

87. FK to Louis Fischer, 22 November 1937, #170, FK MSS.

88. Heywood Broun, "Some Sleeping Beauties," *The Nation* 144 (26 June 1937): 730; FK to OGV, 27 July 1937, f. 2073, OGV MSS.

89. [FK], *The Nation* 143 (5 December 1936): 646.

90. In the 1950s, after he changed his viewpoint, he criticized the *Nation* for its pro-Soviet stance. [FK], *The Nation* 145 (11 December 1937): 632.

91. [FK], "Russia and the World," p. 521.

92. FK, "Conversation with Myself," p. 12, FK MSS.

93. Max Lerner, *It Is Later Than You Think: The Need for a Militant Democracy* (New York: Viking, 1938), p. 24; [FK], *"The Nation's* Future," p. 615.

94. [FK], "Russian Tragedy, Act III," *The Nation* 146 (12 March 1938): 288.

95. FK to Hugo Van Arx, 18 March 1938, p. 2, #108, FK MSS.

96. FK, "European Premier," unpublished manuscript, n.d., #7, FK MSS.

97. FK to MC, October 1938, p. 2, MC private collection.

98. FK, "Gangster Triumphant," *The Nation* 146 (19 March 1938): 321, 322; [FK], "The Great Betrayal," *The Nation* 146 (24 September 1938): 284; see also [FK], "Treaty of Munich," *The Nation* 147 (8 October 1938): 340–341; FK, "Blood and Geography," *The Nation* 148 (8 February 1939): 365.

99. FK to MC, October 1938, p. 3, MC private collection.

100. The summer of 1938, after a year at the University of North Carolina, MC left college for a year of travel through Europe and the Middle East; he entered Harvard College in 1939. EC to MC, 20 September 1938, MC private collection.

101. FK, "Gangster Triumphant," pp. 322, 321; [FK], "The Great Betrayal," pp. 284, 285; FK, "Loving Hitler Less," *The Nation* 148 (25 March 1939): 337, 338.

102. "Munich: Act II," *The Nation* 148 (25 March 1939): 335.

103. FK, "Blood and Geography," p. 366; FK, "Loving Hitler Less," p. 338.

104. James Burkhart Gilbert, *Writers and Partisans: A History of Literary Radicalism in America* (New York: Wiley, 1968), pp. 200–201; Daniel Aaron, *Writers on the Left: Episodes in American Literary Communism* (New York: Harcourt, Brace & World, 1961); pp. 374, 462, 467.

105. FK, "Red Totalitarianism," *The Nation* 148 (27 May 1939): 605.

106. Ibid., p. 606.

107. Her position predated that of noted theologian Reinhold Niebuhr who, five years later, would bring out a similar thesis in *The Children of Light and the Children of Darkness*. Despite their cynicism, Niebuhr would consider Marxists "children of light" foolish since they underestimated "the power of self-interest, both individual and collective, in modern society," while the "children of darkness" were "evil" because they knew no law beyond the self. Reinhold Niebuhr, *The Children of Light and the Children of Darkness: A Vindication of Democracy*

and a Critique of Its Traditional Defense (New York: Scribners, 1944), pp. 9, 10, 32.

108. Sidney Hook to FK, 8 June 1939, #153, FK MSS.

109. FK to Maxwell Stewart, 20 July 1939, #420, FK MSS.

110. Letters to the editors, *The Nation* 149 (26 August 1939): 228; Maxwell Stewart and Max Lerner signed that letter; [FK], *The Nation* 149 (2 September 1939): 231.

111. FK, "Moscow-Berlin Axis," *The Nation* 149 (7 October 1939): 365; OGV, "Issues and Men," *The Nation* 149 (2 September 1939): 247; Louis Fischer, "Europe Goes to War," *The Nation* 149 (9 September 1939): 262; Louis Fischer, "Two Views of the Russian Pact. II. An Inexcusable Treaty," *The New Communism in the 'Red Decade' Revisited* (Bloomington: Indiana University Press, 1966), p. 198. In Warren's *Liberals and Communism*, see "The Collapse of the Popular Front," pp. 193–215, for a thorough treatment of this topic. Richard H. Pells, "The New Mandarins," in *Radical Visions and American Dreams, Culture and Social Thought in the Depression Years* (New York: Harper & Row, 1973), pp. 347–362, is another excellent treatment.

112. FK to Hugo Van Arx, 18 March 1938, p. 3, #108, FK MSS.

113. FK, "Let's Mind Our Own Business," *The Nation* 148 (15 April 1939): 421–422.

6. Political War Years, 1939–1944

1. FK to MC, 5 May 1939, p. 5, MC private collection; FK, "Europe's Last Stand," *The Nation* 149 (2 September 1939): 232.

2. FK to MC, 29 September 1939, p. 1, MC private collection; FK, "Munich Bears Fruit," *The Nation* 149 (9 September 1939): 259–260.

3. FK, "Can We Stay Neutral?" *The Nation* 150 (20 April 1940): 504; FK, "Let's Mind Our Own Business," pp. 421, 422.

4. FK, "Old Liberties," p. 146.

5. FK, unpublished speech, 30 August 1939, pp. 5, 6, #324; unpublished speech, 17 January [?], p. 7, #327; both FK MSS.

6. FK, unpublished speech, 17 January, p. 7.

7. FK, "Taming Mr. Dies," *The Nation* 149 (16 December 1939): 669; FK, "What Dies Is Up To," *The Nation* 155 (3 October 1942): 309–310; FK, "The Law and Mr. Dies," *The Nation* 149 (4 November 1939): 486–487.

8. Michael Wreszin, "The Dies Committee, 1938," in Arthur M. Schlesinger, Jr., and Roger Bruns, eds., *Congress Investigates, A Documented History, 1792–1942* (New York: Chelsea House, 1975), 4 of 5 volumes, p. 2926; FK, "Happy New Year," *The Nation* 150 (6 January 1940): 4–5.

9. FK, "Communists and Democracy," *The Nation* 149 (14 October 1939): 399, 400.

10. Ibid., p. 399.

11. Memorandum, EC to FK, 10 March 1939; FK, unpublished speech, 17 August 1939, pp. 5–6, #324, FK MSS.

12. An excellent treatment of this crisis in the ACLU, along with a rebuttal by Roger Baldwin, is recounted in Jerold S. Auerbach, "The Depression Decade," in Alan Reitman, ed., *The Pulse of Freedom: American Liberties, 1920–1970s*

(New York: Norton, 1975), pp. 85–104. See also *NYT*, 9 May 1940, p. 25; 10 May 1940, p. 22.

13. [FK], *The Nation* 150 (18 May 1940): 610; see also Auerbach, "Depression Decade," pp. 96, 103.

14. FK, "Saving the Front Line," *The Nation* 150 (8 June 1940): 695; FK, "A Democratic Program of Defense," *The Nation* 150 (15 June 1940): 723.

15. FK to OGV, 30 April 1940, p. 1, f. 2073, OGV MSS; parentheses in original.

16. FK, "Escape and Appeasement," *The Nation* 150 (29 June 1940): 773.

17. Ibid., pp. 773, 774.

18. OGV to FK, 13 June 1940, pp. 1–2, #136, FK MSS; OGV, "Valedictory," *The Nation* 150 (29 June 1940): 782. In another letter Villard assured Kirchwey that his feelings toward her as "Freda Kirchwey the woman, as opposed to Freda Kirchwey, the editor, are unchanged." OGV to FK, 20 June 1940, FK MSS. However, in a 1961 letter to Michael Wreszin, FK wrote of the lack of reconciliation between her and OGV. "He continued to express to other people the greatest opposition to *The Nation's* policy and sorrow that he had ever allowed the paper to fall into my hands." FK to Michael Wreszin, 10 March 1961, p. 3, Wreszin private collection.

19. James T. Farrell to FK, 30 October 1939, #414, FK MSS; FK, "Dictator's Dilemma," *The Nation* 149 (18 November 1939): 541.

20. Peter Viereck, "Under Thirty But I'm a Conservative," *Atlantic Monthly* (April 1940), pp. 538–543; Peter Viereck to Editor, *Atlantic Monthly* (28 March 1940), pp. 1, 2; Peter Viereck to Lewis Gannett, 9 April 1940; FK to Peter Viereck, 23 April 1940; all #402, FK MSS.

21. FK, "By Fire and Sword," *The Nation* 149 (9 December 1939): 639, 640; Peter Viereck to FK, 18 April 1940, #402, FK MSS.

22. [FK], *The Nation* 149 (21 October 1939): 427; FK to Archibald MacLeish, 21 September 1939, #406, FK MSS.

23. FK to Franklin D. Roosevelt, 7 December 1939, PPF 5197, FDR MSS; Eleanor Roosevelt, "My Day," 13 February 1940, 3146, ER MSS.

24. Robert Bendiner, "Glossary for 1940," *The Nation* 150 (10 February 1940): 187; FK to Louis Fischer [FK's letter, dated by Fischer 10 January 1939, refers to the *Nation's* seventy-fifth anniversary and so must be 1940], box 2, p. 2, LF MSS.

25. FK to Louis Fischer, 10 January 1939 [1940], box 2, LF MSS; Louis Fischer, "Russia—Twenty-two Years After," *The Nation* 150 (10 February 1940): 182–186, 185, 186.

26. FK, "Old Liberties," pp. 145, 146.

27. FK to MC, 2 April [1940]; EC to MC, n.d.; both MC private collection.

28. Interview with MC, 27 July 1984.

29. Lewis Gannett to FK, 19 May 1941, FK MSS; interview with Caroline Whiting Nash, 10 July 1983; Norman Thomas to FK, 4 June 1941, and clipping; both #356, FK MSS.

30. FK to Louis Fischer, 22 May 1941, box 3, LF MSS; interview with MC, 28 July 1984; FK to Louis Fischer, 22 May 1941, box 3, LF MSS.

31. FK to MC, 17 April 1941, p. 6, MC private collection.

32. FK to Louis Fischer, 22 May 1941, box 3, LF MSS; FK to Jacob Billikopf,

3 July 1941, pp. 2, 3, #188, FK MSS; FK to Hugo Van Arx, 13 January 1941, p. 1, FK MSS.

33. FK to Hugo Van Arx, 13 January 1941, pp. 1, 2, 3, 4, 5.

34. A report of the *New York Post*'s announcement appears in "Should We Declare War?" *The New Republic* 105 (21 July 1941): 72–73, and FK, "Shall We Declare War?" *The Nation* 153 (26 July 1941): 64–65; "For a Declaration of War," *The New Republic* 105 (25 August 1941): 235–236; (1 September 1941): 279–281; (15 September 1941): 341–343; FK, "The Struggle Ahead," *The Nation* 153 (16 August 1941): 132; FK, "What War Is Our War," *The Nation* 153 (30 August 1941): 173.

35. FK, "Prelude to Action," *The Nation* 153 (23 August 1941): 153; FK, "We Move into War," *The Nation* 153 (25 October 1941): 389.

36. [FK], "Our New Board," *The Nation* 153 (13 September 1941): 212.

37. FK, speech, n.d., p. 3, #327, FK MSS; see also FK, "Jews and Refugees," *The Nation* 148 (20 May 1939): 577.

38. FK, "Let in the Refugees!" *The Nation* 150 (1 June 1940): 669, 670; "Bring Them Out!" *The Nation* 150 (29 June 1940): 773.

39. FK, "Nightmare in France," *The Nation* 151 (17 August 1940): 124–125.

40. In Nadav Safran, *Israel—The Embattled Ally* (Cambridge, Mass.: Belknap Press of Harvard University Press, 1978), p. 24, passim; see also Nadav Safran, *The United States and Israel* (Cambridge, Mass.: Harvard University Press, 1963).

41. FK, "No Peace for Palestine," *The Nation* 148 (27 May 1939): 604.

42. OGV, "The Latest Anti-Jewish Horror," *The Nation* 149 (30 December 1939): 735; FK, "Jews in Hitler's Poland," *The Nation* 150 (20 January 1940): 61, 62; Alonzo L. Hamby, *Beyond the New Deal: Harry S. Truman and American Liberalism* (New York: Columbia University Press, 1973), p. 92; FK, "Zionism and Democracy," p. 74.

43. FK, Nation Associates speech, n.d. pp. 2, 3, 4, #327, FK MSS.

44. FK, speech, n.d. [before 25 April 1945], p. 7, #327, FK MSS. The following words referring to the Jews were omitted from the end of this statement when the speech was delivered: "and the entire Jewish people which serves in Nazi mythology as a symbol of democratic internationalism, of tolerance, and of cultural freedom."

45. FK, "Rescue Hungary's Jews!" *The Nation* 159 (26 August 1944): 229; italics in original.

46. FK , "While the Jews Die," *The Nation* 156 (13 March 1943): 366.

47. FK, Nation Associates speech, n.d., p. 1.

48. Ibid., pp. 1, 6.

49. David S. Wyman, *The Abandonment of the Jews: America and the Holocaust, 1941–1945* (New York: Pantheon, 1984), p. 6; Walter Laqueur, *The Terrible Secret: An Investigation Into the Suppression of Information About Hitler's 'Final Solution'* (London: Weidenfeld and Nicolson, 1980), pp. 1–15; Special issue, "Jews Under the Axis, 1939–1942," *Jewish Frontier* 9 (November 1942): 3–41. Philip S. Bernstein, "The Jews of Europe: I. The Remnants of a People," *The Nation* 156 (2 January 1943): 8–9; "The Jews of Europe: How to Help Them," *The New Republic* 109 (30 August 1943): 299–315.

50. Bernstein, "Jews of Europe: I. Remnants," pp. 8–9.

51. FK, book manuscript outline, p. 15.

52. FK , "For a Free World," *The Nation* 153 (27 September 1941): 270–271; FK, book manuscript outline, p. 13.

53. FK, "For a Free World," p. 271; [FK], "Our New Board," p. 212; Louis Fischer to FK, 15 March 1939, box 2; 29 January 1940, box 3, LF MSS; FK to MC, 19 November 1940; FK to MC, 11 December 1940; both MC private collection.

54. J. Alvarez del Vayo, "World War III?" *The Nation* 154 (20 June 1942): 704–708.

55. Carlo Sforza to FK, 17 June 1942, p. 1, FK MSS.

56. Reinhold Niebuhr, "Thoughts on 'World War III?'" *The Nation* 155 (11 July 1942): 32; Michael Straight, "Thoughts on 'World War III?'" *The Nation* 155 (4 July 1942): 12; Carlo Sforza, "Thoughts on 'World War III?'" *The Nation* 155 (4 July 1942): 13; Theodore Dan, "Thoughts on 'World War III?'" *The Nation* 155 (4 July 1942): 14.

57. *The Nation* 155 (22 August 1942): 143; FK, book manuscript outline, p. 13.

58. "Political War," *The Nation* 155 (26 September 1942): 262.

59. FK, "Hapsburg Hopes," *The Nation* 155 (24 October 1942): 402.

60. "Political War," p. 262.

61. J. Alvarez del Vayo, "Primer," *The Nation* 155 (3 October 1942): 298.

62. See, e.g., Argus, *The Nation* 155 (7 November 1942): 478.

63. In 1945, with the discontinuation of the Political War section, Del Vayo was designated European editor; *The Nation* 161 (27 October 1945): 417; in 1949 he was designated foreign editor; *The Nation* 168 (29 January 1949): 114; interview with CMcW, 14 April 1976.

That FK put a foreigner—a controversial one—in charge of the Political War section created tension within and without the *Nation,* and over the years her choice was criticized. Was it advisable to have a foreigner edit the foreign section of an American political journal? Years later CMcW, who became editor of the *Nation* when Kirchwey retired, expressed a strong negative to that question. Others who accused FK of misjudgment alleged that a protracted affair with Del Vayo clouded her thinking and unduly influenced her policies and politics. (Suspicions about that possibility continue into the 1980s.) Since FK and Del Vayo died a decade ago, no one can be certain, but after extensive research in their papers and many interviews, I have concluded that FK and J. Alvarez del Vayo were not lovers; theirs was a platonic relationship. They shared an intense commitment to the cause of a Free Spain and the defeat of Hitler.

Long before she met Del Vayo, FK had developed a sympathetic view of the Soviet Union as a common and necessary ally against fascism. Del Vayo, though accused by some of being a Communist agent, was a lifelong socialist and an incurable optimist about the USSR. Reading his writings and after many interviews, I am convinced of his commitment to socialism only. For charges that he was a Communist, see, e.g., Salvador de Madariaga, *Spain, A Modern History* (New York: Praeger, 1950), p. 450. Burnett Bolloton, who acknowledges that Del Vayo was a socialist, has characterized him as a "Communist at heart," linking him with the Communists' campaign to unite the Socialist and Communist parties during the Spanish Civil War. He is especially critical of Del Vayo for supporting the relatively small Communist Party, thereby offering it a disproportionate influence during the turmoil. Burnett

Bolloton, *The Spanish Revolution* (Chapel Hill: University of North Carolina Press, 1979), quotation on p. 137.

64. Clipping, #40, DKB addenda, 81; GWK to Franklin D. Roosevelt, 10 February 1936, f. 2316, FDR MSS; *National Cyclopaedia of American History* 47: 460–461; Vivian Pierce to Franklin D. Roosevelt, 15 September 1938; Franklin D. Roosevelt to DKB, 6 March 1942; GWK to Franklin D. Roosevelt, 30 October 1938, last three PPF 5516, FDR MSS; DKB to Miriam Van Waters, 1 August 1940, p. 1, #130, MVW MSS; interview with Michael Clark, 28 July 1984; FK to MC, 11 March 1942, MC private collection.

65. FK to MC, 11 March 1942, MC private collection; *The Nation* 155 (22 August 1942): 143.

66. James Wechsler, *The Age of Suspicion* (New York: Random House, 1953), p. 157; FK, "The Indian Dilemma," *The Nation* 150 (22 August 1942): 144.

67. Louis Fischer to FK, 19 September 1942; FK to Louis Fischer, 28 September 1942, box 4, LF MSS.

68. Felix Frankfurter to FK, n.d., Correspondence 1942–46, LF/FDR MSS.

69. Louis Fischer, "Why Cripps Failed," *The Nation* 155 (19 September 1942): 230–234; *The Nation* 155 (26 September 1942): 255–259; FK to Louis Fischer, n.d., Correspondence, 1942–46, LF/FDR MSS; italics in original.

70. Louis Fischer, "Gandhi's Rejected Offer," *The Nation* 155 (22 August 1942), 145–147; G. R. Strauss, M.P., to FK, telegram, 24 September 1942; Graham Spry to FK, n.d., box 4, LF MSS; Graham Spry, "A British Reply to Louis Fischer," *The Nation* 155 (14 November 1942): 501–503; Louis Fischer and FK, "Defending the Empire?" *The Nation* 155 (31 October 1942): 433–434; Reinhold Niebuhr to FK, 30 October 1942, box 4, LF MSS.

71. Louis Fischer to FK, 19 November 1942, box 4, LF MSS; Robert Bendiner to FK, n.d., FK MSS.

72. FK to Louis Fischer, 24 November 1942, box 4, LF MSS; Louis Fischer to FK, late November 1942, FK MSS.

73. FK, unpublished speech, 17 August 1939, p. 1, #7, FK MSS.

74. FK to Isaac Rosengarten, attachment to letter, 17 April 1939, #420, FK MSS.

75. EC to FK, memorandum, 10 March 1939, pp. 1, 2, #147, FK MSS.

76. FK, "Communists and Democracy" (October 1939) pp. 399, 400.

77. FK, "The Fifth Column," *The Nation* 150 (27 April 1940): 529, 530.

78. FK, "Curb the Fascist Press!" *The Nation* 154 (28 March 1942): 357, 358.

79. Ibid.

80. C. I. Claflin to FK, 13 April 1942; FK to C. I. Claflin, 9 April 1942; all #214, FK MSS.

81. Norman Thomas to FK, 3 April 1942, pp. 1, 3, General Correspondence, NT MSS.

82. FK to Norman Thomas, 9 April 1942, pp. 1, 2, General Correspondence, NT MSS.

83. John Haynes Holmes to FK, 13 April 1942, #214, FK MSS.

84. FK, "The Same Old Dragon," *The Nation* 128 (8 May 1929): 560.

85. Dwight Macdonald to Victor Serge, 1 February 1942; John Dos Passos to Dwight Macdonald, 29 January 1942, box 9, f. 212, DMcD MSS.

86. FK et. al. to Eleanor Roosevelt, 3 February 1942, 853, Eleanor Roosevelt

Correspondence; see also 1648, 1942, Eleanor Roosevelt Correspondence, ER MSS.

87. FK to Dwight Macdonald, 9 February 1942, box 9, f. 211, DMcD MSS; FK to Harold Ickes, 10 February 1942, #189, FK MSS.

88. *NYT,* 13 February 1942, p. 5; Richard Rovere, "Ogpu at Work," *The Nation* 154 (7 February 1942): 163–164; letters to the editors, *The Nation* 154 (28 February 1942): 267; Norman Thomas to FK, 5 March 1942, #213, FK MSS.

89. FK to Bertram Wolfe, 2 March 1942, pp. 1, 2, #213, FK MSS; Dwight Macdonald to the editors, *The Nation,* 1 March 1942, series I, box 35, f. 902, DMcD MSS.

90. Editors, letters to the editors, *The Nation* 154 (21 March 1942): 352.

91. FK, "Hitler's Double-Talk," *The Nation* 153 (5 November 1941): 472; FK, "End of the Comintern," *The Nation* 156 (29 May 1943): 762.

92. FK to I. F. Stone, 8 June 1943, FK MSS.

93. XXX (pseudonym of a war-agency executive who was frequently asked by the FBI for character references of personnel), "Washington Gestapo," *The Nation* 157 (17 July 1943): 64–66; XXX, "Washington Gestapo," *The Nation* 157 (24 July 1943): 92–95; I. F. Stone, "XXX and the FBI," *The Nation* 157 (25 September 1943): 342–343; FK, "End the Inquisition," *The Nation* 157 (31 July 1943): 116; see also Penn Kimball, "Opening the Files: The History of *The Nation,*" *The Nation* 242 (22 March 1986): 408.

94. XXX, "Washington Gestapo," p. 66; FK to I. F. Stone, 20 July 1943; FK, "End the Inquisition," p. 116.

95. Anonymous to Attorney General Biddle, 3 August 1943, FK FBI f. 2; John Edgar Hoover to Anonymous, 25 August 1943, FK FBI f. 1; E. E. Conroy to Director, FBI, 31 January 1944, p. 2, FK FBI f. 2.

96. FK to OGV, 7 May 1943, f. 2073, OGV MSS; teletype, 23 August 1943, #343, FK MSS; incorrect spelling in original.

97. FBI Report, 31 January 1944, FK FBI f. 2.

98. Quoted in Kingsley Martin, *Harold Laski* (New York: Viking, 1955), p. 128; interview with Caroline Whiting Nash, 10 July 1983.

99. Memorandum, EC to Bruce Bliven, 28 May 1942, p. 1; Bruce Bliven to EC, 9 June 1942; EC to Bruce Bliven, 12 June 1942; all #398, FK MSS.

100. Statement for the Associated Press, 15 February 1943, pp. 1–2, #102; Thomas Mann to FK, 26 February 1943, #102; John Gunther to FK, 13 April 1943, #114; all FK MSS.

101. FK to Maurice Wertheim, 13 May 1943, p. 1, FK MSS.

102. "The Nation Associates," January 1952, p. 51, FK MSS.

103. "America's Opportunity to Maintain a Lasting Peace," Nation Associates, Library of Congress, Washington, D.C.; FK, "Notice to Readers," *The Nation* 159 (23 September 1944): 337.

104. Raymond Swing to Paul U. Kellogg, 17 December 1943, PUK MSS.

105. Gottlieb Hammer to Raymond Swing, 29 March 1944, p. 1, FK MSS.

106. Tribute Dinner booklet, 27 February 1944, unpaginated, Alpern private collection; hereafter cited as Tribute Dinner booklet.

Archibald MacLeish, "FK and *The Nation*" (New York: The Dinner Committee, 27 February 1944), pp. 1–61 (mimeographed); hereafter cited as Tribute Dinner. Some liberals like Max Eastman refused to attend the dinner. Eastman refused to honor the *Nation's* editor, who, "by apologizing for and upholding the totalitarian regime of the Soviet Union . . . betrayed the cause, not only of liberalism but of democracy and civilized morals"; in John P. Diggins, *Up from Communism: Conservative Odysseys in American Intellectual History* (New York: Harper & Row, 1975), p. 208.

107. J. Alvarez del Vayo to FK, n.d. [1944], FK MSS.

108. Judge Thurman Arnold, Tribute Dinner, p. 17; Dorothy Thompson, Tribute Dinner, p. 22.

109. Reinhold Niebuhr, Tribute Dinner, p. 14.

110. Reinhold Niebuhr, *The Children of Light and The Children of Darkness*, pp. 38, 41, 40, 41.

111. Reinhold Niebuhr, Tribute Dinner, pp. 13, 14.

112. FK, Tribute Dinner, pp. 30, 29, 31.

113. In order to secure a New Deal for the world, FK felt it imperative that FDR be reelected to an unprecedented fourth term. "President Roosevelt has been a man whose greatness shines brightly in times of crisis. He is the only possible leader for the next four years." At a crucial stage of the war, "any change at the top might be disturbing"; besides, Roosevelt had the most logical approach to postwar "jobs at home and peace abroad." As election day drew nearer, FK contacted Eleanor Roosevelt about rumors of the possible loss of Jewish votes in Pennsylvania and New York. Thomas E. Dewey's propaganda had attacked FDR for not doing enough to support Palestine, and FK's Jewish sources said that former FDR supporters might follow their Zionist imperatives and reject him. "Zionists are apt to be fanatic, especially in days like these when the question of Palestine is inevitably bound up in their minds with the extermination of European Jewry." Mrs. Roosevelt thanked FK but said that the President did not have a solution. *The Nation* 159 (22 July 1944): 86; FK, "Parties in Flux," *The Nation* 159 (5 August 1944): 145; FK to Eleanor Roosevelt, 2 October 1944; Eleanor Roosevelt to FK, 4 October 1944; both in 729, 1944, Eleanor Roosevelt Correspondence, ER MSS.

114. FK to MC, 29 April [1944], MC private collection.

115. FK Tribute Dinner, pp. 39, 40, 38.

116. FK, Tribute Dinner, p. 41.

117. The Staff of *The Nation*, Tribute Dinner booklet, p. 2.

7. Postwar Fighting, 1945–1950

1. List of Sponsors, Tribute Dinner booklet; *The Nation* 156 (13 March 1943): 362; Diana Trilling, review of *Jake Home* by Ruth McKenney, *The Nation* 156 (13 March 1943): 388; interview with Diana Trilling, 21 June 1983.

2. FK, "Yalta and San Francisco," *The Nation* 160 (24 February 1945): 201; FK, "The Fight Ahead," *The Nation* 166 (10 March 1945): 265.

3. FK, "Russia and the West," *The Nation* 160 (23 June 1945): 684, 685, 686.

4. Louis Fischer to FK, 5 May 1945, box 7, LF MSS; letters to the editors, *The Nation* 160 (2 June 1945): 631. See also newspaper clippings, #173, FK MSS.

5. Letters to the editors, *The Nation* 160 (2 June 1945): 631.

6. Letters to the editors, *The Nation* 160 (16 June 1945): 706, 708.

7. "The Fischer-Nation Debate," letters to the editors, *The Nation* 160 (30 June 1945): 728; Reinhold Niebuhr to King [Gordon], 2 June [1945], #216, FK MSS.

8. George Orwell, *The Collected Essays, Journalism and Letters of George Orwell*, vol. 3 of 4, *As I Please, 1943–1945*, ed. Sonia Orwell and Ian Angus (New York: Harcourt, Brace & World, 1968), p. 236.

9. FK, speech [before 25 April 1945], p. 13, #327, FK MSS.

10. FK, "San Francisco Clears Its Decks," *The Nation* 160 (5 May 1945): 502.

11. FK, speech [before 25 April 1945], p. 16.

12. FK, AAUW speech [1945], p. 6, #325, FK MSS.

13. FK, speech [before 25 April 1945], p. 2; italics in original.

14. FK, AAUW speech [1945], p. 6, #325, FK MSS.

15. FK, "San Francisco Clears Its Decks," pp. 501, 502.

16. FK, "Fragments of One World," *The Nation* 160 (15 May 1945): 561, 560; *NYT*, 6 May 1945, pp. 1, 28. The EAM was the Greek popular resistance movement, originally composed of all left-wing parties, but soon dominated by the KKE, the Greek Communist Party. See David Sacker, "Background on the Greek Crisis," *The Contemporary Review* 169 (March 1946): 155–159.

17. FK, "Fragments of One World," p. 561; *NYT*, 8 June 1945, p. 12; 10 June 1945, p. 24.

18. FK, "Mirror of Our World," *The Nation* 161 (7 July 1945): 5.

19. FK, "San Francisco Clears Its Decks," p. 502. See also "TRIVIA POLITICA," *The Nation* 161 (27 January 1945): 101; *The Nation* 160 (14 April 1945): 402.

20. FK, "Yalta and San Francisco," *The Nation* 160 (24 February 1945): 201.

21. FK to MC, 18 February [1946], MC private collection; FK to Caroline Whiting, 8 March [1946], pp. 1, 4, #346, FK MSS.

22. [FK], "For Spain!" *The Nation* 159 (16 December 1944): 731. See also "Memorandum on Spain," *The Nation* 162 (13 April 1946): 429–437.

23. FK to Paul U. Kellogg, 5 December 1944, pp. 1, 2; Working Editorial Files (Kirchwey), Survey MSS.

24. FK, news release of speech, 2 January 1945, pp. 1, 3, 4, #325, FK MSS; *NYT*, 3 January 1945, pp. 1, 8; news release of speech, 2 January 1945, p. 4; italics in original.

25. Franklin D. Roosevelt to FK, 20 January 1945, #196, FK MSS; Franklin D. Roosevelt to FK, 5 January 1945, PPF 5107, FDR MSS.

26. FK, speech [before 25 April 1945], pp. 10, 5, #327, FK MSS.

27. "The Fight against Franco Spain," Report of the Activities of the Nation Associates at the Security Council of the United Nations," June 1946, #242, FK MSS.

28. Hamby, *Beyond the New Deal*, pp. xvii, xix; italics in original.

29. FK, "End of an Era," *The Nation* 160 (21 April 1945): 429.

30. FK, "Fragments of One World," 561, 560.

31. *NYT*, 7 August 1945, p. 4.

32. See, e.g., Gar Alperovitz, *Atomic Diplomacy, Hiroshima and Potsdam, The Use of the Atomic Bomb and the American Confrontation with Soviet Power* (New York: Simon and Schuster, 1964); Paul F. Boller, Jr., "Hiroshima and the American Left," *International Social Science Review* 57 (Winter 1982): 13–28; Walter

LaFeber, *America, Russia, and the Cold War, 1945–1971,* 2nd ed. (New York: Wiley, 1967–1972); Herbert Feis, *The Atomic Bomb and the End of World War II* (Princeton: Princeton University Press, 1966); Martin J. Sherwin, *A World Destroyed: The Atomic Bomb and the Grand Alliance* (New York: Knopf, 1975); Len Giovannitti and Fred Freed, *The Decision to Drop the Bomb* (New York: Coward-McCann, 1965); Lisle A. Rose, *After Yalta* (New York: Scribner, 1973); John Toland, *The Rising Sun, The Decline and Fall of the Japanese Empire* (New York: Random House, 1970); Joseph Alsop vs. David Joravsky, "Was Hiroshima Necessary?" *The New York Review of Books* 27 (23 October 1980): 37–42; Paul Fussell, "Hiroshima: A Soldier's View," *The New Republic* 185 (22–29 August 1981): 26–30; Michael Walzer and Paul Fussell, "An Exchange on Hiroshima," *The New Republic* 185 (23 September 1981): 13–14.

33. LaFeber, *America, Russia, and the Cold War,* p. 21.

34. Alperovitz, *Atomic Diplomacy;* Daniel Yergin, *Shattered Peace: The Origins of the National Security State* (Boston: Houghton Mifflin, 1978); Barton J. Bernstein, "The Quest for Security: American Foreign Policy and International Control of Atomic Energy, 1942–1946," *Journal of American History* 60 (March 1974): 1003–1044.

35. FK, "One World or None," *The Nation* 161 (18 August 1945): 150. Historian Paul Boller, Jr., analyzed the reactions of American leftist publications immediately after the bomb was dropped. He argued that the more sympathy a publication had for the Soviet Union, the more it supported dropping the bomb, and he cited editorials in the *Daily Worker* and the *New Masses* approving the action. He quoted Kirchwey at length to document her support, ending the quotation before it reached her bitter criticism of the implications of dropping the bomb. Boller, "Hiroshima and the American Left," pp. 14–19 passim.

36. FK, "One World or None," p. 150.

37. Ibid., pp. 149, 150.

38. "A NATION Forum on Atomic Power," *The Nation* 161 (10 November 1945): 485; *The Nation* 161 (17 November 1945): 511.

39. FK, "Russia and the Bomb," *The Nation* 161 (17 November 1945): 511; King Gordon, "The Bomb Is a World Affair," *The Nation* 161 (24 November 1945): 542; "Economics in the Atomic Age," *The Nation* 161 (1 December 1945): 568. Announcement of Gordon as managing editor in *The Nation* 158 (11 March 1944): 295.

40. *NYT,* 3 December 1945, p. 4; 2 December 1945, p. 16; 4 December 1945, p. 1; Harold C. Urey, "The Task Before Us" in "V. Dinner Forum," *The Nation* 161 (22 December 1945): 719; Edgar Ansel Mowrer, "Unite—or Else," in "IV. The Problem of Control," *The Nation* 161 (22 December 1945): 712; Urey, "The Task Before Us," p. 719.

41. Helen Gahagan Douglas, "The Weapons of Peace," in "II. The Soviet Union and the Bomb," *The Nation* 161 (22 December 1945): 705, italics in original; Walter Millis, "Share and Share Alike," in "II. The Soviet Union and the Bomb," *The Nation* 161 (22 December 1945): 708.

42. FK to MC, 8 December [1945], MC private collection.

43. Harold Laski, "Plan or Perish," *The Nation* 161 (15 December 1945): 651; Thomas K. Finletter, "No Middle Ground," in "IV. The Problem of Control," *The Nation* 161 (22 December 1945): 714; Mowrer, "Unite—or Else," p. 712;

Herbert Vere Evatt, "A Stronger UNO," in "V. Dinner Forum," p. 720.

44. Ivan A. Getting, "Facts About Defense," *The Nation* 161 (22 December 1945): 704; Millis, "Share and Share Alike," p. 708.

45. Harold C. Urey, quoted in Stuart Chase, "The New Energy," in "III. Atoms and Industry," *The Nation* 161 (22 December 1945): 709; Chase, "New Energy," p. 710; Boris Pregel, "Power and Progress," in "III. Atoms and Industry," p. 711.

46. "Resolutions Adopted at the Forum," *The Nation* 161 (22 December 1945): 717.

47. FK, book manuscript outline, p. 19; *Atomic Energy Act of 1946, Statutes at Large,* 60 (1946).

48. EC to FK, 21 June [1946], FK MSS; italics in original; *The Nation* 163 (21 September 1946): 31.

49. FK, "Mr. Hull Should Resign," *The Nation* 154 (3 January 1942): 1, 2; I. F. Stone, "Aid and Comfort to the Enemy," *The Nation* 154 (3 January 1942): 6, 7; *The Nation* 154 (17 January 1942): 50–51; letters to the editors, *The Nation* 154 (31 January 1942): 124; *The Nation* 154 (21 February 1942): 206–207; interview with MC, 12 May 1984.

50. Norman A. Kahl to Editors, letters to the editors, *The Nation* 154 (7 February 1942): 175; Gertrude H. Friedlander to Editors, letters to the editors, *The Nation* 154 (7 February 1942): 175, 176.

51. Victor Bernstein, *The Final Judgment: The Story of Nuremberg* (New York: Boni & Gaer, 1947), p. 265; FK, "Politics and Justice," *The Nation* 163 (12 October 1946): 396, 397; see also Rustem Vambery, "The Law of the Tribunal," *The Nation* 163 (12 October 1946): 400–401; "Law and Legalism," *The Nation* 163 (1 December 1945): 573–575.

52. For treatment of the *Partisan Review,* see, for example, James B. Gilbert, *Writers and Partisans* (New York: Wiley, 1968); Sidney Hook, "The Radical Comedians: Inside *Partisan Review,*" *The American Scholar* 54 (Winter 1984–85): 45–61; William Phillips, *A Partisan View* (New York: Stein and Day, 1983). For a detailed treatment of the change of policy of the *Partisan Review* during World War II, see S. A. Longstaff, "*Partisan Review* and the Second World War," *Salmagundi* 43 (Winter 1979): 108–109; [William Barrett], "The 'Liberal' Fifth Column," *Partisan Review* 13 (Summer 1946): 279–293.

53. Gilbert, *Writers and Partisans,* p. 257.

54. William Barrett, *The Truants* (Garden City, N.Y.: Doubleday, 1982), p. 76. See also Terry A. Conney, "Cosmopolitan Values and the Identification of Reaction: *Partisan Review* in the 1930s," *Journal of American History* 68 (December 1981): 580–598; Barrett, *The Truants,* p. 79.

55. Barrett, "'Liberal' Fifth Column," pp. 280, 288; Barrett, *Truants,* p. 82.

56. In Barrett, "'Liberal' Fifth Column," pp. 291, 289.

57. Barrett, *Truants,* p. 81; Richard H. Pells, *The Liberal Mind in a Conservative Age* (New York: Harper and Row, 1985), p. 99; Hannah Arendt, *The Origins of Totalitarianism* (New York: Harcourt Brace Jovanovich, 1951); see also Stephen J. Whitfield, *Into the Dark: Hannah Arendt and Totalitarianism* (Philadelphia: Temple University Press, 1980).

58. Sidney Hook, "The Future of Socialism," *Partisan Review* 14 (January/February 1947): 23–36; italics in original; quotation on p. 29.

59. Michael Wreszin, "Arthur Schlesinger, Jr., Scholar-Activist in Cold War America: 1946–1956," *Salmagundi* 63/64 (Spring/Summer 1984): 255–285; 263; Pells, *Liberal Mind in Conservative Age,* p. 73.

60. Interview with Sidney Hook, 19 July 1983.

61. Benjamin Stolberg, Oral History Project, Columbia University, New York, N.Y., 1950, p. 21. The oral history of Benjamin Stolberg is copyright 1976 by the trustees of Columbia University in the city of New York; used with permission.

62. William L. O'Neill, *A Better World. The Great Schism: Stalinism and the American Intellectuals* (New York: Simon and Schuster, 1982), p. 123.

63. FK used the terms "liberal" and "progressive" interchangeably. FK, "Liberalism at Los Angeles," *The Nation* 163 (5 October 1946): 369, 370.

64. Robert Bendiner, "C.I.O. Tightrope Act," *The Nation* 163 (30 November 1946): 601, 602.

65. Norman Podhoretz, *Breaking Ranks* (New York: Harper & Row, 1979), p. 7.

66. FK, "Toward a New Beginning," *The Nation* 163 (16 November 1946): 544.

67. Mary Sperling McAuliffe, *Crisis on the Left: Cold War Politics and American Liberals, 1947–1954* (Amherst: University of Massachusetts Press, 1978), p. 5.

68. FK, "Third Party Obstacles," *The Nation* 163 (7 December 1946): 636–638; Helen Fuller, "The Liberals—Split as Usual," *The New Republic* 116 (2 January 1947): 27.

69. See Hamby, *Beyond the New Deal,* pp. 159–161, 162–168.

70. See *NYT,* 5 January, sec. 1, p. 5; 5 January, sec. 4, p. 7; 6 January, p. 12; 31 March, p. 1; 31 March, p. 11; all 1947. For a detailed account of the founding of ADA, see Robert Clayton Pierce's Ph.D. dissertation, "Liberals and the Cold War: Union for Democratic Action and Americans for Democratic Action, 1940–1949," University of Wisconsin—Madison, 1979; on University of Michigan Microfilms, 1979.

71. Quoted in Hamby, *Beyond the New Deal,* p. 162.

72. James Loeb, Jr., "Letter of the Week," *The New Republic* 116 (27 January 1947): 46; correspondence, *The New Republic* 116 (27 January 1947): 45.

73. FK, "Mugwumps in Action," *The Nation* 164 (18 January 1947): 62.

74. Robert Bendiner, "Revolt of the Middle," *The Nation* 164 (4 January 1947): 66.

75. FK, "Mugwumps," p. 62.

76. Keith Hutchinson to FK, memo [February 1947], p. 1, #218, FK MSS.

77. [?] to J. Alvarez del Vayo, 31 January 1947, FK MSS.

78. FK to Sally S. Lindsay, 21 January 1947, FK MSS.

79. Diana Trilling, "Liberal Anti-Communism Revisited, Two Symposiums," in *We Must March, My Darlings* (New York: Harcourt Brace Jovanovich, 1977), p. 5.

80. Margaret Marshall, "Socialism, Communism and the West," *The Nation* 165 (13 September 1947): 246–250. Hook called it "the best article *The Nation* has printed in twelve years." Sidney Hook, letters to the editors, *The Nation* 165 (4 October 1947): 350.

81. Margaret Marshall to William Phillips, 19 October 1964, MM MSS. There is an interesting correspondence between Marshall and Phillips on the issue.

See also B. H. Haggin, "The Editor's Rite," *Partisan Review* 133 (Winter 1965): 114–126. Phillips wrote: "Not everyone who knew *The Nation* during this period will agree with Mr. Haggin's assertion that the back section was not affected by the politics of the front. PR will be happy to publish comments." Quotation, Haggin, p. 117. Marshall also wrote: "I became literary editor at a time when I had become opposed to *The Nation's* political line on the Soviet Union. I was, so to say, a premature anti-Communist; the Popular Front business began as I got off the train. This made my position difficult, but I was not interfered with. I wouldn't have Stalinists as reviewers, at least not knowingly. On the other hand, I didn't conceive it to be my function to carry on a campaign against the 'front of the book.' I thought my job was to run as good a book and arts section as I could—in the Nation tradition as I saw it." Margaret Marshall to Professor Richard Clark Sterne, 5 July 1965, MM MSS. An instance in 1951 illustrates the way FK handled her dismay with the back of the book: "I don't know how other members of the staff feel about it, but it seems to me absurd and undignified to go on using articles from people who regularly attack *The Nation* in public and private. I refer, of course, to Schlesinger, Jr. . . . To go on publishing him seems to me to be carrying other cheekism to a ridiculous point. Perhaps the review you printed this week was an old one but I think we should pay for and kill any we've got and not order any more." Marshall did not kill Schlesinger's reviews which appeared in two issues (172 [27 January 1951]: 91–93; and [3 March 1951]: 280–283), but subsequently she drew from other historians. FK to Margaret Marshall, 24 January 1951, #120, FK MSS.

82. William Phillips, *A Partisan View,* p. 174; interview with Diana Trilling, 21 June 1983; interview with Robert Bendiner, 4 January 1980.

83. Arthur M. Schlesinger, Jr., review of *The Struggle for the World,* by James Burnham, *The Nation* 164 (5 April 1947): 398; FK, "Liberals Beware!" *The Nation* 164 (5 April 1947): 385.

84. Schlesinger, review of Burnham, p. 399.

85. FK, "Liberals Beware!" pp. 384, 385.

86. Ibid., p. 384.

87. FK, "Manifest Destiny, 1947," *The Nation* 164 (22 March 1947): 317; *The New Republic* 116 (24 March 1947): 6.

88. FK, "Behind the Hungarian 'Coup,'" *The Nation* 164 (21 June 1947): 731–732.

89. FK, "Manifest Destiny," p. 318.

90. FK, "Dollars vs. Communism," *The Nation* 164 (31 May 1947): 647.

91. FK, "What America Wants," *The Nation* 164 (3 May 1947): 506; see also "Socialist Union or Holy Alliance?" *The Nation* 166 (31 January 1948): 117.

92. *The New Republic* 116 (16 June 1947): 5; "The Marshall Plan," *The Nation* 164 (14 June 1947): 729; *The Nation* 165 (11 October 1947): 380; "Marshall Plan," p. 731; FK, "Marketing the Plan," *The Nation* 164 (28 June 1947): 759.

93. FK, "Bundles for Europe—Without Strings," *The Nation* 165 (22 November 1947): 546, 547.

94. FK, "E.R.P. and War?" *The Nation* 166 (10 April 1948): 385.

95. FK, "The President's Message," *The Nation* 166 (27 March 1948): 341.

96. William Taubman, *Stalin's American Policy* (New York: Norton, 1982), p. 180.

97. FK, "Prague—A Lesson for Liberals," *The Nation* 166 (6 March 1948): 265; "Farewell and Hail," *The Nation* 168 (8 January 1949): 29.

98. FK, "Prague," p. 266.

99. Taubman, *Stalin's American Policy*, pp. 174, 175.

100. FK, "Masaryk," *The Nation* 166 (20 March 1948): 318; FK, "Eduard Benes," *The Nation* 166 (19 June 1948): 676.

101. FK, manuscript, n.d., 15 pp., Wroclaw trip [1948], pp. 1, 2–3, #326, FK MSS; italics in original. See also Kingsley Martin, "Hyenas and Other Reptiles," *New Statesman & Nation* 36 (4 September 1948): 195.

102. FK, manuscript, 26 August [1948], #349, FK MSS. See *NYT*, esp. 28 August, p. 4; 29 August, p. 1; 30 August, p. 4; 4 September, p. 4; 10 September, p. 21; 12 September, p. 7; all 1948.

103. FK, "East Meets West at Wroclaw," *The Nation* 167 (4 September 1948): 250.

104. FK, "Journey Among Creeds," *The Nation* 167 (30 October 1948): 482.

105. Ibid., pp. 482–483.

106. "P.C.A.'s Quixotic Politics," *The Nation* 165 (27 December 1947): 693.

107. J. W. Gitt to FK, 7 January 1948, #187, FK MSS.

108. Robert Bendiner, "Wallace: The Incomplete Angler," *The Nation* 165 (20 December 1947): 668–669; FK, "Wallace: Prophet or Politician?" *The Nation* 166 (10 January 1948): 29.

109. Interview with Robert Bendiner, 4 January 1980.

110. FK, "A Word to Mr. Wallace," *The Nation* 166 (13 March 1948): 294; FK, "How Are You Going to Vote?" *The Nation* 167 (23 October 1948): 452.

111. "1948: The New Beginning," *The New Republic* 119 (27 September 1948): 32; Michael Straight, *After Long Silence* (New York: Norton, 1983), pp. 207, 213, 219, 221.

112. "To the Victor: An Open Letter from the Editors," *The Nation* 167 (6 November 1948): 505.

113. Eric Goldman, *The Crucial Decade and After: America, 1945–1960* (New York: Knopf, 1956), p. 91, passim.

114. Robert Bendiner, "A Most Unusual Case" *The Nation* 169 (16 July 1949): 52–55.

115. Pells, *Liberal Mind in Conservative Age*, p. 105.

116. FK, "Cold War Inaugural," *The Nation* 168 (29 January 1949): 117.

117. FK, Nation Associates Dinner Forum, 7 April 1949, pp. 2, 5, #326, FK MSS.

118. Arthur M. Schlesinger, Jr., *The Vital Center, The Politics of Freedom* (Boston: Houghton Mifflin, 1949), pp. 36–37, 40.

119. Robert Bendiner, review of *The Vital Center* by Arthur M. Schlesinger, Jr., *The Nation* 169 (17 September 1949): 268.

120. Schlesinger, *Vital Center*, pp. 148, 149.

121. Bendiner, review of Schlesinger, p. 269.

122. FK, letters to the editors, *The Nation* 168 (30 April 1949): 512.

123. FK, "Battle of the Waldorf," *The Nation* 168 (2 April 1949): 377.

124. Diggins, *Up from Communism*, p. 327. See also Gary Wills's Introduction to Lillian Hellman, *Scoundrel Time* (Boston: Little, Brown, 1976); *NYT*, 27 March 1949, p. 1. Quotations from interview with Sidney Hook, 19 July 1983; O'Neill, *Better World*, p. 164.

125. Sidney Hook, letters to the editors, "Waldorf Aftermath," *The Nation* 168 (30 April 1949): 511; FK, "Battle of the Waldorf," p. 378.

126. Ibid; FK, reply, letters to the editors, *The Nation* 168 (30 April 1949): 512; FK to Dr. Sidney Hook, 30 April 1949, #414, FK MSS.

127. FK, reply, letters to the editors, p. 512.

128. FK, Nation Associates Dinner Forum, 7 April 1949, p. 1, #326, FK MSS.

129. Nation Associates Report on Spain, 31 December 1946, #243, FK MSS.

130. See *NYT,* esp. 3 December, pp. 1, 6; 10 December, pp. 1, 4; 13 December, p. 1; 9 December, p. 4, all 1946; *The Nation* 168 (30 April 1949): 485.

131. *The Nation* 168 (30 April 1949): 485.

132. FK to the General Assembly of the United Nations, 29 October 1950, #243, FK MSS.

133. See, e.g., FK, "Prague—A Lesson for Liberals," pp. 265–266; FK, "Masaryk," pp. 317–318; FK, "Eduard Benes," p. 676; "Farewell and Hail," pp. 29–30.

134. See George Orwell, *Homage to Catalonia* (London: Secker & Warburg, 1938). FK never wrote, as *New Republic* editor Malcolm Cowley did, of a "sense of guilt" for carrying on a courtship with Russia during the war years. He told of suppressing some thoughts, of putting observations in his notebook but not publishing them, and he confessed to "various sins of silence, self-protectiveness, inadequacy and something close to moral cowardice." Both Hitler and Stalin were evil; Hitler was "Satan" and Stalin "Beelzebub." But Cowley was convinced that Hitler was more evil than Stalin, and, because it was impossible to fight against both at once, he urged the alliance with Stalin, just as FK did. In 1978 Cowley concluded: "It would have been impossible for the West to have overthrown both tyrants at once. After forty years I am still convinced—as Winston Churchill was at that time—that the only sound policy was to check Hitler by any possible means and with the greatest possible number of allies, including Beelzebub." Malcolm Cowley, "The Sense of Guilt," in *And I Worked at the Writer's Trade, Chapters of Literary History 1918–1978* (New York: Viking, 1978), pp. 133–153, 139, 152.

135. FK to Benjamin V. Cohen, 1 November 1950, #242, FK MSS.

136. EC to FK, 26 April [1946], p. 1, #22, FK MSS.

137. EC to FK, [1945], FK MSS.

138. EC to FK, 24 April [1946], pp. 1–2, #22, FK MSS. All, except J. Alvarez del Vayo, held positions on *The Nation*. Diego del Vayo is the son of J. Alvarez and Luisi del Vayo.

139. EC to FK, n.d. [1945], FK MSS.

140. FK to EC, n.d., 2 February, n.d., p. 4, #22, FK MSS.

141. EC to FK, 26 April [1946], p. 2, #22, FK MSS.

142. Interview with MC, 12 May 1984.

143. Excerpts from FK's diary [1946], May 26, 27, 28, 29 [all 1946], MC private collection; interview with MC, 12 May 1984.

144. FK diary excerpt, 29 May [1946], MC private collection.

145. FK diary excerpt, 1 June [1946], MC private collection.

146. FK, "Palestine and Bevin," *The Nation* 162 (22 June 1946): 737–739. (*The Nation* arrived at the newsstands before 22 June.)

147. Eleanor Roosevelt, "Crisis for the Jews," clipping, *New York World-Telegram,* 22 June 1946, FK MSS. Kirchwey's unswerving support of the Jews and

for a homeland for them was expressed openly in her editorials. When she returned to America that August, her son went to Paris to pursue his idea of starting a European edition of the *Nation*. British refusal to grant an import license hindered those plans. Financial problems also precluded future risks. The *Nation*'s 1946 deficit was "the greatest in the journal's history"; 1947 would be worse. The *Nation* could not even afford Michael's suggestion of a massive promotion campaign to increase European newsstand sales. Hugo Van Arx to MC, 29 January 1947, p. 1, MC private collection.

148. FK, Jewish National Fund speech, 2 January 1947, p. 1, #325, FK MSS.

149. FK, "The Nation Associates and the Jewish State," 30 September 1948, p. 6, passim, #241, FK MSS.

150. FK, Jewish National Fund speech, 2 January 1947, p. 1; FK clung to her belief that Israel embodied the very hope for democracy. As she wrote Otto Nathan: "It is one of the few fine and hopeful places in this grim world of ours and what has been accomplished in the last 15—no, 17—years is almost unbelievable." FK to Otto Nathan, 31 August 1965, pp. 1–2, Otto Nathan private collection.

151. Philip Bernstein, "The Jews of Europe, IV. The Case for Zionism," *The Nation* 156 (6 February 1943): 199.

152. FK, speech [before 25 April 1945], p. 11, #327, FK MSS.

153. FK, Jewish National Fund speech, 2 January 1947, p. 4.

154. See MC, "Behind the Viet-Nam Revolt," *The Nation* 164 (17 May 1947): 564–565. FK to MC, 31 March 1947, MC private collection.

155. FK to MC, 30 April 1947, MC private collection. A medical emergency prevented this. Michael became ill and sought medical care in the U.S. A five-hour operation to remove an intestinal cyst left him in terrible pain, and for a few days he suffered some paralysis. A six-week stay in New York City's Presbyterian Hospital helped him recover mobility and strength. He was not the only family convalescent. Freda Kirchwey was recovering from an operation to remove a benign uterine cyst. Just before Christmas 1947 MC left for France to gather his belongings and to say his goodbyes, before returning to live in the United States. Interview with MC, 13 May 1984.

156. Reference to this Nation Associates invitation in letter from Lessing Rosenthal to Eleanor Roosevelt, 29 September 1947; FK to Eleanor Roosevelt, 8 October 1947; both in 3765, 1945–48, NA-NU, General Correspondence, ER MSS.

157. Eleanor Roosevelt to FK, 14 October 1947, 3765, 1945–48, NA-NU, General Correspondence, ER MSS.

158. FK to Eleanor Roosevelt, 8 October 1947.

159. Nation Associates, "The Record of Collaboration of King Farouk of Egypt with the Nazis and Their Ally, the Mufti," June 1948, #236, FK MSS.

160. Kermit Roosevelt, "The Puzzle of Jerusalem's Mufti," *Saturday Evening Post* 220 (12 June 1948): 26–27, 165–166; FK to Editors, 17 June 1948, pp. 1–2; FK, letters to the editors, *Saturday Evening Post* 221 (28 August 1948): 6, 8.

161. In Abram Leon Sachar, *The Course of Modern Jewish History* (New York: Dell, 1963), p. 461; see also Safran, *United States and Israel*, p. 32.

162. FK, "The Nation Associates and the Jewish State," p. 7.

163. FK, "America and Israel," *The Nation* 166 (22 May 1948): 565; Nation Associates memorandum, "The British Record on Partition," submitted to the

General Assembly of the United Nations, April 1948, in *The Nation* 166 (8 May 1948): pt. II, pp. 1–30. FK's influence did not always work. She consistently asked her friend Supreme Court Justice Felix Frankfurter for support; he just as consistently refused. She asked, for instance, for his assistance in creating the Israeli constitution. "I wish I might comment upon it and particularly do it for you. But my job here precludes doing that as it precludes my doing many things that would give satisfaction to my deep impulses." Another time, close to the expiration of the British mandate, FK went to Bernard Baruch for support. But, she reported to Lillie Shultz: "He said no, he'd used up his influence on Palestine, couldn't do it again." Felix Frankfurter to FK, 1 October 1948, FF MSS; FK, memorandum of Conversation with Bernard Baruch, 4 May 1948, #238, FK MSS. Yet sometimes FK helped plan strategy. She wrote long, detailed suggestions for a speech by Moshe Sharett, foreign minister of Israel: "If I may say so, I think yours should be the voice of morality in the discussions." FK to H. E. Moshe Sharett, 4 April 1949, #240, FK MSS.

164. Paul Blanshard, "The Catholic Church in Medicine," *The Nation* 165 (1 November 1947): 466; "The Sexual Code of the Roman Church," *The Nation* 165 (8 November 1947): 496.

165. Paul Blanshard, "The Catholic Church and Education," *The Nation* 165 (15 November 1947): 525, 528.

166. FK, "*The Nation* Banned," *The Nation* 167 (3 July 1948): 4–6; *The Nation* 166 (17 January 1948): 57; FK, "*The Nation* Banned," p. 4.

167. *The Nation* 165 (22 November 1947): 545; *The Nation* 166 (17 January 1948): 57.

168. Paul Blanshard, "The Roman Catholic Church and Fascism," *The Nation* 166 (10 April 1948): 390–393; "The Catholic Church and Fascism, II," *The Nation* 166 (17 April 1948): 416–417; "The Catholic Church and Fascism, III," *The Nation* 166 (24 April 1948): 432–434; "The Catholic Church as Censor," *The Nation* 166 (1 May 1948): 459–464; "Roman Catholic Science," *The Nation* 166 (15 May 1948): 521–524; "Roman Catholic Science," *The Nation* 166 (29 May 1948): 601, 604–606; "The Catholic Church and Democracy, II," *The Nation* 166 (5 June 1948): 630–632; "Roman Catholic Censorship," *The Nation* 166 (8 May 1948): 499–502.

169. FK, "*The Nation* Banned," pp. 4–6, quotation on p. 4; *The Nation* 166 (17 January 1948): 57; FK, "*The Nation* Banned," p. 4.

170. FK, "*The Nation* Banned," p. 5.

171. *The Nation* 196 (9 February 1963): 111. Blanshard's articles, November 1947 to June 1948, were published as *American Freedom and Catholic Power* (Boston: Beacon, 1949).

172. *The Nation* 167 (4 September 1948): 248.

173. "An Appeal to Reason and Conscience, In Defense of the Right of Freedom of Inquiry in the United States," *The Nation* 167 (16 October 1948): 419–420, 447–449.

174. "Can the Ban Be Justified?" *The Nation* 167 (20 November 1948): 569, 571.

175. FK, "Democracy and Censorship," 31 January 1950, pp. 5, 4, 3, 4, #325, FK MSS.

176. FK to Edward S. Greenbaum, 14 January 1949, FK MSS; FK, Theta Sigma Phi speech, 11 April 1950, pp. 9, 11; both #325, FK MSS.

8. *"The Last Battle"*

1. Richard Rovere, *Senator Joe McCarthy* (New York: Harcourt, 1959), p. 24.

2. FK, "The McCarthy Blight," *The Nation* 170 (24 June 1950): 609.

3. FK, Theta Sigma Phi speech, 11 April 1950, #325, FK MSS. The occasion for FK's attack on McCarthyism was an attempt to excise certain pages of *The Arabian Nights* that offended Jewish sensibilities. She saw a connection between McCarthyism and such convenient attempts at censorship.

4. Robert Griffith, *The Politics of Fear: Joseph R. McCarthy and the Senate* (Lexington: University Press of Kentucky, 1970); Richard M. Fried, *Men against McCarthy* (New York: Columbia University Press, 1976); Rovere, *Senator Joe McCarthy;* Daniel Bell, ed., *The Radical Right* (Garden City, N.Y.: Doubleday, 1963); Owen Lattimore, *Ordeal by Slander* (Boston: Little, Brown, 1950); Murray B. Levin, *Political Hysteria in America: The Democratic Capacity for Repression* (New York: Basic Books, 1971); Victor S. Navasky, *Naming Names* (New York: Viking, 1980); Ellen Schrecker, *No Ivory Tower: McCarthyism and the University* (New York: Oxford University Press, 1986); I. F. Stone, *The Haunted Fifties* (New York: Random House, 1963); Athan Theoharis, *Seeds of Repression: Harry S. Truman and the Origins of McCarthyism* (Chicago: Quadrangle, 1971); James A. Wechsler, *The Age of Suspicion* (New York: Random House, 1953).

5. Joseph C. Goulden, *Korea: The Untold Story of the War* (New York: Times Books, 1982); Lloyd Gardner, ed., *The Korean War* (New York: Quadrangle, 1972); Robert A. Divine, *Eisenhower and The Cold War* (New York: Oxford University Press, 1981); David Rees, *Korea: The Limited War* (New York: St. Martin's, 1964); Matthew B. Ridgway, *The Korean War: How We Met the Challenge* (Garden City, N.Y.: Doubleday, 1967); I. F. Stone, *America's First Vietnam: The Hidden History of the Korean War* (New York: Monthly Review Press, 1952); Dean Acheson, *The Korean War* (New York: W. W. Norton, 1971); Glenn D. Paige, *The Korean Decision, June 24–30, 1950* (New York: Free Press, 1968); Allen S. Whiting, *China Crosses the Yalu to Enter the Korean War* (Stanford: Stanford University Press, 1960).

6. FK to MC, 1 July 1950, MC private collection.

7. Sources on the Hiss trials include: Whittaker Chambers, *Witness* (New York: Random House, 1952); Allen Weinstein, *Perjury: The Hiss-Chambers Case* (New York: Knopf, 1978); George H. Nash, *The Conservative Intellectual Movement in America Since 1945* (New York: Basic Books, 1976).

8. Maxwell S. Stewart to FK, 8 February 1951, #140, FK MSS.

9. Arthur Wubnig to FK, 16 April 1954; FK, Sworn Statement To Whom It May Concern, 30 April 1954; both #145, FK MSS.

10. Sidney Hook, "The Berlin Congress for Cultural Freedom," *Partisan Review* 17 (September—October 1950): 722. See also *NYT,* 17 June 1950, p. 4; *NYT,* 26 June 1950, p. 12.

11. William O'Neill, *Better World,* pp. 297–308.

12. Sidney Hook, "Heresy, Yes—Conspiracy, No," in *Heresy, Yes—Conspiracy, No* (New York: J. Day, 1953); Daniel James, "The Debate on Cultural Freedom," *The New Leader* 35 (7 April 1952): 4, 3; ACCF conference report, 29 March [1952], p. 2, box 9, f. 11, ACCF MSS.

13. Robert Divine, *Blowing in the Wind: The Nuclear Test Ban Debate, 1954–1960* (New York: Oxford University Press, 1978).

14. FK to Max Lerner, 23 March 1950, Box 4, f. 211, ML MSS; John K. Fairbank, "Pinpricks or Policy? II. Can Total Diplomacy Avert Total War?" pp. 488–489; Harrison Brown, "Foreign Policy for the Atomic Era," in "I. The Implications of Atomic War," pp. 481–483, 1–83; Hans Morgenthau, "Power Politics," in "II. Can Total Diplomacy Avert Total War?" pp. 486–487; Norbert Weiner, "Too Big for Private Enterprise," in "IV. The Potential of Atomic Energy for Peace-Time Use," pp. 496–497; Lord Boyd-Orr, "A Challenge to Civilization," in "VI. Dinner Forum—Steps Toward an Agreement Between East and West," p. 503; all in *The Nation* 170 (20 May 1950).

15. FK to MC, 8 May [1950], MC private collection.

16. FK, ed., *The Atomic Era—Can It Bring Peace and Abundance?* (New York: Medill McBride, 1950), p. 7, foreword.

17. FK, book manuscript outline, p. 20.

18. Program of the Nation Associates, October 1950, p. 2, #232, FK MSS, italics in original; FK to Eleanor Roosevelt, 29 September 1950, p. 2, 3855, General Correspondence, ER MSS.

19. The Editors, "The Issue Is Survival," *The Nation* 171 (16 December 1950): 549.

20. Archibald MacLeish, "War or Peace: The Undebated Issue," *The Nation* 171 (16 December 1950): 595, italics in original; 597; Isaac Deutscher, "The War of Ideas," ibid., p. 594.

21. The following also participated in the forum: Harold Isaacs, James P. Warburg, Gerald Bailey, Fritz Sternburg, Andrew Roth, Rayford W. Logan, J. C. Horowitz, and Jesus Silva Herzog. FK to MC, 31 November 1950, p. 3, MC private collection.

22. Robert Bendiner to FK, 9 October 1950, FK MSS.

23. Peter Viereck, "What Kind of Conservatism?" review of *The Case for Conservatism* by Francis Graham Wilson, *The New Leader* 34 (26 March 1951): 23. Diana Trilling, as late as 1976, wrote: "Not all anti-Communists are liberals, but no one can call himself a liberal who is not an anti-Communist." Trilling, "Liberal Anti-Communism Revisited," in *We Must March, My Darlings*, p. 49; Ronald Radosh, review of *We Must March, My Darlings* by Diana Trilling, *The Nation* 224 (18 June 1977): 757–758; Susan Sontag, Philip Green, Diana Trilling, Aryeh Neier, "Communism and the Left," *The Nation* 234 (27 February 1982): 230, 231.

24. Granville Hicks, "Liberals Who Haven't Learned," *Commentary* 11 (April 1951): 319–329.

25. FK to Editor, *Commentary,* 16 April 1951, pp. 1–2, #200, FK MSS. Prior to the conference, Hugo Van Arx reminded Freda of their dialogue concerning the color for the cover of the issue: "I suggested bright burnt orange red. Lillie [Shultz] was against and you agreed. 'No color that has the slightest resemblance to red. People will point at us with an accusing finger and say—see they are reds.'" Hugo Van Arx to FK, 8 December 1950, #110, FK MSS.

26. Elliot E. Cohen to Henry Fleugel Silver, 11 June 1951, pp. 1–2, #200, FK MSS.

27. FK to Editor, *Commentary,* 16 April 1951, pp. 3–4, #200, FK MSS, italics in original.

28. Joseph Short to FK, 19 May 1951; FK to Joseph Short, 22 May 1951, pp.

1–2; Willard Shelton to FK, 23 May 1951, pp. 1–2; all in #200, FK MSS; Hamby, *Beyond the New Deal*, p. 472.

29. "The *Nation* Censors a Letter," *The New Leader* 34 (19 March 1951): 17–18; "Soul-Searching," *Time* 57 (2 April 1951): 44–45; *Time* 57 (9 April 1951): 52.

30. FK to Clement Greenberg, 18 January 1951, box 13, f. 16, ACCF MSS.

31. Letters to the editors, *The Nation* 173 (7 July 1951): 20; Schlesinger letter printed in Peter Viereck, "Sermons of Self-Destruction," *Saturday Review of Literature* 34 (18 August 1951): 39–40; *The Nation* 172 (31 March 1951): 291.

32. FK to Margaret Marshall, 21 March 1951, box 3, MM MSS.

33. EC to Reinhold Niebuhr, 23 May 1951, p. 1, General Correspondence, Nation Associates, RN MSS.

34. Asked to write a critique of J. Alvarez del Vayo, Dwight Macdonald found the evidence less incriminating than he had thought: "I think DV's fellowtravelling is rooted in Popular Front antifascism rather than in partiality for the USSR." Macdonald agreed to pursue evidence of "a more virulent kind of fellowtravelling than appears in his *Nation* pieces." The managing editor of the *New Leader* thought otherwise: "The Spaniards are dead sure that he's an out-and-out CP man (vide Araquistain's *Times* pieces). The problem, of course, is to damn him out of his *Nation* mouth, and not out of Araquistain's. This, I think, may be bridged by using both sources." Dwight Macdonald to Daniel [James], 24 August [1951]; Daniel James to Dwight Macdonald, 25 September 1951, box 36, f. 920, DMcD MSS.

35. Editorial, "Why Did the *Nation* Sue?" *The New Leader* 36 (11 June 1951): 2, 30.

36. [FK], "Why *The Nation* Sued," *The Nation* 172 (2 June 1951): 505.

37. EC to Reinhold Niebuhr, 23 May 1951, p. 2, RN MSS.

38. [FK], "Why *The Nation* Sued," p. 505.

39. Ibid., p. 504.

40. Thomas I. Emerson to Editors, letters to the editors, *The Nation* 173 (7 July 1951): 19; Charles A. Madison to Editors, letters to the editors, *The Nation* 173 (7 July 1951): 20; Letters to the editors, *The Nation* 173 (7 July 1951): 20; Schlesinger letter in Viereck, "Sermons of Self-Destruction," p. 40, italics in original.

41. *The Nation* 172 (5 May 1951): 406; *The Nation* 172 (12 May 1951): 434. Niebuhr remained a member of the Nation Associates (FK to Reinhold Niebuhr, 24 January 1960, The Nation Associates, General Correspondence, RN MSS); "Exit from *The Nation*," *Time* 57 (21 May 1951): 55.

42. EC to Reinhold Niebuhr, 23 May 1951, p. 2, RN MSS.

43. FK to CMcW, 30 August 1955, FK MSS.

44. FK to Margaret Marshall, 21 March 1951, box 3, MM MSS.

45. Viereck, "Sermons of Self-Destruction," pp. 6, 7.

46. Ibid., pp. 6, 39.

47. Ibid., pp. 40, 51.

48. R. Lawrence Siegel to FK, 29 August 1951, pp. 1, 2, #127, FK MSS; letters to the editor, *Saturday Review of Literature* 34 (27 October 1951): 23.

49. Peter Viereck, letters to the editor, *Saturday Review of Literature* 34 (27 October 1951): 26, italics in original; Homer A. Jack to Editors, *Saturday Review of Literature*, 19 August 1951, p. 2, #127, FK MSS, (unpublished).

50. Viereck, letters to the editor, *Saturday Review* (27 October), p. 26; FK to Editor, letters to the editor, *Saturday Review of Literature* 34 (17 November 1951): 25, italics in original.

51. FK to Paul Blanshard, 12 September 1951, p. 3, #127, FK MSS.

52. A settlement with the *New Leader* was one of CMcW's terms for assuming editorship in 1955. Interview with CMcW, 14 April 1976; CMcW, *Education,* p. 150. Letters, *The Nation* 181 (24 September 1955): 272.

53. Special Edition, "How Free Is Free?" *The Nation* 174 (28 June 1951): 615–671, 615.

54. Ibid., p. 615.

55. Zechariah Chafee, Jr., "Spies into Heroes," pp. 618–619; Matthew Josephson, "The Battle of the Books," pp. 619–624; Kirtley F. Mather, "Scientists in the Doghouse," pp. 638–641; Ralph S. Brown, "6,000,000 Second-Class Citizens," pp. 644–647; CMcW, "The Witch Hunt and Civil Rights," 651–653; H. H. Wilson, "Academic Freedom and American Society," pp. 658–661; all *The Nation* 174 (28 June 1952).

56. Irving Kristol, "'Civil Liberties,' 1952–A Study in Confusion," *Commentary* 13 (March 1952): 228–236, 230, 231.

57. O'Neill, *Better World,* p. 285; see also Pells, *Liberal Mind in Conservative Age,* pp. 296–300; James Nuechterlein, "Neoconservatism and Irving Kristol," *Commentary,* 78 (August 1984): 43; Kristol, "Civil Liberties," p. 236.

58. Frederick Woltman, reprint, "Big Names Deny Any Part in Forum," *New York World-Telegram and Sun,* 29 April 1952; *Counterattack* 6 (25 April 1952); both #425, FK MSS; *The New Leader* 35 (28 April 1952): cover page.

59. FK to Stanley Lichtenstein, 28 May 1952 (not sent), #425; FK, book manuscript outline, p. 23; Hernán Santa Cruz to FK, 24 May 1952, #246; all FK MSS.

60. FK to Eleanor Roosevelt, 17 May 1952, pp. 1, 2, 4010 (1952, Nat.), General Correspondence, ER MSS.

61. Eleanor Roosevelt, prefatory remarks to speech "First Need: Resettlement," in evening session, "Arab-Israel Peace—Key to Middle East Stability," *The Nation* 174 (7 June 1952): 556–557; in conference, "Freedom's Stake in the Middle East and North Africa," *The Nation* 174 (7 June 1952): 559; FK to Eleanor Roosevelt, 26 May 1952, 4010 (1952 Nat.), General Correspondence, ER MSS.

62. Statement of facts, 8 February 1952, #249, FK MSS.

63. EC to MC, 7 February 1952; FK to MC, 8 February 1952, MC private collection.

64. FK to President Truman, telegram draft, #249, FK MSS.

65. EC to MC, 7 February 1952, MC private collection; *The Nation* 175 (16 August 1952): 121; CMcW, *Education,* p. 150.

66. *Time* 61 (19 January 1953): 62; Paul Bertram to Editors, letters to the editors, *The Nation* 176 (31 January 1953): 107.

67. FK to MC, [early 1953], MC private collection.

68. FK to Margaret Marshall, 7 January 1953, Correspondence Series, JWK MSS.

69. Margaret Marshall to FK, 9 January 1953, MM MSS.

70. Margaret Marshall to FK, 15 January 1953, MM MSS.

71. FK to Margaret Marshall, 14 January 1953, MM MSS.

72. Announcement, *The Nation* 176 (17 January 1953): 40A; [FK], "A Year To Remember," p. 1, #148, FK MSS.

73. *Time* 61 (19 January 1953): 62; Paul Bertram to Editors, letters to the editors, *The Nation* 176 (31 January 1953): 107; Editors, letters to the editors, *The Nation* 176 (31 January 1953): 107.

74. Margaret Marshall to Editors, letters to the editors, *The Nation* 176 (7 February 1953): 135; Marshall took her grievance to the Newspaper Guild of New York. The *Nation* unit took no further action after it issued a formal expression of support for Marshall and dissatisfaction for the way her termination was handled. Margaret Marshall to Newspaper Guild of New York, 28 January 1953; Paula Turner to FK, 22 January 1953; FK to Paula Turner, 9 February 1953, MM MSS; #134, FK MSS.

75. FK to Joseph Wood Krutch, 14 January 1953, JWK MSS.

76. CMcW, *Education,* p. 189. Of the *Nation*'s union employees, Margaret Marshall and J. Alvarez del Vayo had received the highest salaries in 1952, each earning $8,254.40. Nonunion Hugo Van Arx was paid $8,650; CMcW $10,400, and Lillie Shultz, $12,584, with FK earning only $7,800. The firing of Marshall and Van Arx meant a large saving. Payroll 1952, #129, FK MSS.

77. *The Nation* 176 (21 February 1953): 160.

78. See, e.g., Mark Gayn, "Soviet Russia As It Is," a review of ten books on the Soviet Union, *The Nation* 176 (4 April 1953): 290–292. Mark Gayn, "Lessons of Asia," a review of five books on Asia, *The Nation* 176 (27 June 1953): 545–546; see, e.g., Edgar Snow, review of *Modern China's Foreign Policy* by Werner Levi, *The Nation* 178 (27 January 1954): 182–183.

79. Richard Hofstadter to Margaret Marshall, 20 January 1953; H. Stuart Hughes to Margaret Marshall, 24 January 1953, MM MSS.

80. FK, book manuscript outline, p. 25.

81. FK to CMcW, 2 March 1951, pp. 1–2, 1, #142, FK MSS.

82. FK to CMcW, 6 March 1951, p. 1, #142, FK MSS.

83. CMcW, "Memoirs of *Nation,*" pp. 24–25.

84. FK to CMcW, 22 January 1952, p. 1, #142, FK MSS.

85. EC to MC, 8 April 1952, FK MSS.

86. FK, "Why the Jews?" *The Nation* 176 (31 January 1953): 92. The JDC was a private voluntary organization which rescued Jews during World War II; in postwar times it provided funds for Jewish relief and rehabilitation throughout the world. Most donations to the JDC came from American Jews. Hal Lehrman, "The 'Joint' Takes a Human Inventory," *Commentary* 7 (January 1949): 19–27.

87. "Plea to the Secretary General of the United Nations" (press release for 16 December 1952), box 12, f. 18, ACCF MSS.

88. "A Confidential Report," 19 February 1953, #233, FK MSS. They sent copies to Secretary General of the UN Trygve Lie and the head of the U.S. delegation, Henry Cabot Lodge.

89. See *NYT,* 16 February 1953, p. 7; *NYT,* 17 February 1953, p. 26.

90. FK, "Mercy for the Rosenbergs," *The Nation* 176 (10 January 1953): 24; [FK], "New Kremlin Bid," *The Nation* 176 (21 March 1953): 237; Frank J. Donner, "The Informer," *The Nation* 178 (10 April 1954): 298–309.

91. CMcW, *Education,* p. 186; *NYT,* 14 July 1955, p. 12.

92. CMcW, *Education,* pp. 187, 188.
93. FK to Martin Solow, 22 July 1955, pp. 1, 2, #129, FK MSS.
94. *The Nation* 181 (23 July 1955): 68; see also #129, FK MSS.
95. CMcW, *Education,* p. 188.
96. In "The Nation and Mr. Brownell's 'Justice,'" *The Nation* 181 (23 July 1955): 66.
97. FK to Julie Medlock, 3 March 1955, FK MSS.
98. FK, memorandum to Lillie Shultz, 4 March 1955, pp. 1, 2, #14, FK MSS.
99. Editors, "The 90th Anniversary Forum on Atoms for Peace," *The Nation* 180 (18 June 1955): 515; FK, "Atoms for Peace, 1865–1960," ibid.
100. Bertrand Russell, "The Choice is Ours, Coexistence or No Existence," pp. 515–517; Amos de Shalit, "Irrigating the Negev: Potential Boon for Israel," pp. 531–532; Jacob Sachs, "The Atom in Medicine: Revolutionizing Research," pp. 536–540; Robert W. Fraze, "An Atomic Chronology, From Hiroshima to Now," pp. 559–564; all *The Nation* 180 (18 June 1955).
101. FK, "NINETY YEARS YOUNG: The Future's Challenge," *The Nation* 180 (9 July 1955): 43–44; italics in original.
102. FK, address, 19 June 1955, p. 5, #325, FK MSS.
103. FK to MC, 30 January 1954, MC private collection.
104. EC to MC, 23 February 1954, MC private collection.
105. FK to MC, [1954], MC private collection.
106. EC to MC, 8 June 1955, FK MSS.
107. CMcW to Mary Dreier, 30 June 1955, p. 1, Dreier MSS.
108. Ibid.; CMcW, "Memoirs of *Nation,*" p. 26.
109. FK to CMcW, 30 August 1955, memorandum, p. 2, #107, FK MSS.
110. FK to CMcW, 18 August 1955, #107, FK MSS.
111. FK, "To the Readers of *The Nation,*" *The Nation* 181 (17 September 1955): 233; *NYT,* 15 September 1955, p. 30. The *Nation* reached newsstands prior to 17 September.
112. MC to FK, 2 October 1955, pp. 2–3, FK MSS.
113. EC to MC, 17 August 1955, p. 1, FK MSS.
114. FK, book manuscript outline, p. 25.
115. FK to Louis Fischer, 9 September 1937, p. 1, box 2, LF MSS.
116. FK, book manuscript outline, p. 25.

Epilogue

1. Diggins, *Up from Communism,* pp. 340–341.
2. FK, "To the Readers of *The Nation,*" p. 233.
3. CMcW, *Education,* pp. 193, 195.
4. "Time To Kill Jim Crow," *The Nation* 183 (7 July 1956): 1–22; see, e.g., Ralph Nader, "The Safe Car You Can't Buy," *The Nation* 188 (11 April 1959): 310–313; Larry Agran, *The Cancer Connection And What We Can Do About It* (Boston: Houghton Mifflin, 1977).
5. *The Nation* 181 (17 December 1955): 524; Andrew Roth to FK, 18 May 1959, FK MSS.
6. FK to Doris Tanz, 15 November 1955, p. 1, FK MSS; the civil wedding ceremony, on 2 December 1955 was performed by Jeanné Ruyssen, Edmeé's aunt, who was assistant mayor of Algiers. Edmée, who had a law degree, came

from an upper-middle-class professional family. Her father was Judge of the Algiers Court of Appeals. When Michael met her she was assisting a cousin who was a politician in Algiers; telephone interview with MC, 26 January 1986; FK, "Era of Villard," review of *Oswald Garrison Villard, Liberal of the 1920s* by D. Joy Humes, *The Nation* 192 (14 January 1961): 36–37; FK, "Memoirs of Nation," pp. 27–35.

7. David Wesley to FK, 10 October 1958; FK to David Wesley, 16 August 1958; both #341, FK MSS. See, e.g., FK "Africa, the United Nations and Michael Scott," *The Gazette and Daily* (York, Pa.), 11 December 1958, p. 25; FK to David Wesley, 14 November 1958, #341, FK MSS.

8. Pamphlet, R. M. Whitney, "Peace at Any Old Price," (New York: The Beckwith Press, 13–16 March 1923), p. 30, WILPF MSS; *NYT*, 19 June 1948, p. 4.

9. *NYT*, 21 June 1948, p. 9; FK, "The Challenge of Human Rights," pp. 1–2, FK MSS.

10. FK to Carl T. Rowan, 20 September 1962, pp. 1–2, FK MSS.

11. *NYT*, 23 September 1962, p. 4.

12. Dorothy Hutchinson to Sen. J. William Fulbright, 26 October 1962, telegrams; FK to Dorothy Hutchinson, 9 December 1962, p. 2; both #301, FK MSS.

13. FK to MC, 30 November 1962, FK MSS; One of these commitments was the Medical Aid to Cuba Committee, a humanitarian effort that she and others had formed in March 1962 to provide medicines, medical books, and journals to Cuba. Although the committee described its work as nonpolitical and humanitarian, the House Un-American Activities Committee accused it of being a communist-front organization, and mixed testimony at a subsequent investigation seems to have scared off supporters. Kirchwey's appeal to freedom-of-speech authority Alexander Meiklejohn, did not elicit the requested protest of the HUAC subpoenas. The Medical Aid to Cuba Committee was disbanded in January 1963. Melitta del Villar to FK, 5 March 1962 and 25 January 1963, both #334, FK MSS; *NYT*, 13 November, p. 29, 14 November, p. 8, and 15 November, p. 22; all 1962. Alexander Meiklejohn to FK, 13 November 1962, pp. 1–2, #334, FK MSS; general letter with news release, Medical Aid to Cuba Committee, 25 January 1963 [31 January 1963], #334, FK MSS.

14. Interview with Lillian Elkin, 20 June 1983.

15. FK to Mimi (Edmée) Clark, 20 March 1964, FK MSS. At the same East Side apartment building lived two close friends: Irwin Miness, a lawyer, and Nina Miness, who worked at the UN.

16. CMcW, "The Freda Kirchwey I Knew," *The Nation* 222 (17 January 1976): 39; Lillie Shultz to FK, 8 October 1956, #351; 26 September 1956, #361; Valia Hirsch to FK, 6 July 1965, #352; Lillie Shultz to FK, 7 July 1965, #357; all FK MSS; FK to Otto Nathan, 31 August 1965, Otto Nathan private collection.

17. Suggested itinerary, #352, FK MSS; FK to Otto Nathan, 31 August 1965, Otto Nathan private collection; FK to Marion Hess, 2 September 1965, Marion Hess private collection. Philip was born 29 August 1956, in Algiers. Marie Gabrielle (Mäie) was born in New York on 9 October 1959. The Michael Clarks lived in New York from 1957 to 1960. Edmée and Freda spent some time together then as FK was retired. The Clarks moved to Switzerland in 1960 when

MC was appointed to the International Labor Office. Telephone interview with MC, 26 January 1986.

18. FK to Marion Hess, 2 February 1966, Marion Hess private collection; see also EC diaries for 1965 and 1966, in MC private collection. FK and EC began a routine of renting a small apartment in Santurce (near San Juan), Puerto Rico, during the winter and visiting Michael's family in Switzerland in the summer. Telephone interview with MC, 26 January 1986.

19. C. Wright Mills to FK and Mario de Salegui, 22 November 1960; FK to Katie Ratcliffe, 11 March 1961, p. 2; FK to William L. Shirer, 19 January 1961, pp. 1, 1–4; all FK MSS.

20. *NYT*, 14 February 1961, p. 32; minutes of the Committee for a Democratic Spain, 26 March 1961, #314; FK to Lawrence Fernsworth, 20 April 1961; both FK MSS.

21. Russell Nixon to FK, 27 April 1961, #316, FK MSS.

22. U.S. Senate, Committee on Foreign Affairs, *International Development and Security*, 87th Cong., 1st sess., 1961, pp. 990, 998, 1008, 1001. *Reporter* article filed with FK's testimony: Claire Sterling, "Spain Without Franco: Will We Be Ready?" *The Reporter* 24 (30 March 1961): 17–20.

23. *Act for International Development of 1961, Statutes at Large* 75 (1961).

24. FK to Hon. Clement J. Zablocki, 12 July 1962; FK to Hon. James Roosevelt, 12 July 1962; both #314, FK MSS. The next year when the life of Julian Grimau, a communist foe of Franco, was in danger, Kirchwey urged Assistant Secretary of State for Far Eastern Affairs Averell Harriman and President Kennedy to exert pressure on Franco to show leniency, just as Khrushchev did after resuming communication with Franco to make that direct appeal. Their efforts were to no avail. FK to Hon. Averell Harriman, 13 April 1963, #318, FK MSS; *NYT*, 20 April 1963, p. 1.

25. CDS invitation to 5 January 1967 meeting, Alpern private collection; [FK] to Hon. Joseph S. Clark, 15 February 1967; FK to Ernest Gruening [February 1967], #320, FK MSS; *Spain Today* 6 (April–May 1968); CMcW and FK for Committee to Aid Families of Political Prisoners in Spain, promotion letter, 16 January 1968; FK to Syd Hauskmecht, 29 April 1968, Alpern private collection.

26. See FK to Hugo Van Arx, 23 February 1957, #364, FK MSS; estimated yearly budget; estimated expenses and income; notes on magazine; all #365, FK MSS.

27. FK to [?], 13 April 1960; FK to Stanley Rinehart, Jr., 18 May [1960]; FK to Stanley Rinehart, Jr., 14 August 1960; all #361, FK MSS. FK to Caroline Whiting, 27 October 1960; FK to Barbara Tuchman [1961]; both FK MSS.

28. FK to J. Alvarez del Vayo, 5 August 1962; CMcW to FK, 30 July 1962; FK to Raymond Swing, 5 August 1962; FK to Mimi (Edmée) Clark, 20 March 1964, p. 2; all FK MSS.

29. FK to MC, ca. 2 December 1964 (copy sent on this date), FK MSS. FK, though for the most part pleased with the anniversary issue, expressed some "post-partum complaints" to CMcW. In particular she was distressed by the handling of her last decade as editor and publisher. She felt that some of the important forums were slighted and that Lillie Shultz's specific contributions to them, as Nation Associates executive director, was an untold story. She was also disappointed that articles by some prominent *Nation* contributors, such as

I. F. Stone, Louis Fischer, and J. Alvarez del Vayo, were not included in the issue's "Legacies From Our Past." FK to CMcW, 28 September 1965, #24, DKB addenda, 70s. She did not point out that she herself was noticeably missing from a book anthology also commemorating the *Nation;* none of her scores of editorials appeared in Henry M. Christman, ed., *One Hundred Years of The Nation* (New York: Macmillan, 1965).

30. CMcW, "The FK I Knew," p. 40.

31. FK, book manuscript outline, p. 1.

32. FK to MC, 21 January 1970, MC private collection.

33. FK to Otto Nathan, 14 May 1970, Otto Nathan private collection.

34. *NYT,* 29 August 1970, p. 25; interview with MC, 12 May 1984; interview with Caroline Whiting Nash, 11 July 1983.

35. FK to DKB, [24] February 1971, 23 February 1971; FK to DKB, [24] February 1971; FK to Nina and Irwin Miness, [March 1971], MC private collection; FK to [?], [1971], FK MSS.

36. FK to DKB, 2 March 1971, MC private collection.

37. Irwin Miness to DKB, 5 March 1971, p. 1, MC private collection.

38. Irwin Miness to MC, 15 March 1971, MC private collection.

39. FK to DKB, 31 March 1971, MC private collection.

40. Interview with DKB, 15 October 1974; FK to DKB, 10, 16 March 1971; 6 April 1971, p. 6; 12 April 1971, MC private collection.

41. FK to DKB, 12 April 1971; MC to DKB, telegram, 28 June 1971, MC private collection; FK to Marion Hess, 2 April 1972, Marion Hess private collection.

42. FK to Marion Hess, 2 April 1972; FK to Otto Nathan, 23 April 1972, Otto Nathan private collection.

43. Interview with Diego del Vayo, 30 June 1983.

44. DKB to CMcW, 13 January 1973, FK MSS; DKB to Marion Hess, 7 December 1974, Marion Hess private collection; interview with MC, 13 May 1984; *NYT,* 4 January 1976, p. 47; *Washington Post,* 10 January 1976, sec. E, p. 6; *Barnard Bulletin* 80 (26 January 1976): 3. At the time of her death FK was in a demented state. It is virtually impossible to determine if she or her father suffered from Alzheimer's disease or from arteriosclerosis. Interview with Philip R. Alexander, M.D., 8 February 1985.

Acknowledgments

I am grateful for financial assistance in the form of
fellowships from the American Association of University Women,
the Woodrow Wilson National Fellowship Foundation for research
in Women's Studies, and the University of Maryland Graduate College. The staff of the Schlesinger Library, which holds the papers of
Freda Kirchwey and her sister Dorothy Kirchwey Brown, were particularly helpful. I thank Kathryn Kish Sklar for early suggesting
that I investigate the Kirchwey papers.

Research for this biography was supported in part by funds from
the Andrew W. Mellon Foundation given by Radcliffe College for
research at the Schlesinger Library on the History of Women in
America. The book also has benefited from my participation in John
P. Diggins' NEH summer seminar. My own institution, Texas A&M
University, has provided financial assistance in the form of a College
of Liberal Arts research support grant, a College of Liberal Arts
summer research stipend, a College of Liberal Arts and Department
of History grant from the Program for Excellence, and a Texas
A&M University mini-grant.

Special thanks go to Jo Berg and Susan Pullen, two Texas A&M
University librarians who have been extraordinarily helpful. I wish
to thank the helpful secretarial staff of the Texas A&M University
History department. Carole Knapp, who deciphered many revisions

and typed them into clean prose, died at the age of thirty-three and will never read of my deepest gratitude, not only for her clerical skills but for her interest in and support of this book. My sincere thanks go to Nelda Bravo for picking up the pieces and skillfully bringing the project toward completion.

I am grateful to all the archivists and librarians who assisted me. These include from the staff of the Schlesinger Library: Anne Engelhart, Marie-Helne Gold, Barbara Haber, Patricia King, Katherine Kraft, Eva Moseley, and Elizabeth Shenton. I appreciate the special assistance of Patricia K. Ballou, Ruth Carr, Daria D'Arrienzo, Beth Diefendorf, Mrs. Philip Hartman, James H. Hutson, David Klaassen, J. Richard Kyle, Sandra McCoy Larson, Michael Lordi, Mary MacKenzie, Patricia B. Stark, Esther Togman, and Diana Yount. Thanks go to the helpful staffs of the following libraries and thanks to those libraries that granted me permission to quote: Amherst College Archives; Barnard College Archives; Beinecke Library, Yale University; Franklin D. Roosevelt Library, Hyde Park; Franklin Trask Library, Andover Newton Theological School; Houghton Library, Harvard University; Library of Congress; New School for Social Research Library; New York Public Library; Oral History Project Office, Columbia University; Princeton University Library; Schlesinger Library, Radcliffe College; Social Welfare History Archives, University of Minnesota; Sterling Memorial Library, Yale University; Swarthmore College Peace Collection; Tamiment Library, New York University; Zionist Archives and Library, New York.

For permission to quote from personal letters I am indebted to: Ian Ballantine for Emma Goldman; Daniel Bell for the American Committee for Cultural Freedom; Robert Bendiner; Bruce Bliven, Jr., for Bruce Bliven; Michael Clark for himself and Dorothy Kirchwey Brown, Evans Clark, Dora Wendell Kirchwey, Freda Kirchwey, and George Washington Kirchwey; Diego del Vayo for himself and J. Alvarez del Vayo; Elizabeth Duboff for Grace Epstein; George Fischer for Louis Fischer; Fred S. Fleck and Catherine Fleck-Pastori for Margaret Marshall; Michael R. Gannett for Lewis Gannett; Elizabeth M. Gitt for J. W. Gitt; Jane Perry Gunther for John Gunther; Marion Hess; Roger W. Holmes for John Haynes Holmes; Sidney Hook; H. Stuart Hughes; Gloria Macdonald for Dwight Macdonald; Iris McWilliams for Carey McWilliams; Irwin Miness; Nina Miness; Caroline Whiting Nash; Ursula M. Niebuhr for Reinhold Niebuhr; Cleo Paturis for James T. Farrell; Franklin D. Roosevelt, Jr., for Eleanor Roosevelt; Barbara W. Tuchman for Maurice Wertheim; Helen Van Arx for Hugo Van Arx; Peter Viereck; Oswald Garrison Villard, Jr., for Oswald Garrison Villard; Katherine K. White for William Allen White.

I thank the following publications for permission to quote: *Commentary; International Social Science Review; The Nation; The New Leader; Saturday Review of Literature.*

This book was greatly enriched by interviews. Most of the following knew Kirchwey personally and graciously shared their time and memories with me. I am further indebted to several of them who lent me correspondence or photographs, and to all of them for permitting me to use the material from their interviews in the book. I extend my thanks to all of them: Philip R. Alexander, M.D., Daniel Bell, Robert Bendiner, Selma Bernstein, Victor Bernstein, Michael Clark, Dick Cowen, Diego del Vayo, Lillian Elkin, Grace Epstein, Marion Hess, Sidney Hook, Irving Howe, Keith Hutchinson, Arnold A. Hutschnecker, M.D., George W. Kirchwey, III, Iris McWilliams, Irwin Miness, Nina Miness, Dorothy Conigliaro Moroch, Caroline Whiting Nash, Otto Nathan, Juan Negrin, M.D., Murray Rossant, Andrew Roth, Arthur Schlesinger, Jr., William L. Shirer, I. F. Stone, Michael W. Straight, Diana Trilling, Barbara W. Tuchman, Dorothy Van Doren, Carl Hermann Voss. I deeply regret that Dorothy Kirchwey Brown and Carey McWilliams, who contributed so much to this book, did not live to see it in print.

Many colleagues and friends helped during various stages. Some criticized parts of the manuscript; others contributed their expertise; some cheered me on. The book has benefited from their efforts and I take this opportunity to thank them publicly: Ann Todd Baum, E. P. Black, Joseph Boskin, Keith L. Bryant, Jr., Robert A. Calvert, Jesse Coon, Libby Coon, Richard Costa, Susan Costin, James B. Gilbert, Mary A. Hamilton, Marion Hess, Elsie Kersten, William E. Leuchtenberg, Elizabeth Cowan Neeld, Jerele Neeld, G. Dan Parker, III, Mary Jo Powell, Rosa Richardson, Robert A. Rosenstone, Lynn Shapiro, Patricia Stranahan, Stephan Thernstrom, Dorris B. Turner, Betty M. Unterberger, Frank Warren, Charles Weiner, and Pat Wong.

I am especially grateful to several others. Chester Dunning and John Lenihan helped with rigorous criticism of the manuscript. Michael Keene taught me that writing is a complex, cognitive skill, not a body of knowledge; Paula Michal-Johnson encouraged me to talk through some difficult parts of the book and read more revisions than I had any right to expect her to. Michael Wreszin inspired me to reach beyond my original interest in Kirchwey and toward a biography. I give sincere thanks to James M. Treece for his patience and scholarly interest. Michael Clark not only shared memories, priceless letters, diaries, and photographs of his parents; he also read revisions carefully, correcting only for accuracy, not interpretation. I am grateful to Kathryn Kish Sklar whose reading of the entire manuscript led me to clarify parts of the book. I am indebted to Aida D. Donald and Ann Louise McLaughlin of Harvard University Press for editorial suggestions and demands. Heartfelt thanks go to Ruth Schaffer without whose computer expertise, indefatigable efforts, and collegial support, my index would never have been completed. I appreciate the forbearance of the entire Alpern family. The completion of this book has been lightened by the cheerful sustenance of Peter E. Tarlow and the patient endurance of my son, Josh Frager.

Index

Canada, 170–171, 189
Capitalism, 105, 117–118
Carnegie Endowment for International
   Peace, 204
Carnegie, Andrew, 3
Carolus, 207–208
Carpenter, Edward, 20
Cassin, René, 234
Catholic Church, 200–202
Catt, Carrie Chapman, 44, 158
Catton, Bruce, 221
Censorship, 55, 130, 201, 211, 290n3
Chafe, William, 41
Chafee, Zechariah, Jr., 216
Chamberlain, Neville, 117, 124, 127, 138; at
   Munich, 128
Chambers, Whittaker, 189, 216
Charleston, *South Carolina Gazette,* 42
Chase, Stuart, 108, 173
Chicago Tribune, 93, 189
Child Study, 55
Child Study Association of America, 55, 68
Children, 62–64, 68, 70
Children's Bureau, 44
Churchill, Winston, 73, 163
Ciano, Count Caleazzo, 128
CIO (Congress of Industrial Organiza-
   tions), 168, 179–180
City and Country School, 68, 71
Civic Aid Foundation, 112
Civil liberties, 79, 92, 130, 148–151, 201, 211,
   215–217, 220, 223, 228
Clark, Brewster, 27, 40, 59, 91, 244; death
   of, 254n86
Clark, Edmée, 233, 235
Clark, Evans, 13, 18–19, 21, 29, 34, 48, 53–
   55, 59, 66, 68, 70, 72, 75, 78, 82–84, 87,
   89–91, 94, 96, 124, 134, 145, 156, 167, 174,
   213, 220, 231; background and education, 19, 36; relationship with FK, 14,
   38, 42, 49, 58, 61, 85–86, 100–101, 195;
   and psychoanalysis, 51, 58, 67; travel of,
   81, 195; *Nation* reorganization plan
   (1936), 111; negotiation with *New Republic,* 156
      career of: *Nation* editorials, 34; Rus-
      sian Socialist Federal Soviet Re-
      public Bureau, 35; head of Labor
      Bureau Inc., 37; *New York Times*
      writings, 37, 51, 68, 73–74, 77, 92;
      Committee on Research, Garland
      Fund, 78; Labor Research Bureau,

78; Twentieth Century Fund,
78, 105; chairman, New York NRA
adjustment board, 105; writings,
112
      opinions on: Child Study Association
      Conference, 68; labor causes, 102;
      Wagner-Ellenbogen Public Hous-
      ing Bill, 106; Wagner Act, 107;
      boycott of Italy, 112; race and reli-
      gious freedom, 130; fascist propa-
      ganda, 148
Clark, Mrs. Evans. *See* Kirchwey, Freda
Clark, Fannie, 36, 72
Clark, Grenville, 207
Clark, Jeffrey, 46, 48, 70, 81–91, 93–94,
   242, 254, 266–267n33; death of, 95
Clark, Marie-Gabrielle (Maïe), 235, 296–
   297n17
Clark, Michael, 48, 56–57, 59, 81–82, 91,
   100, 119, 136, 160, 172, 197–198, 220,
   229–231, 235, 242; background and edu-
   cation, 36–37, 60, 68–72, 101, 134; atti-
   tude toward parents, 68–70, 196, 198; in
   Europe, 124, 128; return from Europe,
   129; during World War II, 134–135; 195–
   196; and *Nation,* 198
Clark, Philip, 242, 296–297n17
Cleveland, Grover, 1
Coexistence, 206–207, 228
Cohen, Benjamin, 194
Cohen, Elliot, 178, 209
Cold War, 177, 179, 183, 206–208, 210, 220,
   226
Collective security, 112, 123–124, 161
Collier, John, 209
Collins, Joseph, 63–64, 262n38
Columbia University, 1, 3, 13; Law School,
   2, 13, 18, 144–145; sex barrier, 16; Teach-
   ers' College, 4
Comintern, 117, 178
Commager, Henry Steele, 201
Commentary, 178, 182, 208–209, 216
Committee for Cultural Freedom, 125,
   191–192; manifesto of, 126
Committee for a Democratic Spain
   (CDS), 236–239
Committee to Aid Families of Political
   Prisoners in Spain, 297n25
Communism, 103, 120, 163, 175, 178–179,
   181–186, 189–190, 203–205, 208–209, 213,
   216–217, 219
Communist Party, 177, 205, 292n34; U.S.,

Kirchwey, Freda (*continued*)
engagement, 14–15, 18–19; marriage of, 20, 61, 86; and Brewster, 27; pregnancy, 33, 36, 46, 53; as mother, 36–37, 46, 48, 69, 82–83, 87, 135; ill health of, 36, 92, 111, 155, 234–236, 240, 288n155, 298n44; attitude toward childbearing, 40, 69, 72, 87, 97; attitude toward marriage, 41, 70; attitude toward divorce, 48; on balancing marriage, career, and family, 48, 60, 64, 66–69, 97; miscarrage of, 53; death of parents, 57–58, 144–145; and psychoanalysis, 58, 92, 94–96; traditional values of, 58; self-image of, 65–67, 69; attitude toward school and child-development experts, 70–71; vacations, 73–74, 111, 119; children of, 58, 81–82; as wife, 83, 92, 267–268n45; and Jeffrey Clark, 83–89, 93, 240, 242, 266n12, 267nn34, 44; and Evans Clark, 85–86, 92, 95, 100–101, 174, 195, 213, 229, 240; attitude toward and retreat from work, 87, 91, 93; and Dorothy Kirchwey, 94–95, 242, 263n65; and Michael Clark, 101, 134–135, 160, 172, 195–196, 198, 220, 229–230, 233, 235, 240–242; and retirement, 229–231, 233; travels, 233, 235, 241, 297n18; death of, 242, 298n44
expressed views—international: on Trotsky, 28–29, 119, 272n77; on Soviet Union, 35, 47, 60, 103, 119, 122–123, 125, 127, 132–134, 160, 162, 164–166, 170, 177–178, 183–184, 187, 190–194, 205–207, 209, 212, 215, 226, 277n63, 287n134; on fascism, 99–100, 101, 103, 109, 117, 119, 121, 123–124, 127, 129, 131, 136, 138, 143–145, 149–150, 153, 159–161, 177, 181; and collective security, 113, 118–119, 123–124, 131–132, 153, 161; on Hitler, 113, 114, 124, 126, 129, 167, 225–226, 239, 260; on Nazis, 115, 147, 153, 175, 194; attitude toward European democracy, 117; on need for antifascist unity, 118, 123–126, 150, 164, 177; Great Purge, 118; Moscow Trials,

118; Munich, 118, 124, 128–129; struggle between fascism and democracy, 118; on Spain and Franco, 120–121, 127, 132–133, 153, 159–160, 164, 167–169, 193–195, 231, 236–239, 297n24; on Bukharin trials, 123; on appeasement, 124, 129, 207; European diplomacy, 124; fear of Nazi victory, 125; on Stalin, 126, 177, 216; on Nazi-Soviet Pact, 126; on neutrality, 129; on Finland, 132–133; peace after WWII, 134; as antifascist, 135; political war, 137, 141, 143, 159, 167–168, 184; and refugees, 138; on Britain, 138, 145–146, 159, 166; Jews, 138–141, 196–197, 225, 231, 276n44, 280n113, 287–288n147; on Weizmann, Palestine, 139, 160, 196–199, 280n113; WWII, 143, 159, 160, 161, 167, 174, 178, 199, 239; writings about Axis, 145; India-Britain controversy, 145–147; on communists, communism, 153, 181–184, 186, 191–194, 203, 209, 212, 217; on fifth-column, Nazi invasion of Norway, 148, 149; and Axis, 149, 199; on POUM, 153; on Communist Revolution, Third International, 154; and Laski, 156; New Deal for the world, 159–160; League of Nations, 160; Allies, 161; Yalta, 163; on UN, 165–166, 190, 195, 199; on Argentina, Perón, 166–167; Western press, 166; on Friends of the Spanish Republic, 168; Canada, 170; world government, 170, 173; on French Legion of Honor, 174; concentration-camp survivors, 175; Nuremberg, 175; on Greece, Turkey, 184; on Marshall Plan, 185–186; on Masaryk, 186; at Cultural Congress for Peace, 187; on Atlantic Pact, 190; on Soviet bloc, 194; on Golda Meir, 196; on Middle East, 197, 199, 200, 207, 223; and Israel, 198, 288n150, 289n163; on Arabs, 199; on Germany, 199; on Korea, 204, 207, 223; on atomic disarmament, 206; on detente, 206; on Africa, Asia, 207; on Berlin blockade, 207; on Europe, 207; against anti-